Corrections in the Community by Edward Latessa and Paula Smith is an excellent resource for my class. The text provides a comprehensive introduction to the field of community corrections in a manner that is of interest to my students. The text is relevant to my class and serves to promote a greater understanding of the various components of community corrections.

George Thomas, *Criminal Justice, North Carolina Central University*

Congratulations to Latessa and Smith on the publication of the 6th edition of *Corrections in the Community*! As a frequent user of their earlier editions, I eagerly awaited the publication of this 6th edition because the earlier editions had been so successful in meeting the needs of my students in what I was searching for as a text for my community based corrections classes. Student feedback was extremely positive regarding the earlier editions, but the 6th edition, in particular, will greatly improve on an already solid theoretical and applied foundation. Latessa and Smith have always provided the needed merging of theory and practice for this area of corrections and I find this to be even more evident in this latest iteration. The addition of the new materials on drug courts and specialty courts has greatly enhanced this relatively new area in community based corrections—and rightly so! As one who has been involved in drug court research and evaluation for more than twenty years, I found this timely examination of the research and practice to be a fair and accurate reflection of what is occurring with drug and specialty courts today. It is a very readable and thoughtful book which should greatly enhance the field for both academics and practitioners alike—I highly recommend this book!

Bill Wakefield, *Criminology and Criminal Justice, University of Nebraska at Omaha*

Corrections in the Community is an easy-to-read textbook that provides a comprehensive introduction to probation, parole, alternative sentencing and community programming. While Latessa and Smith deftly cover the major tenets underlying community corrections, their new chapter on problem-solving courts is a timely addition given the recent growth in these courts across the U.S.

Grant Duwe, *Director, Research and Evaluation, Minnesota Department of Corrections*

Corrections in the Community

Sixth Edition

Corrections in the Community, Sixth Edition, examines the current state of community corrections and proposes an evidence-based approach to making programs more effective. As the U.S. prison system approaches meltdown, options like probation, parole, alternative sentencing, and both residential and non-residential programs in the community continue to grow in importance. This text provides a solid foundation and includes the most salient information available on the broad and dynamic subject of community corrections. Authors Latessa and Smith organize and evaluate the latest data on the assessment of offender risk/need/responsivity and successful methods that continue to improve community supervision and its effects on different types of clients, from the mentally ill to juveniles.

This book provides students with a thorough understanding of the theoretical and practical aspects of community corrections and prepares them to evaluate and strengthen these crucial programs. This sixth edition includes a new chapter on specialty drug and other problem-solving courts. Now found in every state, these specialty courts represent a new way to deal with some of the problems that face our citizens, be it substance abuse or re-entry to the community from prison. Chapters contain key terms, boxed material, review questions, and recommended readings, and a glossary is provided to clarify important concepts.

Edward J. Latessa is Professor and Director of the School of Criminal Justice at the University of Cincinnati.

Paula Smith is an Associate Professor in the School of Criminal Justice at the University of Cincinnati.

 A Companion Website is available for this book at www.routledge.com/cw/latessa

Titles of Related Interest from Routledge and Anderson

CORRECTIONS IN THE COMMUNITY

Sixth Edition

Edward J. Latessa and Paula Smith

Routledge
Taylor & Francis Group

NEW YORK AND LONDON

This edition published 2015
by Routledge
711 Third Avenue, New York, NY 10017

and by Routledge
2 Park Square, Milton Park, Abingdon, Oxon, OX14 4RN

Routledge is an imprint of the Taylor & Francis Group, an informa business

© 2015 Taylor & Francis

Library of Congress Cataloging-in-Publication Data
Latessa, Edward J.
  Corrections in the community / Edward J. Latessa, Ph.D. & Paula Smith, Ph.D.,
  School of Criminal Justice, University of Cincinnati. — Sixth edition.
    pages cm
  Includes bibliographical references and index.
  ISBN 978-1-138-85417-8 (hardback : alk. paper) — ISBN 978-0-323-29886-5
  (pbk. : alk. paper) — ISBN 978-0-323-31264-6 (ebook)   1. Corrections—United
  States.   I. Smith, Paula (Paula H.)   II. Title.
  HV9469.L27 2015
  365'.973—dc23

                                                                          2014045622

ISBN: 978-1-138-85417-8 (hbk)
ISBN: 978-0-323-29886-5 (pbk)
ISBN: 978-0-323-31264-6 (ebk)

Typeset in Warnock Pro
by RefineCatch Limited, Bungay, Suffolk, UK

Printed and bound in the United States of America by Sheridan Books, Inc. (a Sheridan Group Company).

This book is dedicated to our families:
Sally, Amy, Jennifer, Michael, Allison and Denise Latessa
Sara Adams and MG

Contents in Brief

Contents in Detail

About the Authors

Edward J. Latessa is Professor and Director of the School of Criminal Justice at the University of Cincinnati. He received his Ph.D. from the Ohio State University in 1979. Dr. Latessa has published more than 140 works in the area of criminal justice, corrections, and juvenile justice. He is co-author of seven books, including *What Works (and Doesn't) in Reducing Recidivism* and *Corrections in America*. Dr. Latessa has directed over 150 funded research projects including studies of day reporting centers, juvenile justice programs, drug courts, prison programs, intensive supervision programs, halfway houses, and drug programs. He has been involved in evaluations of more than 600 correctional programs throughout the United States, and he has provided technical assistance and workshops in over 45 states. Dr. Latessa is a member of the Office of Justice Programs Science Advisory Board's subcommittee for the Bureau of Justice Assistance (appointed 2011) and has been a reviewer for the Office of Juvenile Justice and Delinquency Prevention Model Programs Guide. He is also a Senior Reviewer in the area of Corrections and Courts for the National Institute of Justice and the Office of Justice Programs. Dr. Latessa served as President of the Academy of Criminal Justice Sciences (1989–90). He has also received several awards, including: the Sylvia Boltz Tucker Award for Leadership and Service from the College of Education, Criminal Justice and Human Services, University of Cincinnati (2014); co-recipient of the MacNamara Award for best published paper from the Academy of Criminal Justice Sciences (2014); the Marguerite Q. Warren and Ted B. Palmer Differential Intervention Award presented from the Division of Corrections and Sentencing of the American Society of Criminology (2010); the Outstanding Community Partner Award from the Arizona Department of Juvenile Corrections (2010); the Maud Booth Correctional Services Award in recognition of dedicated service and leadership presented by the Volunteers of America (2010); the Community Hero Award presented by Community Resources for Justice (2010); the Bruce Smith Award for outstanding contributions to criminal justice from the Academy of Criminal Justice Sciences (2010); the George Beto Scholar Award from the College of Criminal Justice, Sam Houston State University (2009); the Mark Hatfield Award for Contributions in public policy research from the Hatfield School of Government at Portland State University (2008); the Outstanding Achievement

Award from the National Juvenile Justice Court Services Association (2007); the August Vollmer Award from the American Society of Criminology (2004); the Simon Dinitz Criminal Justice Research Award from the Ohio Department of Rehabilitation and Correction (2002); the Margaret Mead Award for dedicated service to the causes of social justice and humanitarian advancement from the International Community Corrections Association (2001); the Peter P. Lejins Award for Research from the American Correctional Association (1999); the ACJS Fellow Award (1998); and the ACJS Founders Award (1992). In 2013 he was identified as one of the most innovative people in criminal justice by a national survey conducted by the Center for Court Innovation in partnership with the Bureau of Justice Assistance and the U.S. Department of Justice.

Paula Smith is an Associate Professor in the School of Criminal Justice at the University of Cincinnati. She received her Ph.D. in psychology from the University of New Brunswick in 2006. Her research interests include offender classification and assessment, correctional rehabilitation, the psychological effects of incarceration, program implementation and evaluation, the transfer of knowledge to practitioners and policy makers, and meta-analysis. She has authored more than 60 articles, book chapters, and conference presentations on the aforementioned topics. Dr. Smith has directed numerous research projects and has been involved in evaluations of more than 400 correctional programs throughout the United States. She is a member of the Accreditation Panel for the National Offender Management Service in the UK as well as the Global Consortium on Corrections Research with Griffith University in Australia. In addition to her research experience, Dr. Smith has considerable frontline experience working with a variety of offender populations, including juvenile offenders, sex offenders, and perpetrators of domestic violence. Currently, she provides technical assistance to criminal justice agencies throughout the United States and Canada.

Preface

When the first edition of *Corrections in the Community* was written, the field was experiencing unprecedented incarceration rates, and prison construction and populations were expanding at an alarming rate. Much of what was done in community corrections followed the theme of "getting tough" with crime and offenders. Intensive supervision without treatment, boot camps, shock incarceration, and other sanctions were all tried, with little success in changing offender behavior. Since that time, much has changed. New prisons are not being built, and the prison population is actually in decline. We have also learned a great deal about how to more effectively improve the programs and services we offer our correctional population. Many of these programs operate in the community and we believe that the field is moving away from risk management to one of risk reduction—identifying those most in need of programs and supervision and targeting those criminogenic needs of offenders to actually reduce recidivism rates. Of course, to do that effectively we need to understand what the research and data tell us about designing and implementing evidence-based practices. A great deal of this edition addresses these important topics—risk assessment, improving supervision practices, using data to measure performance and outcomes, and following some empirically derived principles that will allow the system to be more effective and humane, and less costly.

Writing a book on a topic as broad and dynamic as community corrections is a very difficult task. It is extremely hard to know when to stop. The field is changing rapidly and, as a result, information and data are quickly outdated. We believe that we have pulled together some of the most recent and salient information available; however, we accept responsibility for any errors or shortcomings. There are several caveats we would like to make concerning this book.

First, as with prior editions, there are a great many charts and tables with data. Memorizing the numbers is not important, as they change daily. What is important are the trends over time. We want students to see patterns of what is happening in community corrections and to use this information to think critically about the issues facing the field.

Second, we recognize that students are not always interested in the historical aspects of a subject, and we have tried to keep that material to a minimum;

however, we also believe that it is important to understand where we came from and some of the reasons we do things the way we do in corrections. We have also provided key terms, review questions, boxed material, and recommended readings to highlight information that can help the student navigate the book and to better identify some of the key concepts and ideas. In today's world, we have seen an information explosion, and it is easy to find resources to learn more about virtually every topic in this book. We encourage students to be inquisitive and to seek out additional information that can advance their knowledge and understanding.

Third, we have added some new material. Drug and other problem-solving courts are now found in every state, and we felt it was important to expand our discussion of this important movement. It represents a new way to deal with some of the problems that face our citizens, be it substance abuse, or re-entry to the community from prison. These innovations have changed how many courts and communities view the problems that millions of Americans face. More importantly, they also demonstrate that we do not have to always rely on incarceration, and that many of our solutions to the crime problem can be found in the community, especially when various parts of the system work together to seek solutions.

Fourth, you will also become aware of our bias. We believe that we still incarcerate too many of our citizens, that this is not good social policy, and that many can be supervised in the community without seriously jeopardizing public safety. We believe that much public treasure is wasted and human misery increased while incarcerating low-risk offenders. As our good friend Frank Cullen often says, "we are liberal, not stupid." We recognize that some offenders—those who are violent and would likely cause serious harm to others—belong in prison. We do not believe, however, that all or even a majority of the nearly two million or so incarcerated fit that description.

Finally, while probation and parole practices are often slow to change, we do not believe this has to be the case. In just a few short years we have seen more and more agencies and programs move toward evidence-based practices, and if there is one theme to this book it is that we can indeed use research to improve the field and ultimately the lives of those who come into contact with the correctional system. While there is little doubt that change is slow and that old ideas persist, we also believe that the future of community corrections is bright and filled with promise. It is hoped that the instructors and students who use our book will find the subject of community corrections as interesting and stimulating as we do.

Edward Latessa and Paula Smith
Cincinnati, Ohio

Acknowledgments

Writing a book requires a great deal of help and support. We realize that it is a cliché to say that it could not have been possible without the following people, but truer words were never spoken.

There are many people who have allowed us to study and learn about community corrections. They all worked with us over the years, and have contributed immeasurably to our knowledge and experience. In particular, we wish to thank the following friends and colleagues: John Aarons, the late Tim Alley, David Altschuler, Michele Anderson, the late Don Andrews, Sarah Andrews, Dan Aning, Bridget Ansberg, Steve Aos, Brandon Applegate, Troy Armstrong, Jean Atkins, Allen Ault, Bob Balboni, Brad Barnes, John Baron, the late Cheryl Barrett, Jenny Bauer, Julie Baxter, Jeff Beard, Tom Beauclair, Alan Bekelman, Renee Bergeron, Tom Berghausen, Simone Bess, Shay Bilchik, Rick Billak, Claudia Black, Julia Blankenship, Mandy Bley, Jim Bonta, Paul Book, Guy Bourgon, Sue Bourke, Bob Borst, James Bralley, Ann Brewster, Barb Broderick, Ski Broman, Doug Brothers, Kelly Brown, Mike Brown, Bob Brown, Victor Brown, Yvonne Saunders-Brown, Bill Bruinsma, Rob Brusconi, Loren Buddress, Nancy Campbell, Ed Camp, Mark Carey, Mimi Carter, Kelly Castle, Liz Cass, Clint Castleberry, Matt Cate, the late Norm Chamberlain, Brian Center, Karen Chapple, Steve Chapman, John Chin, John Clancy, Elyse Clawson, Todd Clear, Marshall Clements, Rob Clevenger, Diane Coates, Alvin Cohen, Marcia Cohen, Anne Connell-Freund, Linda Connelly, Ron Corbett, Jim Corfman, Caprice Cosper, Brenda Cronin, Chris Cunningham, Nancy Cunningham, Bob Daquilante, Jim Dare, Patti Davis, Ben de Haan, Steve Devlin, Monda DeWeese, the late David Dillingham, Dennis Dimatteo, Gayle Dittmer, Frank Domurad, Mike Dooley, Pam Douglas, Bob Dugan, Joe Ellison, Warren Emmer, Don Evans, Tony Fabelo, Dot Faust, Gretchen Faulstich, Ray Ferns, Joe Fitzpatrick, Nathan Foo, Tonya Gaby, Chris Galli, Gene Gallo, Ryan Geis, Bruce Gibson, Steve Gibson, Rosemary Gido, Barry Glick, Robert Gloeckner, Kathleen Gnall, Michelle Goodman, Ricardo Goodridge, Don Gordon, Mark Gornik, Richard Gray, John Gramuglia, Brian Griffiths, Bill Grosshan, Sharon Haines, Ron Hajime, Patricia Hardyman, Jennifer Hartman, Steve Haas, Alicia Handwerk, Joe Hassett, Sharon Harrigfeld, Angie Hensley, Tomi Hiers, Ed Heller, Martha Henderson, Domingo Herraiz, Doug Herrmann, Chris Heywood, Rick

xxii   *Acknowledgments*

Hoekstra, Buzz Hoffman, LaRon Hogg, Deborah Holmberg, Dorothy Holmes, Steve Holmes, Alex Holsinger, Martin Horn, Dana Jones Hubbard, Mary Kay Hudson, Mindy Hutcherson, Butch Huyandi, Norma Jaeger, Linda Janes, Bob Jester, Phil Kader, Maureen Kiehm, Kevin Knight, Authur Jones, Justin Jones, Dan Joyner, Colleen Kadleck, George Kaiser, Sharon Kennedy, Bill King, Peter Kinziger, Lea Klingler, Melissa Knopp, Ed Kollin, Rosemary Kooy, Sally Kreamer, Bill Kroman, Don Kuhl, Fred LaFluer, Steve Lamberti, Glen Lammon, Jim Lawrence, Mike Link, Dominic Lisa, Shelley Johnson Listwan, Mary Livers, Fransaia LoDico, Dan Lombardo, Kirk Long, Denise Lord, Arthur Lurigio, Jennifer Luther, Pam McClain, Cindy McCoy, Scott MacDonald, David McGriff, Alan Mabry, Tom Madeo, Marty Magnusson, Lauren Maio, Joe Marchese, Vicki Markey, Bob Markin, Cheryl Marlow, Carole Martin, Ginger Martin, Betsy Matthews, Tina Mawhorr, Terry McDonald, Robert Mecum, Harvey Milkman, Michael Minor, Linda Modry, Gary Mohr, Sandy Monfort, Chris Monroe, Melissa Moon, Chris Money, Ernie Moore, Tom Muhleman, Linda Murken, Larry Muse, Geraldyne Nagy, Steve Nelson, Maria Nemec, Mike Nickols, Wendy Niehaus, Linda Nixon, Phil Noone, Michael Noyes, Tom O'Connor, Denise O'Donnell, Julie Okamoto, Steve Oldenstadt, Gaylon Oswalt, Sharon Owsley, Beth Oxford, Ted Palmer, Mario Paparozzi, Evalyn Parks, George Parks, Grafton Payne, Marc Pelka, Linda Penner, Geno Natalucci-Persichetti, Dan Peterca, Candi Peters, Ellyn Peterson, Sharon Pette, Merel Pickenpaugh, Dianne Poindexter, Bruce Ponder, Vince Polito, Dan Pompa, Jerry Powers, Rocco Pozzi, John Prevost, John Prinzi, Craig Prysock, Nina Ramsey, Harvey Reed, Brent Reinke, Ed Rhine, Sue Righthand, Bryan Riley, Debbie Rios, Carole Roberts, Denise Robinson, Jim Robinson, Renee Robinson, Casey Rogers, Claudia Rowlands, Kathy Russell, Loretta Ryland, Reece Satin, John Schneider, Pat Schreiner, Dave Schroot, Jane Seigel, Richard Seiter, Tim Shannon, Nancy Shomaker, Cliff Simonsen, Jerry Smith, Linda Smith, Mary Smith, Larry Solomon, Bill Sondervan, Kim Sperber, Mary Spotswood, Barry Stodley, Colleen Stoner, Susan Storm, Tom Strickrath, Kathleen Strouse, Mary Jo Sullivan, Jodi Sundt, Bill Sawyer, Bob Swisher, Scott Taylor, Mike Tardy, Faye Taxman, Richard Tewksbury, Yvette Thériault, Morris Thigpen, Mike Thompson, John Thurston, Neil Tilow, Jim Toner, Julie Truschel, Mike Turner, Cecilia Velasquez, Vicki Verdeyen, Ute Vilfroy, John Vivian, Dennis Waite, Myra Wall, Mike Walton, Bernie Warner, Kathy Waters, Ralph Watson, Beth Weiman, Carey Welebob, Bonita White, Jim Wichtman, Reggie Wilkinson, Diane Williams, Larry Williams, Gary Yates, the late George Yefchek, Gary Zajac, Andrew Zalman, Carole Rapp-Zimmerman, and Linda Zogg.

A number of current and former research assistants and graduate students at the University of Cincinnati assisted us with this and previous editions of the book: Kristin Bechtel, Lesli Blair, Lori Brusman-Lovins, Angela Estes, Tony Flores, Lia Gormsen, Jessica Halliday, Erin Harbinson, Alex Holsinger, Debi Koetzle, Ryan Labrecque, Rich Lemke, Brian Lovins, Christopher Lowenkamp, Matthew Makarios, Kelsey Mattick, AJ Myer, Kristin Ostrowski, Jennifer Pealer, Ryan Labreque, Charlene Taylor, and Jessica Warner. Special thanks to Amanda Pompoco for assisting with some of the more complicated charts in this version. We wish them well with their careers, and hope that they adopt the book! A special word of thanks to several University of Cincinnati full-time staff members for all of their help and support: Ashley Bauman, Erin Cochran, Jean Gary, Eva Kishimoto, Jenni Lux, Janice Miller, Kelly Pitocco, Chandra Reeves, John Schwartz, Mindy Schweitzer, Jen Scott, Jodi Sleyo, Carrie Sullivan, and Cara Thompson.

We also wish to thank Dr. Pamela Chester, the Acquisitions Editor at Taylor & Francis Publishing, as well as the old Anderson crew, for all of their help and support over the years. Much of the copyediting, proofing, and sundry tasks associated with the production of a book were in the very capable hands of Ellen Boyne, who has been a very good friend and supporter of our book. We would also be remiss not to mention the assistance and support of our good friend Mickey Braswell, and the helpful review of the first edition from John Whitehead at East Tennessee State University.

To our colleagues and friends, without whose support and expertise this book would never have been possible: Harry Allen, Frank Cullen, Robin Engel, Chris Eskridge, Jim Frank, Paul Gendreau, Claire Goggin, Bob Langworthy, Chris Sullivan, Larry Travis, Patricia Van Voorhis, Jerry Vito, and John Wright.

Finally, we wish to thank Amy, Jennifer, Michael, and Allison, who reminded Ed that delinquency prevention begins at home, as well as Sara and Kiara, who allow Paula to test early intervention strategies on a daily basis. And to Sally and Michael for your endless support and care, we love you.

Edward Latessa
Paula Smith

Chapter 1

THE CRIMINAL JUSTICE SYSTEM

Key Terms

community corrections
corrections
criminal justice system
incarceration

jail
parole
prison
probation

> It is hard to identify the benefits inmates gain from prison, but the harm done there is readily seen. If you want to increase the crime problem, incite men to greater evil, and intensify criminal inclinations and proclivities, then lock violators up in prison for long periods, reduce their outside contacts, stigmatize them and block their lawful employment when released, all the while setting them at tutelage under the direction of more skilled and predatory criminals. I know of no better way to gain your ends than these.—Harry E. Allen

Crime is everywhere, in all nations great and small, and in this nation. In the United States, crime is a violation of criminal statutes passed by elected representatives. These statutes are enforced by a variety of social control agencies, including law enforcement, prosecution, court, and post-adjudication components (e.g., prisons, probation, and parole). These varied agencies and actions, along with their philosophical bases and objectives, are usually called the "criminal justice system."

No one imposed this specific set of agencies on the nation. We invented them ourselves and, if there is something amiss with an agency or mission, it can be changed. One fact about the American criminal justice system is that it is rapidly evolving and changing as a result of the volume of crime, emerging national priorities, available funding, and changing political ideologies. Behaviors deemed particularly heinous in one epoch may become regulated, if not accepted, behavior in another. For example, the "Great Experiment" of prohibition attempted to protect our national character and youth, increase productivity, lessen collateral problems of idleness, and improve the moral fiber of those using alcohol. It was later abandoned as a national crusade; earlier twentieth-century law enforcement efforts instead lapsed into strategies to regulate alcohol as a controlled substance, concerned only in large part with keeping alcohol out of the hands of youthful consumers and collecting taxes. More recently we have seen several states legalize marijuana, when not so long ago one could be imprisoned for its use.

One component of the criminal justice system is **corrections**, defined as "post-adjudication processing of convicted criminal offenders." This definition, if it were ever adequate, probably best fits the correctional scene of the early twentieth century, when the major sentencing options available to sentencing courts were committing the offender to prison or granting probation. In fact, the study of post-adjudication processing of criminal law offenders was, until about 1969, commonly referred to as "penology." As shown in subsequent chapters, post-adjudication has become much more complex in the United States.

The field of corrections, like most of the justice system, has undergone rapid change in the past three decades. Programs have been developed to allow prosecutors to suspend prosecution of alleged criminals, provided they became and remained actively involved in seeking personal development and rehabilitation under the "deferred prosecution" program. Pretrial detention of accused law violators is now used less frequently due to the development of personal recognizance programs that reduced the importance of bondsmen in the pretrial portion of the system. In addition, the tools of technology have grown greatly in the past two decades, expanding probation supervision into conventional probation, intensive supervised probation, house arrest (with or without electronic monitoring or global position tracking), community service, day attendance centers, and restitution programs. There are even probation variations that combine serving a sentence in jail before probation begins, and several probation programs that require a period of imprisonment prior to return to the community under probation supervision. These latter programs, incidentally, are part of the "intermediate sanctions" that have emerged in the past 30 years: offender control programs that fall somewhere between probation and imprisonment.

What has corrections become? How can we best define it at the present time? For us, corrections is the social control agency that provides societal protection through incarceration and community supervision and rehabilitation services to persons accused or convicted of criminal law violating behavior. This definition includes restorative justice and pretrial diversion programs, as well as the more traditional probation and parole services. It also embraces intermediate sanctions and alternative early release programs for inmates in prisons across the nation. In sum, corrections involves social control of persons whose behavior has brought them to the attention of the justice system. The missions, objectives, procedures, and even

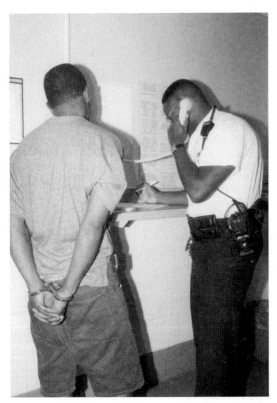

Booking into local jail.
[Photo courtesy of Beth Sanders]

principles that govern our definition of corrections are continually changing. In this book, we hope to describe the recent developments and emerging dimensions that define community corrections today.

CORRECTIONS IN THE COMMUNITY

This book describes and explains corrections in the community, or "community corrections." This term refers to numerous and diverse types of supervision, treatment, reintegration, control, restoration, and supportive programs for criminal law violators. Community corrections programs, as shown later, are designed for offenders at many levels of both juvenile and criminal justice systems. First, community corrections programs are found in the pre-adjudication level of the justice systems and include diversion and pretrial release programs, as well as treatment programs provided by private sector agencies, particularly for juveniles (Allen et al., 2012).

As correctional clients enter the justice system, community corrections programs have been developed and designed to minimize their further processing and placement into more secure settings. These pre-imprisonment programs include restitution, community services, active probation, intensive supervised probation, house arrest, and residential community facilities, such as halfway houses (please note that all of these programs are described in detail in later chapters). One assumption underlying this effort to minimize offender penetration into the justice system is that community corrections is more effective at reducing future crime and is more cost-efficient. Community corrections is certainly no less effective in reducing recidivism than is prison, and there is strong evidence that community correctional programs, if administered properly, can significantly reduce recidivism.[1]

Another assumption is that community corrections is more humane, although there is some contemporary debate over whether corrections should be humane rather than harsh.

Community corrections continues after incarceration (and in some cases is combined with incarceration),[2] and among the many programs found at this level are split sentences (jail followed by probation), shock incarceration and shock probation, prison furlough programs, work and educational release, shock parole, and parole programs and services.[3]

The various points at which community corrections programs have been developed are suggested in Figure 1.1, which identifies the flow of clients into and through the justice system.

The diagram shown in Figure 1.1 first appeared in President Lyndon Johnson's Crime Commission report, *The Challenge of Crime in a Free Society* (1969). It outlined the basic sequence of events in the criminal justice process. Police, courts, and corrections were thus viewed as elements that were interrelated and interdependent. The idea was to demonstrate the manner in which successful crime prevention was the goal of the entire system. Community corrections fits squarely into this goal: offenders whose criminal behavior is reduced or

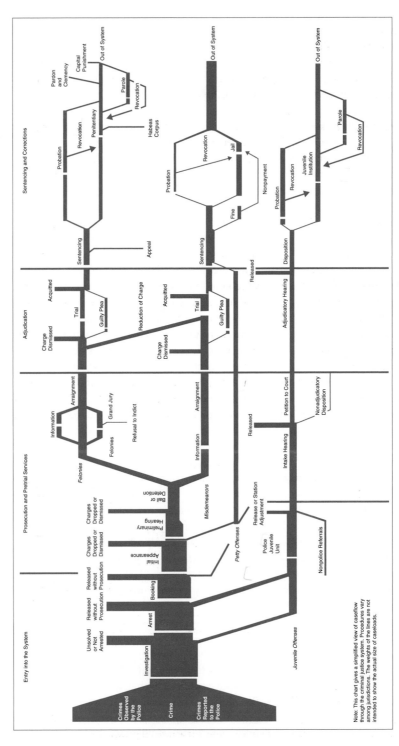

Figure 1.1 What is the Sequence of Events in the Criminal Justice System?

Source: Adapted from President's Commission on Law Enforcement and Administration of Justice (1969).

Box 1.1
Probation and Parole

[Probation is a sentence imposed by the court that does not usually involve confinement and imposes conditions to restrain the offender's actions in the community.] The court retains authority to modify the conditions of the sentence or to re-sentence the offender if he or she violates the conditions.

　　[Parole is the release of an offender from confinement prior to expiration of his or her sentence on condition of good behavior and supervision in the community.]

---

eliminated through programs in the community will commit fewer if any crimes in the future.[4]

Two major factors should be pointed out in Figure 1.1. [First, the major ways out of the system are probation and parole,] shown here as system outputs. The [second conclusion is that the number of cases flowing through the system decreases as offenders are processed at the various decision points (prosecutor, court, sentencing, and release from prison). The majority of offenders under correctional control are in the community.] It is also noteworthy that [since 2009 the correctional population has declined. This four-year trend halts what had been an ever-growing number of Americans in the correctional system.]

The percentage of offenders in each major correctional sanction can be found in Figure 1.2. [Non-incarceration sentences were imposed for 56 percent of offenders in 2012.] Another 12 percent who were sentenced were released from

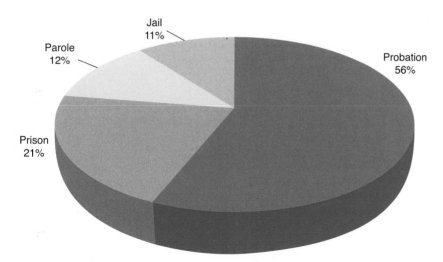

Figure 1.2 Correctional Populations in the United States, 2012.

Source: Glaze, L.E., Herberman, E.J. (2013). *Correctional populations in the United States, 2012.* Washington, DC: U.S. Department of Justice, Bureau of Justice Programs.

↗68% of Individuals on Parole/Probation

prison onto parole supervision. Together this represents nearly 4.8 million offenders. Even a large part of those offenders sentenced to jail may be released onto probation as part of a split sentence. It should be obvious that community corrections handles a large proportion of the offenders in the nation. For example, the Bureau of Justice Statistics (2013) reported that one in every 35 adult residents of the nation was under correctional control at the start of 2013. This is the lowest rate since 1997. It was also estimated that one in every 50 adults was supervised on probation or parole. On the basis of 100,000 adult residents in the nation, 1,875 were on probation, 353 on parole, and 920 in prison or in jail (see Table 1.1). These rates have dropped over the past few years. More than two out of three offenders were living in the community on a given day in 2012. A list of the incarceration rate for each state is shown in Table 1.2. Louisiana leads the nation with a rate of 865 per 100,000, and Maine has the lowest with 147 (Glaze & Herberman, 2013).

Table 1.1 Number of Adults under Correctional Supervision in 2006 and 2012 per 100,000 Residents

	Rate per 100,000	
	2006	**2012**
Probation	1,875	1,633
Parole	353	353
Prison or jail	1,000	920
Total correctional population	3,190	2,870

Sources: Glaze, L.E., Herberman, E.J. (2013). *Correctional populations in the United States, 2012.* Washington, DC: U.S. Department of Justice, Bureau of Justice Programs; Maruschak, L.M., Bonczar, T. (2014). *Probation and parole in the United States, 2012.* Washington, DC: U.S. Department of Justice, Bureau of Justice Statistics.

Table 1.2 Ranking of States by Prison Incarceration Rates, 2012 (Inmates per 100,000 Residents)

1. Louisiana	865
2. Mississippi	690
3. Alabama	650
4. Texas	633
5. Oklahoma	632
6. Arizona	589
7. Georgia	547
8. Arkansas	545
9. Florida	537
10. Missouri	512

11.	Idaho	487
12.	Kentucky	479
13.	South Carolina	473
14.	Virginia	468
15.	Nevada	461
16.	Indiana	443
17.	Tennessee	443
18.	Ohio	441
19.	Michigan	434
20.	Delaware	439
21.	Colorado	427
22.	South Dakota	426
23.	Pennsylvania	403
24.	Alaska	399
25.	California	393
26.	Wisconsin	385
27.	Wyoming	382
28.	Maryland	380
29.	Illinois	376
30.	Oregon	373
31.	Montana	367
32.	West Virginia	367
33.	North Carolina	362
34.	Connecticut	350
35.	New Mexico	329
36.	Kansas	324
37.	Iowa	295
38.	New York	283
39.	Hawaii	282
40.	New Jersey	269
41.	Washington	260
42.	Vermont	255
43.	Nebraska	244
44.	Utah	243
45.	North Dakota	206
46.	Massachusetts	205
47.	New Hampshire	198
48.	Rhode Island	197
49.	Minnesota	183
50.	Maine	147
51.	Federal System	63
	U.S. Total:	492

Source: Carson, E.A., Golinelli, D. (2013). *Prisoners in 2012—advance counts*. Washington, DC: U.S. Department of Justice, Bureau of Justice Statistics.

Box 1.2
Jail

A jail is a confinement facility, usually administered by a local law enforcement agency, intended for adults but sometimes containing juveniles, that holds persons detained pending adjudication and/or persons committed after adjudication for sentences of generally one year or less. Some states do allow longer sentences to be served in jail, although these are the exception. Jails are usually supported by local tax revenues and, as such, are particularly vulnerable to resource reductions.

Additional categories of jail inmates include mentally ill persons for whom there are no other facilities or who are awaiting transfer to mental health authorities, parolees and probationers awaiting hearings, court-detained witnesses and persons charged with contempt of court, federal prisoners awaiting pick-up by marshals, and offenders sentenced to state departments of corrections for whom there is not yet space but who cannot be released ("holdbacks").

Box 1.3
Prison

A **prison** is a state or federal confinement facility having custodial authority over criminal law-violating adults sentenced to confinement for usually more than one year.

Probation in America

The majority of the adults under correctional care or custody are on probation, the largest single segment of the community correctional system. As shown in Table 1.3, Georgia had the largest number of its citizens on probation, and the highest rate: 5,919 per 100,000 adult residents. Four other states each had a rate of more than 2,500: Ohio, Rhode Island, Idaho, and Minnesota. The lowest state rate was New Hampshire (390 per 100,000).

In all, it is clear that a great number of convicted persons are now being placed on probation. In most cases, probation agencies monitor the offender's compliance with the conditions of probation release (restitution, community service, payment of fines, house arrest, drug/alcohol rehabilitation, etc.). The crucial roles that probation plays in community corrections and the justice system become even more apparent when institutional and parole population figures are examined.

Table 1.3 Community Corrections among the States, 2012

Ten states with the largest community corrections populations	Number supervised
Probation	
Georgia	457,217
Texas	408,472
California	297,917
Ohio	252,901
Florida	245,040
Michigan	185,984
Pennsylvania	177,851
Illinois	125,442
Indiana	124,976
New Jersey	114,611
Ten states with the highest rates of supervision	**Persons supervised per 100,000 adult U.S. residents***
Georgia	5,919
Ohio	2,886
Rhode Island	2,848
Idaho	2,691
Minnesota	2,625
Indiana	2,441
Michigan	2,338
Delaware	2,185
Maryland	2,117
Texas	2,107
Ten states with the lowest rates of supervision	**Persons supervised per 100,000 adult U.S. residents***
New Hampshire	390
Nevada	536
Utah	575
West Virginia	582
Maine	652
New York	701
Kansas	784
Virginia	832
North Dakota	863
Oklahoma	882
Parole	
Ten states with the largest community corrections population	**Number supervised**
California	111,703
Texas	105,996
Pennsylvania	94,581

Ten states with the largest community corrections populations	Number supervised
New York	47,243
Louisiana	27,092
Illinois	26,208
Georgia	25,489
Michigan	22,598
Oregon	22,463
Missouri	21,140

Ten states with the highest rates of supervision	Persons supervised per 100,000 adult U.S. residents*
Arkansas	1,041
Pennsylvania	1,008
Louisiana	828
Texas	583
Missouri	446
Wisconsin	453
Kentucky	428
Idaho	328
New Mexico	322
California	308

Ten states with the lowest rates of supervision	Persons supervised per 100,000 adult U.S. residents*
Maine	2
Florida	29
Virginia	31
North Carolina	58
Rhode Island	60
North Dakota	78
Delaware	84
Oklahoma	80
Nebraska	99
Connecticut	99

Note: This table excludes the District of Columbia, a wholly urban jurisdiction; Georgia probation counts, which included probation case-based counts for private agencies; and Idaho probation counts in which estimates for misdemeanors were based on admissions.

*Rates are computed using the U.S. adult resident population on January 1, 2013.

Source: Maruschak, L.M., Bonczar, T. (2014). *Probation and parole in the United States, 2012.* Washington, DC: U.S. Department of Justice, Bureau of Justice Statistics.

The U.S. Prison Population

Because the rate of parole in a given state is affected by the size of the prison population, it is necessary to examine the size of the U.S. prison population before considering parole figures. A census of state and federal corrections institutions is conducted at mid-year and year-end by the Bureau of Justice Statistics. At the end of 2012, the number of people incarcerated in prison was 1,483,900, a decline of more than 21,000 from 2011 (Glaze & Herberman, 2013). Figures from the Bureau also reveal that 59 percent of all those incarcerated are either black or Hispanics (Carson & Golinelli, 2013). See Figure 1.3 for the number of persons under correctional supervision in 2000, 2010, and 2012.

These figures are important to the parole rates in part because they represent the source of clients for the parole system. In many states prisoners enter the parole system by a parole board decision or by fulfilling the condition of mandatory release. Typically, at some time between their minimum and maximum sentences, inmates are released from prison and placed on parole. Mandatory releasees enter parole supervision automatically at the expiration of their maximum terms (minus sentence reductions for time credit accumulated for good time, jail time, and other "gain" procedures). Traditionally, this has been the manner in which a parole system operated under the indeterminate sentencing model presently in force in one-half of the states. The "abandon parole" movement began in 1976, and a number of states have changed their statutes to remove the authority of the parole board to release offenders before the expiration of their sentences. This issue is discussed in more detail in the chapters that follow.

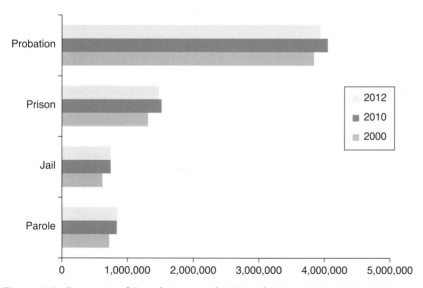

Figure 1.3 Correctional Populations in the United States: 2000, 2010, 2012.

Source: Glaze, L.E., Herberman, E.J. (2013). *Correctional populations in the United States, 2012.* Washington, DC: U.S. Department of Justice, Bureau of Justice Programs.

Parole in America

Adults on parole at the beginning of 2013 are found in Table 1.1 and totaled 851,200, down slightly from 2011. Table 1.3 shows that the parole rate ranged from a high of 1,041 in Arkansas to a low of two in Maine. Maine abolished parole in the late 1970s, which explains the low rate; only those sentenced to parole before 1976 continue to be supervised.

In sum, parole statistics reveal the relationship between the size of the prison population and the number of parolees. These figures indicate that both prison and parole populations increased dramatically from 1995 through 2008, and only began abating since 2009. Changes in sentencing options and sentence length have also meant that prisoners were actually serving longer sentences than they were in 1995.

SUMMARY

This brief consideration of statistics from major components of the correctional system (probation, prisons, and parole) demonstrates their crucial linkage within the criminal justice system. Imagine what would happen if probation and parole were abolished completely and all convicted persons were required to serve their full prison terms; if this happened today, the prison population would be over seven million! Naturally, the prison system is not equipped to handle such a large number of inmates, nor would it be good social policy to attempt such a foolish venture.

We do not wish to suggest that all offenders could and should be released to community corrections. At least 15–25 percent of the prison population are too dangerous or pose too great a threat to community safety to allow their immediate release, even onto "intensive supervised parole" (Allen et al., 2012).

It is the function of probation and its many variants (the so-called "intermediate sanctions"), as well as parole, to determine how the population of convicted persons can be managed in a fashion consistent with not only the capacity of the prison population but also the goals of societal protections and offender rehabilitation and reintegration.

In short, the examination of corrections in the community is the theme of this text. We consider such key issues as what are the best methods for classifying and supervising offenders? What background, education, and training should various community corrections agents possess? How effective are community corrections programs in terms of public safety? And at what cost? What are the recent innovations in community corrections and intermediate sanctions? How effective are these compared to incarceration? How are juveniles handled in the community? The consideration of these (and other) issues will provide readers with the opportunity to form their own opinions and ideas concerning the proper use of community correctional programs and how to coordinate these in the criminal justice system.

Review Questions

1. What is corrections in the community?
2. What is meant by the funnel effect and how does it occur?
3. If probation and parole were abolished completely, what effect would this have on the prison systems?
4. Develop an argument for increased use of community corrections.
5. How are offenders generally released from prison?
6. Describe the current distribution of offenders across the main components of the criminal justice system.

Notes

1 An extensive body of research has demonstrated that community correctional programs can have a substantial effect on recidivism provided certain empirically derived principles are met. For a summary of this research see Latessa and Lowenkamp (2007).
2 For example, in Ohio, the state funds "community-based correctional facilities." These facilities are operated by local community corrections boards, they are designed to provide treatment, and they often utilize local community services. They are, however, secure facilities and after being released offenders are usually on probation. Texas funds similar facilities.
3 Some would argue that many so-called "community" correctional programs are essentially institutional correctional facilities because they are state run. However, we believe that state-operated programs can indeed be considered community correctional programs, provided they include some type of supervision in the community. For a different perspective on this issue, see Duffee (1990). See also Burke (1997); and Gendreau et al. (2000).
4 See Lowenkamp et al. (2006); and Wilson et al. (2000).

Recommended Readings

Allen, H.E., Latessa, E.L., Ponder, B. (2012). *Corrections in America: An introduction.* 12th edn. Upper Saddle River, NJ: Pearson/Prentice Hall.
Latessa, E.J., Holsinger, A. (2011). *Correctional Contexts: Contemporary and classical readings.* Los Angeles: Roxbury.

References

Allen, H.E., Latessa, E.L., Ponder, B. (2012). *Corrections in America: An introduction.* 12th edn. Upper Saddle River, NJ: Pearson/Prentice Hall.
Burke, P.B. (1997). *Policy driven responses to probation and parole violations.* Washington, DC: U.S. Department of Justice.

Carson, E.A., Golinelli, D. (2013). *Prisoners in 2012—Advance county.* Washington, DC: U.S. Department of Justice, Bureau of Justice Statistics.

Duffee, D.E. (1990). Community characteristics: The presumed characteristics and argument for a new approach. In: D.E. Duffee, E.F. McGarrell, eds. *Community corrections: A community field approach.* Cincinnati: Anderson.

Gendreau, P., Goggin, C., Smith, P. (2000). Generating rational correctional policies. *Corrections Management Quarterly* 4(2), 52–60.

Glaze, L.E., Herberman, E.J. (2013). *Correctional populations in the United States, 2012.* Washington, DC: U.S. Department of Justice, Bureau of Justice Programs.

Latessa, E.J., Lowenkamp, C. (2007). What works in reducing recidivism. *St. Thomas Law Journal* 3, 521–535.

Lowenkamp, C.T., Latessa, E.J., Holsinger, A. (2006). The risk principle in action: What we have learned from 13,676 offenders and 97 correctional programs. *Crime & Delinquency* 51(1), 1–17.

Maruschak, L.M., Bonczar, T. (2014). *Probation and parole in the United States, 2012.* Washington, DC: U.S. Department of Justice, Bureau of Justice Statistics.

President's Commission on Law Enforcement and Administration of Justice (1969). *The challenge of crime in a free society.* Washington, DC: U.S. Government Printing Office.

Wilson, D.B., Gallagher, C., MacKenzie, D. (2000). A meta-analysis of corrections-based education, vocation, and work programs for adult offenders. *Journal of Research in Crime and Delinquency* 37(4), 347–368.

Chapter 2

SENTENCING AND COMMUNITY CORRECTIONS

Key Terms

community service

day-reporting center

determinate sentence

deterrence

electronic monitoring

fine

indeterminate sentencing

intensive supervision

intermediate sanctions

jail

mandatory release

parole

parole boards

penitentiary plea bargaining pretrial release

prison

restitution

retribution

selective incapacitation

sentencing disparity

split sentence

"three-strikes" sentencing laws

tourniquet sentencing

work release

> Justice is itself the great standing policy of civil society; and any eminent departure from it, under any circumstances, lies under the suspicion of being no policy at all.—Edmund Burke

CONTEMPORARY SENTENCING PRACTICES

Historically, the American criminal justice system was an adversarial combat between the state and the accused defendant in a criminal trial. The accused denied committing the alleged offense, and the trial jury was charged with determining the fact of innocence or guilt. If the accused was found guilty, the presiding judge, using all available information and guided by the pre-sentence investigation report ordered previously from the court's investigators, would then impose sentence on the guilty in the interest of justice and to achieve some recognizable correctional objective. Such objectives could include punishment, rehabilitation, reintegration, retribution, reparation, or deterrence.

Table 2.1 Types of Felony Sentences Imposed in State Courts in 2006 (percent)

Crime	Nonincarceration	Incarceration	
	Probation	Jail	Prison
Murder	3	2	93
Sexual assault	16	18	64
Robbery	13	14	71
Aggravated assault	25	30	43
Burglary	24	24	49
Larceny	28	34	34
Motor vehicle theft	15	41	42
Drug trafficking	29	26	41
All	27	28	41

Source: Rosenmerkel, S., Durose, M., Farole, D. (2009). *Felony sentences in state courts, 2006: Statistical tables.* Washington, DC: U.S. Department of Justice, Bureau of Justice Statistics.

Perhaps this model typified the justice system a half-decade ago, but it is atypical of sentencing practices in the 2000s. Some 1,132,290 persons were convicted of a felony offense in state courts in 2006, including 197,030 for a violent felony (Rosenmerkel et al., 2009). A large number of convictions were for drug possession and trafficking, about 33 percent of the total number of felony convictions and almost two times the number of convictions for all crimes of violence totaled together (murder, robbery, rape, and aggravated assault). Federal courts convicted 78,009 persons of a felony in 2006. That number represents only 6 percent of the combined state and federal convictions in that year. See Table 2.1 for the types of sentences imposed by state courts.

Determination of guilt, however, is seldom decided by a jury. Instead, most of those convicted (95 percent) pleaded guilty for considerations, and the judge usually complied with the negotiated plea struck by the prosecutor and defense counsel. Only 5 percent of the total convicted cases were found guilty through trial, and 60 percent of those were convicted by the judge in a bench trial (Durose & Langan, 2007). A definition of plea bargaining is found in Box 2.1.

Regardless of the avenue of conviction, 69 percent of those convicted felony offenders were sentenced to incarceration (either prison or jail). The remaining 31 percent were sentenced to probation. Of course, probation is the umbrella and the workhorse of corrections, under which many other community-based alternatives reside. Before we look at sentencing options it is important to examine overall sentencing approaches.

Box 2.1
Plea Bargaining

Plea bargaining is exchange of prosecutorial and/or judicial concessions, commonly a lesser charge, the dismissal of other pending charges, a recommendation by the prosecutor for a reduced sentence, or a combination thereof, in return for a plea of guilty.

THE DEVELOPMENT OF PAROLE AND THE INDETERMINATE SENTENCE

A basic tenet underlying sentencing in the nineteenth century was a belief in the perfectibility of humans. The American Revolution engendered a great deal of interest and enthusiasm for reform. The emerging nation threw off the dread yoke of British imperialism, including the harsh and widely hated British laws in place throughout the colonies that relied so heavily on the death penalty. In its place, a more rational system of "corrections" arose—the ideal of certain but humane punishment believed to most certainly deter offenders from criminal careers. America entered the "Progressive Era" in which "rational men" would be able to pursue their best interests and maximize gain and reward while avoiding penalties or pain. This famous principle ("hedonistic calculus") was accepted wholeheartedly as a guiding objective in the question being asked by concerned citizens, lawmakers, and public officials: "Who are offenders and what shall we do with them?" Under British codes, they were seen as inherently evil and thus to be punished, killed, or disabled. Under the Progressive Era, the answer that emerged was quite different: They are people out of touch with God and, given a chance to change by thinking about their crime and relationship with God and fellow humans, they will opt to repent and change. Prison was the answer to the policy question of what to do with offenders, and America embraced prisons with its general zeal for humanitarianism and enthusiasm, building huge "fortress" prisons that emphasized reform and repentance. The American **penitentiary** ("place to do penance") was a contribution to corrections throughout the world.

Yet in the emerging penitentiary and later reformatory movements there remained the philosophical quandary: What to do with the reformed offender who continued to be held in prison years after actual reformation. Sentencing codes were determinate or "flat" and inmates were expected to serve their sentences to the day. In this philosophical environment, correctional administrators began to innovate.

In the British outpost of Australia, offenders who had been sentenced to exile by transportation to Australia occasionally continued their violent criminal behavior. Transported felons were failures because they had committed crimes in England; when they continued their miscreant behavior in Australia, they were shipped to Norfolk Island, onto a bleak and inhospitable shore some 1,000 miles to the east. These "double failures" of Australia who were subsequently sentenced to death thanked God, but those sentenced to Norfolk Island sank into the deepest depression and sadness. Such was the place that Captain Alexander Maconochie inherited when he was posted as managing officer in 1842.

Maconochie quickly determined that the violence, treachery, and staff–inmate confrontations had to stop and seized upon what is now known as the "mark" system (also known now as a form of token economy). Assembling the inmates, he promised that there was hope of freedom if any inmate could amass 100 marks (credits). Each inmate was to be billed for food, clothing, and tools; marks were to be assigned for quantity and quality of work. Through hard work and frugal living, inmates could save marks; when an inmate amassed 100 marks, he was free from correctional control, to marry and live on the island, and conduct himself with proper behavior. Assault and violence immediately declined with this innovative and constructive management approach, but the Royal Marines assigned to prison officer duty thought Maconochie was too lenient and that he mollycoddled offenders. Maconochie was quickly removed, and Norfolk Island slid rapidly back into the slough of despair it was before Maconochie's innovative management.

Fortunately, Maconochie's ideas spread: imprisonment could be used to prepare an offender for a productive life and eventual return to the community under what could be seen as an "indeterminate sentence." The implications of this demonstration were that sentence length should not be an arbitrary or "flat" sentence but one related to the reform and rehabilitation of the inmate. Sir Walter Crofton in Ireland used Maconochie's concepts when he developed what became known as the "Irish" system.

Crofton reasoned that if penitentiaries were places where offenders reflect on their crimes and decide to stop their criminal activities ("repent"), then there should be some mechanism or scheme to detect when the reform had occurred, as well as releasing the offender when this had happened. Crofton established a three-stage system, each of which would bring the convict closer to freedom within the community. Phase One consisted of solitary confinement and tedious work such as picking oakum (separating coconut fibers for the purpose of making rope). After six months, the convict could be assigned to public works on a team, each member of which was responsible for the behavior of every other team member (an early use of "peer pressure"). Anyone who misbehaved would cause all team members to be returned to Phase One. The last phase was assignment to a transitional prison permitting unsupervised day work outside the prison. If the inmate's behavior was good and he could find employment in the community, he was given a "ticket of leave," in effect extending the limits of confinement to include placement in the county on "conditional pardon." While the ex-inmate could not leave the county and was required to produce his "ticket" upon demand by law enforcement agents, he was nonetheless free of correctional control for the duration of his sentence. Of course, if his conduct was bad, the ticket could be revoked and the offender returned to prison (Phase One). In effect, Crofton established conditional liberty in the community, what would now be called **parole**.

By 1870, prison crowding in the United States had become so massive and the related management problems so complex that a conference was deemed necessary. Prison administrators, wardens, religious leaders, concerned leaders, and innovators met in Cincinnati, Ohio in 1870 in the first meeting of what would become the American Correctional Association. Spurred on by Crofton and empowered by eloquent oratory by Zebulon Reed Brockway, the assembly adopted standards and principles that addressed new types of buildings to be constructed, as well as an early release system. In 1876, Brockway initiated parole in the nation by the ticket of leave system. New York quickly passed enabling legislation and parole became a reality.

Box 2.2
Indeterminate Sentencing

Under the **indeterminate sentencing** system, the sentencing judge pronounces a minimum and maximum period of incarceration, such as from 3 to 5 or 5 to 10, or 1 to 20 years, and so on. Correctional personnel were expected to assist the offenders in changing their behavior and preparing for eventual return to the community, and the parole board was to monitor offender behavior and change. The actual decision on parole readiness and release was detailed to a parole board, charged with protecting society and releasing offenders onto community correctional supervision. The actual conditions of parole were set by the parole board, which retained authority to return nonadjusting offenders to the prison for further treatment and punishment. In essence, the sentencing judge shares sentence length determination with the executive branch in which parole boards are located.

Box 2.3
Pretrial Release

Pretrial release is the process by which those accused of a crime are released prior to trial. Mechanisms for release include posting bond, or release on recognizance (a promise to return to stand trial).

Other states responded by changing their sentencing structures as well by authorizing parole as a mechanism for releasing reformed offenders. The resultant sentencing system was the indeterminate sentence, the dominant sentencing structure in the United States until the mid-1970s.

RAPID CHANGE IN SENTENCING

By 1930, most states and federal courts were operating under the indeterminate sentencing structure. The wide range of sentence lengths reflected the dominant rehabilitation goal of the correctional system and the belief that once the offender had been rehabilitated, the parole board would detect the change and then order parole release.[1] Using their authority of discretionary release, parole boards actually determined the length of the sentence served.

Following a very long period of relative inactivity (1930–74), American sentencing laws and practices began to undergo rapid change, a fundamental restructuring of the sentencing process. The causes have been identified (Allen et al., 2012):

1. Prison uprisings (such as at Attica in New York and others in California, Florida, New Mexico, and Oklahoma) indicated that inmates were particularly discontented with the rhetoric of rehabilitation and the reality of the prison environment.
2. The abuse of discretion caused concerns about individual rights, as prosecutors, judges, and parole boards were immune from review and some practiced arbitrary uses of discretion.
3. Court orders and decisions led to a movement that demanded accountability in official decision making and outcomes.
4. The rehabilitation ideal was challenged, both empirically and ideologically, which undermined the rationale of the indeterminate sentence's "parole after rehabilitation" corollary.
5. Experimental and statistical studies of judicial sentencing found substantial disparity and both racial and class discrimination. Such inconsistencies and disparities fostered the conclusion that sentencing practices were unfair. (Sentencing disparity occurs when offenders committing the same crimes under the same circumstances are given different sentences by the same judge.)
6. Crime control and corrections became a political football, useful for those seeking election to public office. Such political opportunists led the general public to believe that lenient judges and parole boards were releasing dangerous offenders back into the community, with little concern for public safety.

Box 2.4
Sentencing Disparity

Sentencing disparity is the divergence in the types and lengths of sentences imposed for the same crimes, with no evident reason for the differences. It is also known as unequal treatment of similarly situated offenders.

NEW GOALS

Although corrections in the 1970s generally reflected the utilitarian goal of rehabilitation, other discussions from the reform movement brought additional correctional goals to the forefront in the 1980s, such as the incapacitation of persons likely to commit future crimes and its variant of selective incapacitation, in which the highest-risk offenders would receive much longer sentences in order to prevent any more criminal activity. The specific deterrence of sentenced offenders—and the general deterrence of those contemplating committing a crime—was legitimized as a social policy goal. One emerging example of this new goal is the "three-strikes" policy many states have adopted, particularly in California,[2] mandating long-term incarceration (at least 25 years) for those persons convicted of a serious or violent third felony. In addition, retribution as a goal

---

Box 2.5
Deterrence

Deterrence is the prevention of criminal behavior through the threat of detection, apprehension, and punishment.

As a policy, deterrence programs can be directed against individuals or the general society. Individual or specific deterrence is designed to prevent a person from committing a crime and can take such forms as punishment, persuasion, deprivation of liberty, or even death. "Scared Straight" programs that fleetingly mix hardened convicts with impressionable juveniles are believed by some to be a specific deterrent.

A societal deterrence program reminds potential offenders of what may happen to them if they violate the law. Driving automobiles while intoxicated, for example, is believed to be prevented or discouraged by a well-planned and coordinated television advertisement, linked to staunch enforcement by local policing agencies and mandatory loss of driving privileges or short periods of incarceration in jail. The death penalty is frequently cited as a general deterrent.

---

became attractive, inasmuch as it would impose deserved punishment. (Such a "just deserts" strategy looks back to the offender's personal culpability, focuses on the nature of the act, and considers the harm done.)

REFORM OPTIONS

As a result of the reform movement, sentencing practices were changed in the belief that such practices would limit disparity and discretion and establish more detailed criteria for sentencing or new sentencing institutions. These contradictory options included:

1. abolishing plea bargaining;
2. establishing plea-bargaining rules and guidelines;
3. setting mandatory minimum sentences;
4. establishing statutory determinate sentencing;
5. setting voluntary or descriptive sentencing guidelines or presumptive or prescriptive sentencing guidelines;
6. creating sentencing councils;
7. requiring judges to provide reasons for their sentences;
8. setting parole guidelines to limit parole board discretion;
9. abolishing parole;
10. adopting or modifying good-time procedures; and
11. routinizing appellate review of sentences (Allen et al., 2007, pp. 68–69).

Those options represent only the principal steps designed to limit unbridled discretion under the guise of making sentencing fairer, enhancing justice, and lessening discrimination.

Reform Effects

Over the past three decades, dramatic changes in sentencing structures and practices thus became evident. Discretionary release by a parole board was abolished in at least 18 states, and parole sentencing guidelines had been established in one-half of the others. See Table 2.2 for a list of states that have abolished or severely limited parole board release. In 1987, the U.S. Federal Sentencing Guidelines were promulgated, and fewer federal offenders are paroled by the U.S. Parole Commission. Across the country, the number of inmates released on discretionary parole has been considerably less than those released on mandatory parole until 2012. See Figure 2.1 for entries to parole by method of release.

Table 2.2 States that have Abolished or Severely Limit Parole Board Release

State	Year
Arizona	1994
Arkansas	1994
California	1976
Delaware	1990
Florida	1983
Illinois	1978
Indiana	1977
Kansas	1993
Maine	1976
Minnesota	1980
Mississippi	1995
New Mexico	1979
North Carolina	1994
Ohio	1996
Oklahoma	2000
Oregon	1989
South Dakota	1996
Virginia	1995
Washington	1984
Wisconsin	2000

Source: Association of Paroling Authorities International (2005). *Paroling Authorities Survey.* www.apaintl.org.

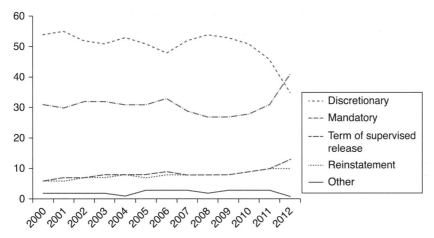

Figure 2.1 Entries to Parole by Type of Entry, 2000–2012.

Source: Maruschak, L.M., Bonczar, T. (20013). *Probation and parole in the United States, 2012.* Washington DC: U.S. Department of Justice, Bureau of Justice Statistics.

Box 2.6
Parole Release

Discretionary parole release means that the parole board opted to release an offender before the maximum sentence was met. **Mandatory release** means the offender had to be released because the maximum sentence (or its equivalent) had been attained. Both imply parole supervision in the community.

Determinate Sentencing

Critics have identified several unwarranted and unwanted problems with indeterminate sentencing, as well as parole board decision making. Reformers, neoclassical theorists, politicians, and organized political action groups with punitive agendas coalesced to attack rehabilitation and parole. The primary substitute for the indeterminate sentence is the determinate sentence, a throwback to the tradition of "flat time" in our earlier history. A determinate sentence is a fixed period of incarceration imposed on the offender by the sentencing court. The ideology underlying determinate sentencing is retribution, just deserts, incapacitation, and selective incapacitation.

Travis and Petersilia (2001) found that 18 states have created sentencing commissions whose guidelines have restricted judicial sentencing discretion, that legislation creating mandatory minimum sentences has been enacted in all 50 states, and that 40 states now have sentencing laws requiring inmates to serve

Table 2.3 Truth-in-Sentencing Requirements by State

Meet Federal 85% requirement	50% of minimum requirement	100% of minimum requirement		Other requirements
Arizona	Missouri	Indiana	Idaho	Alaska
California	New Jersey	Maryland	Nevada	Arkansas
Connecticut	New York	Nebraska	New	Colorado
Delaware	North Carolina	Texas	Hampshire	
Dist. of Col.	North Dakota	Massachusetts	Kentucky	
Florida	Wisconsin			
Georgia	Oklahoma			
Illinois	Oregon			
Iowa	Pennsylvania			
Kansas	South Carolina			
Louisiana	Tennessee			
Maine	Utah			
Michigan	Virginia			
Minnesota	Washington			
Mississippi				
Ohio				

Source: Ditton, P., Wilson, D. (1999). *Truth in sentencing in state prisons* . Washington, DC: U.S. Bureau of Justice Statistics, p. 2.

at least 50 percent of their sentences in prison. Of those 50 states, 27 (and the District of Columbia) have statutes requiring offenders to serve at least 85 percent of their sentence in prison. See Table 2.3 for a list of truth-in-sentencing requirements by state.

SENTENCING GUIDELINES

Sentencing guidelines for structuring the penalty decisions of judges work by providing decision makers with criteria and weights on which the sanction decision should be based (Hoffman & DeGostin, 1975). By explicitly stating factors deemed relevant to the sentence decision and by providing guidance to the sentencer, these guidelines ensure a greater degree of uniformity in criminal penalties. Explicit sentencing guidelines then work to limit the effect of extralegal factors on the sentencing decision.

Such a sentencing structure limits judicial control over sentencing, as the legislature heavily influences the sentence length. Whether there are unforeseen problems in presumptive sentencing remains to be proved, but the Federal Bureau of Prison's population problems may well be due to a corollary of presumptive sentencing: abolition of parole board early release authority that has been used to control prison overcrowding in the past (the Federal Bureau of Prisons is now the largest single prison system in the world).

Mandatory prison-term statutes now exist in all states. Those statutes apply for certain crimes of violence and for habitual criminals, and the court's discretion in such cases (regarding, e.g., probation, fines, and suspended sentences) has been eliminated by statute. In some states, imposition of a prison term is constrained by sentencing guidelines, such as those shown in Figure 2.2. Guidelines are usually set by a governor's commission, including a cross-section of the state population. As noted by a major study (Coleman & Guthrie, 1988, p. 142):

> A sentencing commission in each state monitors the use of the guidelines and departures from the recommended sentences by the judiciary. Written explanations are required from judges who depart from guideline ranges. The Minnesota Sentencing Guidelines Commission states that "while the sentencing guidelines are advisory to the sentencing judge, departures from the presumptive sentences established in the guidelines should be made only when substantial and compelling circumstances exist." Pennsylvania sentencing guidelines stipulate that court failure to explain sentences deviating from the recommendations "shall be grounds for vacating the sentence and resentencing the defendant." Furthermore, if the court does not consider the guidelines or inaccurately or inappropriately applies them, an imposed sentence may be vacated upon appeal to a higher court by either the defense or the prosecution.

The range and particular format for sentencing guidelines can include such things as specifically worded statutes and grids with a range of judicial options. Similarly,

Offender: ____________________ Docket number: __________

Judge: ____________________ Date: __________

Offense(s) convicted of: ____________________

____

Crime score:

A. Injury
  0 = No injury
  1 = Injury
  2 = Death ______ +

B. Weapon
  0 = No weapon
  1 = Weapon
  2 = Weapon present and used ______ +

C. Drugs
  0 = No sale of drugs
  1 = Sale of drugs ______ = [ ] Crime score

Figure 2.2 Sentencing Guidelines. *(continued)*

Offender score:
- A. Current legal status
  - 0 = Not on probation/parole, escape
  - 1 = On probation/parole, escape _____ +
- B. Prior adult misdemeanor convictions
  - 0 = No convictions
  - 1 = One conviction
  - 2 = Two or more convictions _____ +
- C. Prior adult felony convictions
  - 0 = No convictions
  - 2 = One conviction
  - 4 = Two or more convictions _____ +
- D. Prior adult probation parole revocations
  - 0 = None
  - 1 = One or more revocations _____ +
- E. Prior adult incarcerations (over 60 days)
  - 0 = None
  - 1 = One incarceration
  - 2 = Two or more incarcerations _____ =

Offender
score

Guideline sentence: _____

Actual sentence: _____

Reasons (if actual sentence does not fall within guideline range): _____

_____

Crime score

	0–1	2–4	5–7	8–10
4–5	4–6 years	5–7 years	6–8 years	8–10 years
3	3–5 years	4–6 years	6–8 years	6–8 years
2	2–4 years	3–5 years	3–5 years	4–6 years
1	Probation	Probation	2–4 years	3–5 years
0	Probation	Probation	Probation	2–4 years

Offender score

The sentencing judge first determines the crime score, typically concerned with the actual crime, injury, weapon used, and drug sale. Points are assigned as above under "Crime score." Second, the judge scores the offender's prior behavior, using those items identified under "Offender score." Determining the guideline sentence entails finding the grid cell that corresponded to the crime and offender score, and then imposing a sentence that falls within the suggested range.

Figure 2.2 Continued.

Source: Kress, J., Calpin, J.C., Gelman, A.M., Bellows, J.B., Dorworth, B.E., Spaid, O.A. (1978). *Developing sentencing guidelines: Trainers handbook.* Washington, DC: National Institute of Criminal Justice.

parole guidelines are sometimes closely prescribed, and sometimes wide discretion is afforded to the parole board. The amount of flexibility in such decisions can directly enhance or detract from the efforts to relieve crowded prison conditions. Because most parole decisions are not based on time but on perceived "risk to the community," tighter and tighter criteria make it difficult to manage prison population size by such decisions.

THREE-STRIKES LAWS

No discussion of sentencing changes would be complete without exploring "**three-strikes" sentencing laws**. Although sentence enhancement statutes exist in most states (such as habitual or repeat offender laws), legislation that specifically identified a group of repeat offenders for lengthy incapacitation began to bloom in 1993 when Washington became the second state to enact three-strike legislation.[4] Currently, 27 states and the federal government have enacted so-called three-strikes laws, all designed to remove offenders convicted of repeated serious offenses from society for a long period of time, if not for life. In California, for example, the minimum sentence under three-strikes legislation is 25 years, with no "good time" credit. Time served will be no less than 25 years. As might be expected, some unusual cases have arisen in California. For example, one defendant was given a 25-years-to-life sentence for shoplifting golf clubs (with previous convictions for burglary and robbery with a knife). In one particular notorious case, Kevin Weber was sentenced to 26-years-to-life for stealing four chocolate chip cookies after two previous convictions (Ellingwood, 1995). California also has a two-strikes law that doubles the presumptive sentence. In 2000, California voters did support an amendment to scale back punishment that provides drug treatment instead of life imprisonment for most offenders convicted of possessing drugs; and in 2012, voters passed an amendment that would have required the third felony to be either "violent" or "serious" in order for a 25-years-to-life sentence. See Table 2.4 for a list of states that have enacted some sort of three-strikes sentencing law.

While the Supreme Court has upheld the constitutionality of using prior convictions as aggravating factors in determining a sentence, there are many critics of three-strikes legislation, there is little evidence that three-strikes laws are contributing significantly to reductions in crime rates, and there is no reason to believe that this sentencing effort will be appreciably different from other attempts to limit discretion.[5]

This review of the changes in sentencing practices and their consequences in the last decade clearly shows the shifts that have taken place. Although discretion in determining sentence length has been somewhat removed from the sentencing judge and parole board, it was reduced by legislatures through their enactment of new sentencing structures. In turn, in many jurisdictions, the prosecutor's discretion was increased.[6] The prison population has continued to climb as increasingly more offenders are committed and serve increasingly longer sentences (Wooldredge, 1996).

Let's now look at some of the other sentencing options that exist.

Table 2.4 States That Have Some Sort of a
Three-Strikes Sentencing Law

State	Year adopted
Arizona	2006
Arkansas	1995
California	1994
Colorado	1994
Connecticut	1994
Florida	1995
Georgia	1994
Indiana	1994
Kansas	1994
Louisiana	1994
Maryland	1994
Massachusetts	2012
Montana	1995
Nevada	1995
New Jersey	1995
New Mexico	1994
North Carolina	1994
North Dakota	1995
Pennsylvania	1995
South Carolina	1995
Tennessee	1994
Texas	1974
Utah	1995
Vermont	1995
Virginia	1994
Washington	1993
Wisconsin	1994

SENTENCING OPTIONS

In the plea-bargaining process, defense counsel may negotiate sentence outcome to avoid incarceration of the accused. Thus, the decision to incarcerate may, in part, depend on the outcome of negotiated justice. The two major incarceration outcomes are imprisonment in a penal facility or in a jail. The major alternative to incarceration is probation and such other intermediate punishments as weekend confinement, house arrest, electronic monitoring, fines, restitution and work centers, intensive supervised probation, and so on. These are discussed here.

If the decision is to place the offender on probation or other intermediate punishment, usually as a condition of probation, the offender is typically supervised by an

---

Box 2.7
Tourniquet Sentencing

Tourniquet sentencing is tightening or increasing the conditions of probation to encourage the client to conform to legal and supervisory expectations. A probation officer requests the court to order additional restrictions
or to mandate participation in identified programs. The correctional
objective is reintegration or avoidance of criminal activity. One example of
tourniquet sentencing is the probationer convicted of indecent exposure
who continues to consume alcohol. The court may order participation in
substance abuse treatment, as well as house arrest with electronic monitoring, or that the probationer takes Antabuse (disulfiram), a medication
that generally sickens the person who imbibes alcohol.

Source: The term "tourniquet sentencing" is attributed to
Judge Albert Kramer, District Judge, Quincy, MA. Klein, A. (1980).
Earn it: the story so far. Waltham, MA: Brandeis University.

---

officer of the local or state probation department. Conditional freedom under
probation requires the probationer to meet certain conditions of behavior (see
Chapter 3). If the probationer is in danger of substantively violating these conditions
or is determined to be in need of additional service or more intensive supervision,
the supervising officer may request that the judge increase the conditions of
supervision to include additional restrictions or program participation. The intent
of this practice, often called tourniquet sentencing, is to lessen the risk of failure
and recidivism and assist the probationer to decide to conform to court expectations. The implicit alternative to nonconforming behavior is incarceration,
frequently in the local jail, for a period of time to be imposed by the judge. To
understand tourniquet sentencing, it is necessary to examine the jail and its role
as a hub of community corrections.

THE JAIL

The local detention facility, usually administered by a county law enforcement
agency, is generally known as the "jail." There are nearly 3,400 jails across the
nation, housing more than 700,000 persons in midyear 2013 (Minton & Golinelli,
2014). Jails incarcerate a wide variety of people. Jails receive individuals pending
arraignment and hold them awaiting trial, conviction, and sentencing. They
also readmit probation, parole, bail-bond violators, and absconders, as well as
temporarily detain juveniles pending transfer to juvenile authorities. Further, they
hold mentally ill persons pending their movement to appropriate health facilities,
as well as individuals for the military, for protective custody and contempt, and for
the court as witnesses. In addition, jails release convicted inmates to the
community upon completion of their sentence and transfer inmates to state,

Table 2.5 Persons under Jail Supervision, Midyear 2013

Confinement status and type of program	Number
Total	790,649
Held in jail	731,208
Supervised outside of a jail facility[a]	59,441
Weekender program	10,950
Electronic monitoring	12,023
Home detention[b]	1,337
Day reporting	3,683
Community service	13,877
Other pretrial supervision	7,542
Other work programs[c]	5,341
Treatment programs[d]	2,002
Other	2,687

[a] Excludes persons supervised by a probation or parole agency.
[b] Includes only persons without electronic monitoring.
[c] Includes persons in work release programs, work gangs, and other work alternative programs.
[d] Includes persons under drug, alcohol, mental health, and other medical treatment.

Source: Minton, T.D., Golinelli, D. (2014). *Jail inmates at midyear 2013*. Washington, DC: U.S. Department of Justice, Bureau of Justice Statistics.

federal, and other local authorities. They temporarily incarcerate convicted felons sentenced to prisons but for whom there are no bed spaces (Minton & Golinelli, 2014) and relinquish custody of temporary detainees to juvenile and medical authorities (Beck & Karberg, 2001). Finally, they sometimes operate community-based programs as **work release** programs and other alternatives to incarceration and hold inmates sentenced to short terms (generally under one year) (see Table 2.5). It is small wonder that local jails admitted 11.7 million in a 12-month period ending in midyear 2013 (Minton & Golinelli, 2014).

Box 2.8
California Public Safety Realignment

On May 23, 2011, the U.S. Supreme Court upheld the ruling by a lower three-judge court that the State of California must reduce its prison population to 137.5 percent of design capacity (approximately 110,000 prisoners) within two years to alleviate overcrowding. In response, the California State Legislature and governor enacted two laws—AB 109 and AB 117—to reduce the number of inmates housed in state prisons starting October 1, 2011.

The Public Safety Realignment (PSR) policy is designed to reduce the prison population through normal attrition of the existing population while placing new nonviolent, non-serious, non-sex offenders under county jurisdiction for incarceration in local jail facilities. Inmates released from local jails will be placed under a county-directed post-release community supervision program instead of the state's parole system. The state is giving additional funding to the 58 counties in California to deal with the increased correctional population and responsibility; however, each county must develop a plan for custody and post-custody that best serves its needs.

After record low jail populations between year-end 2010 and year-end 2011, the California jail population increased by an estimated 7,600 inmates between year-end 2011 and midyear 2012 and by an estimated 3,500 inmates between midyear 2012 and midyear 2013.

NON-JAIL SENTENCING OPTIONS

Sentencing judges make decisions to incarcerate offenders in jails or prisons or to place them on probation with its numerous ancillary programs ("in" or "out" decisions). If the decision is to retain the offender in the community under probation or its supplemental programs, the judge increasingly has a large number of supervision and control strategies from which to pick, known as intermediate sanctions (Allen et al., 2012; Gowdy, 1993). Selected programs are not capriciously imposed but are designed to achieve a correctional objective, such as community protection, reintegration, and treatment and rehabilitation. Court officers, usually probation officers, oversee the implementation of, and offender compliance with, court conditions. If the offender appears to be failing at technical conditions (such as no alcohol or attending treatment programs), the judge may tighten the requirements by imposing mandatory daily attendance. In extreme cases, a request for medical intervention (e.g., methadone maintenance for heroin addicts) may be issued. If these conditions are not met or are insufficient for the particular client, the court may further increase the conditions of control by imposing weekend confinement in jail or house arrest. If these are insufficient, the judge may order a short term of jail incarceration to be followed by additional control programs, such as house arrest with electronic monitoring. In extreme cases, the court may order an interlock device installed in the offender's vehicle, as well as intensive supervision. Tightening the conditions and restraints is commonly called "tourniquet sentencing" (see Box 2.7). We turn now to a brief description of major ancillary control ("probation-plus") programs.

INTERMEDIATE CONTROLS

Intermediate punishments are explored in greater detail in Chapter 10. For our purposes, the major intermediate control programs are listed with brief descriptions. The reader will notice that each increases the level of "penal harm" and crime control. For many offenders, such preventive control is necessary for them

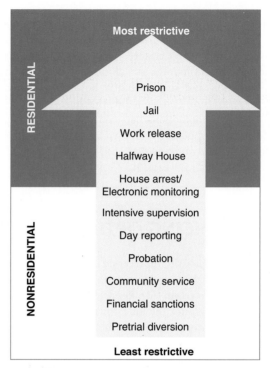

Figure 2.3 Sample of Sanctions.

to begin to deal with their rehabilitation needs. The discussion moves from least to most punishment approaches. For a sample of sanctions ranging from most to least restrictive, see Figure 2.3.

Fines

The penalties that courts impose on offenders require specific sums of money to be paid, cash payments of a dollar amount. Judges may impose fines based on a fixed schedule published and used throughout the court or on an individual basis.

Box 2.9
Reintegration

A broad correctional ideology stressing acquisition of legitimate skills and opportunities by criminal offenders, and the creation of supervised opportunities for testing, using, and refining those skills, particularly in community settings.

Box 2.10
Incapacitation

Incapacitation is a crime prevention strategy based on specific deterrence that would disable the potential offender from committing another crime by isolating the instant offender. The most common form of incapacitation is imprisonment.

Box 2.11
Rehabilitation

Rehabilitation is a change in behavior of the offender produced by treatment and services. The offender chooses to refrain from new crimes rather than being unable to do so.

Community Service

Community service or work orders represent court-ordered nonpaid work for a specified number of hours that offenders must perform, usually for some charitable organization or public service, such as working as a volunteer hospital orderly, doing interstate and street cleaning, performing maintenance or repair of public housing, or providing services to indigent groups (Anderson, 1998; Caputo, 1999). Professionals such as dentists or doctors can be ordered to provide free services for the indigent, welfare recipients, or probationers, whereas sports stars may be required to speak to youth groups or at schools.

Restitution

This court-ordered condition of probation requires the offender to repair the financial, emotional, or physical damage done (a reparative sentence) by making financial payment of money to the victim or, alternatively, to a fund to provide services to victims. Restitution programs may also be ordered in the absence of a sentence to probation (Seiter, 2000). Restitution is usually a cash payment by the offender to the victim of an amount considered to offset the loss incurred by the victim (medical expenses, insurance deductibles, time lost from work due to the victim's injuries, etc.). Payments may be made in installments in most jurisdictions, and sometimes services benefitting the victim directly or indirectly may be substituted for cash payments.

Box 2.12
Retribution

Philosophically, this term generally means "getting even" with the perpetrator. *Social revenge* suggests that individuals cannot exact punishment, but that the State will do so in their name.

Retribution assumes that offenders will fully choose to commit the evil acts, are responsible for their own behavior, and should receive the punishment they deserve. The just-deserts movement in sentencing reflects the retribution philosophy. For many, it provides a justifiable rationale for the death penalty.

Probation

Probation is the conditional freedom granted by a judicial officer to an alleged offender, or adjudicated adult or juvenile, as long as the person meets certain conditions of behavior. Unsupervised probation resembles *sursis*, or "no action by the court as long as there are no further incidents" but, generally, probation includes the requirement to report to a designated person or agency over a period of time.

Box 2.13
Selective Incapacitation

This doctrine of isolating the offender, or causing "social disablement," proposes "adopting a policy of incarcerating those whose criminal behavior is so damaging or probable that nothing short of isolation will prevent recidivism." This "nothing-else-works" approach would require correctly identifying those offenders who should receive long-term imprisonment and diverting others into community corrections. Thus, we would be able to make maximum use of prison cells, a scarce resource, to protect society from the depredations of such dangerous and repetitive offenders. The "three strikes and you're out" approach is a continuation of this theme.

Current correctional technology does not permit us to correctly identify those who require incapacitation. Rather, the evidence is that we would probably incarcerate numerous noneligibles (a "false positive" problem) and release to lesser control many of those eligible (a "false negative" problem). Whatever benefits might accrue to this sentencing doctrine have thus far eluded corrections.

Box 2.14
Parole Board

A **parole board** is any correctional person, authority, or board that has the authority to release on parole those adults (or juveniles) committed to confinement facilities, to set conditions for behavior, to revoke from parole, and to discharge from parole. Parole boards also recommend executive clemency through pardon or sentence commutation (shortening), as well as set policies for supervision of parolees.

Day-Reporting Centers

Certain persons on pretrial release, probation, or parole may be required to appear at a **day-reporting center** on a frequent and regular basis in order to participate in services or activities provided by the center or other community agencies. Failure to report or participate is a violation that could cause revocation of pretrial release, conditional release, or community supervision.

Reports on the national scene indicate that offenders in these programs must not only report to their centers physically, but also provide a schedule of planned activities and participate in designated activities (McDevitt et al., 1997).

Intensive Supervised Probation

These are court-ordered programs of community supervision by probation officers working with very small caseloads to provide **intensive supervision**. Such programs are usually linked to impromptu (and scheduled) alcohol and other drug testing, curfews, restitution, volunteer sponsors, probation fees, and other punitive intrusions (Anderson, 1998; Maxwell & Gray, 2000).

Box 2.15
Jail

A **jail** is a confinement facility, usually administered by a local law enforcement agency, intended for adults, that holds persons detained pending adjudication and/or persons committed after adjudication for sentences usually of one year or less.

House Arrest

House or home arrest is a more intensive program that requires the offender to remain secluded in his or her own home except for work, grocery shopping, community service, or other minor exceptions. Alcohol and other drug use or possession in the residence is a violation of house arrest and can result in increased intervention.[8] Frequently, house arrest may be intensified by requiring the offender to wear an electronic device that signals a computer that the offender is at home or by requiring electronic breath analyzer testing to determine any alcohol use. House arrest can be used as an alternative to parolees with nonviolent technical violations (Stanz & Tewksbury, 2000).

Electronic Monitoring

An **electronic monitoring** program requires an offender to wear a bracelet or anklet that will emit an electronic signal, confirming via telephone contact that the offender is located at a specific, required location. Strict curfews are required, and restrictions on visitors may be imposed. Some monitoring systems have the capability to emit signals that can be picked up by cellular listing posts within a community to signal to a computer monitor that the offender is moving within the community (not at home). Frequently, the electronic monitoring system is buttressed by scheduled probation officer visits, drug testing, and other surveillance options. Electronic monitoring is used with both pretrial releasees and for convicted offenders on community release. In either case, clients pay for at least part (if not all) of the cost of leasing the monitoring equipment.

Global Positioning Systems

Modern technology has advanced to the point where some offenders can be tracked using global positioning systems. These devices are gaining use for sex offenders and domestic violence offenders and allow a probation officer to track the whereabouts of the offender to make sure that they are not in an area prohibited by the court.

Box 2.16
Fine

A **fine** is a penalty imposed on a convicted person by the court, requiring that he or she pay a specified sum of money. The fine is a cash payment of a dollar amount assessed by the judge in an individual case or determined by a published schedule of penalties. Fines may be paid in installments in many jurisdictions in the nation.

Community Residential Centers

Formerly known as halfway houses, community residential centers are nonconfining residential facilities for adjudicated adults or juveniles, or for those subject to criminal or juvenile proceedings. They are intended as an alternative to jail incarceration for persons in danger of failing on probation or who need a period of readjustment. Increasingly, correctional and victim services (such as services and treatment for battered women, drunk drivers, drug abusers, mentally ill sex offenders, etc.) are offered in these 24-hour facilities.

Box 2.17
Prison

A **prison** is a confinement facility, usually administered by a state agency, having custodial authority over adults sentenced to confinement for more than one year.

Box 2.18
Intermediate Sanctions

Intermediate sanctions, ranging in severity from day fines to shock incarceration ("boot camps"), are interventions that fill the sentencing gap between jails and prisons at one extreme, and probation at the other. Lengthy incarceration periods may be inappropriate for some offenders; for others, probation may be too inconsequential and may not provide the degree of public supervision necessary to ensure public safety. By expanding sentencing options, intermediate sanctions enable the criminal (and juvenile) justice system to tailor punishment more closely to the nature of the crime and the criminal, to maximize offender compliance with court objectives, and to hold offenders strictly accountable for their actions.

Box 2.19
Sentencing: Concurrent or Consecutive?

If the offender is to be sentenced for more than one crime and receives a concurrent sentence, the offender would start serving time for all his or her crimes beginning on the day of arrival in prison. If a consecutive sentence is imposed, the offender must generally serve the minimum sentence for the

> first crime before beginning to serve time for the second offense. Offenders obviously prefer the concurrent over the consecutive sentence option because they would be eligible for release from prison much earlier.

Split Sentences

Frequently, sentencing judges impose a short term of incarceration in the local jail to be followed by a term of probation. For example, the **split sentence** (jail plus probation) is the most frequently imposed sentence for felony convictions in California (Lundgren, 2001).

A variation on "jail plus" is weekend confinement. To lessen the negative impacts of short-term incarceration and allow offenders to retain current employment, as well as keep their dependants off welfare rolls, some jurisdictions permit sentences to be served during nonworking weekends. Such weekend confinement allows offenders to check into the jail facility on Friday after work and to leave Sunday morning, sometimes early enough to attend religious services. A "weekender" serving his or her sentence over a number of months would generally be credited with three days of confinement per weekend. Some jurisdictions have so many "weekenders" that specific buildings are set aside for their short-term detention. In larger jurisdictions in which sufficient numbers of offenders work on weekends but not every day during the ordinary working week, those buildings operate all week but at reduced staffing levels.

SUMMARY

The primary mission of the correctional system is protection of the public. Programs must be designed with that objective in mind or they will be doomed to early failure and public rejection. What seems to be needed is a system that offers as many alternatives to incarceration as are possible for the individuals who appear to have some hope of benefitting from them and who will present little, if any, danger to the community. The residual population may be required to remain in more secure institutions until new treatments can be found for them. The prison, in a modified form, has a valuable place in a correctional system for the estimated 15 to 20 percent of the convicted offenders who require this level of control. For most convicted offenders, however, the use of either partial or total alternatives to imprisonment is a more reasonable and less costly response than is incarceration.

Prisons should be the "last choice" of sentencing judges faced with the difficult decision of how to manage offenders before them and how best to attain the correctional objective being sought. Judges are increasingly turning to "tourniquet sentencing" as a promising strategy for determining those sanctions.

Whatever good prisons do is difficult to measure, but the damage done is detected easily. If our objective is the protection of society from criminal recidivism, long-term strategies must be developed. If we are determined to control offenders and lower the costs of overincarceration, it will become necessary to develop a system of community corrections that includes extensive program alternatives and increasing levels of control over the offender in the arms of the law. Developing an effective community corrections program will require formulating social policy that requires handling local problems in the community, setting priorities for control of crime, and making resources available to develop and maintain the proposed system. Probation is one of the major elements in such a system.

Review Questions

1. Compare past sentencing practices to more contemporary ones.
2. What is the difference between a determinate and an indeterminate sentence?
3. What alternatives to incarceration can help alleviate jail crowding?
4. What are sentencing guidelines?
5. How is the jail the center of community corrections?
6. What are the main purposes of imprisonment?
7. What are alternatives to "bricks and mortar" as a solution to prison over-crowding?
8. How do prisons eventually contribute to the workloads of community corrections?
9. Does your state use determinate or indeterminate sentencing?
10. What is a split sentence?
11. What are some of the causes given for rapid changes in the U.S. sentencing laws?

Notes

1 Some historians argue that the noble ideals of rehabilitation were never really implemented and that the "convenience" of punishment won out over the "conscience" of rehabilitation. See Rothman, D. (1980). *Conscience and convenience: The asylum and its alternatives in progressive America*. Boston, MA: Little, Brown. See also Irwin, J., Schiraldi, V., Ziedenberg, J. (2000). America's one million non-violent prisoners. *Social Justice* 27(2), 135–147.
2 California recently revised its law to impose life sentences only when the new felony conviction is "serious or violent."
3 DeClan Roche (1999). Mandatory sentencing: Trends and issues. *Australian Institute of Criminology* 138(1), 1–6.
4 Texas is credited with being the first state to enact such a law in 1974 with a mandatory life sentence.
5 King, R., Mauer, M. (2002). *State sentencing and corrections policy in an era of fiscal restraint*. Washington, DC: The Sentencing Project.
6 Austin, J., Clark, J., Hardyman, P. (1999). The impact of "Three strikes and you're out." *Punishment and Society* 1(2), 131–162; Burt, G., Wong, S., Vander Veen, S. (2000). Three strikes and you're out. *Federal Probation* 64(2), 3–6.

7 The "material" witness detained in jails to ensure presence at trial is a seldom-studied actor in the justice system; hence, little is known about this category of jail inmate.

8 Technical violators among those on intermediate sanctions can be a large component of the offenders. See Taxman, F. (1995). Intermediate sanctions: Dealing with technical violators. *Corrections Today* 57(1), 46–57. See also Marciniak, L. (2000). The addition of day reporting to intensive supervised probation. *Federal Probation* 64(2), 34–39.

Recommended Readings

Clear, T. (1994). *Harm in American penology: Offenders, victims, and their communities.* Albany, NY: State University of New York Press.

Irwin, J., Austin, J. (1997). *It's about time: America's imprisonment binge.* Belmont, CA: Wadsworth.

Petersila, J. (2003). *When prisoners come home.* New York: Oxford Press.

Rothman, D. (1980). *Conscience and convenience: The asylum and its alternatives in progressive America.* Boston, MA: Little, Brown.

Travis, J. (2000). *But they all come back: Rethinking prisoner reentry.* Washington, DC: National Institute of Corrections.

References

Allen, H., Latessa, E., Ponder, B., Simonsen, C. (2007). *Corrections in America.* Upper Saddle River, NJ: Pearson Prentice Hall.

Allen, H.E., Latessa, E.L., Ponder, B. (2012). *Corrections in America: An introduction.* Upper Saddle River, NJ: Pearson Prentice Hall.

Anderson, D.C. (1998). *Sensible justice: Alternatives to prison.* New York: New Press.

Beck, A. (1995). *Profile of jail inmates: 1989.* Washington, DC: U.S. Department of Justice.

Beck, A. (2000). *State and federal prisoners returning to the community: Findings from the Bureau of Justice Statistics.* www.ojp.usdoj.gov/bjs/pub/pdf/sfprc.pdf (accessed July 20, 2001).

Beck, A., Karberg, J. (2001). *Prison and jail inmates at midyear 2000.* Washington, DC: Bureau of Justice Statistics.

Caputo, G. (1999). Why not community service? *Criminal Justice Policy, Review* 10(4), 503–519.

Coleman, S., Guthrie, K. (1988). *Sentencing effectiveness in preventing crime.* St. Paul, MN: Criminal Justice Statistical Analysis Center.

Ditton, P., Wilson, D. (1999). *Truth in sentencing in state prisons.* Washington, DC: U.S. Bureau of Justice Statistics.

Durose, M.R., Langan, P.A. (2007). *Felony sentences in State Courts, 2004.* Washington, DC: U.S. Department of Justice (NCJ 215646).

Ellingwood, K. (1995). Three-time loser gets life in cookie theft. *Los Angeles Times,* October 1–28.

Glaze, L.E., Bonczar, T.P. (2009). *Probation and parole in the United States, 2008.* Washington, DC: U.S. Department of Justice, Bureau of Justice Statistics.

Gowdy, V. (1993) *Intermediate sanctions.* Washington, DC: U.S. Department of Justice.

Harrison, P., Beck, A. (2006) *Prisoners in 2005.* Washington, DC: Bureau of Justice Statistics. www.ojp .usdoj.gov/bjs/pub/pdf/p00.pdf.

Hoffman, P., DeGostin, L. (1975). An argument for self-imposed explicit judicial sentencing standards. *Journal of Criminal Justice* 3, 195–206.

Jones, M.A., Austin, J. (1995). *The 1995 NCCD national prison population forecast.* San Francisco, CA: National Council on Crime and Delinquency.

Kress, J., Calpin, J.C., Gelman, A.M., Bellows, J.B., Dorworth, B.E., Spaid, O.A. (1978). *Developing sentencing guidelines: Trainers handbook.* Washington, DC: National Institute of Criminal Justice.

Lundgren, D. (2001). *Crime and delinquency in California, 2000: Advance release.* Sacramento, CA: Department of Justice.

Maxwell, S., Gray, K. (2000). Deterrence. *Sociological Inquiry* 70(2), 117–136.

McDevitt, J., Domino, M., Baum, K. (1997). *Metropolitan day reporting center: An evaluation.* Boston, MA: Northeastern University Press.

Minton, T.D., Golinelli, D. (2014). *Jail inmates at midyear 2013.* Washington, DC: U.S. Department of Justice, Bureau of Justice Statistics.

Rosenmerkel, S., Durose, M., Farole, D. (2009). *Felony sentences in state courts, 2006: Statistical tables.* Washington, DC: U.S. Department of Justice, Bureau of Justice Statistics.

Seiter, R. (2000). Restorative justice 3. In: R. Seiter (ed.) *Corrections Management Quarterly* 4, 1–85.

Stanz, R., Tewksbury, R. (2000). Predictors of success and recidivism in a home incarceration program. *The Prison Journal* 80(3), 326–344.

Travis, J., Petersilia, J. (2001). Re-entry reconsidered: A new look at an old question. *Crime & Delinquency* 47(3): 291–313.

Wooldredge, J. (1996). Research note: A state-level analysis of sentencing policies and inmate crowding in state prisons. *Crime Delinquency* 42(3), 456–466.

Chapter 3

PROBATION IN AMERICA

Key Terms

Cesare Beccaria
Community work orders
conditions of probation
individualized justice
intermittent incarceration
John Augustus
Killits decision
presentence investigation report
probation

probationer fees
restitution
revocation
selective incapacitation
sentencing hearings
shock probation
split sentences
victim impact statement

> I can forgive, but I cannot forget, is only another way of saying, I will not forgive. Forgiveness ought to be like a canceled note—torn in two, and burned up, so that it never can be shown against one.—Henry Ward Beecher

In many respects, probation is a way of giving an offender another chance. Probation represents one of the unique developments within the criminal justice system; it provided a mechanism to divert offenders from further involvement with the correctional system, which was a crucial aspect of the rise of the rehabilitation model in this country. Any study of probation must begin with an analysis of its predecessors. This chapter begins with a historical review that will help explain how probation, both for adults and for juveniles, developed into its current forms and practices. The second portion of this chapter focuses on the granting of probation and how it exists today.

Probation is a conditional sentence that avoids an offender being incarcerated; in other words, it is an alternative disposition available to the court. While probation is an outcome of the offender's conviction in a criminal court, it neither confines him or her in an institution nor allows the offender's release from court authority. Supervision by a probation officer is almost always a condition of release.

Box 3.1
Definition of Probation: Adults

Probation is a sentence not involving confinement that imposes conditions and retains authority in the sentencing court to modify the conditions of a sentence or to resentence the offender if the offender violates the conditions. Such a sentence should not involve or require suspension of the imposition or execution of any other sentence.

As indicated by the National Advisory Commission on Criminal Justice Standards and Goals (1973), probation can also refer to other functions, activities, and services. It is a status, given to the convicted offender, that falls somewhere between that of free citizen and incarcerated felon (or misdemeanant). As a subsystem of criminal justice, it refers to the agency or organization that administers the probation process. As a process, it refers to those activities that include the preparation of reports for the court, the supervision of probationers, and provision of services for those probationers. These activities are undertaken by the probation officer as a part of his or her regular duty. Finally, as Reed (1997) notes, probation can serve to lower prison populations.

The rationale for the use of probation has been clearly stated by Dressler (1962, p. 26):

> the assumption that certain offenders are reasonably safe risks in society by the time they appear in court; it would not facilitate their adjustment to remove them to institutions, and the move might well have the opposite effect. Meantime, the community would have to provide for their dependents. And the effect of such incarceration upon the prisoner's family would be incalculable. If, then, the community would not be jeopardized by a defendant's presence, and if he gave evidence of ability to change to a law-abiding life, it served both society and the individual to give him the chance, conditionally, under supervision and guidance.

Probation is thus clearly tied to the correctional goals of rehabilitation and reintegration, providing potential benefits to the offender as well as to the community.

FOUNDERS OF PROBATION

John Augustus of Boston is commonly recognized as the originator of probation, but there were other contributors to its development both before and after his unique contribution.

Dressler (1962, pp. 12–13) cites the 1841 activities of Matthew Davenport Hill of Birmingham, England. In Warwickshire, Hill observed that, in the case of youthful offenders, magistrates often imposed token sentences of one day with the special condition that the defendant remain under the supervision of a guardian. This experiment represented a mitigation of the punishment; no other conditions were imposed and there was no provision for revocation. When Hill became a magistrate, he modified this procedure; he suspended the sentence and placed the offender under the supervision of a guardian, under the assumption that "there would be better hope of amendment under such guardians than in the [jail] of the county." Hill's program has some of the same elements as Augustus's method: selected cases, suspended sentences, and if the defendant got into trouble again no sanctions were levied. Hill was not unwilling to take action against repeaters, however: "That the punishment should be such as to show that it was from no weakness, from no mistaken indulgence, from no want to resolution on the part of the court to perform its duty" that the previous sentence had been suspended. Hill also demonstrated his concern for the safety of the community by requesting that the superintendent of police investigate the conduct of persons placed under a guardian's supervision.

In this country, one of the earliest proponents of leniency was Judge Peter Oxenbridge Thatcher of Boston. In 1836, Massachusetts passed legislation promoting the practice of releasing petty offenders upon their recognizance with sureties at any stage of the proceedings.[1]

It is a court volunteer, John Augustus, who is most often given credit for the establishment of probation in the United States. Augustus first appeared in police court in Boston when he stood bail for a man charged with drunkenness and then helped the offender find a job. The court ordered the defendant to return in three weeks, at which time he demonstrated great improvement. Instead of incarcerating this individual, the judge imposed a one-cent fine and ordered the defendant to pay costs.

From this modest beginning, Augustus proceeded to bail out numerous offenders, supervising them and offering guidance until they were sentenced. Over an 18-year period (from 1841 until his death in 1859), Augustus "bailed on probation" 1,152 men and 794 women (Barnes & Teeters, 1959, p. 554). He was motivated by his belief that "the object of the law is to reform criminals and to prevent crime and not to punish maliciously or from a spirit of revenge" (Dressler, 1962, p. 17). Augustus obviously selected his candidates carefully, offering assistance "mainly to those who were indicted for their first offense, and whose hearts were not wholly depraved, but gave promise of better things." He also considered the "previous character of the person, his age and influences by which he would in the future be likely to be surrounded and, although these points were not rigidly adhered to, still they were the circumstances which usually determined my action" (United Nations, 1976, p. 90). In addition, Augustus provided his charges with aid in obtaining employment, an education, or a place to live and also made an impartial report to the court. The task was not without its frustrations, as Augustus noted (Barnes & Teeters, 1959, p. 554):

> While it saves the country and state hundreds and I might say thousands of dollars, it drains my pockets instead of enriching me. To attempt to make money by bailing poor people would prove an impossibility. The first two years of my labor I received nothing from anyone except what I earned by my daily labor.

His records on the first 1,100 individuals whom he bailed out revealed that only one forfeited bond (Dressler, 1962). It is also important to note that virtually every basic practice associated with probation was initiated by Augustus, including the idea of a presentence investigation, supervision conditions, case work, reports to the court, and revocation of probation supervision (Probation in the United States, 1997). When Augustus died in 1859, he was destitute—a most unfitting end for a humanitarian visionary.

PHILOSOPHICAL BASES OF PROBATION

Probation emerged in the United States during the nineteenth century, a period of considerable social turmoil and conflict. It was a development widely influenced by certain thoughts, arguments, and debates in Europe. In a larger sense, proba-tion is an extension of Western European philosophical arguments about the functions of criminal law and how offenders should be handled and punished. The punishment philosophy generally advocated by the kings, emperors, and other rulers of Europe focused on the crime and attempted to treat all crimes equally. They viewed the purposes of criminal law as to punish, to deter others, and to seek revenge and vengeance for violations of the "king's peace." Widespread use of the death penalty, torture, banishment, public humiliations, and mass executions resulted from "disturbing the king's peace."

In the eighteenth century, French philosophers created a controversy by focusing on liberty, equality, and justice. Famous French philosophers and lawyers attempted to redefine the purpose of criminal law in an effort to find some way to make the criminal justice system of their age more attuned to the humanitarian ethos of the Age of Enlightenment. A major figure of the time was **Cesare Beccaria**, a mildly disturbed Italian genius who only left his country once, when invited to visit Paris to debate the French philosophers.

When Beccaria (1764) published his classic work, *Essay on crimes and punishments*, he established the "Classical School" of criminology, which attempted to reorient the law toward more humanistic goals. This would include not torturing the accused in order to extract confessions, no secret indictments and trials, the right to defense at a trial, improvement of the conditions of impris-onment, and so on. His work focused on the offense and not on the offender. He believed that punishment should fit the crime. His work was widely read throughout Europe and even attracted the attention of Catherine the Great, the Russian empress, who invited Beccaria to revise Russian criminal law. Unfortunately, he never took her up on her offer.

The philosophical ferment of the period quickly spread to England and, from there, to the colonies. When the United States emerged from the Revolutionary War, the remaining vestiges of the harsher English penal codes were resoundingly abandoned. What emerged was a constitutional system that incorporated the major components of the humanitarian philosophy, along with a populace imbued with the belief in the inherent goodness of humankind and the ability of all persons to rise to their optimal level of perfectibility.

The difference between the earlier approach to handling offenders (harsh punishments openly administered, and corporal and capital punishments) and the emerging reformation emphasis of the last decade of the eighteenth century was primarily in (1) the way offenders were viewed, and (2) the focus and intent of the criminal law. Prior to the Revolutionary War, offenders were seen as inherently evil, deserving punishment so that they might "get right with God." After the Civil War, Americans had generally recognized that humankind was not basically evil. The focus shifted to dealing with individual offenders rather than focusing on the crime that had been committed. The Civil War further added to the movement toward democracy, the rise of the reformation movement, and the further individualization of treatment and punishment. Eventually the following question arose: Do all offenders need to be imprisoned in order for them to repent and stop their criminal behavior? It was in this philosophical environment that Massachusetts began to answer the question, and the concern was juvenile probation.

THE GROWTH OF PROBATION

Influenced by Augustus's example, Massachusetts quickly moved into the forefront of probation development. An experiment in providing services for children (resembling probation) was inaugurated in 1869, under the auspices of the Massachusetts State Board of Health, Lunacy, and Charity (Johnson, 1928). A statute enacted in that year provided that, when complaints were made in court against a juvenile under 17 years of age, a written notice must be furnished to the state. The state agent was then given an opportunity to investigate, to attend the trial, and to safeguard the interest of the child.

Despite the early work of Augustus and others with adult offenders, probation was supported more readily for juveniles. It was not until 1901 that New York passed the first statute authorizing probation for adult offenders, more than 20 years after Massachusetts passed a law for juvenile probation (Lindner & Savarese, 1984). Although the development of probation for adults lagged behind that of juveniles, by 1923, most states had a law authorizing probation for adults, and by 1956 all states had adopted adult and juvenile probation laws. Historical data on select states can be found in Table 3.1. Surprisingly, it was the federal government that resisted probation.

PROBATION AT THE FEDERAL LEVEL

Although probation quickly became almost universal in the juvenile justice system, no early specific provision for probation was made for federal offenders, either juvenile or adult. As a substitute, federal courts suspended sentence in instances in which imprisonment imposed special hardships. However, this practice was quickly called into question by several sources.

The major question was a legal one: Did federal judges have the constitutional authority to suspend a sentence indefinitely or did this practice represent an

Table 3.1 States with Juvenile and Adult Probation Laws: 1923

Year enacted

State	Juvenile	Adult
Alabama	1907	1915
Arizona	1907	1913
Arkansas	1911	1923
California	1903	1903
Colorado	1899	1909
Connecticut	1903	1903
Delaware	1911	1911
Georgia	1904	1907
Idaho	1905	1915
Illinois	1899	1911
Indiana	1903	1907
Kansas	1901	1909
Maine	1905	1905
Maryland	1902	1904
Massachusetts	1878	1878
Michigan	1903	1903
Minnesota	1899	1909
Missouri	1901	1897
Montana	1907	1913
Nebraska	1905	1909
New Jersey	1903	1900
New York	1903	1901
North Carolina	1915	1919
North Dakota	1911	1911
Ohio	1902	1908
Oklahoma	1909	1915
Oregon	1909	1915
Pennsylvania	1903	1909
Rhode Island	1899	1899
Tennessee	1905	1915
Utah	1903	1923
Vermont	1900	1900
Virginia	1910	1910
Washington	1905	1915
Wisconsin	1901	1909

Source: Adapted from Johnson, F. (1928). *Probation for juveniles and adults*. New York: Century Co., pp. 12–13.

encroachment upon the executive prerogative of pardon and reprieve, and was it, as such, an infringement upon the doctrine of separation of powers? This issue was resolved by the U.S. Supreme Court in the *Killits* decision (*Ex parte United States* 242 U.S. 27, 1916). In a case from the northern district of Ohio, John M. Killits suspended the five-year sentence of a man who was convicted of embezzling $4,700 from a Toledo bank. The defendant was a first-time offender with an otherwise good background and reputation who made full restitution for this offense. The bank officers did not wish to prosecute. The government contended that such action was beyond the powers of the court. A unanimous opinion, delivered by Chief Justice Edward D. White, held that federal courts had no inherent power to suspend sentence indefinitely and that there was no reason "to continue a practice which is inconsistent with the Constitution, as its exercise in the very nature of things amounts to a refusal by the judicial power to perform a duty resting upon it and, as a consequence thereof, to an interference with both the legislative and executive authority as fixed by the Constitution." However, instead of abolishing this probationary practice, the *Killits* decision actually sponsored its further development. Interested parties interpreted the reversal of the "doctrine of inherent power to suspend sentences indefinitely" to mean that enabling legislation should be passed that specifically granted this power to the judiciary.

At the federal level, the National Probation Association (then headed by Charles Lionel Chute) carried on a determined educational campaign and lobbied for federal legislation. These efforts did not go unopposed, however. For example, prohibitionists feared that the growth of probation would take the sting out of the provisions of the Volstead Act.[2]

> What we need in this court is not a movement such as you advocate, to create new officials with resulting expense, but a movement to make enforcement of our criminal laws more certain and swift. . . . In this county, due to the efforts of people like yourselves, the murderer has a cell bedecked with flowers and is surrounded with a lot of silly people. The criminal should understand when he violates the law that he is going to a penal institution and is going to stay there. Just such efforts as your organization is making are largely responsible for the crime wave that is passing over the country today and threatening to engulf our institutions.

Objections also arose from the Justice Department. For example, Attorney General Harry M. Daugherty wrote that he hoped "that no such mushy policy will be indulged in as Congress turning courts into maudlin reform associations . . . the place to do reforming is inside the walls and not with lawbreakers running loose in society." A memorandum from the Justice Department further revealed this sentiment against probation: "It is all a part of a wave of maudlin rot of misplaced sympathy for criminals that is going over the country. It would be a crime, however, if a probation system is established in the federal courts."

Approximately 34 bills to establish a federal probation system were introduced in Congress between 1909 and 1925. Despite such opposition, a bill passed on its sixth introduction to the house. The bill was sent to President Coolidge who, as a former governor of Massachusetts, was familiar with the functioning of probation. He signed the bill into law on March 4, 1925. This action was followed by an appropriation to defray the salaries and expenses of a limited number of probation officers, to be chosen by civil service (Burdress, 1997; Lindner and Savarese, 1984; Meeker, 1975). Table 3.2 highlights some of the significant events in the development of probation.

Table 3.2 Significant Events in the Development of Probation

Date	Event
Middle Ages	*Parens patriae* established to protect the welfare of the child in England
1841	John Augustus becomes the "Father of Probation"
1869	Massachusetts develops the visiting probation agent system
1875	Society of the Prevention of Cruelty to Children established in New York, paving the way for the juvenile court
1899	The first juvenile court in America was established in Cook County (Chicago) Illinois
1901	New York passes the first statute authorizing probation for adults
1925	Congress authorizes probation at the federal level
1927	All states but Wyoming have juvenile probation laws
1943	Federal Probation System formalizes the presentence investigation report
1954	Last state enacts juvenile probation law
1956	Mississippi becomes the last state to pass authorizing legislation to establish adult probation
1965	Ohio is the first state to create "shock probation," which combines prison with probation
1967	*In re Gault* decided by the U.S. Supreme Court
1969	Jerome Miller is appointed Youth Commissioner in the State of Massachusetts and begins to decarcerate state institutions
1971	Minnesota passes the first Community Corrections Act
1973	National Advisory Commission on Criminal Justice Standards and Goals endorses more extensive use of probation
1974	Congress passes the Juvenile Justice and Delinquency Prevention Act establishing the Federal Office of Juvenile Justice and Delinquency Prevention
	Restorative justice and victim/offender mediation programs begin in Ontario, Canada
1975	The state of Wisconsin receives funding from the Law Enforcement Assistance Administration to develop a case classification system. Four years later, the Risk/Needs Assessment instruments are designed and implemented
1980	American Bar Association issues restrictive guidelines to limit use of preadjudication detention

(Continued)

Table 3.2 (Continued)

Date	Event
1982	"War on Drugs" begins
1983	Electronic monitoring of offenders begins. Georgia establishes the new generation of Intensive Supervised Probation program
1984	Congress passes Sentence Reform Act to achieve longer sentences, "just deserts," and equity in sentencing
1989	President Bush displays clear plastic bag of crack on primetime television
1994	American Bar Association issues proposals to counteract the impact of domestic violence on children
1998	National Institute of Corrections begins national correctional training on implementing community restorative justice programs
2000	American Probation and Parole Association issues monograph: *Transforming Probation through Leadership: The Broken Windows Model*
2001	Evaluation of sex-offender notification on probation in Wisconsin finds high cost to corrections in terms of personnel, time, and budgetary resources
2003	Evaluation of strategies to enforce drug court treatment by aggressive probation officer involvement results in significant drop in drug use in Maryland
2008	Evaluation of strategies to more fully integrate the principles of effective intervention into face-to-face interactions between probation and parole officers and offenders
2009	Probation populations begin to decline for the first time in many years

Source: Compiled by authors.

PROBATION TODAY

Because probation is a privilege and not a right, it is essentially an "act of grace" extended by the sentencing judge who presided over the trial (although a few states permit the jury that determined guilt to award or recommend probation). Of all the principal groups of offenders under correctional control in America—probationers, jail inmates, prison inmates, and parolees—the largest group is probationers. Figure 3.1 shows how the number of adults on probation has grown over the past 25 years, from just under two million in 1985 to more than four million in 2005. During the past several years the numbers have begun to decline, and in 2012 there were 38,300 fewer offenders on probation than in the previous year. The United States Bureau of Justice Statistics reveals that nearly 57 percent of all convicted offenders were on probation, 12 percent were on parole, 21 percent were in prison, and about 11 percent were in jail. Numerically, at the beginning of 2013, there were nearly

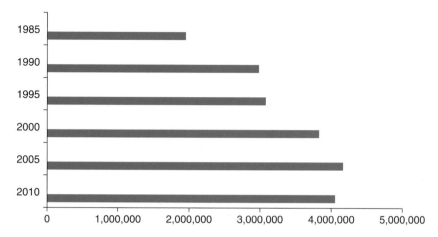

Figure 3.1 Adults on Probation: 1985–2012 (in millions)

Source: Maruschak, L.M., Bonczar, T. (20013). *Probation and parole in the United States, 2012.* Washington, DC: U.S. Department of Justice, Bureau of Justice Statistics.

four million probationers supervised by at least 20,000 probation officers. Although the average caseload size varies tremendously from jurisdiction to jurisdiction, it is estimated that the average caseload is about 180 offenders per officer. It is estimated that approximately 53 percent of offenders on probation are for felonies, with the other 47 percent for misdemeanors.

Table 3.3 illustrates the most serious offense for offenders on probation in 2012. As might be expected, probation tends to be granted more prevalently for non-violent offenders. In general, offenders convicted of nonviolent crimes (e.g., property or drug law violations) were more likely to receive probation than those convicted of violent offenses (e.g., sexual assault). So, what is probation, why is it used so frequently, and what is the process by which so large a proportion of offenders are placed on probation?

Table 3.3 Adults on Probation in 2012: Most Serious Offense

Offense	Percent
Sex offense	3
Domestic violence	4
Other violent offense	12
Property offense	28
Drug law violations	25
Driving under the influence	15
Other traffic offenses	2
Other	11

Source: Maruschak, L.E., Bonczar, T. (2013). *Probation and parole in the United States, 2012.* Washington, DC: U.S. Bureau of Justice Statistics.

OBJECTIVES AND ADVANTAGES OF PROBATION

As stated earlier, both state and federal jurisdictions enacted statutes that permit the granting of probation and define certain categories of offenses for which probation may not be granted. These acts could include all crimes of violence, crimes requiring a life sentence, armed robbery, rape or other sex offenses, use of a firearm in a crime, or multiple-convicted offenders.

However, despite the existence of legislatively defined exclusion, granting probation is a highly individualized process that usually focuses on the criminal rather than on the crime. The following are the general objectives of probation:

1. Reintegrate amenable offenders.
2. Protect the community from further antisocial behavior.
3. Further the goals of justice.
4. Provide probation conditions (and services) necessary to change offenders and to achieve the aforementioned objectives.

While probation granting is individualized, judges and corrections personnel generally recognize the advantages of probation:

1. Use of community resources to reintegrate offenders who are thus forced to face and hopefully resolve their individual problems while under community supervision.
2. Fiscal savings over imprisonment.
3. Avoidance of imprisonment, which tends to exacerbate the underlying causes of criminal behavior.
4. Keeping offenders' families off local and state welfare rolls.
5. A relatively successful process of correcting offenders' behavior (60–90 percent success rates have been reported).[3]
6. A sentencing option that can permit "selective incapacitation."

Probation, the most frequent disposition for offenders and widely recognized for its advantages (Dawson, 1990), has also received strong endorsement from numerous groups and commissions, including the prestigious National Advisory Commission on Criminal Justice Standards and Goals (1973), the General Accounting Office (1982), and the American Bar Association (ABA) (1970). The National Advisory Commission recommended that probation be used more extensively, and the ABA endorsed probation as the presumed sentence of choice for almost all nonviolent felons. Others have argued (Finn, 1984) that universal use of probation would reduce prison populations. It is important to remember that prison space is a limited and, some would say, scarce, resource. The economics of corrections are such that probation is essential if the system is going to manage its finite resources effectively (Clear et al., 1989). Figure 3.2 illustrates the cost per offender for probation supervision. Even when we consider specialized supervision (e.g., intensive, electronic), daily supervision still averages less than $4 per day. When is probation an appropriate sentence and how is it granted?

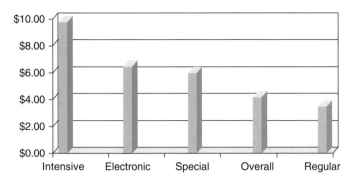

Figure 3.2 Average Daily Cost per Probationer by Supervision Type.

Source: Camp, C., Camp, G. (2003) *The corrections yearbook adult corrections 2002.* Middletown, CT: The Criminal Justice Institute, p. 206.

GRANTING PROBATION

Sentencing is a complicated process, and sentencing judges frequently find that the disposition of the case (sentence) has already been determined—by the prosecutor, not by the judge. This is because, prior to the determination of guilt, the prosecuting attorney and defense counsel have engaged in plea bargaining. During this interaction, any (or even all) of the following trial elements may have been negotiated:

1. The defendant's pleading guilty to a lesser crime but one that was present in the illegal behavior for which the penalty is considerably more lenient.
2. The frequency of the crime ("number of counts") to which the defendant will plead guilty.
3. The number of charges that will be dropped.
4. Whether the prosecutor will recommend that the defendant receives probation or be sentenced to incarceration in jail or prison.
5. The recommended length of time (months or years) of incarceration.
6. If sentence will be consecutive or concurrent.

It appears that the judiciary tends to accept and acquiesce to the negotiation outcomes (Dixon, 1995; Glaser, 1985). However, in many cases, judges still decide the sentence, one alternative of which may be probation.

The process of granting probation begins after the offender either pleads guilty (frequently for favorable personal considerations) or is judged guilty following a trial. For those offenders whose crime falls within the list of probation-eligible offenses or in those states where mandated by law, a presentence investigation will be ordered. One of the major functions of a presentence investigation report is to assist the court in determining the most appropriate sentence.

Based on observations of the defendant at trial—including demeanor, body language, evidence of remorse, and behavior—as well as the recommendation in presentence reports and the prosecutor's recommendation for sentence, judges attempt to determine the appropriate sentence for a particular individual. Judges are aware that **individualized justice** demands that the sentence fit not only the crime but also the criminal.[4]

A number of factors can influence the sentencing decision, such as the nature of the offense, the demeanor of the offender, the harm done to the victim, judicial and community attitudes, and many other considerations. Many of these factors are brought forth in a document called the **presentence investigation report** (PSI).

Perhaps, the most important criterion is the recommendation of the probation officer who composes the PSI. The role of the presentence report recommendation is a major factor, for the extent of concurrence between the probation officer's recommendations and the judge's sentencing decision is quite strong. Liebermann et al. (1971) found that, when probation was recommended, judges followed that recommendation in 83 percent of cases; Carter (1966) found an even stronger agreement: 96 percent of the cases. Liebermann and colleagues (1971) also found that when the recommendation was for imprisonment, the judge agreed in 87 percent of the cases. Macallair (1994) found that defense-based disposition reports for juveniles that recommended probation alternatives consistently lowered commitments to state correctional facilities. So what is the PSI?

THE PRESENTENCE INVESTIGATION REPORT

One of the primary responsibilities of probation agencies is investigation. This includes gathering information about probation and technical violations, facts about arrest, and, most importantly, completing the PSI for use in **sentencing hearings**.

The concept of the PSI developed with probation.[5] Judges originally used probation officers to gather background and personal information on offenders to "individualize" punishment.[6] In 1943, the Federal Probation System formalized the PSI as a required function of the federal probation process. The PSI can have a great deal of significance in the sentencing process, as 80–90 percent of defendants plead guilty and the judge's only contact with the offender is during sentencing (The Presentence Report, 1970). The judge's knowledge of the defendant is usually limited to the information contained in the presentence report. As Walsh concludes (1985, p. 363), "judges lean heavily on the professional advice of probation."

In a study of the acceptance of the PSI recommendation, Latessa (1993) examined 285 cases in Cuyahoga County, Ohio (which includes the city of Cleveland). He found that judges accepted the recommendation of the probation department in 85 percent of the cases when probation was recommended and in 66 percent when prison was the recommendation.

As mandatory minimum sentences have become more popular some jurisdictions report that fewer PSIs are being prepared. However, for others the PSI remains an important function for probation. For example, in terms of the agency workload, almost one-half (45 percent) of agencies that conduct presentence investigations reported that more than 25 percent of their workloads were devoted to these reports.

At the federal level, federal sentencing guidelines have increased the importance of the presentence investigation and the role and responsibility of the probation officer (Dierna, 1989; Jaffe, 1989; McDonald & Carlson, 1993; Steffensmeier & Demuth, 2000).

Functions and Objectives

The primary purpose of the PSI is to provide the sentencing court with succinct and precise information upon which to base rational sentencing decisions. Judges usually have a number of options available to them: they may suspend sentence, impose a fine, require restitution, incarcerate, impose community supervision, and so on. The PSI is designed to aid the judge in making the appropriate decision, taking into consideration the needs of the offender as well as the safety of the community.

Over the years, many additional important uses have been found for the presentence report. Basically, these functions include the following:[7]

1. Aiding the court in determining sentence.
2. Assisting correctional authorities in classification and treatment in release planning.
3. Giving the parole board useful information pertinent to consideration of parole.
4. Aiding the probation officer in rehabilitation efforts during probation.
5. Serving as a source of information for research.

In those jurisdictions in which probation and parole services are in the same agency, the PSI can be used for parole supervision purposes.

A PSI includes more than the simple facts about the offender, as is seen later. If it is to fulfill its purpose, it must include all objective historical and factual information significant to the decision-making process, an assessment of the character and needs of the defendant and the community, and a sound recommendation with supporting rationale that follows logically from the evaluation (Bush, 1990). A reliable and accurate report is essential, and the officer completing the report should make every effort to ensure that information contained in the PSI is reliable and valid. Information that has not been validated should be indicated.

Content

The PSI is not immune from a lack of consistency across jurisdictions, but there seem to be some common elements that illustrate its uses and content. A survey of 147 probation agencies across the nation (Carter, 1976) revealed that the cover

Table 3.4 Common Elements Contained in Presentence Reports

1. Name of defendant	10. Plea
2. Name of jurisdiction	11. Date of report
3. Offense	12. Sex
4. Lawyer	13. Custody or detention
5. Docket number	14. Verdict
6. Date of birth	15. Date of disposition
7. Address	16. Marital status
8. Name of sentencing judge	17. Other identifying numbers
9. Age	

Source: Carter, R. (1976). *Prescriptive package on pre-sentence investigations.* Washington, DC: Law Enforcement Assistance Administration.

sheets contained 17 pieces of identical information in more than 50 percent of the agencies surveyed. Information that appears most often across the various jurisdictions is included in Table 3.4.

While content requirements for a presentence investigation vary from jurisdiction to jurisdiction, there appear to be some common areas that are included and generally consist of the following:

1. Offense
   Official version
   Defendant's version
   Codefendant information
   Statement of witnesses, complainants, and victims
2. Prior record
   Juvenile adjudications
   Adult record
3. Personal and family data
   Defendant
   Parents and siblings
   Marital status
   Employment
   Education
   Health (physical, mental, and emotional)
   Military service
   Financial condition
   Assets
   Liabilities
4. Evaluation
   Alternative plans
   Sentencing data
5. Recommendations

Basically, these areas reflect the recommendation of Carter (1976, p. 9), who states that "in spite of the tradition of 'larger' rather than 'shorter,' there is little evidence that more is better." At a minimum, the PSI should include the five basic areas outlined earlier. This permits flexibility by allowing for expansion of a subject area and increased detail of circumstances as warranted. However, a subsection may be summarized in a single narrative statement.

Carter believes it is not necessary to know everything about an offender. Indeed, there is some evidence that in human decision making, the capacity of individuals to use information effectively is limited to five or six items of information. Quite apart from questions of reliability, validity, or even relevance of the information are the time and workload burdens of collecting and sorting masses of data for decision making. The end result may be information overload and impairment of efficiency.

A sample outline of a PSI from the Montgomery County Adult Probation Department (Dayton, Ohio) is shown in Figure 3.3. A thorough PSI is not complete without a plan of supervision for those individuals selected for probation. If this type of information is developed while preparing the PSI, supervision can begin on day 1, not several weeks into the probation period. During development of the PSI, special attention is also given to seeking innovative alternatives to traditional sentencing dispositions (jail, fines, prison, or probation). More recently, there has been increased attention given to the victim (Roy, 1994; Umbreit, 1994). Many probation departments now include a section pertaining to the victim as part of their PSI report. An example of a victim impact statement from the Montgomery County is presented in Figure 3.4. This section includes an assessment of the harm done to the victim and may include their comments concerning the offense and offender.

Evaluation and Recommendation

Two of the most important sections of the PSI are the evaluation and the recommendation. Although the research evidence is mixed, there appears to be a high correlation between the probation officer's recommendation and the judge's decision (Hagan, 1975; Walsh, 1985). There is also some evidence that these are the sections most widely read by the judge.

The evaluation should contain the probation officer's professional assessment of the objective material contained in the body of the report. Having gathered all the facts, the probation officer must now consider the protection of the community and the need of the defendant.

First, the probation officer should consider the offense. Was it situational in nature or indicative of persistent behavior? Was violence used? Was a weapon involved? Was it a property offense or a personal offense? Was there a motive?

Second, the community must be considered. For example, does the defendant pose a direct threat to the safety and welfare of others? Would a disposition other than prison deprecate the seriousness of the crime? Is probation a sufficient deterrent? What community resources are available?

```
Prosecutor:                              Defense Attorney:

_____ I. Case Information _____

A.  Case No.:                       C.  Jail Status:
      Referred:                             Amount of Bond:
      Disposition:                          Days in Custody:

B.  Name                            D.  Urinalysis Ordered Yes___No___
      Alias(es):                            Urine(s) Collected:
      Address:                              Result(s) Positive:
                                            Result(s) Negative:
      Phone:                                Probation Officer:


      Date of Birth:                E.  Codefendant Status:


      Social Security No.:          F.  Restitution:

_____ II. Charge Information _____

A.  Current Adjudicated Charge(as)/
      O.R.R./Penalty:
                                    D.  Other Pending Cases/Detainers:

                                    E.  Prior Felonies:
B.  Indicated Charge:
                                    F.  Repeat Offender Status:

C.  Original Jurisdiction:          G.  Eligibility for Conditional Probation:

_____ III. Client Information _____

A.  Physical
      Sex_____Race_____Height_____
      Weight_____Eyes_____Hair_____
      Present Health_____

B.  Social
      Marital Status_____
      No. of Dependants_____
      Custody of Children if Sentenced_____
      _____
      Employment Status_____
      Last Grade Completed_____
      Social Service Involvement_____
      Past_____
      _____
      Present_____
      _____
      Limitations:
                    Rec. Bailiff_____Date/Time_____
```

Figure 3.3 The Montgomery County Common Pleas Court Adult Probation Department Presentence Report.

Source: The Montgomery County Adult Probation Department.

```
                          Part I. The Offense


                     Part II. Criminal Record Section

A.   Juvenile

B.   Adult


                Part III. Employment/Other Pertinent Data


                      Part IV. Recommendation
Reasons:

1.

2.

3.

4.

Respectfully Submitted,

_____

Team Supervisor_____
```

Figure 3.3 Continued.

```
   Judge:

   Case No.:

   Name of Defendant:

   Disposition Date:

   A.   Economic Loss

   B.   Physical Injury

   C.   Change in Personal Welfare of Familial Relationships

   D.   Psychological Impact

   E.   Comments
```

Figure 3.4 Victim Impact Statement.

Source: The Montgomery County Adult Probation Department.

Finally, the probation officer has to consider the defendant and his or her special problems and needs, if any. What developmental factors were significant in contributing to the defendant's current behavior? Was there a history of antisocial behavior? Does the defendant acknowledge responsibility or remorse? Is the defendant motivated to change? What strengths and weaknesses does the defendant possess? Is the defendant employable or supporting any immediate family? The probation officer should also provide a statement of sentencing alternatives available to the court. This does not constitute a recommendation, but rather informs the court which services are available should the defendant be granted probation.

A sound recommendation is the responsibility of the probation officer. Some alternatives may include the following:

Anger management programs	Restitution
Cognitive behavioral groups	Fine
Probation	Mandatory drug treatment
Work release	House arrest/electronic monitoring
Incarceration	Community service
Split sentence	Psychiatric treatment
Shock probation	Day fines
Halfway house	Victim mediation
Family counseling	Shock incarceration
Day reporting	No recommendation

If commitment were recommended, the probation officer would indicate any problems that may need special attention on the part of the institutional staff. In addition, if the defendant were considered a security risk, the investigator would include escape potential, as well as any threats made to or received from the community or other defendants.

Regardless of the recommendation, the probation officer has the responsibility to provide a supporting rationale that will assist the court in achieving its sentencing goals.

Factors Related to Sentencing Decisions

As mentioned previously, the PSI involves a great deal of a probation department's time and resources. The presentence report is the primary comprehensive source of information about the defendant available to the sentencing judge. Although most judges agree that the PSI is a valuable aid in formulating sentencing decisions, there appear to be some differences of opinion about the value of the recommendations section of the report.[8]

Several studies have attempted to identify those factors that appear to be of primary importance to sentencing judges. Carter's 1976 survey found that the two most significant factors were the defendant's prior criminal record and the current offense. An earlier study by Carter and Wilkins (1967) found that the most important factors for judges in making a decision to grant probation included the defendant's educational level, average monthly salary, occupational level, residence, stability, participation in church activities, and military record. But, again, when factors were ranked according to their importance in the sentencing decision, the current offense and the defendant's prior record, number of arrests, and number of commitments were ranked most important. Welch and Spohn (1986) also concluded that prior record clearly predicts the decision to incarcerate; however, their research suggests that a wide range of indicators have been used to determine "prior record," but that the safest choice to use is prior incarceration.

In another study, Rosecrance (1988, p. 251) suggests that the PSI report serves to maintain the myth that criminal courts dispense individualized justice. His conclusions are "that present offense and prior criminal record are the factors that determine the probation officer's final sentencing recommendation." Rosecrance (1985) also believes that probation recommendations are designed to endorse prearraigned judicial agreements and that probation officers structure their recommendations in the "ball park" in order to gain judicial acceptance. Rogers (1990) argues, however, that the presentence investigation individualizes juvenile justice.

In another study, Latessa (1993) examined both the factors that influenced the probation officer's recommendation, as well as the actual judicial decision. He found that offenders were more likely to be recommended for prison if they were repeat offenders, committed more serious offenses, there was a victim involved, and whether the offender had a prior juvenile record. Factors that influenced the actual sentencing decision included the recommendation, drug history, mental health history, seriousness of offense, and having been incarcerated previously in a state prison. Latessa concluded that in this jurisdiction sentencing factors are based mainly on offense and prior record factors and on other relevant information, such as the presence of a victim. It is important to note that demographic factors, such as race, sex, and age, did not play a factor in either the recommendations or the decisions of the judges.

CONDITIONS OF PROBATION

When probation is granted, the court may impose certain reasonable conditions on the offender, which the probation officer is expected to monitor in the supervision process. The **conditions of probation** must not be capricious and may be both general (required of all probationers) and specific (required of an individual probationer). General conditions include obeying laws, submitting to searches, reporting regularly to the supervising officer, notifying the officer of any change in job or residence, and not being in possession of a firearm, associating with known criminals, refraining from excessive use of alcohol, or not leaving the court's jurisdiction for long periods of time without prior authorization. A partial list of services provided by probation jurisdictions can be found in Figure 3.5.

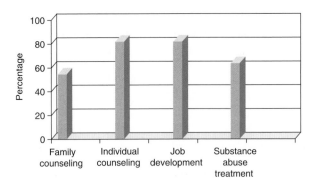

Figure 3.5 Percentage of Probation Agencies Offering Specific Services.

Source: Camp, C., Camp, G. (2003) *The corrections yearbook adult corrections 2002.* Middletown, CT: The Criminal Justice Institute, p. 215.

Specific conditions are generally tailored to the needs of the offender or philosophy of the court. For reintegration or other such purposes, the court may impose conditions of medical or psychiatric treatment; residence in a halfway house or residential center; intensive probation supervision, electronic surveillance, house arrest, community service, and active involvement in Alcoholics Anonymous; participation in a drug abuse program; restitution or victim compensation; no use of psychotropic drugs (such as cocaine or marijuana); observing a reasonable curfew; no hitchhiking; staying out of bars and poolrooms (particularly if the probationer is a prostitute); group counseling; vocational training; or other court-ordered requirements. Such required conditions are specifically designed to assist the probationer in the successful completion of probation. An example of standard conditions of probation from federal courts is presented in Figure 3.6.

Probation Fees

As part of the conditions of probation, many jurisdictions have included **probation fees** as part of the probation experience. These fees are levied for a variety of services, including the preparation of presentence reports, electronic monitoring, ignition interlock devices, work-release programs, drug counseling and testing, and regular probation supervision (Ring, 1988; Lansing, 1999). Fees range anywhere from $10 to $120 per month, with the average estimated to be about $32 per month. The imposition of supervision fees has increased dramatically over the years (Baird et al., 1986; Lansing, 1999; Camp & Camp, 2003). In addition, some states, such as Ohio, now require probation officers to assist in collecting child support payments from parents under probation supervision.

Critics of probation fees argue that it is unfair to assess a fee to those most unable to pay. Others argue that probationer fees will result in a shift from

PROB 7A
(Rev. 10/89)   Conditions of Probation and Supervised Release

UNITED STATES DISTRICT COURT

FOR THE

_____

Name _____   Docket No. _____

Address _____

Under the terms of your sentence, you have been placed on probation/supervised release (strike one) by the Honorable _____ , United States District Judge for the District of _____ . Your term of supervision is for a period of _____ , commencing _____ .

While on probation/supervised release (strike one) you shall not commit another Federal, state, or local crime and shall not illegally possess a controlled substance. Revocation of probation and supervised release is mandatory for possession of a controlled substance.

CHECK IF APPROPRIATE:

☐ As a condition of supervision, you are instructed to pay a fine in the amount of _____ ; it shall be paid in the following manner _____ .

☐ As a condition of supervision, you are instructed to pay restitution in the amount of _____to _____ ; it shall be paid in the following manner _____ .

☐ The defendant shall not possess a firearm or destructive device. Probation must be revoked for possession of a firearm.

☐ The defendant shall report in person to the probation office in the district to which the defendant is released within 72 hours of release from the custody of the Bureau of Prisons.

☐ The defendant shall report in person to the probation office in the district of release within 72 hours of release from the custody of the Bureau of Prisons.

It is the order of the Court that you shall comply with the following standard conditions:

(1)   You shall not leave the judicial district without permission of the Court or probation officer.

(2)   You shall report to the probation officer as directed by the Court or probation officer, and shall submit a truthful and complete written report within the first 5 days of each month.

(3)   You shall answer truthfully all inquiries by the probation officer and follow the instructions of the probation officer.

(4)   You shall support your dependents and meet other family responsibilities.

(5)   You shall work regularly at a lawful occupation unless excused by the probation officer for schooling, training, or other acceptable reasons.

(6)   You shall notify the probation officer within 72 h of any change in residence or employment.

Figure 3.6 Conditions of Probation and Supervised Release, U.S. District Court.

(7)   You shall refrain from excessive use of alcohol and shall not purchase, possess, use, distribute, or administer any narcotic or other controlled substance, or any paraphernalia related to such substances, except as prescribed by a physician.

(8)   You shall not frequent places where controlled substances are illegally sold, used, distributed, or administered.

(9)   You shall not associate with any persons engaged in criminal activity, and shall not associate with any person convicted of a felony unless granted permission to do so by the probation officer.

(10)   You shall permit a probation officer to visit you at any time at home or elsewhere, and shall permit confiscation of any contraband observed in plain view by the probation officer.

(11)   You shall notify the probation officer within 72 h of being arrested or questioned by a law enforcement officer.

(12)   You shall not enter into any agreement to act as an informer or a special agent of a law enforcement agency without the permission of the Court.

(13)   As directed by the probation officer, you shall notify third parties of risks that may be occasioned by your criminal record or personal history or characteristics, and shall permit the probation officer to make such notifications and to confirm your compliance with such notification requirement.

The special conditions ordered by the Court are as follows:

Upon a finding of violation of probation or supervised release, I understand that the Court may (1) revoke supervision or (2) extend the term of supervision and/or modify the conditions of supervision.

These conditions have been read to me. I fully understand the conditions, and have been provided a copy of them.

(Signed) _____   _____
                                    Defendant   Date

_____   _____
U.S. Probation Officer/Designated Witness   Date

Figure 3.6 Continued.

treatment and surveillance to fee collection, which in turn will turn probation officers into bill collectors.

Others, however, believe that probation fees can be a reasonable part of the probation experience (Wheeler et al., 1989a, 1989b). Harlow and Nelson (1982, p. 65) point out that successful fee programs serve a dual purpose: "both an important revenue source and an effective means of communicating to the offender the need to pay one's own way."[9]

It appears that probation fees are rapidly becoming a fixture in probation. Not only are they a means of raising revenue and offsetting the costs of supervision, treatment, and surveillance but they can also be used as a form of punishment (or to promote responsible behavior depending on your viewpoint).

Restitution and Community Service

Two more recent but related trends in conditions the court may impose are restitution and community work orders. **Restitution** requires the offender to make payment (perhaps monetary) to a victim to offset the damages done in the commission of the crime. If the offenders cannot afford to repay at least a part of the loss suffered by the victim, it is possible to restore the victim's losses through personal services. Probation with restitution thus has the potential for being a reparative sentence, and Galaway (1983) argues that it should be the penalty of choice for property offenders. Restitution can lessen the loss of the victim, maximize reconciliation of the offender and community, and marshal community support for the offender, perhaps through enlisting a community sponsor to monitor and encourage the offender's compliance. A good example of this can be seen in California, where in 1982 voters passed a victim's bill of rights. Part of this initiative was a crime victim restitution program that enables the court to order offenders to repay victims and the community through restitution or community service (see van Dijk et al., 1999).

Community work orders as conditions of probation appear to be used increasingly in conjunction with probation, particularly if there are no direct victim losses or the nature of the crime demands more than supervised release. Examples of community work orders would include requiring a dentist convicted of driving while intoxicated to provide free dental services to a number of indigents or ordering a physician to provide numerous hours of free medical treatment to jail inmates, perhaps on Saturday mornings. Juveniles may frequently be ordered to work for community improvements through litter removal, cutting grass, painting public buildings or the homes of elderly people, or driving shut-ins to market or to visit friends and relatives. Both restitution and community work orders can serve multiple goals: offender punishment, community reintegration, and reconciliation. The four reasons cited most commonly for using community service are as follows:

1. It is a punishment that can fit many crimes.
2. The costs of imprisonment are high and are getting higher.
3. Our jails and prisons are already full.
4. Community service requires an offender to pay with time and energy.

Another increasingly popular probation program is day reporting, a slightly structured nonresidential program often using supervision, volunteers, sanctions, and services coordinated from a central location. Providing offenders with access to treatment services, day attendance centers can help reduce jail and prison overcrowding, hold offenders accountable for their behavior, and help them address such risk factors as unemployment, addiction, and lack of education (see Williams & Turnage, 2001).

ALTERNATIVE PROBATION PROCEDURES

In addition to the most frequent procedures described earlier, there are six other variations of granting probation that need to be discussed before we consider the legal process of revoking probation of those who cannot or will not abide by court-imposed conditions of liberty in the community:

1. Prosecutorial probation
2. Court probation without adjudication
3. Shock probation
4. Intermittent incarceration
5. Split sentences
6. Modification of sentence.

While probation is imposed most frequently by a trial judge after a guilty plea or trial, it may also replace the trial completely, in which case it is called "probation without adjudication." In practice, the process embraces two separate programs: one operated by the prosecutor (a form of deferred prosecution) and the other by the judge in those limited numbers of jurisdictions in which state legislation permits a bifurcated process (determining guilt, followed by adjudication as a felon). Both result in probation but are vastly different.

Deferred Prosecution Probation

Part of the broad power accorded a prosecutor in the United States is the ability to offer the accused deferred prosecution. In those programs in which the prosecutor grants deferred prosecution, the accused will generally be asked to sign a contract accepting moral (but usually not legal) responsibility for the crime and agreeing to make victim restitution, to undergo specific treatment programs (substance abuse, methadone maintenance, anger management, etc.), to report periodically to a designated official (usually a probation officer), and to refrain from other criminal acts during the contract period. If these conditions are satisfied, the prosecutor dismisses (*nolle pros*) the charge. If the accused does not participate and cooperate actively in the program the prosecutor can, at any time during the contract period, carry the case forward to trial. Deferred prosecution can, although it is infrequent, lead to a unique probation organization within the office of the prosecutor.

Probation by Withholding Adjudication

This process refers to a judge's optional authority available in those states (such as Florida) where statutes permit a bifurcated process: first determine guilt and then declare the defendant a convicted felon. By refraining from declaration of a guilty felon, the judge can suspend the legal process and place the defendant on probation for a specific time period, sometimes without supervision being required (a "summary" or non-reporting probation). Thus the judge gives the offender a chance to demonstrate his or her ability and willingness to adjust and reform. The offenders know that they can still be returned to court for adjudication of guilt and sentencing, and frequently imprisonment.

The advantages of this option fit squarely in the general philosophy of probation and may be of particular use in intimate-partner assaults (Canales-Portalatin, 2000). Not only is treatment in the community emphasized but the collateral benefits are also considerable (Allen et al., 1981: pp. 361–362):

> [The judge] places him or her on probation without requiring him to register with local law enforcement agencies as a previously convicted felon; without serving notice on prospective employers of a previous conviction; without preventing the offender from holding public office, voting, or serving on a jury; without impeding the offender from obtaining a license that requires "reputable character"; without making it more difficult than others to obtain firearms; in short, without public or even private degradation.

Shock Probation

In 1965, Ohio became the first of at least 14 states to enact an early release procedure generally known as "**shock probation.**" Shock probation combined the leniency of probation with a short period of incarceration in a penal institution. The assumptions and features underlying this innovative program were described by the then-director of the Ohio Adult Parole Authority (Allen & Simonsen, 2001, p. 226). They were as follows:

1. A way for the courts to impress offenders with the seriousness of their actions without a long prison sentence.
2. A way for the courts to release offenders found by the institution to be more amenable to community-based treatment than was realized by the courts at time of sentence.
3. A way for the courts to arrive at a just compromise between punishment and leniency in appropriate cases.
4. A way for the courts to provide community-based treatment for rehabilitable offenders while still observing their responsibilities for imposing deterrent sentences where public policy demands it.
5. [A way to afford] the briefly incarcerated offender a protection against absorption into the "hard rock" inmate culture.

Critics have argued that shock probation combines philosophically incompatible objectives: punishment and leniency. Other criticisms (Reid, 1976) are that the defendant is further stigmatized by the incarceration component of shock probation, and the existence of a shock probation sentence may encourage the judiciary to rely less on probation than previously. The most damaging criticism was presented by Vito and Allen (1981) when they concluded that the negative effects of incarceration were affecting the performance of shock probationers.

Vito (1984, pp. 26–27) has drawn some conclusions about shock probation based on his long-term work in this area as follows:

1. The level of reincarceration rates indicates that the program has some potential.
2. If shock probation is utilized, it should be used with a select group of offenders who cannot be considered as good candidates for regular probation.
3. The period of incarceration must be short in order to achieve the maximum deterrent effect while reducing the fiscal cost of incarceration.
4. In this time of severe prison overcrowding, the use of shock probation can only be justified as a diversionary measure to give offenders who would otherwise not be placed on probation a chance to succeed.

Although shock probation was used for more than 30 years, in the mid-1990s, Ohio eliminated it as a sentencing option; however, it is still an option for first-time offenders in Kentucky.

Combining Probation and Incarceration

There are a number of alternatives to placing an offender on probation, other than shock probation, that include a period of incarceration (Parisi, 1980). The U.S. Department of Justice (Bureau of Justice Statistics, 1997) notes:

> Although the courts continue to use [probation] as a less severe and less expensive alternative to incarceration, most courts are also given discretion to link probation to a term of incarceration—an option selected with increasing frequency.

Combinations of probation and incarceration include the following:

- **Split sentences**: where the court specifies a period of incarceration to be followed by a period of probation (Parisi, 1981).
- Modification of sentence: where the original sentencing court may reconsider an offender's prison sentence within a limited time and change it to probation.
- **Intermittent incarceration**: where an offender on probation may spend weekends or nights in jail (Bureau of Justice Statistics, 1997).

PROBATION REVOCATION

The judge usually imposes the conditions that must be observed by the offender while on probation and has absolute discretion and authority to impose, modify, or reject these conditions. Some examples of conditions a judge might impose are routine urine testing to detect drug use and abuse, participation in a substance abuse program if the probationer has an alcohol or other drug problem, driving limits, restitution to victims of the probationer (but probation may not be revoked if the offender cannot make payments because of unemployment (*Bearden v. Georgia*, 1983)),[10] and not leaving the court's jurisdiction without prior approval. Many cases have challenged the conditions that courts might impose, but case law has determined that any condition may be imposed if it is constitutional, reasonable, clear, and related to some definable correctional goal, such as rehabilitation or public safety. These are difficult to challenge and leave the court with broad power and tremendous discretion in imposing conditions. Such discretion has contributed to the volume of civil rights lawsuits (del Carmen, 1985).

Once placed on probation, offenders are supervised and assisted by probation officers who are increasingly using existing community agencies and services to provide individualized treatment based on the offender's needs. Assuming that the offender meets the court-imposed conditions, makes satisfactory progress in resolving underlying problems, and does not engage in further illegal activities, probation agencies may request the court to close the case. This would terminate supervision of the offender and probation. Probation may also be terminated by completion of the period of maximum sentence or by the offender having received "maximum benefit from treatment." Table 3.5 shows the various ways that adult offenders terminated probation in 2012. Fortunately, most offenders completed their term of probation successfully.

Table 3.5 Reasons for Termination from Probation in 2012

Type of Exit	Percent
Completion	68
Incarceration	15
Absconder	3
Other Unsatisfactory	9
Other	5

Source: Maruschak, L.E., Bonczar, T. (2013). *Probation and parole in the United States, 2012.* Washington, DC: U.S. Bureau of Justice Statistics.

In supervising a probationer, officers should enforce the conditions and rules of probation pragmatically, considering the client's particular and individual needs, the legality of decisions they must make while supervising clients (Watkins, 1989), the clarity of anticipation by the probationer of assistance from the supervising officer (and expectations of the probationer), and the potential effects of enforcing rules on a client's future behavior and adjustment (Koontz, 1980). Because many clients have alcohol and other drug problems, they must be tested for substance abuse.

Probationers vary in their ability to comply with imposed conditions, some of which may be unrealistic, particularly those that require extensive victim restitution or employment during an economic period of high unemployment (Smith et al., 1989). Some probationers are also indifferent or even hostile, unwilling, or psychologically unable to cooperate with their probation supervisor or the court. Others commit technical violations of court orders that are not new crimes *per se* but are seen as harbingers of future illegal activity. In these circumstances, probation officers must deal with technical probation violations.

Probation officers, charged with managing such cases, may determine that technical violators need a stern warning or that court-imposed conditions should

---

Box 3.3
Technical Violation of Probation

A technical violation refers to an infraction of a court order, often in the form of a probation condition. It is generally not considered a new crime *per se*, but can be used by the probation officer to bring an offender back in front of the judge. An example of a technical violation would be failure of a probationer to meet with his or her probation officer as scheduled. Technical violations can lead to the revocation of probation and the imposition of incarceration or another sanction.

---

be tightened (or relaxed, depending on individual circumstances). These determinations may lead to an offender's reappearance before the court for a warning or redefinition of conditions. Judges and probation officers, ideally, collaborate in such cases to protect the community or increase the probability of successful reintegration. Offenders are frequently returned to probation, and supervision and treatment continue.

If the warning and new conditions are not sufficient, if the offender repetitively violates conditions of probation or is arrested for an alleged new crime, a probation revocation hearing may be necessary. If the probationer is not already in jail for the alleged new crime, a warrant may be issued for his or her arrest. It is also clear that technical violations can be a major source of failures in probation and that rates can vary considerably from jurisdiction to jurisdiction.

A probation **revocation** hearing is a serious process, posing potential "grievous loss of liberty" for the offender. Both probation officers and judges vary considerably as to what would constitute grounds for revoking probation and resentencing to imprisonment. Punitive probation officers may contend that technical violations are sufficient for revoking probation; judges may believe that the commission of a new crime would be the only reason for revocation.

Revocation and Legal Issues

Probation is a privilege, not a right (del Carmen, 1985). This was decided in *United States v. Birnbaum* (1970).[11] Once granted, however, the probationer has an interest in remaining on probation, commonly referred to as an entitlement. The due process rights of probationers at a revocation hearing were generally ignored until 1967, when the U.S. Supreme Court issued an opinion regarding state probationers' rights to counsel at such a hearing (*Mempa v. Rhay*, 1967). This case provided right to counsel if probation were revoked under a deferred sentencing statute, but this decision did not specify that a court hearing was required. That issue was resolved in *Gagnon v. Scarpelli* (1973), a landmark case in due process procedures in probation. The U.S. Supreme Court ruled that probation cannot be

---

Box 3.4
Modifications of Conditions of Sentence

Probation officers supervise clients assigned by sentencing courts and, during the period of community release, may find that certain probationers refuse to abide by the court-imposed rules or that their clients' personal circumstances change so markedly that additional court direction may be needed.

If the client has difficulty accepting the legitimacy of community control, probation officers may recommend additional surveillance or treatment options. These range from imposing house arrest to electronic monitoring or daily surveillance by the officer. Clients may also be required to reside in a residential setting, such as a halfway house, or appear daily at a day reporting program until their behavior or circumstances change.

Increasing the requirements for conformity to court-ordered liberty is frequently referred to as "tourniquet sentencing." Conditions may be relaxed as behavior improves.

---

withdrawn (revoked) unless certain basic elements of due process are observed. If a court is considering removing the offender from probation (through a "revocation" hearing), the following rights and procedures must ensue: the probationer must (1) be informed in writing of the charge against him or her, (2) have the written notice in advance of the revocation hearing, and (3) attend the hearing and be able to present evidence on his or her own behalf. The probationer also has a right (4) to challenge those testifying against him or her, (5) to confront witnesses and cross-examine them, and (6) to have legal counsel present if the charges are complicated or the case is so complex that an ordinary person would not be able to comprehend the legal issues.[12]

The probation officer is responsible for seeing that conditions imposed by the court are met and, if not, for calling violations to the attention of the court. As such, the probation officer functions both as a helper and as a supervisor of the probationer. Legal liability is greater for the probation officer than the court; although an agent of the court, the probation officer does not enjoy the absolute immunity from liability that the court enjoys.

Some areas of potential liability for the probation officer include acts taken or protective steps omitted. For example, a probation officer may be liable for failing to disclose a probationer's background to a third party if this results in subsequent serious injury or death. Case decisions have generally held that the probation officer should disclose the past behavior of the probationer if he or she is able to reasonably foresee a potential danger to a specific third party. This would include an employer hiring a probationer as an accountant in a bank when the instant crime was embezzlement or hiring a child molester to work in a grade school position. Insurance for certain liabilities can be obtained from the American Correctional Association.[13]

As a counselor to probationers, probation officers are often faced with the problem of encouraging their clients to share their problems and needs. Frequently, during the monthly contact, a probationer will reveal involvement in criminal activities. Under these noncustodial circumstances, probation offers are required to warn the probationer against self-incrimination through *Miranda* warnings[14] or the evidence cannot be used in a court of law. Any discussion with a probationer under detention circumstances must be preceded by *Miranda* warnings. Litigation is so extensive within the probation area that the probation officer must frequently take an active role as a law enforcement officer rather than a helper, a sad development from the original role John Augustus initiated and correctional personnel usually pursue.

SUMMARY

This chapter began by tracing historical, philosophical, and legal developments in the field of probation over the past two centuries. While John Augustus is given credit as the "father" of probation, we have seen that many others played an important part in developing and shaping probation. Probation continues to serve the bulk of adult offenders. This chapter also described court options and procedures for placing offenders on probation, as well as some issues in supervising offenders. It should be obvious that probation requires a judge to weigh the "individualization" of treatment as well as the "justice" or "just deserts" associated with the crime that was committed. In addition, this chapter examined the presentence investigation report. Because the PSI is one of the primary responsibilities of probation agencies, its importance is highlighted by the fact that the vast majority of defendants plead guilty and that their only contact with the judge is during sentencing.

Finally, the imposition of conditions, and the probation officer's monitoring of offenders' behavior, are important parts of the probation process. Accordingly, revoking probation is not an action that is taken lightly, as it often results in the incarceration of the offender. Granting probation and supervising probation clients are complicated procedures requiring considerable skill and dedication, issues that are also raised in granting parole.

Review Questions

1. How did philosophical precursors of probation contribute to its development?
2. Why was probation established much earlier for juvenile offenders than for adult offenders?
3. Define probation.
4. Should probation be the disposition of choice for most nonviolent offenders?
5. What are the general objectives of probation?
6. Describe the advantages of probation.
7. How is justice individualized?

8. What functions does the presentence investigation serve?
9. What is the potential value of a victim impact statement?
10. Identify and define five supervision conditions that might be included in the PSI recommendation.
11. List five conditions of probation generally required of all probationers.
12. What are three grounds for revoking probation and sentencing to incarceration?
13. List five possible sentencing recommendations that can be made.
14. Explain why probation revocation rates might be higher in rural versus urban areas.

Notes

1 Sureties refer to cash, property, or bond posted by an offender to be forfeited if he or she fails to conform to such conditions as to appear in court for trial or to avoid further criminal behavior over a specified time period. It can also refer to a pledge by another responsible person to assure that the accused will appear or behave properly.

2 The Volstead Act authorized the enforcement of anti-alcohol legislation—the "Great Experiment" of the Thirteenth Amendment to the U.S. Constitution. As Evjen (1975, p. 5) has demonstrated, letters from judges to Chute clearly denounced the practice of probation.

3 While some dispute the effectiveness of probation (Petersilia, 1985), other researchers (McGaha et al., 1987; Vito, 1986) have found probation generally to be effective.

4 Some evidence shows that sentencing is in part influenced by judges' personal goals, such as potential for promotion to a higher court (Cohen, 1992; Macallair, 1994).

5 For a thorough discussion of early development of the PSI, see The Presentence Report (1970).

6 See Sieh (1993).

7 These functions are adapted from the Administrative Office of the U.S. Courts (1978). The Presentence Report. Washington, DC: U.S. Government Printing Office. See also Marvell (1995).

8 For example, in Cincinnati, Ohio, a single probation department serves both the municipal court and the court of common pleas, yet each court requires a different PSI. The court of common pleas does not permit probation officer recommendations to be included in the report, but the municipal court requires one.

9 For a description of the Texas Program, see Finn and Parent (1992).

10 10 461 U.S. 660 (1983).

11 421 F.2d 993, *cert. denied*, 397 U.S. 1044 (1970).

12 411 U.S. 778, 93 S. Ct. 1756 (1972).

13 The current mailing address for the American Correctional Association is 4380 Forbes Boulevard, Lanham, MD 20706–4322 (www.cworrections.com/aca).

14 *Miranda* warnings: (1) that the suspect has the right to remain silent; (2) that any statement he does make may be used as evidence against him; (3) that he has a right to the presence of an attorney; and (4) that if he cannot afford an attorney, one will be appointed for him prior to any questioning if he so desires.

Recommended Readings

del Carmen, R. (1985). Legal issues and liabilities in community corrections. In: L.F. Travis (ed.) *Probation, parole and community corrections*. Prospect Heights, IL: Waveland, pp. 47–70. [This chapter does an excellent job of summarizing the legal issues surrounding probation, including release, conditions, and supervision.]

Dressler, D. (1962). *Practice and theory of probation and parole*. New York: Columbia University Press. [A cogent and well-documented analysis of the historical development of probation.]

Evjen, V. (1975). The Federal Probation System: The struggle to achieve it and its first 25 years. *Federal Probation* 39(2), 3–15. [A very thorough description of the rise of the federal probation system.]

Gowdy, V. (1993). *Intermediate sanctions*. Washington, DC: U.S. Department of Justice. [An excellent overview of the range of and issues surrounding intermediate punishments.]

Jones, M., Johnson, P. (2012). *History of criminal justice*, 5th edn. Boston, MA: Elsevier (Anderson Publishing). [This book provides a history of criminal justice and probation and examines the philosophy of individualized justice.]

Lindner, C., Savarese, M. (1984). The evolution of probation: early salaries, qualifications and hiring practices; the evolution of probation: the historical contributions of the volunteer; the evolution of probation: university settlement and the beginning of statutory probation in New York City; and The evolution of probation: university settlement and its pioneering role in probation work. *Federal Probation* 48 (1–4). [This four-part series examines the early rise of probation in the United States.]

Rothman, D. (1980). *Conscience and convenience: The asylum and its alternatives in progressive America*. Boston, MA: Little, Brown. [Chapter 3 provides a critical assessment of the early use of probation and development of the presentence investigation.]

References

Allen, H., Simonsen, C. (1989). *Corrections in America*. New York: Macmillan.

Allen, H., Simonsen, C. (2001). *Corrections in America*. Upper Saddle River, NJ: Prentice Hall.

Allen, H., Friday, P., Roebuck, J., Sagarin, E. (1981). *Crime and punishment*. New York: The Free Press.

American Bar Association (1970). *Project standards for criminal justice: Standards relating to probation*. New York: Institute of Judicial Administration.

American Correctional Association (2001). *Probation and parole directory 2000–2003*. Lanham, MD: ACA.

Baird, C., Holien, D., Bakke, J. (1986). *Fees for probation services*. Washington, DC: National Institute of Corrections.

Barnes, H., Teeters, N. (1959). *New horizons in criminology*. Englewood Cliffs, NJ: Prentice-Hall.

Bearden v. Georgia, 461 U.S. 660 (1983).

Beccaria, C. (1764). *Essay on crimes and punishments*. Indianapolis, IN: Bobbs-Merrill (H. Paulucci, trans., 1963).

Black's Law Dictionary 5th edn (1994). St. Paul, MN: West.

Burdress, L. (1997) The Federal Probation and Pretrial Services System. *Federal Probation* 61(1), 5–111.

Bureau of Justice Statistics (1997). *Correctional populations in the United States*. Washington, DC: U.S. Department of Justice.

Bureau of Justice Statistics (2001). *National correction population reaches new high, grows by 126,400 during 2000 to total 6.5 million adults*. Washington, DC: U.S. Department of Justice.

Bureau of Justice Statistics (2006). *Probation and parole in the United States, 2005*. Washington, DC: U.S. Department of Justice.

Bush, E.L. (1990). Not ordinarily relevant? Considering the defendant's children at sentencing. *Federal Probation* 5(1), 15–22.

Camp, C., Camp, G. (1997). *The corrections yearbook*. South Salem, NY: The Criminal Justice Institute.

Camp, C., Camp, G. (2003). *The corrections yearbook adult corrections 2002*. Middletown, CT: The Criminal Justice Institute.

Canales-Portalatin, D. (2000). Intimate partner assailants. *Journal of Interpersonal Violence* 15(8), 843–854.

Carter, R. (1966). It is respectfully recommended. *Federal Probation* 30(2), 38–40.

Carter, R. (1976). *Prescriptive package on pre-sentence investigations*. Washington, DC: Law Enforcement Assistance Administration: unpublished draft.

Carter, R., Wilkins, L. (1967). Some factors in sentencing policy. *Journal of Criminal Law, Criminology and Police Science* 58(4), 503–514.

Citizens Committee for Children (1982). *Lost opportunities: A study of the promise and practices of the [New York City] department of probation's family court*. New York: Citizens Committee for Children.

Clear, T.R., Clear, V.B., Burrell, W.D. (1989). *Offender assessment and evaluation: The presentence investigation report*. Cincinnati, OH: Anderson.

Cohen, M. (1992). The motives of judges: Empirical evidence from antitrust sentencing. *International Review of Law and Economics* 12, 13–30.

Cornelius, W. (1997). *Swift and sure: Bringing certainty and finality to criminal punishments*. Irvington-on-Hudson: Bridge Street Books.

Dawson, J. (1990). *Felons sentenced to probation in state courts*. Washington, DC: U.S. Department of Justice.

del Carmen, R.V. (1985). Legal issues and liabilities in community corrections. In: L.F. Travis (ed.) *Probation, parole and community corrections*. Prospect Heights, IL: Waveland, pp. 47–70.

del Carmen, R.V., Bonham, G. (2001). Overview of legal liabilities. *Perspectives* 25(1), 28–33.

Dierna, J. (1989). Guideline sentencing: Probation officer responsibilities and inter-agency issues. *Federal Probation* 53(3), 3–11.

Dixon, J. (1995). The organizational context of criminal sentencing. *American Journal of Sociology* 100, 1157–1198.

Dressler, D. (1962). *Practice and theory of probation and parole*. New York: Columbia University Press.

Dubois, P. (1981). Disclosure of presentence reports in the United States District Courts. *Federal Probation* 45(1), 3–9.

DuRose, M., Levin, D., Langan, P. (2001). *Felony sentences in state courts, 1998*. Washington, DC: Bureau of Justice Statistics

Evans, S., Scott, J. (1983). Social scientists as expert witnesses: Their use, misuse and sometimes abuse. *Law and Policy Quarterly* 5, 181–214.

Evjen, V. (1975). The Federal Probation System: The struggle to achieve it and its first 25 years. *Federal Probation* 39(2), 3–15.

Ex parte, 1916 *U.S. 242* 27–53.

Finn, P. (1984). Prison crowding: The response of probation and parole. *Crime & Delinquency* 30, 141–153.

Finn, P., Parent, D. (1992). *Making the offender foot the bill: A Texas program*. Washington, DC: U.S. Department of Justice.

Fruchtman, D., Sigler, R. (1999). Private pre-sentence investigation: Procedures and issues. *Journal of Offender Rehabilitation* 29(3/4), 157–170.

Gagnon v. Scarpelli, 411 U.S. 778 (1973).

Galaway, B. (1983). Probation as a reparative sentence. *Federal Probation* 46(3), 9–18.

General Accounting Office (1982). *Federal parole practices*. Washington, DC: GAO.

Gitchoff, T. (1980). *Expert testimony of sentencing. American jurisprudence proof of facts*, vol. 21. Rochester, NH: Lawyers Cooperative Publishers, pp. 1–9.

Gitchoff, T., Rush, G. (1989). The criminological case evaluation of sentencing recommendation: An idea whose time has come. *International Journal of Offender Therapy and Comparative Criminology* 33(1), 77–83.

Glaser, D. (1985). Who gets probation and parole: Case study versus actuarial decision-making. *Crime & Delinquency* 31, 367–378.

Granelli, J. (1983). Presentence reports go private. *National Law Journal* 15, 1–23.

Greenwood, P., Turner, S. (1993). Private presentence reports for serious juvenile offenders: Implementation issues and impacts. *Justice Quarterly* 10, 229–243.

Hagan, J. (1975). The social and legal construction of criminal justice: A study of the presentence report. *Social Problems* 22, 620–637.

Harlow, N., Nelson, K. (1982). *Management strategies for probation in an era of limits*. Washington, DC: National Institute of Corrections.

Higgins, J. (1964). Confidentiality of presentence reports. *Albany Law Review* 28, 31–47.

Hoelter, H. (1984). Private presentence reports: Boon or boondoggle? *Federal Probation* 48(3), 66–69.

Jaffe, H. (1989). The presentence report, probation officer accountability, and recruitment practices: Some influences of guideline sentencing. *Federal Probation* 53(3), 12–14.

Johnson, F. (1928). *Probation for juveniles and adults.* New York: Century Co.

Johnson, H., Wolfe, N., Jones, M. (2008). *History of criminal justice,* 4th edn. Newark, NJ: LexisNexis Matthew Bender.

Kane, R. (1995). A sentencing model for modernizing sentencing practices in Massachusetts' 68 District Courts. *Federal Probation* 59(3), 10–15.

Koontz, J.B. (1980). Pragmatic conditions of probation. *Corrections Today* 42, 14–44.

Kulis, C. (1983). Profit in the private presentence report. *Federal Probation* 47(4), 11–16.

Lansing, S. (1999). *Parental responsibility and juvenile delinquency.* Albany, NY: New York State Division of Criminal Justice Services.

Latessa, E. (1993). *An analysis of pre-sentencing investigation recommendations and judicial outcome in Cuyahoga County adult probation department.* Cincinnati: Department of Criminal Justice, University of Cincinnati.

Latessa, E., Travis, F., Holsinger, A. (1997). *Evaluation of Ohio's community correctional act programs by county size.* Cincinnati: Division of Criminal Justice, University of Cincinnati.

Liebermann, E., Schaffer, S., Martin, J. (1971). *The Bronx Sentencing Project: An experiment in the use of short-form presentence report for adult misdemeanants.* New York: Vera Institute of Justice.

Lindner, C., Savarese, M. (1984). The evolution of probation: Early salaries, qualifications and hiring practices. *Federal Probation* 48(1), 3–9.

Macallair, D. (1994). Disposition case advocacy in San Francisco's juvenile justice system: A new approach to deinstitutionalization. *Crime & Delinquency* 40, 84–95.

Macallair, D. (1996). Violence in America: How we can save our children. *Stanford Law and Policy Review* 7(1), 31–41.

Marshall, F., Vito, G. (1982). Not without the tools: The task of probation in the eighties. *Federal Probation* 46(4), 37–40.

Maruschak, L.E., Bonsczar, T. (2013). *Probation and parole in the United States, 2012.* Washington, DC: U.S. Bureau of Justice Statistics.

Marvell, T. (1995). Sentencing guidelines and prison population growth. *The Journal of Criminal Law and Criminology* 85, 696–707.

McDonald, D., Carlson, K. (1993). *Sentencing in the federal courts: Does race matter?* Washington, DC: U.S. Bureau of Justice Statistics.

McGaha, J., Fichter, M., Hirschburg, P. (1987). Felony probation: A re-examination of public risk. *American Journal of Criminal Justice* 12, 1–9.

Meeker, B. (1975). The federal probation system: The second 25 years. *Federal Probation* 39(2), 16–25.

Mempa v. Rhay, 389 U.S. 128 (1967).

National Advisory Commission on Criminal Justice Standards and Goals (1973) *Corrections.* Washington, DC: U.S. Government Printing Office.

Parisi, N. (1980). Combining incarceration and probation. *Federal Probation* 46(2), 3–10.

Parisi, N. (1981). A taste of the bars. *Journal of Criminal Law and Criminology* 72, 1109–1123.

Parker, L. (1997). A contemporary view of alternatives to incarceration in Denmark. *Federal Probation* 61(2), 67–73.

Petersilia, J. (1985). Probation and felony offenders. *Federal Probation* 49(2): 4–9.

Petersilia, J. (1997). Probation in the United States. In: M. Tonry (ed.) *Crime and justice: A review of research,* vol. 22. Chicago, IL: University of Chicago Press, pp. 149–200.

Reed, T. (1997). *Apples to apples: Comparing the operational costs of juvenile and adult correctional programs in Texas.* Austin, TX: Texas Criminal Justice Policy Council.

Reid, S. (1976). *Crime and criminology.* Hinsdale, IL: Dryden Press.

Ring, C. (1988). *Probation supervision fees: Shifting costs to the offender.* Boston: Massachusetts Legislative Research Bureau.

Rodgers, T., Gitchoff, T., Paur, I. (1979). The privately commissioned pre-sentence report: A multidisciplinary approach. *Criminal Justice Journal* 2, 271–279.

Rogers, J. (1990). The predispositional report: Maintaining the promise of individualized justice. *Federal Probation* 54(1), 43–57.

Rosecrance, J. (1985). The probation officers' search for credibility: Ball park recommendations. *Crime & Delinquency* 31: 539–554.

Rosecrance, J. (1988). Maintaining the myth of individualized justice: Probation presentence reports. *Justice Quarterly* 5, 235–256.

Roy, S. (1994). Victim offender reconciliation program for juveniles in Elkhart County, Indiana: An exploratory study. *Justice Professional* 8(2), 23–35.

Shockley, C. (1988). The federal presentence investigation report: Sentence disclosure under the freedom of information act. *Administrative Law Review* 40(1), 79–119.

Sieh, E. (1993). From Augustus to the progressives: A study of probation's formative years. *Federal Probation* 57(3), 67–72.

Smith, B., Davis, R., Hillenbrand, S. (1989). *Improving enforcement of court-ordered restitution.* Chicago, IL: American Bar Association.

Sourcebook of Criminal Justice Statistics (2001). *Adults on probation, in jail or prison, and on parole.* Albany, NY: State University of New York.

Steffensmeier, D., Demuth, S. (2000). Ethnicity and sentencing outcomes in U.S. Federal Courts. *American Sociological Review* 65(5), 705–729.

The Presentence Report (1970). An empirical study of its use in the federal criminal process. *Georgetown Law Journal* 58, 12–27.

The Presentence Investigation Report (1978). *Federal Rules of Criminal Procedure, Rule 32 (Appendix A),* Publication No. 105. Washington, DC: Administrative Office of the United States Courts.

Umbreit, M. (1994). *Victim meets offender: The impact of restorative justice and mediation.* Monsey, NY: Criminal Justice Press.

United Nations (1976). The legal origins of probation. In: R.N. Carter, L.T. Wilkins (eds) *Probation, parole and community services.* New York: John Wiley and Sons, pp. 81–88.

United States v. Birnbaum, 421 F.2d 997, cert. denied, 397 U.S. 1044 (1970).

van Dijk, J.J.M., van Kaam, R.G.H., Wemmers, J.A.M. (1999). In: van Dijk-Kaam, J., Wemmers, J. (eds) *Caring for crime victims*. Monsey, NY: Criminal Justice Press, pp. 1–12.

Vito, G.F. (1978). Shock probation in Ohio: A comparison of attributes and outcomes. Ohio State University: unpublished doctoral dissertation.

Vito, G. (1984). Development in shock probation: A review of research findings and policy implications. *Federal Probation* 48(2), 22–27.

Vito, G. (1986). Felony probation and recidivism: Replication and response. *Federal Probation* 50(4), 17–25.

Vito, G., Allen, H. (1981). Shock probation in Ohio: A comparison of outcomes. *International Journal of Offender Therapy and Comparative Criminology* 25, 70–75.

Walsh, A. (1985). The role of the probation officer in the sentencing process. *Criminal Justice and Behavior* 12, 289–303.

Watkins, J.C. (1989). Probation and parole malpractice in a noninstitutional setting: A contemporary analysis. *Federal Probation* 53(3), 29–34.

Welch, S., Spohn, C. (1986). Evaluating the impact of prior record on judges' sentencing decisions: A seven-city comparison. *Justice Quarterly* 3, 389–407.

Wheeler, G., Macan, T., Hissong, R., Slusher, M. (1989a). The effects of probation service fees on case management strategy and sanctions. *Journal of Criminal Justice* 17, 15–24.

Wheeler, G., Rudolph, A., Hissong, R. (1989b). Do probationers' characteristics affect fee assessment, payment and outcome? *Perspectives* 3(3), 12–17.

Williams, D.J., Turnage, T. (2001). Success of a day reporting center program. *Corrections Compendium* 26(3), 1–2.26.

Zastrow, W.G. (1971). Disclosure of the presentence investigation report. *Federal Probation* 35(4), 20–23.

Chapter 4

PAROLE IN AMERICA

Key Terms

American Prison Association
conditional release
deterrence
discretionary release
flopped
good-time credits
incapacitation
indeterminate sentence
mandatory release
mark system
pardon

parole
parole board
parole conditions
parole guidelines
parole revocation
penal colony
presumptive sentencing
program credits
sentencing disparity
sentencing guidelines
transportation

The most vivid disagreements over the matter of rights were caused by the ticket-of-leave system. There were only three ways in which the law might release a man from bondage. The first, though the rarest, was an absolute pardon from the governor, which restored him all rights including that of returning to England. The second was a conditional pardon, which gave the transported person citizenship within the colony but no right of return to England. The third was the ticket-of-leave.—Robert Hughes

A couple was driving through the country one fall day when they came upon a large house with a sign hanging from the porch. The sign said: "Dr. E. Smith, Veterinarian and Taxidermist." This seemed like an odd combination, so the couple drove closer. Under the name, it said: "Either way, you get your dog back."—Anonymous

THE DEVELOPMENT OF PAROLE

The way prisoners are released has changed dramatically over the years (Pew, 2014). Some are released by a **parole board** (discretionary release, about 55 percent in 1980 and only 33 percent in 2011), others finish their entire sentences and are released with no supervision (mandatory release, 22 percent in 2012), and still others are given mandatory release with supervision. For example, in 2012, about 33 percent of all prisoners were released with no supervision (Carson & Golinelli, 2013). We also know that parole is implemented differently from state to state. So what is parole, and how did we get to this point?

⌐**Parole** is a correctional option that often evokes strong feelings.⌐There are those who argue that it should be abolished entirely, whereas others believe that it provides men and women with an opportunity to demonstrate that they can re-enter society and lead law-abiding and productive lives.⌐ Regardless of one's position, parole is an important part of the American correctional system. Furthermore, because⌐in 2012 more than 637,000 inmates were released to the community, many of whom will be under some form of correctional supervision,⌐ it is important that we understand the roots of parole and how it is granted.

Although the percentage of prisoners released on discretionary parole has been growing since 2011, the rate is still low compared to the not too distant past. Of those released to parole in 2012, about 41 percent were released by a parole board. Thus, parole remains a commonly used mechanism by which offenders may be released from a correctional institution after completion of a portion of the sentence. Figure 4.1 shows the rate of parole exits in 2012 by the type of exit. Contemporary parole also includes the concepts of supervision by state, release on condition of good behavior while in the community, and return to prison for failing to abide by these conditions or for committing a new crime. As we shall see, earlier parole practices saw the development of these elements.

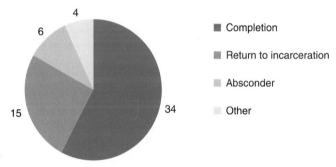

Figure 4.1 Rate of Parole Exits by Type, 2012.

Source: Maruschak, L.M., Bonczar, T.P. (2013). *Probation and parole in the United States, 2012*. Washington, DC: U.S. Dept. of Justice, Offices of Justice Programs, Bureau of Justice Statistics.

THE ROOTS OF AMERICAN PAROLE

Although⌐parole had its roots elsewhere, the widespread use of parole from prison, like the prison itself, is primarily an American innovation.⌐ It emerged from a philosophical revolution and a resulting tradition of penal reform established in the late eighteenth century in the newly formed United States. As with many other new ideas that emerged in early America,⌐parole had its roots in the practices of English and European penal systems.⌐

Early punishments, for offenses were often what Langbein (1976, pp. 35–63) called "blood punishments." Capital and corporal punishment were accepted penal practices in Europe and the United States well into the nineteenth century. This was so, in part, because the technology and economy of these principally rural societies were unable to process and control large inmate populations, and also because these societies had strong traditions of corporal punishment that were rooted in the Old Testament.[2]

In the late seventeenth and early eighteenth centuries, two massive social changes occurred that altered the direction of Western civilization and, consequently, had an impact on criminal law and penalties. The first was the Enlightenment, which gave rise to a conception of the human being as a rational and ultimately perfectible being and, along with this, a belief in basic human equality. Second, urbanization and the earliest movements toward industrialism simultaneously changed the nature of social interactions and created a new social class, the urban working class.

The writing of such thinkers as Locke, Voltaire, Beccaria, and Montesquieu both created and reflected a changing conception of man and the social order. These writers believed that government or society existed because individuals allowed it to exist. In other words, a "social contract" governed society. In order to be secure in their persons and possessions, free and equal individuals banded together and surrendered certain of their freedoms to the government on condition that it protect them from their enemies.

Among those enemies were criminals. The State assumed the responsibility of controlling crime and, by administering justice, punishing offenders. Individuals surrendered their "rights" to seek revenge and to commit crimes or avenge themselves. The social contract was the product of rational, free individuals. Because rational and free people had control of their own fates, they could be held responsible for their actions.

A crime was considered a "breach of contract," an offense against all parties to the social contract, not just the injured party. This state of affairs enabled the establishment of a central body of law (such as the Common Law in England) and centralized control of enforcement. Finally, rational individuals, presumed to have prior knowledge of the law and its penalties, were expected to perceive that it was in their own interest not to violate the law and suffer the penalties. **Deterrence** was the rationale of the criminal law and its sanctions, which were severe so as to enhance the deterrent effect of the law (Beccaria, 1764). In fact, more than 200 offenses carried the death penalty in England at one time. During the reign of Henry VIII, some 74,000 major and minor thieves were sent to the gallows. Under the reign of his daughter, Elizabeth I, 300 to 400 at a time were hanged, attracting large crowds where pickpockets flourished—even though pickpocketing was an offense punishable by death (Rennie, 1978).

Because the criminal law in colonial America developed from the English Common Law, it was also very harsh. Judges and magistrates in the English system had the option to impose a variety of penalties less severe than death, such as branding, maiming, the stocks, fines, or any combination of these.

As a reaction against cruel punishments, the "benefit of clergy" was developed to mitigate punishment for clerics and the wealthy. Initially designed to separate church and state, the "benefit" was eventually extended to all literate British citizens, even to those who could feign literacy (Clear, 1978, pp. 6–7; Briggs et al., 1996).

The reluctance of juries to convict and judges to impose sentences that were perceived to be disproportionate to the severity of most offenses did much to detract from the deterrent effect of the law. In addition, the inequity evident in sentencing, coupled with the potential and actual practices of abuses of the power to suspend sentences altogether, led to calls for reform in the English eighteenth-century criminal code, particularly for a reduction in the severity of penalties. A gradual shift in the conception of humankind and concomitant re-evaluation of the effectiveness and severity of punishment contributed significantly to the origins of parole as it exists today (Fogel, 1975).

Other writers, however, felt that poverty and lack of education, or heredity and biological inferiority, were factors that gave rise to crime. The shifting conception of humankind as being at least partly at the mercy of forces beyond their control reduced the degree to which they could be held responsible for criminal actions and paved the way for a reduction in the severity of many penalties. These changes in the philosophical conception of crime and punishment brought a new factor into the determination of sentences. Instead of imposing uniformly harsh sanctions for nearly all offenders, judges began to mitigate penalties for those "unfortunates" whom they "deemed to be worthy."

In England, orders of **transportation** were thought to be a severe punishment. In the eighteenth century, banishment, a common penalty for the aristocracy or nobility for centuries, was imposed on the common offender for the first time. The judge would order that the common offender should be transported to the colonies rather than to the gallows or pillory. The criminal would be allowed to go at liberty in the new land, sometimes for a period of indenture (Pisciotta, 1982), on the condition of not returning to England for a specified time period (such as 10 years), if at all (Hawkins, 1971). The concept of transportation thus avoids the extreme harshness of existing criminal law, while at the same time serving incapacitative purposes of those penalties. The serious felony offender, of course, was still sentenced to death.

While transportation was a partial solution to England's crime problem and, for a time, helped settle and develop new lands (the colonies, however, had no similar outlet for their offenders, with the exception of casting them into the wilderness, with usually the same results as the death penalty), it was only a temporary one. As a result of the American Revolution, England was forced to transport her convicts elsewhere (Campbell, 1994), and for a time they were sent to Australia; until, eventually, even Australia closed its doors to English convicts.[4]

Criminologists commonly accept punishment by transportation as the principal forerunner of parole (Hawkins, 1971). They argue that transportation was an organized, uniform process by which thousands of convicts were punished

---

Box 4.1
Incapacitation

Incapacitation is a crime prevention strategy based on specific deterrence that would disable the potential offender from committing another crime by isolating the instant offender. Common forms of incapacitation include transportation to other countries or colonies, committing the offender to an asylum or mental hospital, and lifelong imprisonment.

A contemporary version of this strategy is "selective incapacitation," a policy that would reserve prison beds for the most hardened, rapacious, and dangerous offenders. It would also require the use of community corrections for less severe offenders.

Two major problems with selective incapacitation are the inability of corrections to devise classification devices that would accurately predict which offenders would repeat (recidivate) or would not commit another crime. The second problem is more intractable: the widespread but erroneous belief that all offenders are dangerous and cannot be controlled in the community. The latter has been a major impediment to the creation of community corrections.

---

in a manner short of execution or corporal punishment, as it was a system wherein offenders eventually obtained their freedom. In addition, transportation did not necessarily involve a period of incarceration.

THE RISE OF EARLY PRISON REFORM

The Treaty of Paris in 1783 acknowledged the creation of the first republic in Western civilization since the fall of the Roman Empire. The United States of America, free from the English monarchy and founded on the teachings of the Enlightenment, became fertile ground for the development of a new system of criminal justice.

While the influence of English Common Law, with its harsh penalties, was strong in the new republic, even stronger were anti-British sentiment and the desire to abandon the oppressive regime of the English king. American reformers moved away from the archaic, tyrannical sanctions of colonial law and toward a more humane and rational penalty of incarceration.[5]

Chief among the reform groups were the Quakers (Offutt, 1995). The Judiciary Act of 1789 established imprisonment as the penalty for most crimes in Pennsylvania. In a nation that had newly acquired independence, what more fitting penalty could be found than the deprivation of liberty? When Patrick Henry uttered his now-famous line, "Give me liberty or give me death," little did he know that he had identified the perfect penalty for crime. Prison replaced the penalty of death and yet denied liberty to its inmates. Much to the dismay of these first reformers, their efforts were not rewarded by a reduction in crime. Rather, the first penal institutions were dismal failures (Rothman, 1971, p. 62):

> The faith of the 1790s now seemed misplaced; more rational codes had not decreased crime. The roots of deviancy went deeper than the certainty of punishment. Nor were the institutions fulfilling the elementary task of protecting society, since escapes and riots were commonplace occurrences.

The search for the causes of crime continued. Reformers still believed that offenders were rational people who would strive to improve themselves, but the manner in which they could be convinced to obey the law was still unknown. In a time of rapid social change and movement from an agrarian to an industrial society, environmental factors came to be viewed as criminogenic: cities, poverty, and idleness were believed to be the hotbeds of crime.

The proposed solution that emerged was to remove the offender from bad environments and teach the benefits of industry and morality. Offenders needed to be shown the error of their ways. Criminal law was required to do more than punish and deter; it should change the prisoner into a productive citizen. Punishment should serve to allow the prisoner to repent, to be trained, and to be reformed into a good citizen. A place to repent was thus needed, and prisons were developed to fulfill that need.

The original basis of prison was the reformation of the offender, and the ideal of reformation placed high value on discipline and regimentation. In short, in the newly created free society, incarceration itself was punishment and, while incarcerated, the goal was to reform the prisoner. Offenders were expected to obey strict rules of conduct and to work hard at assigned tasks (Johnson, 1994). In this milieu, it was believed that the offender would learn the benefit of discipline and industry.

Founders of penitentiaries were mindful that prison was a means to an end; their successors were not (Rothman, 1971). Reformation of inmates came to be identified solely with confinement, and custody eventually grew to be the ultimate goal of incarceration (Rothman, 1971). Furthermore, inmates posed significant threats to the security of the penitentiaries. Prison officials resorted to severe corporal punishments in order to maintain control within the prison—a penalty the development of prisons was supposed to replace.

The second generation of prison officials also saw another way of keeping the inmates out of trouble. American industry in the mid-1800s was labor-intensive, and prison populations were ideal sources of inexpensive labor. Inmate labor was expected to generate the money necessary to run the prisons, and prison administrators were thus receptive to offers to hire entire populations. This situation led to grossly underpaid prison labor, antagonism from unemployed free citizens, and the emergence of the labor contractor as a major force in institutional administration.[6] The Report of the Massachusetts General Court Joint Special Committee on Contract Convict Labor (1880, p. 16) illustrates the problem:

In the State Prison, contracts have been made which have no clause [giving] the State power to annul [them]. . . . Such bargains are bad, and, carried out to the fullest extent with large contracts, may naturally be expected to lead to a condition of affairs that has existed in other States given ground to the popular assertion that contractors, and not the State, control the prison.

EARLY PRACTICES IN OTHER NATIONS

The first operational system of **conditional release** was started by the governor of a prison in Spain in 1835. Up to one-third of a prison sentence could be reduced by good behavior and a demonstrated desire to do better (Carter et al., 1975). A similar system was enacted in Bavaria in the 1830s, and many prison reformers in France in the 1840s advocated the adoption of similar conditional release systems. In fact, the term "parole" comes from the French *parole d'honneur*, or "word of honor," which characterized the French efforts to establish parole release. Prisoners would be released after showing good behavior and industry in the prison[7] and on their word of honor that they would obey the law.

Despite the fact that these efforts predate those of Alexander Maconochie, it is he who is usually given credit as being the father of parole. In 1840, Captain Maconochie was put in charge of the English **penal colony** in New South Wales at Norfolk Island, about 1,000 miles off the coast of Australia. To this colony were sent the criminals who were "twice condemned." They had been shipped from England to Australia, and then from Australia to Norfolk (Allen & Simonsen, 2001). Conditions were allegedly so bad at Norfolk Island that men reprieved from the death penalty wept and those who were to die thanked God (Barry, 1957, p. 5). The conditions on Norfolk Island were so unbearable that suicide became a means of escape and an act of solidarity. Hughes (1987, p. 468) describes it in vivid terms:

> A group of convicts would choose two men by drawing straws: one to die, the other to kill him. Others would stand by as witnesses. There being no judge to try capital offenses on Norfolk Island, the killer and witnesses would have to be sent to Sidney for trial—an inconvenience for the authorities but a boon to the prisoners, who yearned for the meager relief of getting away from the "ocean of hell," if only to a gallows on the mainland. And in Sidney there was some slight chance of escape. The victim could not choose himself; everyone in the group apparently, had to be equally ready to die, and the benefits of his death had to be shared equally by all survivors.

It was under these conditions that Maconochie devised an elaborate method of granted conditional release. Maconochie's plan was based on five basic principles (Barnes & Teeters, 1959, p. 419):

1. Release should not be based on the completion of a sentence for a set period of time, but on completion of a determined and specified quantity of labor. In brief, time sentences should be abolished, and task sentences substituted.
2. The quantity of labor a prisoner must perform should be expressed in a number of "marks" that he must earn, by improvement of conduct, frugality of living, and habits of industry, before he could be released.
3. While in prison he should earn everything he receives. All sustenance and indulgences should be added to his debt of marks.
4. When qualified by discipline to do so, he should work in association with a small number of other prisoners, forming a group of six or seven, and the whole group should be answerable for the conduct of labor of each member.
5. In the final stage, a prisoner, while still obliged to earn his daily tally of marks, should be given a proprietary interest in his own labor and be subject to a less rigorous discipline to prepare him for release into society.

Under his plan, referred to as the **mark system**, prisoners were awarded marks and moved through stages of custody until finally granted release. His system involved indeterminate sentencing, with release based on the number of marks earned by prisoners for good conduct, labor, and study. The five stages, based on the accumulation of marks, each carried increased responsibility and freedom, leading to a ticket of leave or parole resulting in a conditional pardon and, finally, to full restoration of liberty.

Maconochie has been described as a zealot (Hughes, 1987); however, his reforms made life bearable at Norfolk Island and can be described as revolutionary in comparison to the horrible conditions that existed there before his arrival. While Maconochie's reforms transposed Norfolk Island from one of despair to one of hope, it was short-lived. Petty bureaucrats and a general mistrust of Maconochie's ideas led to his recall as commandant in 1843.

Sir Walter Crofton, director of the Irish prison system in the 1850s, built upon foundations laid by Maconochie. He decided that a transitional stage between prison and full release was needed and developed a classification scheme based on a system in which the prisoner progressed through three stages of treatment. The first was segregated confinement with work and training provided to the prisoner. This was followed by a transition period from confinement to freedom, during which the prisoner was set to work on public projects with little control being exercised over him. If he performed successfully in this phase, he was released on "license" (Clare & Kramer, 1976; Maguire et al., 1996).

Release on license was constrained by certain conditions, violations of which would result in reimprisonment. While on license, prisoners were required to submit monthly reports and were warned against idleness and associating with other criminals. Prisoners on license, then, had to report, could be reimprisoned for violating the conditions of release, and had not been pardoned. These distinctions from earlier systems of release were large steps toward modern parole.

EARLY AMERICAN PRACTICES

Convicts sentenced to prison in America in the early 1800s received definite terms; a sentence of five years meant the offender would serve five years in prison. This strict sentencing structure led to overcrowded prisons and widespread problems in the institutions. It was not uncommon for a governor to grant pardons to large numbers of inmates in order to control the size of prison populations. In some states, this pardoning power was even delegated to prison wardens (Sherrill, 1977).

This method of rewarding well-behaved prisoners with reductions in sentence was first formalized in 1817 by the New York State legislature. In that year, the first "good-time" law was passed. This law authorized a 25 percent reduction in length of term for those inmates serving five years or more who were well behaved and demonstrated industry in their prison work. By 1869, 23 states had good-time laws, and prison administrators supported the concept as a method of keeping order and controlling the population size (Sherrill, 1977).

Liberal use of the pardoning power was continued in those states that did not have good-time laws, and the mass pardon was not uncommon even in those states that already allowed sentence reductions for good behavior. These developments are important because they represent the first large-scale exercise of sentencing power by the executive branch of government, the branch in which parole boards would eventually be located.

Another philosophical base for American parole was the indenture system established by the New York House of Refuge. Although not called parole, for all intents and purposes, a parole system was already operational for juveniles committed to the House of Refuge in New York. The House of Refuge had developed a system of indenture whereby youths were released from custody as indentured servants of private citizens. Unfortunately, this system permitted corruption.[8]

To combat these abuses, the New York House of Refuge developed a system supervising the indentured. A committee was formed that selected youths for indenture, defined the conditions under which they served their indentureships,

---

Box 4.2
Pardon

A **pardon** is an act of executive clemency that absolves the offender in part or in full from the legal consequences of the crime and conviction. Probably the most famous example is President Gerald Ford's pardon of President Richard Nixon for his role in the Watergate crimes.

Executive clemency can include gubernatorial action that results in the release of an inmate from incarceration, as well as pardoning current and former inmates. Camp and Camp (2000) reported that pardons and other acts of clemency were awarded to 722 inmates.

Source: Camp and Camp (2000).

Box 4.3
Parole Board

A **parole board** is any correctional person, authority, commission, or board that has legal authority to parole those adults (or juveniles) committed to confinement facilities, to set conditions for behavior, to revoke from parole, and to discharge from parole.

Parole boards can usually also recommend shortening a prisoner's sentence (commuting sentences), recommend pardons to a governor, set parole policies, and, in some jurisdictions, recommend reprieve from execution. An example of parole policy would be a "zero-tolerance" policy for parolees whose urine samples indicate recent use of illicit drugs, usually resulting in certain return to confinement.

---

and established rules both for the superintendent of the House of Refuge and for the persons to whom youths were indentured.

There was no formal mechanism for releasing the youths from custody, but they were able to work off their contracts and thus obtain their freedom. Their masters could break the contracts and return the youths to the House of Refuge at any time. In essence, a parole system was operating.

In addition to these forms of release from custody before expiration of the maximum term, the concept of supervising released offenders had also been operationalized. It is important to note, however, that supervision of released prisoners prior to the creation of parole in America only required providing assistance and not crime control duties.[9]

In 1845, the Massachusetts legislature appointed a state agent for discharged convicts and appropriated funds for him to use in assisting ex-prisoners in securing employment, tools, clothes, and transportation. Other states followed this example and appointed agents of their own. As early as 1776, however, charitable organizations, such as the Philadelphia Association for the Alleviation of Prisoners' Miseries, were already providing aid to released convicts (Sellin, 1970). By the late 1860s, dissatisfaction with prisons was widespread, and a concerted effort to establish a formal parole release and supervision system began. In 1867, prison reformers Enoch Wines and Louis Dwight reported that "There is not a state prison in America in which reformation of the convicts is the one supreme object of discipline, to which everything else is made to bend" (Rothman, 1971, pp. 240–243).

In 1870, the first meeting of the American Prison Association was held in Cincinnati, Ohio.[10] Reform was the battle cry of the day, and the meeting took on an almost evangelical fervor (Fogel, 1975). Both Sir Walter Crofton and American warden F.B. Sanborn advocated the Irish system (Lindsey, 1925).

Armed with the success of the meeting, the focus of prison reformers shifted from incarceration as the answer to crime and, instead, concentrated on the return of offenders to society. Prisons remained central, but they were now seen

---

Box 4.4
Indeterminate Sentencing

Originally, the **indeterminate sentence** had no minimum length of period of incarceration. Later, legislatures changed this practice to require a minimum period of incarceration.

Indeterminate sentences typically require a minimum and maximum period (1–3, 2–10, 10–25 years, etc.). Offenders ordinarily will be released during some point in the spread of years pronounced by the sentencing judge.

Both minimum and maximum terms can be reduced by certain credits allowable under legal statute and practice. These include time spent in jail awaiting trial or sentence, good-time credits for behaving while in prison, and **program credits** awarded frequently for completion of institutional programs (attaining the equivalent of a high-school diploma, active involvement in Alcoholic Anonymous, basic welding classes, etc.).

---

almost as a necessary evil, not as an end in themselves. Prison reformers everywhere began to advocate adoption and expansion of good-time laws, assistance to released prisoners, adoption of the ticket-of-leave system, and parole. In 1869, the New York State legislature passed an act creating the Elmira Reformatory and an indeterminate sentence "until reformation, not exceeding 5 years."

This law created the reformatory as a separate institution for young offenders, expressly designed to be an intermediate step between conviction and return to a law-abiding life. Administrators of the reformatory were empowered to release inmates upon demonstration of their reformation. Such release was conditional, and released offenders were to be supervised by a state agent (Lindsey, 1925).

With the passage of this law, parole in the United States became a reality. It soon spread to other jurisdictions, and by 1944, every jurisdiction in the nation had a parole authority (Hawkins, 1971). Table 4.1 illustrates the rapid growth of parole in the United States up to the year 1900. Between 1884 and 1900, parole was adopted in 20 states. The rapid growth of parole, however, was fraught with difficulties and criticism.

THE SPREAD OF PAROLE

Parole release was adopted by the various state jurisdictions much more rapidly than the indeterminate sentence. By 1900, some 20 states had adopted parole; by 1944, every jurisdiction had a parole system (see Table 4.2). The expansion of parole has been characterized as being a process of imitation (Lindsey, 1925), yet a great deal of variation in the structure and use of parole was observed.[11]

Table 4.1 States with Parole Laws by 1900

State	Year enacted
Alabama	1897
California	1893
Colorado	1899
Connecticut	1897
Idaho	1897
Illinois	1891
Indiana	1897
Kansas	1895
Massachusetts	1884
Michigan	1895
Minnesota	1889
Nebraska	1893
New Jersey	1895
New York	1889
North Dakota	1891
Ohio	1896
Pennsylvania	1887
Utah	1898
Virginia	1898
Wisconsin	1889

Source: Adapted from Lindsey, E. (1925). Historical origins of the sanction of imprisonment for serious crime. *Journal of Criminal Law and Criminology* 16, 9–126.

The growth and expansion of modern parole were assisted by a number of factors. One of the most important was the tremendous amount of support and publicity that prison reformers gave the concept at the National Congress on Penitentiary and Reformatory Discipline. Its inclusion in the Congress's Declaration of Principles, coupled with the publicity of Alexander Maconochie's work in New South Wales, provided the necessary endorsement of correctional experts.

In addition, it was quickly recognized that a discretionary release system solved many of the problems of prison administration. A major factor in favor of parole was that it supported prison discipline. A number of writers pointed out that by placing release in the inmate's own hands, the inmate would be motivated both to reform and comply with the rules and regulations of the prison.[12] Finally, parole provided a safety valve to reduce prison populations, which were generally over-crowded (Wilcox, 1929).

A third contributory factor was that the power to pardon was being exercised liberally in a number of states. The effect of liberal pardoning policies was to initiate parole even though it was not yet authorized by law.

Table 4.2 Significant Developments in Parole

Date	Development
1776	Colonies reject English Common Code and begin to draft their own codes.
1840	Maconochie devises mark system for release of prisoners in the Australian penal colony, a forerunner of parole.
1854	Crofton establishes ticket-of-leave program in Ireland.
1869	New York State legislature passes enabling legislation and establishes indeterminate sentencing.
1870	American Prison Association endorses expanded use of parole.
1876	Parole release adopted at Elmira Reformatory, New York.
1931	Wickersham Commission criticizes laxity in early parole practice.
1944	Last state passes enabling legislation for parole.
1976	Maine abolishes parole.
1979	Colorado abolishes parole release.
1984	Federal system abolishes parole as an early release mechanism.
1985	Colorado reinstates parole release.
1996	Ohio becomes 11th state to abolish parole.
2011	Kansas abolishes its Parole Board and established a three-member Prisoner Review Board
2012	637,411 inmates were released from prison, down from a high of 734,144 in 2008.

Source: Compiled by authors.

These early parole systems were controlled by state legislators that, in general, rigidly defined which prisoners could be paroled. Most legislation authorizing parole release restricted it to first offenders convicted of less serious crimes. Through the passage of time and a gradual acceptance of the idea of discretionary early release, the privilege was eventually extended to serious offenders.

Because early parole systems were operated primarily by persons with a direct interest in the administration of prisons, decisions on parole release and those who acted as parole officers were institution based. Eligibility was strictly limited, at the inception of parole, and was expanded only gradually to include more serious offenders. Supervision of released inmates was nominal, and the seeds of corruption and maladministration were present.

EARLY PUBLIC SENTIMENTS

The decade between 1925 and 1935 was a turbulent time, including both the economic boom (and the Prohibition Era) and the Great Depression. Crime, particularly as sensationalized in the mass media, appeared to be rampant. As crime rates increased, the public felt increasingly more that crime was "public enemy number one."[13] This period also saw the rise of attempts by the federal government to stem interstate crimes, particularly kidnapping, bootlegging, bank robbery, and a host of newly enacted legislation that considerably widened the net of crime the government would seek to prevent and prosecute. Two significant events reflecting public concern about crime[14] were the establishment of the maximum-security federal prison on Alcatraz and a crusade headed by J. Edgar Hoover, chief of the Federal Bureau of Investigation, against interstate crime. Hoover's pronouncements assumed a political nature, as he strongly advocated neoclassical responses to crime: long-term prison sentences, abolition of parole, increased incarceration of offenders, use of the death penalty, and so on.[15]

Both the releasing and the supervising functions of parole were criticized sharply and roundly. The major concern of these criticisms was the failure of parole to protect the public safety. The Report of the Advisory Commission on Penal Institutions, Probation, and Parole to the Wickersham Commission in the 1931 summarized the problems with parole, stating:

Parole is defective in three main respects:

1. In the chasm existing between parole and preceding institutional treatment.
2. In the manner in which persons are selected for parole.
3. In the quality of supervision given to persons on parole.

In short, parole was seen as failing to be effective in attaining the promised and lofty goals. Primary arguments were that convicted criminals were being set loose on society, supervised inadequately, and unreformed. The concept of parole and the general ideology of reform were not yet under attack; it was the means and not the ends that were being criticized.

The decade of the 1930s saw the publication of two documents concerning parole: the 1931 Wickersham Commission Report, noted earlier, and, in 1939, the Attorney General's Survey of Release Procedures (Hawkins, 1971). As with the reports of Wines and Dwight and the International Prison Congress of more than 50 years earlier, the 1931 and 1939 documents pointed to flaws in the operation of American corrections and advocated reforms to improve both prisons and parole services.[16]

Simultaneously, the correctional medical model was on the rise. This criminogenic approach was based on a belief that human beings are basically moral and that crime is a deviation from humankind's basic behavior inclinations. Unlike earlier views that humans were, at heart, bestial, but restrained their primitive drives because reason informed them that by doing so they would be safe, the idea that humans are basically good led to the inevitable conclusion that there must be something fundamentally wrong with those who were bad. The job of corrections should, then, be to diagnose the problems, prepare and administer the treatment programs, and make offenders well again. Offenders committed crimes when social, personal, or psychological forces and factors overwhelmed them. Hence, the development of new habits, the threat of deterrent sanctions, and the giving of religious instruction dealt only with the symptoms of a deeper disorder. The real causes of crime remained deep within the personality structure of the offender. If

Box 4.5
Parole

Parole is release of an inmate from confinement to expiration of sentence on condition of good behavior and supervision in the community. This is also referred to as post-incarceration supervision or, in the case of juveniles, aftercare.

the prisons were to be hospitals, the parole board was to release the patient when "well"; that is, when able to deal with all phases of everyday life. This development had significant implications for parole.

Between the adoption of parole release in Elmira in 1876 and the enactment of enabling legislation for parole in Mississippi in 1944, the concept of parole faced two critical challenges. The first involved the issue of legality of executive control over sentencing and indeterminate sentences. The second centered on the administration of parole systems. Toward the end of the first quarter of the twentieth century, a new behavioral technology came into its own and grew to be a predominant goal of corrections and sentencing. The rehabilitative ideal gave new legitimacy to parole, endorsing discretion.

LEGAL CHALLENGES TO PAROLE

The basic legal challenge raised against parole was that the placing of control over sentence length and criminal penalties in the hands of a parole board was unconstitutional. The specific arguments varied across individual lawsuits, but they were basically of two types. First, questions of infringement on the principle of the separation of powers' clauses of the federal and state constitutions were raised in several states (Lindsey, 1925).

These suits claimed that parole release was an impairment of judicial sentencing power, an improper delegation of legislative authority to set penalties, and usurpation of the executive branch's power of clemency (Hawkins, 1971). For the most part, parole authorities emerged victorious from these court battles, and those constitutional questions of parole were laid to rest.

A further rationale behind challenges to the constitutionality of parole release was based on the Eighth Amendment prohibition against cruel and unusual punishment. Although the issue was weighty, most criminal penalties were limited by legislatively set maximum terms. The most common judicial response to these arguments was that indeterminate sentences could be interpreted as sentences that would not extend the maximum terms as set by the legislature or judge, thereby rendering moot the issue of cruelty by virtue of uncertainty (Hawkins, 1971).

Box 4.6
Eighth Amendment

Excessive bail shall not be required, nor excessive fines imposed, nor cruel and unusual punishment inflicted.

ADMINISTRATIVE CHALLENGES

We have seen that, in the late nineteenth and early twentieth centuries, parole practices were criticized for failing to protect the public. The basic arguments were that parole authorities were not following procedures that would lead to the release of only deserving inmates and that the lack of subsequent parole supervision placed the community in danger. Such were the complaints reflected by the Wickersham Commission and the Attorney General's Survey. These were not the only critical voices.[17]

One salient argument, supported by ample evidence, was that parole had become a commonplace method of reducing prison populations. In several states, most inmates were released immediately upon expiration of their minimum terms. Only those inmates whose conduct records within prison showed a failure to conform were held longer. The problem was defined as inadequate or improper release decision making.

Blanket release policies were felt to be inappropriate for several reasons. First, because parole boards failed to consider that risk and parole supervision was inadequate, such wholesale release practices were felt to endanger public safety. Second, because most parole boards were dominated by prison officials, it was believed that too much weight was attached to prison conduct and the needs of the prison administration. Finally, failure to consider reformation efforts of the inmate, or the prison, worked to hamper the success of prisons in reforming criminals.

Proposed solutions were varied and involved beefing up parole supervision staffs and increasing postrelease surveillance of parolees. It was believed that these actions could enhance public protection. Additionally, there were calls for professional parole boards composed of trained, salaried, full-time decision makers who would be removed from the pressures of day-to-day prison administration and its needs and who were skilled in identifying those inmates who were reformed.

These proposals arose at about the same time behavioral sciences expanded into the world of public policy. Psychology and sociology were beginning to develop practical components in addition to their traditional theoretical bases. The new professions of clinical psychologist, social worker, and criminologist were developing. An ability to predict, change, and control undesirable human behavior was promised.[18] Corrections and parole seemed ideal places in which these professions could have their most positive impact. The dawn of the rehabilitative model was at hand, and this model caused radical changes in the practice and organization of the American parole system, as we shall see.

GRANTING PAROLE

As noted earlier, parole was originally implemented as a method of releasing reformed inmates at the ideal time. The primary focus of parole was the rehabilitation and eventual reintegration of the offender to society, although it also functioned to incapacitate violent and dangerous offenders whose probability of reoffending was believed to be unacceptably high. Parole also serves as a decompression period that helps the offender make the adjustment between the institution and the outside world. As such, parole is an integral component of the re-entry process. Figure 4.2 shows that the number of offenders on parole has grown dramatically since 1985: from 300,000 to more than 800,000 in 2012. This

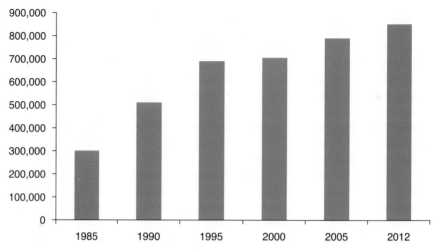

Figure 4.2 Number of Parolees, 1985–2012.

Source: Maruschak, L.M., Bonczar, T.P. (2013). *Probation and parole in the United States, 2012.* Washington, DC: U.S. Dept. of Justice, Offices of Justice Programs, Bureau of Justice Statistics.

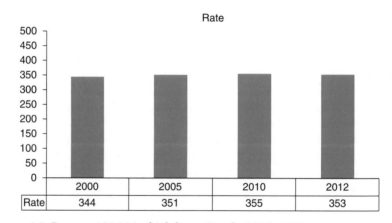

	2000	2005	2010	2012
Rate	344	351	355	353

Figure 4.3 Rate per 100,000 of Adults on Parole, 2000–2012.

Source: Maruschak, L.M., Bonczar, T.P. (2013). *Probation and parole in the United States, 2012.* Washington, DC: U.S. Dept. of Justice, Offices of Justice Programs, Bureau of Justice Statistics.

dramatic increase is due to the incarceration binge that occurred in the 1980s and 1990s. Despite the large number of offenders on parole, the rate per 100,000 has remained relatively steady since 2000 (see Figure 4.3).

OVERVIEW OF THE PAROLE PROCESS

The parole process begins in the courtroom when the judge sentences an individual to a determinate or indeterminate prison sentence. The latter includes fixing a term by stating the minimum and maximum length of time the individual is to serve. At the expiration of a certain portion of that sentence, less credit granted for good behavior and performance of duties, an individual becomes eligible for parole. The amount of the sentence that must be served and the amount of credit that can be given for good behavior and performance of duties vary from state to state. In Nebraska, someone sentenced to a three- to five-year term can become eligible for parole at the end of two years and five months if they have behaved "properly" within the institution.[19] This does not mean that a release will actually occur; it only means that the individual is eligible to be released. A number of states have mandatory parole release statutes which state that at the expiration of a certain portion of the sentence, inmates must be released on parole, unless the inmate chooses not to be released. A small number of inmates refuse to be released on parole because they do not want to be subject to a parole officer's supervision and consequently they choose to serve their entire prison sentence ("max out").

Regardless of whether these individuals wish to max out or receive parole, institutional officers compile information concerning their personal characteristics and backgrounds. Treatment progress is updated continually and, at some point in time, the staff begin working with the offender's friends, family, and employers to develop a release plan.

The information, along with the presentence and institutional progress reports, is periodically brought to the attention of the releasing authority, usually a parole board. Some states review inmates' progress on a yearly basis, even though they are not eligible for release. In accordance with the eligibility guidelines and an interview with the offender, the parole board decides whether to release the offender on parole. If the decision is to deny release, a future rehearing date is usually set. If a release is to be effected, the parole board then determines when and where the release is to be made. A contract, usually including very specific conditions of parole, is also established. Once a release has been achieved, inmates (now called parolees) come under the supervision of parole officers. Figure 4.4 shows the percentage of prisoners released on conditional release between 1988 and 2012. As seen, this percentage has dropped over the years.

Box 4.7
Maxing Out

A recent study by Pew (2014) found that between 1990 and 2012 the number of inmates who maxed out of their sentences in prison grew 119 percent, from less than 50,000 to more than 100,000 and in 2012 the rate was about 22 percent of all inmates. They also found that the max-out rates varied widely from state to state, ranging from less than 10 percent in Arkansas, California, Louisiana, Michigan, Missouri, Oregon, New Hampshire, and Wisconsin, to more than 40 percent in Florida, Mains, Massachusetts, New Jersey, North Carolina, Ohio, Oklahoma, South Carolina, and Utah.

Source: Pew (2014).

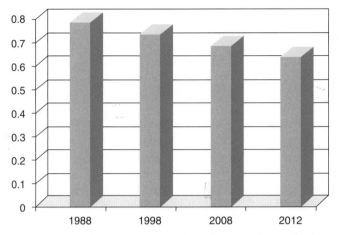

Figure 4.4 Percentage of U.S. Prisoners Released on Conditional Release, 1988–2012.

Source: Carson, E., Golinelli, D. (2013). *Prisoners in 2012: Trends in admissions and releases, 1991–2012.* Washington, DC: U.S. Dept. of Justice, Office of Justice Programs, Bureau of Justice Statistics.

**Box 4.8
Good-time Credits**

Statutes in almost every state allow for the reduction of a prison term based on an offender's behavior in prison ("good time") or for participation and completion of certain educational or treatment programs ("program time"). Reduction in time is awarded; such awards reduce the date to the parole board or minimum sentence, and maximum time to be served.

Good-time credits are earned by a formula established within correctional settings, sometimes set into law but usually decided by institutional administrators in collaboration with the parole board. In California, the award is four months for each eight months served (four for eight, or 1:2). If an offender is serving a three-year sentence (36 months) and earns maximum good time, that offender will be in prison for no more than 24 months.

Some jurisdictions award time for pretrial detention and postconviction jail time while awaiting transport to prison. There are thousands of jail inmates who have been sentenced to prison but are being held back pending availability of prison space and transport to prison. These inmates generally earn "jail credits" at a 1:1 ratio and will bring those credits to the parole board, further reducing the maximum time they will serve as prison inmates.

Finally, to encourage participation in institutional work and rehabilitation programs, credits may be awarded for participation in and completion of specific programs: welding, masonry, car repair, general educational development (GED), drug treatment, and so on. The awards across jurisdictions vary, but usually approximate the "good-time credit" ratio.

Thus, an inmate sentenced to three years in prison but detained for four months on a pretrial basis and held for four months in jail after sentencing before being transported to prison would bring eight months of jail time credit and would generally receive an additional four months for good time, the equivalent of serving one year against the term of punishment. If the offender participates in and graduates from a drug treatment program within the first 12 months, that offender will usually serve less than 16 months before being released as having served the maximum sentence ("max out"): 36 months.

Box 4.9
Discretionary and Mandatory Release

Discretionary release is parole of an inmate from prison prior to expiration of the maximum sentence, according to the boundaries set by the legislature and sentence. Discretionary release is associated with the indeterminate sentence and implies that the offender is ready for release and continued treatment within the community.

Mandatory release is required release of the offender by the parole board because the statutes mandate release of any inmate who has served the equivalent of the maximum sentence. Mandatory release implies that the parole board refused to release an inmate prior to attainment of maximum sentence imposed by the court. Mandatory release means time served behind prison walls, when added to time credits for jail time, good time, and earned time, totals the sentence imposed by the sentencing court. About one in five inmates leave prison under mandatory release (Pew, 2014).

Current Operations

Parole is a complex procedure and has many functions and processes that differ from one jurisdiction to another. Traditionally, parole has five basic functions:

1. Selecting and placing prisoners on parole.
2. Establishing conditions of supervision (frequently case specific).
3. Aiding, supervising, assisting, and controlling parolees in the community.

4. Returning parolees to prison if the conditions of parole are not met.

5. Discharging parolees when supervision is no longer necessary or when the sentence is completed.

[Parole, unlike probation, is an administrative process located within the executive branch of every state, as well as the federal government] This may soon change, however, for a[number of states (Arizona, California, Delaware, Florida, Illinois, Indiana, Kansas, Maine, Minnesota, Mississippi, North Carolina, Ohio, Oregon, Virginia, Washington, Wisconsin, and the federal prison system) have virtually eliminated the discretionary release power of these parole boards.] Connecticut abolished parole in 1981 but reinstated it nine years later, after prison costs surged.[20] Similarly, Colorado abolished parole release in 1979 and reinstated it in 1985. Thirty other jurisdictions have developed various system-wide[**parole guidelines** that have restricted the discretionary powers of the parole boards.[21] The operation of parole, obviously, is not all uniform.[22] [State parole systems vary widely in terms of their organizational makeup and administrative process.[23] Most parole boards are independent state agencies that only administer parole. Depending on the state, there are anywhere from 3 to 19 members on a parole board (Camp & Camp, 2000). Only 22 states have any statutory requirements for specific qualifications for parole board members, and even those are usually stated in such broad terms as "possessing good character" or "judicious temperament." In 1967, the President's Commission on Law Enforcement and Administration of Justice recommended that parole board members be appointed solely on the basis of competence; however, in many states, appointment to the parole board appears to be based on political consider-ations. For example, only two states, Wisconsin and Ohio, appoint parole board

---

Box 4.10
Parole Board Members

Governors appoint parole board members in 45 jurisdictions, usually with the advice and consent of the state legislature. The most frequent term is four years, and most states stagger the terms of office of members to achieve continuity of parole boards regardless of changes in the governor's mansion or philosophy. Five-, six-, and seven-year terms are found in Alabama, Arizona, Georgia, and so on. Ohio parole board members serve an indefinite term. In Utah, parole board members are appointed by the Board of Corrections and serve six-year terms.

There are no statutory qualifications for parole board membership in 29 jurisdictions, but the other 22 jurisdictions have qualifications that speak to length of time and experience in corrections (or such related fields as welfare, religion, or law enforcement). Seven jurisdictions set the minimal educational level as at least a bachelor's degree.

members from a civil service list. The governor is directly responsible for parole board appointments in 45 states.

Parole Selection Process

In most jurisdictions, individual cases are assigned to individual members of the parole board, who review each case and make initial recommendations. These recommendations are usually accepted, although occasionally the board as a whole may seek to obtain more details. While there are some jurisdictions that make the final release decision solely on the basis of written reports, most states conduct some type of a formal hearing. The hearing may be with one member of the parole board or the assembled board as a whole (en banc) or may be handled by a hearing examiner with no members of the board present. Occasionally, prison staff are also interviewed. Some states send the board members and/or hearing examiners to the institutions to conduct the hearings, whereas others bring those to be interviewed to the board/examiners.

Parole selection guidelines differ widely from state to state. The U.S. Supreme Court has consistently held parole to be a privilege and, consequently, held that a full complement of due process rights do not need to be afforded at parole-granting hearings (*Greenholtz v. Inmates of the Nebraska Penal and Correctional Complex*, 99 S. Ct. 2100 (1979)). As a result, the states have been given the opportunity to establish whatever inmate privileges they feel are appropriate at parole-granting hearings.

Inmates are permitted the use of counsel in 21 states and are allowed to present witnesses in 19 states. The rationale for the parole decision must be formally articulated in 11 parole jurisdictions. Most states have established regulations as to the amount of time an inmate is required to serve prior to parole eligibility. In 16 states, eligibility is obtained upon completion of the minimum sentence. In 10 states, as well as the federal system, eligibility is achieved upon completion of one-third of the maximum sentence. Other states use the number of prior felony convictions and length of prior sentences to calculate eligibility rules. Even in states that use the same eligibility guidelines, there is such a wide variation in the length of the minimum and maximum prison terms handed down for the same offense that, in reality, there are literally as many variations in eligibility as there are parole jurisdictions.[24] In addition to time factors, some states restrict the use of parole for those convicted of various serious personal offenses, such as first-degree murder, kidnapping, and aggravated rape.[25]

If an inmate does not meet parole standards, the sentence is continued and a date is set for the next parole review. If parole is approved, the individual is prepared for release to the parole field service authority. Just how long an inmate must wait to hear the verdict varies greatly. In many jurisdictions, the inmate receives word immediately. In others, and in those jurisdictions where no hearings are held, inmates are notified by the prison staff or by mail. Receipt by the inmate of formal written notification varies from immediately in several states to as long as three to four weeks in New Jersey.

Box 4.11
Sexually Violent Predators

California enacted a statute in 1996 that seeks to ensure that sexual predators in prison suffering from mental disorders and deemed likely to reoffend are treated in a secure facility through civil commitment and are not released prematurely into society to victimize others.

The Board of Prison Terms screens cases to determine if inmates meet criteria specified in the statute and then refers inmates to the California Department of Mental Health for clinical evaluations by two clinicians. If both clinicians concur that the inmate meets the criteria, a county district attorney may file a petition for civil commitment.

If the judge determines that probable cause exists, the prisoner is scheduled for a court trial. A jury hears the case and, based on the "beyond a reasonable doubt" test, may determine that the offender meets the statutory criteria. In such cases, the offender is civilly committed to a Department of Mental Health facility for two years of treatment. Annual examinations are conducted; the offender may petition the court for conditional release (parole). At the end of two years, the prisoner is re-evaluated and the court may enter an order for a new trial to seek a new commitment of the offender. Since 1996, more than 300 sex offenders have been found to be sexually violent predators and committed to the Department of Mental Health for treatment.

The parole-granting hearing is a very significant event for inmates. Regardless of the outcome, the result affects their lives greatly. They realize that a single inappropriate word or action could jeopardize their freedom for years to come. Yet despite the significance of the decision, the national average is probably between 12 and 15 minutes per case. This means that parole boards are hearing approximately 15 to 20 cases per day. It is difficult to determine exactly how long a parole board deliberates because they operate in relative secrecy. In many cases, parole hearings are at least partially closed, and decision-making criteria are not really known to outsiders. Indeed, a major criticism of the parole process is a reluctance on the part of most parole boards to clearly articulate standards and guidelines for release.

Box 4.12
Flopped

"**Flopped**" is inmate argot for being denied early release by the parole board for failing to meet parole board standards or expectations. When flopped, the inmate is usually given a "next review date" by the board, and his or her case will be heard again at that time. Frequently, the board suggests treatments, programs, or goals the offender is expected to complete before the next review (learning to read and write, AA involvement, life skills, etc.).

FACTORS INFLUENCING PAROLE DECISIONS

In theory, parole decisions should be based on the factors outlined in state statutes. In practice, however, it appears that parole boards are influenced by a wide variety of criteria, not all of which are articulated by law. Furthermore, some states do not have any legal guidelines.

In one of the first studies to examine parole board release decision criteria, Scott (1974) studied 325 males and 34 females facing a parole decision in a Midwest state in 1968. He determined that the seriousness of the crime, a high number of prison disciplinary reports, age (older inmates), a low level of education, a marital status of single, and (surprisingly) a good institutional record were factors that lengthened an inmate's sentence. Prior record and race were determined to have no effect upon the parole decision.

As suggested by Dawson (1966), there appear to be three major release criteria that influence parole boards:

1. Factors for granting parole based on the probability of recidivism.
2. Factors for granting parole other than probability of recidivism.
3. Factors for denying parole other than probability of recidivism.

Probability of Recidivism

Perhaps the most basic aspect of the decision-making process is estimating the probability that an individual will violate the law if and when he or she is released on parole.[26] This is known as the recidivism factor. Parole boards, as quasi-political entities, are extremely sensitive to the public criticism that may arise when parolees violate parole, especially if they commit a serious offense. Just how parole boards determine the probability of recidivism is unclear. As early as 1923, Hart advocated the need to develop methodologically sound prediction tables for potential parolees that were based on data. Since this observation, many such scales and tables have been developed (Babst et al., 1970; Bromley & Gathercole, 1969; Burgess, 1928; Glaser, 1962; Gottfredson et al., 1958; Gottfredson & Gottfredson, 1993; Loza & Loza, 2000; Wilkins & MacNaughton-Smith, 1964). For more than 50 years, the value of prediction devices has been recognized as a means of standardizing parole release and assessing recidivism probability more accurately. At least one-half of all parole boards use formal risk assessment (Burke, 1997).[27]

Box 4.13
The Ohio Risk Assessment System Re-entry Tool

In 2009, researchers from the University of Cincinnati developed the Ohio Risk Assessment System (ORAS). One of the tools in this system is the Re-entry Tool. After examining the recidivism of inmates who had served at

---

least two years in prison prior to release, 17 items were identified in three basic domains: Criminal History, Social Support, and Criminal Attitudes and Behavioral Patterns that helped classify those exiting prison into three risk categories: low (with a 20 percent probability of failure,) moderate (40 percent), and high risk (60 percent). Given the nature of the prison environment, many traditional risk factors are controlled, such as current employment and substance use, and were not found to be important in predicting risk at release.

Source: Latessa et al. (2010).

Factors for Granting Parole Other Than Probability of Recidivism

There are occasions when inmates are granted parole despite the parole board's belief that they possess a relatively high probability of recidivism. In instances when offenders are believed to be unlikely to commit a crime of a serious nature, the parole board may vote to grant parole. This factor is often accompanied by a determination that the inmate will gain little additional benefit from further institutionalization. For example, although an inmate may be an alcoholic with a long record of public intoxication arrests, the parole board may grant a release because it feels that the individual is relatively harmless and that continued institutionalization will very likely have little further impact upon the alcoholism problem. Compassionate release of inmates dying of cancer and AIDS also falls under this category (Pagliaro & Pagliaro, 1992).[28]

Occasionally, situations arise in which inmates have only a short period of time to serve before the completion of their sentences. When such circumstances arise, parole boards frequently give these individuals parole, despite what may be a high perceived probability of recidivism, in order to provide even a brief period of supervisory control and, more importantly, to assist the parolee in the environmental decompression and social reintegration process.

An additional criterion that may swing a parole board, despite an apparent high recidivism probability, is the length of time served. If an inmate has failed to respond to institutional treatment but has served a relatively long sentence, the parole board may grant parole under the conviction that these individuals have paid their dues and that perhaps they will succeed on parole to avoid being sent back. Occasionally, the maturation process will play an important role. When lengthy sentences are mandated for young persons, the parole board may effect an early release, noting the general process of maturation that will enable these individuals to adopt more acceptable patterns of behavior once released.

Factors for Denying Parole Other Than Probability of Recidivism

There are circumstances in which individuals may not be granted a release despite a relatively low recidivism probability. For example, when inmates have demonstrated occasional outbursts of violent and assaultive behavior, parole boards tend to be somewhat reluctant to grant release. As noted previously, parole boards are extremely sensitive to public criticism, and while the probability of a violent attack may be very small, the seriousness of the incident would likely attract considerable media attention. Consequently, release in such a situation will often be denied. Community attitudes and values often play major roles in overriding the recidivism probability factors. For example, murderers have traditionally been good parole risks in terms of likelihood of parole success. However, whether and how quickly they should be paroled is often a function of community attitudes. If a community attitude is unfavorable, parole is likely to be denied, for the release of such an inmate might expose the parole board to bitter public criticism, and most parole boards prefer to keep an inmate in prison rather than incur the public's anger.

There are also occasions when parole is used as a tool to support and maintain institutional discipline. Individuals may possess very high potential for success on parole, but violate institutional rules and regulations continually. In these situations, parole will frequently be denied. Occasionally, an inmate with a drug abuse problem may be counseled by the parole board to enroll in an existing drug-dependency program, sending a clear message to the inmate population that such rehabilitation programs are appropriate and functional for release. In this way, parole can be viewed as an incentive for good behavior and a sanction against inappropriate conduct. There are even situations in which parole may be denied so as to benefit the inmate. Circumstances occasionally arise when inmates are making rapid progress in academic pursuits or may be receiving and responding to necessary medical and/or psychological treatment. The parole board may temporarily postpone such a case for a few months to give these individuals the opportunity to complete their high school work, for example, or recover from medical treatment they are undergoing.

Box 4.14
Parole Board Functions

The most visible function of a parole board is the discretionary release of an inmate from confinement prior to the expiration of his or her sentence on condition of good behavior in the community. This is commonly known as the parole release decision. However, parole boards have extensive authority to undertake a variety of other functions seldom acknowledged in the justice area.

Setting policy. The parole board enunciates and refines broad policy governing specific areas of parole, such as directives to community supervision officers on offenders whose drug tests show illicit drug use. Some policies require the officer to hold a revocation hearing under *Morrissey v. Brewer*; other jurisdictions may only suggest that officers tighten up the conditions of parole ("motivational" jail time, house arrest, or NA). When parole boards establish a "zero-tolerance" policy, a large portion of drug-abusing parolees may be returned to prison.

Modification of presumed release date. If an offender is given a presumed release date, it is usually based on conformity to institutional rules. When inmates persistently violate those, a decision may be made to delay release ("extend the time") based on institutional behavior. In effect, the parole board reinforces control of prison inmates and encourages participation in institutional programs.

Commutation of sentence. Inmates serving life sentences or double-life or life-plus-a-day or minimum sentences of several hundred years have few hopes of ever leaving the facility alive. It is possible, however, to petition the executive branch for commutation, a reduction in sentence length. A parole board, whose recommendation for commutation is seriously considered by the governor, usually hears the initial plea. "Lifers" who receive commutations usually leave the penal institution shortly thereafter.

Revocation from parole. If a supervising officer requests a hearing for revocation of parole under Morrissey and the hearing officer finds reasonable cause, the case will be heard by the parole board (or its authorized designee) and the offender's grant of parole may be revoked. The offender is then returned to prison to serve additional time.

Pardon. Only the executive branch may grant a pardon, absolving the offender in part or in full from the legal consequences of the crime and conviction. Governors usually receive such petitions after they have been considered by the parole board, generally authorized to advise the governor on these matters.

Reprieve. A reprieve is a stay in imposition of sentence, typically associated with death row inmates nearing their execution date. Parole boards, sometimes in conjunction with the governor's cabinet, may recommend reprieve to a governor.

Incapacitation. Some offenders have demonstrated a pattern of violent and dangerous criminal behavior that continues unabated in prison. By denying parole and thus forcing such inmates to serve longer prison sentences, parole boards protect the public through disabling future violent crime. This function is seldom recognized.

Finally, there are situations in which the parole board may feel that individuals are good risks but ineligible for release because they have not served the minimum terms as fixed by the sentencing judge. Some have expressed a concern over the fact that the courts occasionally err in handing down sanctions more severe than necessary. Correctional officials, after more careful observation and evaluation than the courts could originally consider, may clearly document greater progress than the court expected. Nevertheless, as noted previously, state parole statutes may mandate a minimum time to be served (calculated as a percentage of the minimum or maximum sentence) that even the parole board cannot ignore. Such inmates may be released, however, under work furlough programs.

PAROLE BOARD RELEASE DECISIONS

All persons eligible for parole are not automatically granted a release. Occasionally, parole boards will not release individuals who could be released safely. This is partially a desire by parole boards to minimize the number of persons who are classified as good risks and released, but whom the board feel are, in reality, bad risks and expected to fail on parole. Failed parole is a problem the boards seek to minimize (Wiggins, 1984).

Our ability to predict future recidivism has improved over the years; however, it is not without its critics (Gottfredson & Gottfredson, 1994; Monahan, 1981; Smykla, 1984). Furthermore, our ability to predict future violent behavior is limited, and as a result, there is a general tendency to overpredict dangerousness, which results in more persons being classified as bad risks,[29] fewer persons being granted parole, and an increase in prison populations (Monahan, 1981). Although such tendencies have come under intense criticism, overprediction of dangerousness continues (Morris, 1974; Smykla, 1984). This is probably due to the perception that overprediction is viewed as having smaller short-term costs. In the short run, it may be less expensive to incarcerate larger numbers of offenders than to permit a few dangerous persons to roam the streets and commit crimes. Such an approach is quite costly in the long run, however, as more and more persons are housed and cared for within the prison system. Furthermore, indications show that after extended prison sentences are served, some former inmates will commit more serious crimes more frequently than they would have prior to their incarceration.

While the courts have ruled that parole cannot be denied on the basis of race, religion, or national origin,[30] they have really not become involved in parole board policies and practices. This is due in large part to the fact that the Supreme Court has defined parole as a privilege rather than a right (*Greenholtz*, 1979). Consequently, there is no constitutional mandate that there even be any formal parole release guidelines, no right to obtain access to institutional files, and no right to counsel at the hearing. Indeed, there is no constitutional requirement that there even be a formal hearing. The state is under no constitutional obligation to articulate the reason for denial of parole, and there is no right of appeal, except as given by an individual state.

Most states have adopted laws and/or administrative policies that outline parole procedures. Some allow inmates access to their files and permit the presence of legal counsel. As of 1977, the U.S. Parole Commission[31] and 23 states offered inmates the opportunity to internally appeal parole release hearing decisions (O'Leary & Hanrahan, 1977). Up to this point, however, courts have continued to refuse to become involved in any type of review of a negative parole board decision.

CONDITIONS OF PAROLE

Parole is, in essence, a contract between the state and the offender. If the offender is able to abide by the terms of the contract, or **parole conditions,** freedom is maintained. If a violation of these conditions occurs or if a parolee is charged with a new crime, the parole board may revoke parole and return the offender to prison. The offender must abide by the contract and stay under parole supervision for the period of time outlined by the parole board. While every state has its own policies and procedures (see Figure 4.5), parole usually lasts more than two but less than

GENERAL/SPECIAL PAROLE AND POST-PRISON SUPERVISION CONDITIONS

Parole/Post-Prison Supervision is subject to all listed General Conditions and the designated Special Conditions. Prior to release the Board may modify the conditions at any time. After parole/post-prison supervision has commenced, conditions may be added upon your signed consent or after opportunity to be heard, orally or in writing.

Parole may be revoked for violation of any of these conditions and/or you may be returned when parole is not in your best interest or the best interest of society.

The Board may, at its discretion, sanction violations of Post-Prison Supervision Conditions; sanctions may include returning you to the Department of Corrections custody.

As used in this exhibit, the following words have the following meanings: "Offender" means persons released to parole or post-prison supervision. "Parole Officer" shall also mean the supervisory authority under the post-prison supervision system.

GENERAL CONDITIONS

1. Pay supervision fees, fines, restitution, or other fees ordered by the Board.

2. Not use or possess controlled substances except pursuant to a medical prescription.

3. Submit to testing of breath or urine for controlled substance or alcohol use if the offender has a history of substance abuse or if there is a reasonable suspicion that the offender has illegally used controlled substances.

4. Participate in a substance abuse evaluation as directed by the supervising officer and follow the recommendations of the evaluator if there are reasonable grounds to believe there is a history of substance abuse.

5. Remain in the State of Oregon until written permission to leave is granted by the Department of Corrections or a county community corrections agency.

6. If physically able, find and maintain gainful full-time employment, approved schooling, or a full-time combination of both. [Any waiver of this requirement must be based on a finding by the court stating the reasons for the waiver.]

7. Change neither employment nor residence without prior permission from the Department of Corrections or a county community corrections agency.

Figure 4.5 Oregon Parole Board Conditions of Parole.   *(Continued)*

8. Permit the supervising officer to visit the offender or the offender's residence or work site, and report as required and abide by the direction of the supervising officer.

9. Consent to the search of person, vehicle, or premises upon the (required) request of a representative of the supervising officer if the supervising officer has reasonable grounds to believe that evidence of a violation will be found, and submit to fingerprinting or photographing, or both, when requested by the Department of Corrections or a county community corrections agency for supervision purposes.

10. Obey all laws, municipal, county, state, and federal.

11. Promptly and truthfully answer all reasonable inquiries by the Department of Corrections or a county community corrections agency.

12. Not possess weapons, firearms, or dangerous animals.

SPECIAL CONDITIONS

1. Offender shall be evaluated by a mental health evaluator and follow all treatment recommendations.

2. Offender shall follow a psychiatric or psychotropic medication monitoring program with a physician per the physician's instructions.

3. Offender shall have no contact with minor females and shall not frequent any place where minors are likely to congregate (e.g., playgrounds, school grounds, arcades) without prior written approval from their supervising officer.

4. Offender shall have no contact with minor males and shall not frequent any place where minors are likely to congregate (e.g., playgrounds, school grounds, arcades) without prior written approval from their supervising officer.

5. Offender shall submit to random polygraph tests as part of a sex offender surveillance program. Failure to submit to the tests may result in return to Department of Corrections custody. Specific responses to the tests shall not be the basis for return to Department of Corrections custody.

6. Offender shall enter and complete or be successfully discharged from a recognized and approved sex offender treatment program which may include polygraph and/or plethysmograph testing and a prohibition on possession of printed, photographed, or recorded materials that the offender may use for the purpose of deviant sexual arousal.

7. Offender shall pay court-ordered restitution to the clerk of the court of the county of sentencing (ORS 137.106, OAR 255-65-005).

8. When criteria applies, the Department of Corrections may notify the community of the sex offender's status pursuant to ORS 181.507-509, OAR291-28-010 to 291-28-030.

9. Offender shall not use intoxicating beverages.

10. Other: Special conditions may be imposed that are not listed above when the Board of Parole and Post-Prison Supervision determines that such conditions are necessary.

11. Offender shall have no contact with those listed below.

Figure 4.5 Continued.

seven years. Some states in fact permit discharge from parole after a very short time, as long as the offender has diligently adhered to the prerelease contract. While the exact content of the contracts varies from state to state and from individual to individual, the following federal guidelines[32] cover the majority of conditions that are usually adopted:

- You shall go directly to the district showing on this CERTIFICATE OF PAROLE (unless released to the custody of other authorities). Within 3 days after your arrival, you shall report to your parole advisor if you have one, and to the United States Probation Officer whose name appears on this certificate. If in an emergency you are unable to get in touch with your parole advisor, or your probation officer or his office, you shall communicate with [the United States Parole Commission].
- If you are released to the custody of other authorities, and after your release from physical custody of such authorities, you are unable to report the United States Probation Officer to whom you are assigned within 3 days, you shall report instead to the nearest United States Probation Officer.
- You shall not leave the limits of this CERTIFICATE OF PAROLE without written permission from the probation officer.
- You shall notify your probation officer immediately of any change in your place of residence.
- You shall make a complete and truthful written report (on a form provided for that purpose) to your probation officer between the first and third day of each month, and on the final day of parole. You shall also report to your probation officer at other times as he directs.
- You shall not violate any law. Nor shall you associate with persons engaged in criminal activity. You shall get in touch immediately with your probation officer or his office if you are arrested or questioned by a law-enforcement officer.
- You shall not enter into any agreement to act as an "informer" or special agent for any law-enforcement agency.
- You shall work regularly, unless excused by your probation officer, and support your legal dependants, if any, to the best of your ability. You shall report immediately to your probation officer any change in employment.
- You shall not drink alcoholic beverages to excess. You shall not purchase, possess, use, or administer marijuana or narcotics or other habit-forming or dangerous drugs, unless prescribed or advised by a physician. You shall not frequent places where such drugs are illegally sold, dispensed, used, or given away.
- You shall not associate with persons who have a criminal record unless you have permission of your probation officer.
- You shall not have firearms (or other dangerous weapons) in your possession without the written permission of your probation officer, following prior approval of the United States Board of Parole.
- You shall, if ordered by the Board pursuant to Section 4203, Title 18, U.S.C., as amended October 1970, reside in and/or participate in a treatment program of a Community Treatment Center operated by the Bureau of Prisons, for a period not to exceed 120 days.

The U.S. Parole Commission's authority and reach are declining rapidly.[33]

PAROLE REVOCATION

In 1972, the U.S. Supreme Court established procedures for **parole revocation** with the case of *Morrissey v. Brewer*, 408 U.S. 471 (1972). In this case, the Supreme Court said that once parole is granted, it is no longer just a privilege but a right. Consequently, the court ruled that parolees should be granted certain due process rights in any parole revocation proceeding. While the court did not grant a full array of due process rights in *Morrissey*, it did advance the mandate of fundamental fairness. The court required the following minimum due process rights in the event of a parole revocation proceeding:

- Parolee given advanced written notification of the inquiry, its purpose, and alleged violation.
- A disclosure to the parolee of the evidence against him or her.
- The opportunity to be heard in person and present witnesses and documentary evidence.
- The right to confront and cross-examine adverse witnesses.
- A neutral and detached hearing body.
- A written statement by the hearing body as to the evidence relied upon and reasons for revoking parole.

The *Morrissey* case also established a dual state procedure, including a preliminary inquiry at the time of the alleged parole violations as well as a formal revocation hearing. Left unanswered, however, was the right to counsel, and whether the exclusionary rule should apply to revocation cases. One year later, in the case *Gagnon v. Scarpelli*, 411 U.S. 778 (1973), the court held that parolees do have a limited right to counsel in revocation proceedings and that the hearing body must determine, on a case-by-case basis, whether counsel should be afforded. While it need not be granted in all cases, "Counsel should be provided where, after being informed of his right, the . . . parolee requests counsel, based on a timely and colorable claim that he had not committed the alleged violation or, if the violation is a matter of public record or uncontested, there are substantial reasons in justification or mitigation that make revocation inappropriate."

The exclusionary rule issue remains unanswered. Although illegally seized evidence cannot be used in a criminal trial, many states do permit such evidence to be used in parole revocation cases, where the standard is "probable cause." To date, the courts have generally upheld this practice.

PROBLEMS WITH PAROLE BOARD DISCRETIONARY POWER

Beginning in the 1970s, dramatic shifts began in the field of corrections. Dissatisfied with high recidivism rates, many states opted to amend the traditional indeterminate sentencing model and adopt some of the aspects of a determinate or fixed sentencing model. Use of the indeterminate sentence in the United

States represented a grand experiment in controlling, if not eliminating, criminal behavior. Indeterminate sentencing, in which the judge sets limits within legislatively determined minimum and maximum sentences (e.g., one to seven years for burglary), would focus on the individual criminal and his or her needs rather than establishing a fixed penalty for certain types of crime. It sought to maximize the possibility of criminal rehabilitation through the use of various educational, vocational, and psychological treatment programs in the institution, and the use of a parole board that would release the inmate on parole at the optimum moment when change had occurred.

Through this "medical model of corrections," it was argued that such parole board decision making would offer several benefits:

- It would provide an incentive for rehabilitation by linking it to release from prison.
- This incentive would also apply as a mechanism to control the prison population, ensuring inmate discipline and safety.
- Another latent function of parole would be to provide a mechanism to control the size of the prison population.
- Similarly, the parole board would share the responsibility for societal protection with the judiciary through its control over prison release procedures. The board could also serve as a check and balance to judicial discretion by reducing sentencing disparities (such that inmates who committed the same crime would serve approximately the same amount of actual time in prison).

However, a number of factors combined to question the efficacy and fairness of this medical model. Penologists, such as Martinson (1974) and MacNamara (1977), reviewing the outcome of research reports on correctional rehabilitation programs, concluded that the medical model failed to cure criminals, reduce recidivism, or protect the public.[34] Others (Morris, 1974) argued that the medical model harmed inmates because the program participation was tied to and dependent on such participation. From the inmates' point of view, the decisions of the board were arbitrary, capricious, prejudicial, unpredictable, and not subject to external review by any other governmental body (Irwin, 1977). In fact, a number of studies (see Goodstein, 1980) have indicated that inmate frustration over failure to obtain release on parole is a factor that contributes to prison violence (Hassine, 2004).

PAROLE BOARD DECISION-MAKING GUIDELINES

Concerns over some of these issues led a number of jurisdictions, including the Federal Parole System, to adopt parole release guidelines. The U.S. Parole Commission developed its system of parole decision-making guidelines in 1974. The major complaint against parole board decision making has been, and remains, the great amount of discretionary power. The parole decision-making guidelines propose to structure this discretionary power to promote equity and fairness[35]

Box 4.15
Presumptive Sentencing

One alternative to limiting sentencing disparity is the *presumptive senten-cing* system, a variation of the determinate sentence. In presumptive senten-cing, the state legislature sets minimum, average, and maximum terms, allowing the judge to select a term based on the characteristics of the offender and any aggravating or mitigating circumstances proven in court. The sentence imposed will be the time served, less any credits against that sentence that the offender earns (jail time, good time, and program time). California has a presumptive sentencing structure that provides three options to the sentencing judge, as seen here for the crime of burglary.

1. Aggravating circumstances: seven years.
2. Presumptive (average) sentence: five years.
3. Mitigating circumstances: three years.

Ordinarily, the judge would decide if the offender should be placed on probation or imprisoned (the "in-out" decision). Assuming imprisonment to be the answer, the judge would impose the average or presumed term of five years, unless mitigating circumstances were present at the time of the offense (such as the offender being under the influence of a controlled substance at the time of the offense or because he or she had a weak person-ality and was easily led into committing crime for peer approval). If mitig-ating circumstances were proven, the judge would impose the lowest sentence (three years). However, if aggravating circumstances were proven in court, the judge must impose the highest sentence (seven years). Examples of aggravating circumstances are gross bodily harm to the victim, prior incarceration in prison, or victim extremely vulnerable (blind, frail, para-plegic, over 60 years of age, and so on).

---

and also to reduce sentencing disparity. The task was to make the decisions of the parole board less arbitrary and more explicit.

These guidelines usually involve a consideration of the seriousness of the commit-ment offense and a "risk" score that includes factors predictive of failure or success on parole. Recommended terms of incarceration are predetermined. For example, if the offender is rated as a "good" risk level and has committed a less serious offense, his or her recommended term of incarceration might fall between six and nine months. Conversely, an offender rated as a "high risk" and convicted of a more serious offense might serve a much longer term prior to consideration for parole.

In this fashion, the guidelines system attempts to structure the discretionary power of the parole board while at the same time maintaining equity and fairness (Hoffman, 1983).

Board examiners are also permitted to deviate from the guidelines. Examiners can shorten or lengthen the amount of time specified by the guidelines when, in their judgment, the case at hand appears to merit such consideration. However, when such a step is taken, the examiner is usually required to state the specific factors present that led to such a judgment.

Research indicates that guidelines appear to have some effect in reducing sentencing disparity among inmates. Sentencing disparity is divergence in the types and lengths of sentences imposed for the same crimes, with no evident reason for the differences. The use of parole board decision-making guidelines attempts to deal with the traditional problems of the parole process. They do not represent a panacea, but they are an alternative to the typical method, outright abolition, or use of determinate sentencing. There is evidence of more widespread adoption and use of formal risk assessment, as well as toward structural revocation decision making (Runda et al., 1994; Samra et al., 2000).

GET-TOUGH SENTENCES

While some criminologists and practitioners have been content to alter various aspects and procedures of the parole process, others have called for its complete abolition. A number of states have, for all intents and purposes, abolished parole. Whatever the change, one should be aware of the argument by Bill Woodward, former Director of Criminal Justice in Colorado (Gainsborough, 1997. p. 3): "The problem with abolishing parole is you lose your ability to keep track of the inmates and the ability to keep them in treatment if they have alcohol and drug problems." As seen in Table 4.3, the attack on parole release has been ongoing for more than 20 years.

Table 4.3 Some Significant Events in the Abolition of Parole Release

1976	Maine abolishes parole
1978	California abolishes indeterminate sentences and discretionary parole release
1980	Minnesota abolishes parole
1983	Florida abolishes parole
1984	Washington abolishes parole
1985	Colorado re-establishes parole
1986	Congress abolishes parole at the federal level
1990	Delaware abolishes parole
1994	Arizona and North Carolina abolish parole
1995	Virginia abolishes parole
1996	Ohio abolishes parole
1998	New York passes *Jenna's Law*, which eliminates discretionary release for all violent felony offenders
2011	Kansas abolishes the parole board and replaces it with a three-member prison review board under the Department of Corrections

Source: Compiled by authors.

Box 4.16
Sentencing Guidelines

In an attempt to limit, if not remove, **sentencing disparity**, many jurisdictions have implemented a set of guidelines to help judges decide what sentence should be imposed given the seriousness of the offense and the characteristics of the offender. **Sentencing guidelines** are based on past experience by a large number of sentencing judges and represent average sentences imposed by sentencing peers in similar cases. Obviously, inasmuch as the determinations are guidelines, judges are not required to impose the recommended sentence (but must at least state in writing why they are deviating from the recommended range).

One such guideline to determine sentence length is from Minnesota. Across the top of the guideline grid is a score for the characteristics the offender brings to the sentencing hearing: number of prior juvenile adjudications, adult convictions for misdemeanors and felonies, number of times the offender has been previously incarcerated, employment status and educational attainment, and so on. Obviously, the higher the score, the worse the criminal history and the longer the recommended sentence length.

The severity of the offense is found on the left side of the grid, ranked from the least severe to highest offense. After the judge calculates the criminal history score, she or he locates the offense category and reads across to see what other judges have done in terms of sentence length. The sentencing judge then imposes a sanction within the suggested range. Obviously, such guidelines must be revalidated frequently.

One example of shifts in sentencing can be seen in the development of three-strikes sentencing statutes across the United States. While some argue that they have the potential to reduce violent crime committed by repeat offenders by selective incapacitation of up to 25 years, the multiple-billion-dollar costs for prison construction, operations, and maintenance are considerable. Further, locking up second- and third-time offenders for long periods of time will not (1) address the successive waves of juveniles and young offenders who will take the place of those incarcerated for 25 years, (2) reduce the risk factors of individuals involved in crime, nor (3) be accurate enough to isolate the truly dangerous from the truly stupid. Three-strikes sentencing assumes that offenders operate as rational persons in a middle-class background and are driven by free will to commit crimes. Most criminals are neither so simplistic nor pure. A number of states and the federal government have enacted these laws since 1993 (Campaign for an Effective Crime Policy, 1996). California has used these statutes more extensively than other states, and at least 49,000 offenders have been sentenced to at least twice to three times the sentence they would have received, absent these "enhancement" laws. Recently, California amended its law to apply only to those who committed three "serious" offenses. One untoward outcome is that geriatric inmates (those over age 50) have become an increasing proportion of the prison population, even though studies show that this group of offenders pose the least risk to recidivate.

RE-ENTRY: THE NEW CHALLENGE

The large number of incarcerated offenders in the United States has led to the inevitable result—a large number of offenders who will re-enter society each year. In fact, re-entry has become the new buzz-word used by policy makers to describe the process by which offenders come back into the community. Some have argued that parole is essential to this process (Travis and Petersilia, 2001), whereas others (Austin, 2001) believe that because a high percentage of offenders pose minimal risk to public safety, parole supervision should be eliminated or shortened to about six months. As it is estimated that a significant percentage of offenders who will be returning to the community will have a number of important needs (Lowenkamp & Latessa, 2005; Lurigio, 2001), there is little doubt that services and treatment in the community should be an important part of the re-entry process. Indeed, several states have already created re-entry programs designed to coordinate efforts and services among the institution, parole, and community correctional programs and treatment providers.

Designing effective entry programs has become a major challenge facing both correctional officials and the community. In order to be effective, re-entry programs need to focus on higher-risk offenders, remove barriers, but stay focused on criminogenic needs, and provide high-quality programs and services that provide offenders with the skills they need to be successful (Latessa, 2008).

SUMMARY

Although the early beginnings of parole can be traced to Europe and Australia, the process as it is known today is almost exclusively an American invention. Once embraced by early reformers, parole spread quickly and, by 1944, every state jurisdiction had a parole system. Despite growth, parole was not without its detractors. Early criticism of parole included a suspicion of the way in which prisoners were selected for release, concern over a lack of community supervision, and extensive abuse by prison authorities. Many of the criticisms leveled at parole continue today.

There is considerable contemporary discussion relative to the value of parole. Indeed, there are those who oppose the indeterminate sentencing mode in general and wish to see parole abolished in particular. Concerns over these issues, and the perceived ineffectiveness of the present parole system, have led jurisdictions to either abolish parole altogether or adjust the entire parole process dramatically. Of all community programs, parole faces perhaps the greatest challenge. There are new indications, however, that pragmatism in the form of simple economics may renew an interest in parole. As our jail and prison populations swell above capacity, criminal justice planners and politicians will be forced to either continue to construct new facilities or develop alternative models. Parole emerges as a relatively inexpensive alternative model and, perhaps more importantly, one that is already in place. There is a need, though, to improve both the parole process and supervision so as to overcome the deficiencies detailed earlier.

Even if this apparent renewed interest in parole phases out, and parole as we know it is abolished in a stampede toward the determinate sentencing model, the need to assist inmates in their transition from the institution to the free community will remain. The problems facing released inmates are usually temporal or material—obtaining employment, suitable housing, financial aid, alcohol and other drug abuse, and so on.

As parole moves toward structuring release and revocation decisions to remove unwanted discrepancies and as jurisdictions consider abolition of parole as a release mechanism (whether assisted by guidelines or from clinical experience), two facts remain. First, parole has always served as a "release valve" or mechanism to prevent (or lower) prison overcrowding, a fact sadly ignored by policy makers and politicians. Second, discretionary parole has within it the authority to retain dangerous persons whose behavior would lead reasonable persons, citizens, and experienced correctional practitioners alike to protect society by not paroling dangerous offenders. If the nation is to avoid the even more extreme of hiking sentences by multiples of current statutory terms, parole authorities should have the ability to protect the public by selective incapacitation of those who have several convictions for crimes against a person (murder, rape, aggravated assault, robbery, etc.). Of course, it is important to remember that parole board members are human, and as such they cannot be expected to be infallible. Some inmates invariably are released who should not be, whereas others are kept far longer than necessary. Outcomes such as these require consideration of ways and means to intended objectives, as well as justice.

Review Questions

1. Contrast the punishment model with the reform model of corrections.
2. How did Maconochie contribute to the development of parole?
3. How did parole develop in the United States?
4. What were the early criticisms of parole in America?
5. What were three elements of corruption that emerged in American corrections between 1790 and 1930?
6. Contrast the view of criminals offered by Maconochie with that of J. Edgar Hoover.
7. How did the decade from 1925 to 1935 affect attitudes of the American public toward parole?
8. Debate the following resolution: Discretionary parole from prison should be abolished.
9. What functions do parole boards serve?

10. If parole boards could not release offenders into the community, would they be abolished? Why or why not?
11. How do sentencing guidelines work? Parole guidelines?
12. How can parole boards use and implement intermediate sanctions?
13. How can three-strikes laws affect corrections?

Notes

1   Various forms of conditional release from incarceration were developed in other countries before an American state adopted a parole system. However, the core elements of a parole system administrative board making release decisions and granting conditional, supervised release with the authority to revoke it were first created by legislation in New York State (1869).

2   For a view of the impacts of conservative Christian beliefs on punishment of offenders, see Gramich and McGill (1994). In the area of impact of evangelical and fundamentalist religion on the death penalty, see Gramich et al. (1993). For contrasting evidence, see Sandys and McGarrell (1997); and Johnson (2000).

3   For an excellent reading of the movement as it relates to the study of crime, see Rennie (1978).

4   For an excellent description of transportation to Australia, see Hughes (1987). Pretransportation detention was usually in hulks, dilapidated and unseaworthy naval vessels. See Campbell (1994).

5   For a conflicting interpretation of the political purposes intended for prisons, see Durham (1990). It was argued that fair, simple laws, backed by certain and humane punishment, would eradicate crime.

6   For a review of the contemporary issues in the prison privatization movement, see Shichor (1993). See also Vardalis and Decker (2000).

7   See Chayet (1994).

8   It was not uncommon for juveniles to be indentured without a careful investigation of those who would hold the indenture contracts. Thus, juveniles were sometimes indentured to criminals, and the conditions of their indentureships were virtually uncontrolled.

9   The first legislatively authorized "parole officer" position was established in 1937 in Massachusetts. The officer was charged with assisting released convicts to obtain shelter, tools, and work. The legislation made no mention of any surveillance duties.

10   For a history of the American Correctional Association, see Travisono and Hawkes (1995).

11   See Lindsey (1925). Lindsey writes, "There has been considerable modification and variation in various phases of the system as it has spread from one state to another. Methods of administration are also widely different." For an update on parole practices, see Runda et al. (1994).

12   Perhaps chief among these were Wines and Dwight who, in 1867, published a report to the New York Prison Association entitled *Prisons and reformatories*

of the United States and Canada. Other state committees echoed the call for a parole system. See Report of the Massachusetts General Court Joint Special Committee on Contract Convict Labor (1880). See also Roberts et al. (2000).

13 For a remarkably similar view of contemporary corrections and public fears, see Murphy and Dison (1990). See also Chiricos et al. (2000).

14 On media influence on citizen perception and fear of crime, see Barlow et al. (1995); Bennett and Flavin (1994); Wright et al. (1995); and Chiricos et al. (1997).

15 But see DeLoach (1995).

16 Authors of these reports were joined by others. Reformers wanted full-time, paid parole authorities who had to meet certain qualifications and who were as far removed as possible from political patronage. See Colvin (1992).

17 Field (1931). For sentiments of inmates denied parole, see West-Smith et al. (2000).

18 Predicting postrelease behavior is difficult. See Gottfredson and Gottfredson (1994), and Heilbrun et al. (2000).

19 The offender's mandatory release date in Nebraska is calculated as follows: For all odd-numbered maximum terms $MR = (Max - 1)/2 + 11$ months. For all even-numbered minimum terms $MR = Max/2 + 5$ months.

20 Editors (1995).

21 Runda et al. (1994).

22 Such intrastate variations may also be true within states. For example, Sutton observed that the decision to place an individual in prison or not, and the length of the sentence *per se*, may be more a function of the county where the sentence was handed down than the nature of the offense. See Sutton (1981). But see Turner et al. (1997).

23 Rhine et al. (1992).

24 Florida Office of Program Policy Analysis and Government Accountability (1996).

25 English et al. (1996).

26 Oregon Intermediate Sanctions for Female Offenders Policy Group (1995). *Intermediate sanctions for females.* Salem, OR: Oregon Department of Corrections.

27 Sutton (1981).

28 Pagliaro and Pagliaro (1992). See also Hammett et al. (1994a, 1994b).

29 Monahan and Steadman (1994).

30 See *Block v. Potter*, 631 E2d 233 (3d Cir. 1980); *Candelaria v. Griffin*, 641 E2d 868 (10th Cir. 1980); *Farris v. U.S. Board of Parole*, 384 F.2d 948 (7th Cir. 1973).

31 Gottfredson and Gottfredson (1994).

32 Hoffman (1994).

33 Violators of federal statutes sentenced after November 1, 1987 do not fall under the authority of the U.S. Parole Commission but are instead sentenced under new federal sentencing guidelines, a form of determinate sentencing that emphasizes just deserts. Sentencing guidelines were developed by the U.S. Sentencing Commission and are quite similar to the system used under the Parole Commission.

34   The weight of evidence has shifted against the "nothing works in corrections" argument. Overwhelming evidence shows that programs designed specifically for offenders'needs and delivered in a coherent manner by trained intervention personnel assisted by competent supervisors work and are effective. See Cullen and Gendreau (2001).

35   As defined by Gottfredson et al. (1973), equity and fairness mean that "similar persons are dealt with in similar ways in similar situations. Fairness thus implies the idea of similarity and of comparison."

Recommended Readings

Hughes, R. (1987). *The fatal shore*. New York: Alfred A. Knopf. [This is the definitive book on the history of Australia as a penal colony, and the roots of parole as developed by Captain Maconochie.]

Rothman, D.J. (1971). *The discovery of the asylum: social order and disorder in the New Republic*. Boston, MA: Little, Brown. [This book presents an excellent history of the use of punishments and corrections in early colonial America.]

Rothman, D.J. (1980) *Conscience and convenience: the asylum and its alternatives in progressive America*. Boston, MA: Little, Brown. [A fastidious discussion of the modern effort to reform the programs that have dominated criminal justice in the twentieth century.]

References

Allen, H.E., Simonsen, C.E. (2001). *Corrections in America*, 9th edn. Upper Saddle River, NJ: Prentice Hall.

Austin, J. (2001). Prisoner reentry: Current trends, practices, and issues. *Crime & Delinquency* 47, 314–334.

Babst, D.V., Inciardi, J.A., Jarman, D.R. (1970). *The uses of configural analysis in parole prediction research*. New York: Narcotics Control Commission.

Barlow, M., Barlow, D., Chiricos, T. (1995). Economic conditions and ideologies of crime in the media: A content analysis of crime news. *Crime & Delinquency* 43, 3–19.

Barnes, H.E., Teeters, N.D. (1959). *New horizons in criminology*. Englewood Cliffs, NJ: Prentice Hall.

Barry, J.V. (1957). Captain Alexander Maconochie. *The Victorian Historical Magazine* 27, 1–18.

Beccaria, C. (1764). *On crimes and punishments*. Indianapolis: Bobbs-Merrill (H. Paulucci, trans., 1963).

Bennett, R., Flavin, J. (1994). Determinants of the fear of crime: The effects of cultural setting. *Justice Quarterly* 11, 357–381.

Block v. Potter, 631 F.2d 233 (3d Cir. 1980).

Bottomley, K.E. (1990). Parole in transition: A comparative study of origins, developments, and prospects for the 1990s. In: M. Tonry, N. Morris (eds) *Crime and justice: a review of research,* vol. 12. Chicago, IL: University of Chicago Press.

Briggs, J., Harrison, C., McInnes, A. (1996). *Crime and punishment in England: An introductory history*. New York: St. Martin's Press.

Bromley, E., Gathercole, C.E. (1969). Boolean predication analysis: A new method of prediction index construction. *British Journal of Criminology* 17, 287–292.

Burgess, E.W. (1928). Factors determining success or failure on parole. In: B. Harmo, E.W. Burgess, C.L. Landeson (eds) *The workings of the indeterminate sentence law and the parole system in Illinois*. Springfield, IL: Illinois State Board of Parole.

Burke, P. (1997). *Policy driven responses to probation and parole violators*. Washington, DC: U.S. National Institute of Justice.

Camp, C., Camp, G. (2000). *The 2000 corrections yearbook: Adult corrections*. Middletown, CT: Criminal Justice Institute.

Campaign for an Effective Crime Control Policy (1996). *The impact of "Three Strikes and You're Out" laws: What have we learned?* Washington, DC: CFECP.

Campbell, C. (1994). *The intolerable hulks: British shipboard confinement*. Bowie, MD: Heritage Books.

Candelaria v. Griffin, 641 F.2d 868 (10th Cir. 1980).

Carson, A.E., Golinelli, D. (2013). *Prisoners in 2012 trends in admissions and releases 1991–2012*. Washington, DC: U.S. Dept. of Justice, Office of Justice Programs, Bureau of Justice Statistics.

Carter, R.M., McGee, R.A., Nelson, K.E. (1975). *Corrections in America*. Philadelphia, PA: J.B. Lippincott.

Chayet, E. (1994). Correctional "good time" as a means of early release. *Criminal Justice Abstracts* 26, 521–538.

Chiricos, T., Escholz, S., Gertz, M. (1997). Crime, news and fear of crime. *Social Problems* 44(3), 342–357.

Chiricos, T., Padgett, K., Gerz, M. (2000). Fear, TV news and the reality of crime. *Criminology* 38(3), 755–785.

Clare, P.K., Kramer, J.H. (1976). *Introduction to American corrections*. Boston, MA: Holbrook Press.

Clear, T.R. (1978). *A model for supervising the offender in the community*. Washington, DC: National Institute of Corrections.

Colvin, W. (1922). What authority should grant paroles? If a Board, how should it be composed? *Journal of Criminal Law and Criminology* 12, 545–548.

Criminal Courts Technical Assistance Project, January (1982). *Judicial and executive discretion in the sentencing process: Analysis of felony state code provisions*. Washington, DC: American University.

Cullen, F., Gendreau, P. (2001). From nothing works to what works: Changing professional ideology in the 21st century. *The Prison Journal* 81(3), 313–338.

Dawson, R.O. (1966). The decision to grant or deny parole: A study of parole criteria in law and practice. *Washington University Law Quarterly* June, 248–285.

DeLoach, C. (1995). *Hoover's FBI: The inside story by Hoover's trusted lieutenant*. Washington, DC: Regenery.

Durham, A.M. (1990). Social control and imprisonment during the American Revolution: Newgate of Connecticut. *Justice Quarterly* 7, 293–323.

English, K., Colling, C., Pullen, S. (1996). *How are adult felony sex offenders managed on probation and parole: A national assessment.* Denver, CO: Colorado Department of Public Safety.

Farris v. U.S. Board of Parole, 1973 *384 F.2d 948* (7th Cir.).

Field, H.E. (1931). The attitudes of prisoners as a factor in rehabilitation. *The Annals* 157–162.

Florida Office of Program Policy Analysis and Government Accountability (1996). *Information brief of control release workload of the Florida Parole Commission.* Tallahassee: FOPPAGA.

Fogel, D. (1975). *We are the living proof . . . the justice model for corrections.* Cincinnati: Anderson.

Gagnon v. Scarpelli, 1972 *411 U.S. 788.*

Gainsborough, J. (1997). Eliminating parole is a dangerous and expensive proposition. *Corrections Today* 59(4), 23.

Glaser, D. (1962). Prediction tables as accounting devices for judges and parole boards. *Crime & Delinquency* 8, 239–258.

Glaze, L., Bonczar, T. (2009). *Probation and parole in the United States, 2008.* Washington, DC: U.S. Department of Justice Statistics, Bureau of Justice Statistics.

Goodstein, L. (1980). Psychological effects of the predictability of prison release: implications for the sentencing debate. *Criminology* 18, 363–384.

Gottfredson, D.M., Babst, D.V., Ballard, K.B. (1958). Comparison of multiple regression and configural analysis techniques for developing base expectancy tables. *Journal of Research in Crime and Delinquency* 5, 72–80.

Gottfredson, D.M., Hoffman, P.B., Sigler, M., Wilkins, L. (1973). Making parole policy explicit. *Crime and Delinquency* 52: 52–58.

Gottfredson, S., Gottfredson, D. (1993). The long-term predictive utility of the base expectancy score. *Howard Journal of Criminal Justice* 32, 276–290.

Gottfredson, S., Gottfredson, D. (1994). Behavioral prediction and the problem of incapacitation. *Criminology* 32, 441–474.

Gramich, H., McGill, A. (1994). Religion, attribution style, and punitiveness toward offenders. *Criminology* 32(1), 23–46.

Gramich, H., Cochran, J., Burish, J., Kimpel, M. (1993). Religion, punitive justice, and support for the death penalty. *Justice Quarterly* 10(2), 289–314.

Greenholtz v. Inmates of the Nebraska Penal and Correctional Complex, 1979 *442 U.S. 1.*

Hammett, T., Harrold, L., Epstein, J. (1994a). *Tuberculosis in correctional facilities.* Washington, DC: U.S. Department of Justice.

Hammett, T., Harrold, L., Gross, M. (1994b). *1992 update: HIV/AIDS in correctional facilities: issues and options.* Washington, DC: U.S. Department of Justice.

Hart, H. (1923). Predicting parole success. *Journal of Criminal Law and Criminology* 14, 405–414.

Hassine, V. (2004). *Life without parole: Living in prison today,* 3rd edn. Los Angeles, CA: Roxbury.

Hawkins, K.O. (1971). Parole selection: The American experience. University of Cambridge: unpublished doctoral dissertation.

Heilbrun, K., Brock, W., Waite, D., et al. (2000). Risk factors for juvenile criminal recidivism. *Criminal Justice and Behavior* 27(3), 275–291.

Hoffman, P. (1983). Screening for risk. *Journal of Criminal Justice* 11(6), 539–547.

Hoffman, P. (1994). Twenty years of operational use of a risk prediction instrument: The United States Parole Commission's salient factor score. *Journal of Criminal Justice* 22, 477–494.

Hughes, R. (1987). *The fatal shore*. New York: Alfred A. Knopf.

Irwin, J. (1977). Adaptation to being corrected: Corrections from the convict's perspective. In: R.G. Legar, J.R. Stratton (eds) *The sociology of corrections*. New York: John Wiley and Sons, pp. 276–300.

Johnson, E. (1994). Opposing outcomes of the industrial prison: Japan and the United States compared. *International Criminal Justice Review* 4(1), 52–71.

Johnson, S. (2000). The Bible and the death penalty. *Journal of Contemporary Criminal Justice* 11(1), 15–23.

Kanvensohn, M. (1979). *A national survey of parole-related legislation*. San Francisco, CA: Uniform Parole Reports.

Langbein, J.H. (1976). The historical origins of the sanction of imprisonment for serious crime. *Journal of Legal Studies* 5, 35–63.

Latessa, E. (2008). *What science says about designing effective prisoner reentry programs*. Wisconsin Family Impact Seminars, University of Wisconsin. Available at www.familyimpactseminars.org/index.asp?p=2&page=seminar&seminarid= 168&siteid=50.

Latessa, E., Smith, P., Lemke, R., Makarios, M., Lowenkamp, C. (2010). The creation and validation of the Ohio Risk Assessment System (ORAS). *Federal Probation* 74(1).

Lindsey, E. (1925). Historical origins of the sanction of imprisonment for serious crime. *Journal of Criminal Law and Criminology* 16, 9–126.

Lowenkamp, C., Latessa, E. (2005). Developing successful reentry programs: Lesson learned from the "what works" research. *Corrections Today* (April).

Loza, W., Loza, F. (2000). Predictive validity of the self-appraisal questionnaire (SAQ). *Journal of Interpersonal Violence* 15(11), 1183–1191.

Lurigio, A.J. (2001). Effective services for parolees with mental illnesses. *Crime & Delinquency* 47, 446–461.

MacNamara, D.E.J. (1977). The medical model in corrections: Requiescat in Pax. *Criminology* 14, 435–438.

Maguire, M., Peroud, B., Dison, J. (1996). In: Maguire, M., Peroud, B., Dison, J. (eds) *Automatic conditional release: the first two years*. London: Her Majesty's Stationery House.

Martinson, R. (1974). What works? Questions and answers about prison reform. *Public Interest* 25(spring), 22–25.

Maruschak, L.M., Bonczar, T.P. (2014). *Probation and parole in the United States, 2012*. Washington, DC: U.S. Dept. of Justice, Offices of Justice Programs, Bureau of Justice Statistics.

Monahan, J. (1981). *Predicting violent behavior: An assessment of clinical techniques*. Beverly Hills, CA: Sage.

Monahan, J., Steadman, H. (1994). In: Monahan, J., Steadman, H. (eds) *Violence and mental disorder: Developments in risk assessment*. Chicago, IL: University of Chicago Press.

Morelli, R.S., Edelman, C., Willoughby, R. (eds) (1981). In: Morelli et al. (eds) *A survey of mandatory sentencing in the U.S.* Pennsylvania Commission on Crime and Delinquency.

Morris, N. (1974). *The future of imprisonment*. Chicago, IL: University of Chicago Press.

Morrissey v. Brewer, 1972 *408 U.S. 471*.

Murphy, J.W., Dison, J. (1990). *Are prisons any better? Twenty years of correctional reform*. Newbury Park, CA: Sage.

National Commission of Law Observance and Enforcement (1939). *George W. Wickersham, Chairman. Report on penal institutions, probation and parole*. Washington, DC: U.S. Government Printing Office.

Offutt, W. (1995). *Of "good laws" and "good men:" Law and society in the Delaware Valley, 1680–1710*. Chicago, IL: University of Chicago Press.

O'Leary, V., Hanrahan, K. (1977). *Parole systems in the United States: A detailed description of their structure and procedure*, 3rd edn. Hackensack, NJ: National Council on Crime and Delinquency.

Pagliaro, P., Pagliaro, A. (1992). Sentenced to death: HIV infections and AIDS in prison—current and future concerns. *Canadian Journal of Criminology* 34(2), 201–214.

Pew (2014). *Max out the rise in prison inmates released without supervision*. www.pewtrusts.org/en/research-and-analysis/reports/2014/06/04/max-out.

Pisciotta, A. (1982). Saving the Children: The promise and practice of Parens Patria, 1838–1898. *Crime & Delinquency* 28(3), 410–425.

President's Commission on Law Enforcement and Administration of Justice (1969). *The challenge of crime in a free society*. Washington, DC: U.S. Government Printing Office.

Rennie, Y. (1978). *The search for criminal man*. Lexington, MA: D.C. Heath.

Report of the Massachusetts General Court Joint Special Committee on Contract Convict Labor (1880). *Report of the Massachusetts General Court Joint Special Committee on Contract Convict Labor*. Boston, MA: State of Massachusetts.

Rhine, E., Smith, W., Jackson, R. (1992). *Paroling authorities: Recent history and current practices*. Laurel, MD: American Correctional Association.

Roberts, J., Nuffield, J., Hahn, R. (2000). Parole and the public. *Empirical and Applied Criminal Justice Research Journal* 1(1), 1–25.

Rothman, D.J. (1971). *The discovery of the asylum: Social order and disorder in the new republic*. Boston, MA: Little, Brown.

Runda, J., Rhine, E., Wetter, R. (1994). *The practice of parole boards*. Lexington, KY: Council of State Governments.

Samra, G., Pfeifer, J., Ogloff, J. (2000). Recommendations for conditional release suitability. *Canadian Journal of Criminology* 42(4), 421–447.

Sandys, M., McGarrell, E. (1997). Beyond the Bible belt: The influence (or lack thereof) of religion on attitudes toward the death penalty. *Journal of Crime and Justice* 20(1), 179–190.

Scott, J. (1974). The use of discretion in determining the severity of punishment for incarcerated offenders. *Journal of Criminal Law and Criminology* 65, 214–224.

Sellin, T. (1970). The origin of the Pennsylvania system of prison discipline. *The Prison Journal* 50(13), 13–15, 17.

Sherrill, M.S. (1977). Determinate sentencing: History, theory, debate. *Corrections Magazine* 3, 3–13.

Shichor, D. (1993). The corporate context of private prisons. *Crime, Law and Social Change* 20(2), 113–138.

Smykla, J.O. (1984). *Prediction in probation and parole: Its consequences and implications*. Paper presented at the annual meeting of the Academy of Criminal Justice Sciences, Chicago, IL.

Sutton, P.L. (1981). *Criminal sentencing in Nebraska: The feasibility of empirically based guidelines*. Williamsburg, VA: National Center for State Courts.

Travis, J., Petersilia, J. (2001). Reentry reconsidered: A new look at an old problem. *Crime & Delinquency* 47: 291–313.

Travisono, A., Hawkes, M. (1995). *Building a voice: The American Correctional Association, 125 years of history*. Lanham, MD: ACA. www.corrections.com/aca/history/html.

Turner, M., Cullen, F., Sundt, J. (1997). Public tolerance for community-based sanctions. *Prison Journal* 77(1), 6–26.

Vardalis, J., Decker, F. (2000). Legislative opinions concerning the private operations of state prisons. *Criminal Justice Policy Review* 11(2), 136–148.

West-Smith, M., Pogebrin, M., Poole, E. (2000). Denial of parole: An inmate perspective. *Federal Probation* 64(2), 3–10.

Wiggins, M.E. (1984). *False positives/false negatives: A utility cost analysis of parole decision making*. Paper presented at the annual meeting of the Academy of Criminal Justice Sciences, Chicago, IL.

Wilcox, C. (1929). Parole: Principles and practice. *Journal of Criminal Law and Criminology* 20, 345–354.

Wilkins, L.E., MacNaughton-Smith, P. (1964). New prediction and classification methods in criminology. *The Journal of Research in Crime and Delinquency* 1, 19–32.

Wines, E.C., Dwight, T.W. (1867). *Prisons and reformatories of the United States and Canada*. Albany, NY: New York Prison Association.

Wright, J., Cullen, E., Blankenshin, M. (1995). The social construction of corporate violence: Media coverage of the imperial food products fire. *Crime & Delinquency* 41(1), 20–36.

Chapter 5

WHAT WORKS IN PROBATION AND PAROLE

Key Terms

community residential centers
cost-effectiveness
faith-based programs
furlough
length of follow-up

parole conditions
principles of effective intervention
shock probationers
therapeutic communities

> How could "nothing works" prevail and punishment be promoted when, at a minimum, the research evidence suggested that at least some programs appeared to be working for some offenders under some circumstances? The evidence was not consistent with the myths of sociological criminology.—D.A. Andrews and James Bonta

THE IMPORTANCE OF EVALUATING CORRECTIONAL PROGRAMS

The importance of evaluating correctional programs has never been more pronounced, especially given the current economic crisis. With vast sums of money being spent on corrections, the public is demanding programs that work. The critical questions considered in this chapter are as follows. What works? What do we know about program effectiveness? What harm is done when we fail to develop effective programs? Moreover, this chapter provides an evidence-based framework for discussing research and practice on community corrections throughout this book.

One of the most important areas of contemporary concern for corrections officials is the design and operation of effective correctional intervention programs. This is particularly relevant, as there is consistent evidence that the public supports rehabilitation programs for offenders (Pew, 2012). Survey research also reveals strong support for public protection as an important goal of corrections (Applegate et al., 1997). As a result, disagreements are not uncommon about what the best methods are to achieve these goals. On one side are advocates for more punitive policies, such as an increased use of incarceration, "punishing smarter" strategies (e.g., boot camps), or simply increasing control and monitoring of offenders. The limits of these approaches have been outlined and debated by others (Currie, 1985; Bennett et al., 1996; Petersilia & Cullen, 2014).

As Cullen and Applegate (1998) imply, the most disheartening aspect of these "get-tough" policies is their dismissal of the importance of programming designed to rehabilitate offenders. Cullen and Applegate further question whether this rejection of rehabilitation is sound public policy. As many states have found, simply locking up offenders and "throwing away the key" has proven to be a very expensive approach to crime control. This approach is also very limited, as the vast majority of offenders will one day return to society. Many will return at best unchanged, and at worst with many more problems and intensified needs for service (Petersilia, 1992). For those advocating incapacitation, one must also ask: What should be done with offenders while they are incarcerated? Some scholars, such as Cullen and Applegate, do not believe that incapacitation and rehabilitation are mutually exclusive. Furthermore, because the vast majority of offenders are supervised in the community at differing degrees of intensity, it is even more important that we develop programs that work toward reducing recidivism.

What Does the Research Tell Us?

Many of the "intermediate sanctions" that have been developed over the past years are but a few examples of "programs" that often fail to live up to their expectations, particularly in terms of reductions in recidivism (Fulton et al., 1997; Latessa et al., 1997; Petersilia, 1997). While programs such as boot camps, Scared Straight, and other "punishing smarter" programs have been popular, there is little evidence that they will lead to reductions in recidivism. Figure 5.1 shows some of the results from various studies. Unfortunately, evidence seems to indicate that in some cases, punishing smarter programs actually lead to increases in recidivism rates. One of the main problems with such approaches is that they only send a message about what the offender should *not* do; these approaches do not teach them the skills that they need to address high-risk situations in the future.

In a study funded by the National Institute of Justice, Sherman and colleagues (1998) summarized what does not work in reducing recidivism:

- correctional boot camps using traditional military basic training;
- drug prevention classes focused on fear and other emotional appeals, including self-esteem, such as DARE;
- school-based leisure-time enrichment programs;
- "Scared Straight" programs in which juvenile offenders visit adult prisons;
- shock probation, shock parole, and split sentences adding time to probation or parole;
- home detention with electronic monitoring;
- intensive supervision;
- rehabilitation programs using vague, unstructured counseling;

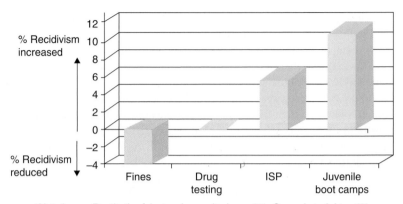

*Not shown: Restitution/electronic monitoring = 3%, Scared straight = 4%

Figure 5.1 Effects of Punishing Smarter Programs on Recidivism.

Sources: Gendreau, P., Goggin, C., Cullen, F., Andrews, D. (2000). The effects of community sanctions and incarceration on recidivism. *Forum on Corrections Research* 12, 10–13; Aos, S., Phipps, P., Barnoski, R., Lieb, R. (1999). *The comparative costs and benefits of programs to reduce crime.* Olympia, WA: Washington State Institute for Public Policy.

■ residential programs for juvenile offenders using challenging experiences in rural settings.

Despite the punitive movement, increasing evidence shows that correctional treatment can be effective in reducing recidivism among offenders (Andrews et al., 1990; Cullen & Gendreau, 1989; Gendreau & Andrews, 1990; Latessa & Lowenkamp, 2006; Redondo et al., 1999; Van Voorhis, 1987). Nonetheless, some scholars remain unconvinced (Antonowicz & Ross, 1994; Lab & Whitehead, 1988; Logan & Gaes, 1993; Farabee, 2005). The debate surrounding treatment effectiveness has been ongoing since Martinson's proclamation that "nothing works," with many still clinging to this mantra, despite evidence to the contrary. Primary among the reasons for disbelief in the potential effectiveness of correctional programming is the failure to measure outcome by looking at effects by risk level of the offender and the lack of quality programs.

Gendreau (1996) examined hundreds of correctional and rehabilitation programs that attempt to intervene with offenders. His results indicated that 64 percent of the offender rehabilitation studies (that had control groups) reported reductions in favor of the treatment group; in fact, the average reduction in recidivism was 10 percent. Others have subsequently conducted similar studies (Lipsey & Wilson, 1997) and have come to the same conclusion: rehabilitation can be effective in reducing recidivism. For example, Figure 5.2 is based on a meta-analysis (or quantitative review of the literature) conducted by Lipsey (1999). Results showed the expected recidivism rates when various programming characteristics are factored into probation.

Gendreau and Paparozzi (1995) also found that when rehabilitation programs incorporated at least some of the eight principles of effective intervention, those programs reduced recidivism in the range of 25 to 70 percent, with the average about 50 percent. Some principles of effective intervention are as follows:

1. Programs should have intensive services that are cognitive-behavioral in nature, that occupy 40 to 70 percent of the offender's time in a program, and that are from 3 to 9 months in duration. Cognitive-behavioral programs incorporate elements of cognitive theories, behavioral theories, and social learning theories (see Spiegler & Guevremont, 2009).
2. Programs should target the criminogenic needs of high-risk offenders, such as antisocial attitudes, peer associations, personal and emotional factors (e.g., aggression, deficits in self-control), substance abuse, family and marital problems, and education/employment deficits.
3. Programs should incorporate responsivity among offender, therapist, and program. Simply said, treatment programs should be delivered in a manner that allows the offender to learn new pro-social skills and address potential barriers.
4. Program contingencies and behavioral strategies are enforced in a firm but fair manner; positive reinforcers outnumber punishers by at least 4:1.
5. Staff should relate to offenders in interpersonally sensitive and constructive ways and are trained and supervised accordingly. Treatment is systematically delivered by competent therapists and case managers.
6. Program structure and activities disrupt the delinquency network by placing offenders in situations (with people and in places) where pro-social activities predominate.
7. Provide relapse prevention in the community by such tactics as planning and rehearsing alternative pro-social responses, anticipating problem situations, training significant others (family and friends) to provide reinforcement for pro-social behavior, and establishing a system for booster sessions.
8. A high level of advocacy and brokerage as long as the community agency offers appropriate services.

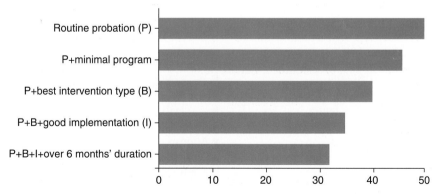

Figure 5.2 Expected Recidivism with Various Intervention Characteristics for Noninstitutionalized Juvenile Offenders.

Source: Lipsey, M. (1999). Can intervention rehabilitate serious delinquents? *Annals of the American Academy of Political and Social Science* 564, 142–166.

In a study of the effects of using behavioral reinforcement, Widahl and his colleagues (2011) examined the effects of increasing rewards for probationers. Completion rates increased dramatically as the ratio of rewards to punishers grew. At 4:1 the completion rates were over 70 percent. Figure 5.3 shows the increases in completion rates, and Table 5.1 shows the list of rewards and punishments used by the probation department.

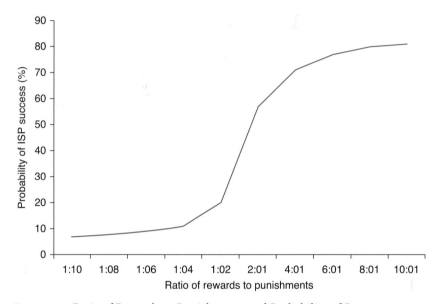

Figure 5.3 Ratio of Rewards to Punishments and Probability of Success on Intensive Supervision.

Source: Widahl, E.J., Garland, B., Culhane, S.E., McCarty, W.P. (2011). Utilizing behavioral interventions to improve supervision outcomes in community-based corrections. *Criminal Justice and Behavior* 38(4), 386–405.

Table 5.1 Sanctions and Rewards

Sanctions	**Rewards**
■ Verbal reprimand	■ Verbal praise and reinforcement
■ Written assignment	■ Remove from EM
■ Modify curfew hours	■ Level advancement
■ Community service hours	■ Increased personal time
■ Restrict visitation	■ Approved special activity
■ Program extension or regression	■ Fees reduced
■ Electronic monitoring	■ Approve of extend special visitation
■ Inpatient or outpatient txt	
■ Detention time	

Source: Widahl, E.J., Garland, B., Culhane, S.E., McCarty, W.P. (2011). Utilizing behavioral interventions to improve supervision outcomes in community-based corrections. *Criminal Justice and Behavior* 38(4).

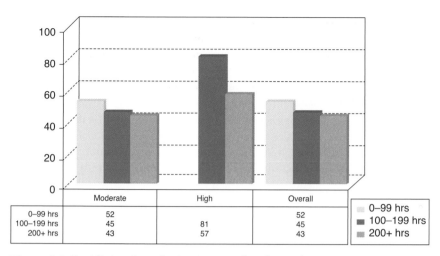

	Moderate	High	Overall
0–99 hrs	52		52
100–199 hrs	45	81	45
200+ hrs	43	57	43

Legend: 0–99 hrs; 100–199 hrs; 200+ hrs

Figure 5.4 Recidivism Rates by Intensive and Risk Level.

Source: Sperber, K., Latessa, E.J., Makarios, M.D. (2013). Examining the interaction between level of risk and dosage of treatment. *Criminal Justice and Behavior* 40(3), 338–348.

Another new exciting line of research focused on these principles is around the dosage of treatment required to reduce recidivism. While many have argued that higher-risk offenders should receive "intensive" services, until recently the question of what constitutes intensive programming has remained undefined. Sperber et al. (2013) examined the effects of increasing the hours of cognitive behavioral treatment that adult male felons received in a community-based facility. Figure 5.4 shows that increasing the dosage of treatment for moderate-risk offenders results in a modest reduction in recidivism; however, when dosage was increased for high-risk offenders, the reductions were more substantial. This research clearly indicates that we cannot continue to have "one-size-fits-all" programs for offenders.

Gendreau (1996) has also listed those interventions that have not been found to be effective in reducing recidivism:

- talking cures;
- nondirective, relationship-oriented therapy;
- traditional medical model approaches;
- intensive services directed to low-risk offenders;
- intensive services oriented to noncriminogenic needs (or factors unrelated to future criminal behavior).

One example of a program that was not effective in reducing recidivism is found in Box 5.1. In a review of substance abuse treatment, Lightfoot (1999) identified effective and ineffective types of treatment. Interestingly, the types of effective and ineffective treatment models for substance abusers mirror findings from studies of other offender types. Taxman (2000) made similar conclusions after reviewing the research on substance abuse treatment. Her findings are summarized in Table 5.2.

Box 5.1
Acupuncture Treatment for Drug-dependent Offenders

Acupuncture is defined as "the Chinese medical art of inserting fine needles into the skin to relieve pain or disability" (Wensel, 1990, p. 5). A number of advocates claim that acupuncture can be an effective remedy for drug addiction (Smith et al., 1982, 1984). In 1992, Latessa and Moon published results from a study they conducted on an outpatient drug treatment program for felony probationers. Program participants were divided randomly into three groups: an experimental group, which received acupuncture on a regular basis; a control group, which did not receive acupuncture; and a placebo group, which received an acupuncture-like simulation. They concluded that "With regard to outcome there is no evidence that acupuncture had any appreciable effect on program completion, arrests, convictions, or probation outcome" (1992, p. 330).

Source: Latessa and Moon (1992).

Table 5.2 Review of Drug Treatment Effectiveness by Taxman (2000)

What treatment types were successful at reducing recidivism?
- Directive counseling
- Behavior modification
- Therapeutic community
- Moral reasoning
- Social competency cognitive behavior models
- Emotional skill development
- Cognitive skills
- Behavioral skills

What treatment types showed no clear evidence of effectiveness of reduced recidivism?
- Nondirective counseling
- Reality therapy
- Psychosocial education
- 12-step or other self-help groups
- Psychoanalytical

Source: Taxman, F. (2000). Unraveling "what works" for offenders in substance abuse treatment services. *National Drug Court Institute Review* 2 (2).

Despite the stereotypical belief that nothing works, many studies show that substance abuse treatment can be effective in reducing recidivism rates. The research on substance abuse treatment can be summarized as follows:

- There is no "magic bullet"—no one treatment approach works with everyone.
- In general, treatment is superior to no treatment.
- Drug addiction is a chronic relapsing condition. Applying short-term, education-based treatment services will not reduce it effectively. Treatment should be at least 100 hours of direct service over a period of three to four months; however, intensive treatment programs lasting more than one year might begin to see diminishing results.
- Traditional models used by substance abuse programs, such as drug/alcohol education and 12-step programs, have not been found to be as effective as cognitive-behavioral models.
- Aftercare services increase treatment effectiveness.
- Criminality is a significant factor that independently affects a treatment outcome.

It appears from these summaries that the most effective approaches are based on cognitive–behavioral, social learning approaches, and skill-building techniques rather than talk therapy and self-help approaches.

PAROLE EFFECTIVENESS

What is actually known about the effectiveness of probation and parole, and other community correctional alternatives, and what should be future research priorities? The next section summarizes what is generally concluded about selected topic areas of interest in parole effectiveness. This discussion of topic areas is basically organized along the general flow of criminal justice decision points as they relate to parole; however, most of the findings also pertain to probation, particularly those on supervision and innovative programs.

Institutional Factors

Several aspects of the institutional experience are thought to be related to parole and its effectiveness, such as length of time incarcerated, prison behavior, institutional programs, and parole conditions imposed as conditions of release.

Time Served

Early research that examined the effects of the amount of time served in prison on parole has generally concluded that the shorter the amount of time served, the greater the likelihood of successful parole (Eichman, 1965; Gottfredson et al., 1977).

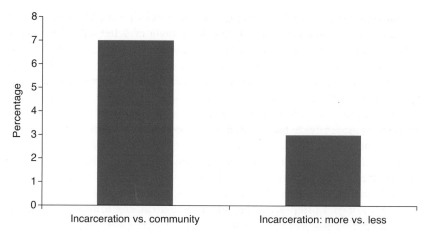

Figure 5.5 Percent Increase in Recidivism by Type of Sanction.

Source: Smith, P., Goggin, C., Gendreau, P. (2002). *The effects of prison sentences and interme-diate sanctions on recidivism: general effects and individual differences.* A Report to the Corrections Research Branch. Ottawa, Ontario: Solicitor General of Canada.

Similarly, Smith et al. (2002) conducted a meta-analysis of the prison literature. Results included a total of 27 studies comparing community-based offenders (e.g., probationers) to inmates, as well as 23 studies comparing prisoners who served longer sentences with prisoners who served shorter sentences. Results indicated that offenders who were imprisoned had recidivism rates approximately 7 percent higher than community-based offenders, and inmates who served longer sentences had a recidivism rate that was 3 percent higher than inmates with shorter sentences. Figure 5.5 shows these results.

Most researchers, however, have concluded that longer prison terms have an adverse effect on a parolee's chances of success, implying that the negative aspects of prisonization seem to intensify with time. For example, in his study of **shock probationers**, Vito (1978) concluded that even a short period of incarceration has a negative impact. The question that remains unanswered by this research is: Are there any characteristics of inmates who have served more time that are also associated with an unfavorable parole outcome?

Prison Programs

Does participation in prison programs have an effect on recidivism? Existing research on the effectiveness of institutional programs and prison behavior has been limited in its scope. Most such programs are analyzed in relation to institutional adjustment, disciplinary problems, and impact of program participation on the parole-granting process. The few evaluations that included a parole period usually show little if any positive effects with regard to recidivism. A study by

Smith and Gendreau (2007), however, examined the relationship between program participation and recidivism in a Canadian sample of 5,469 federal offenders. Results indicated that programs targeting criminogenic needs reduced postrelease recidivism by 9 percent for moderate-risk offenders and 11 percent for high-risk offenders. German correctional researchers evaluated the effectiveness of social therapy programs across eight prisons, and the results were remarkably similar (Egg et al., 2000). The overall average reduction in recidivism for what is generally described as moderate- to high-risk adult incarcerates was 12 percent.

Most research that has examined prison behavior has not found a relationship between prison behavior and success on parole (Morris, 1978; von Hirsch & Hanrahan, 1979). However, a study by Gottfredson et al. (1982) found that there is some relation between institutional infractions and infractions while on parole, after controlling for prior record. French and Gendreau (2006) also examined the relationship between participation in prison-based programs and misconducts/postrelease recidivism using meta-analytic techniques. Prison-based programs targeting criminogenic needs reduced misconducts by 26 percent and reduced postrelease recidivism by 14 percent (French & Gendreau, 2006). Overall, however, there has not been a great deal of attention given to the relationship among institutional programs, prison behavior, and subsequent success or failure on parole.

Work and Education Programs

Two areas that have received some attention are work and education programs for offenders. Although the literature on education programs over the years has found mixed results, evidence does seem to suggest that educational programs can affect inmate behavior and recidivism positively (Ayers et al., 1980; Eskridge & Newbold, 1994; Linden & Perry, 1982; Roberts & Cheek, 1994; Wilson et al., 2000; Aos et al., 2006; Davis et al., 2013). For example, in several meta-analyses, the reductions in recidivism for inmates who participated in correctional education programs ranged from 11 percent (Wilson et al., 2000) to 13 percent in a more recent study (Davis et al., 2013). While the research on correctional education programs has mostly been positive, studies on prison work programs do not convincingly demonstrate reduced recidivism (Vito, 1985b; Zeisel, 1982; MacKenzie & Hickman, 1998; Bouffard et al., 2000; MacKenzie, 2012). At least one meta-analysis found that correctional industries were effective (Aos, 2005); however, the results were based on only three studies. Gendreau and Ross (1987), however, do provide some principles that should be followed with regard to work programs: (1) they must enhance practical skills, (2) develop interpersonal skills and minimize prisonization, and (3) ensure that work is not intended as punishment alone.

Therapeutic Communities

In recent years, prison-based **therapeutic communities** (TCs) have made a resurgence (see Box 5.2). This is due in part to increased federal funding. Although

Box 5.2
Therapeutic Communities

Therapeutic communities, or TCs as they are commonly known, are eclectic in nature and offer an intense self-help model that focuses on the whole person. Staff and offenders are intimately involved in the treatment process. Confrontation and accountability are key ingredients of a TC. Offenders who engage in appropriate behavior are given "pull-ups" (positive reinforcement) by other offenders and staff, while those who engage in behavior detrimental to them or others are given "haircuts" (confronted about their behavior). One of the criticisms leveled at TCs is their use of shaming and other degrading sanctions. For example, some TCs have been known to have offenders wear diapers like a baby, sit in chairs for long periods of time, wear dunce hats, and hand out other punishments designed to change the behavior of the participant.] - limitation of TCs

there is a great deal of variation in how therapeutic communities operate, the essential ingredient is the principle that all staff and offenders provide therapeutic experiences. TCs are more common in prisons, but many operate in community-based facilities, such as halfway houses.]

[A number of studies have shown that TCs can have an appreciable effect on recidivism rates, especially when community follow-up aftercare is provided](see Knight et al., 1999; Martin et al., 1999; Wexler et al., 1999). Figure 5.6 shows results from one such program operating in Delaware.

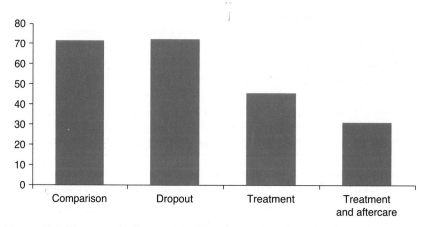

Figure 5.6 Therapeutic Community Treatment: Arrest Rates after a Three-year Follow-up (percent arrested).

Source: Martin, S., Butzin, C., Saum, C., Inciardi, J. (1999). Three-year outcomes of therapeutic community treatment for drug-involved offenders in Delaware. *The Prison Journal* 79, 294–320.

Faith-based Programs

One of former President George W. Bush's initiatives was the expansion of faith-based programs in human service. While faith-based programs have a long history in corrections, there has been surprisingly little empirical research conducted on their effectiveness, and results are mixed. Religious programs in prisons may help inmates cope; however, research indicates that offenders who had poor coping skills prior to prison have poor coping skills in prison (Porporino & Zamble, 1984). Since 1985, at least 23 studies have explored the relationship between religion and deviance in the general population. Eighteen of those studies show evidence that religiosity reduces deviance (i.e., people of strong faith are generally less criminal than nonbelievers); however, this does not appear to translate well into correctional programming.

Two studies have examined effects of religious participation on institutional adjustment and infractions. In 1984, Johnson studied 782 inmates in Florida. Results indicated no differences in disciplinary problems or institutional adjustment for religious and nonreligious inmates. In 1992, Clear and his colleagues studied a nonrandom sample of 769 inmates in 20 prisons in 12 states. They concluded that a prisoner's religious participation had a significant and positive relationship to prison adjustment. They also found that other factors, such as age and race of offender, played a role.

Similarly, three studies have examined religion and post-release behavior. In 1987, Johnson and colleagues studied inmates released from four adult male prisons in New York. One group participated in the Prison Fellowship Program (PFP); one did not. Results from this research indicated that the level of participation influenced prison adjustment; however, the direction was not always as anticipated:

- Participants with a high level of involvement in PFP were less likely to commit infractions than low- or moderate-level participants.
- However, high-PFP participants received more serious infractions.
- High-PFP participants were significantly less likely to be rearrested during the follow-up, but this relationship was strongest for whites and non-significant for African Americans.

Young et al. (1995) followed a group of 180 federal inmates trained as volunteer prison ministers who attended special seminars and a matched control group. Overall, the seminar group had a significantly lower rate of recidivism and maintained a higher survival rate than the control group. Seminars were most effective with lower-risk subjects, whites, and women.

A study by Sumter (1999) followed inmates from the Clear et al. (1992) study. There were no differences in the recidivism rates between "religious" and "nonreligious" inmates; furthermore, regardless of how many times they attended chapel, inmates who had a greater religious orientation in terms of values were less likely to recidivate. Sumter also found that offenders who attended religious programs upon release were less likely to recidivate; however, no relationship existed between attending inside and outside prison. Participation in religious programs was certainly no panacea: 66 percent of "religious" prisoners experienced one or more arrests in the follow-up period. Sumter concluded that religion as a correctional program is complicated and multifaceted—as personal as it is social—and becomes more complicated in a prison setting. Inmates embrace religion for a number of reasons, some heartening (spirituality and coping mechanism) and some cynical (get snacks, time out of cell, more freedom, looks good for parole). What we do know is that prisons distort everything. What may seem like a quest for spiritual awakening on the surface can simply be a way to get around the strictures of confinement. Related to this is the fact that we have little understanding of precisely how religion works or what the best definition of "religious" might be (conversion, weekly service attendance, number of books read in Bible study, punitive vs. redemptive orientation, or frequency of participation in religious rites such as attending church, participation in services, tithing, frequency of prayer, or proselytizing). Regardless of the findings on faith-based correctional programs, most of us would agree that pursuit of religious understanding is a basic human right—prisoners who wish to engage in spiritual expression should be encouraged to do so, but this is true regardless of what the research finds. It does not mean that faith-based programs will have a significant effect on recidivism rates.

Given all the contradictions from the research, it is often difficult to determine what, if any, effects prison-based treatment has on offender behavior. In a large study conducted by researchers in Washington State (Aos et al., 1999), the research examined all the available studies and conducted a meta-

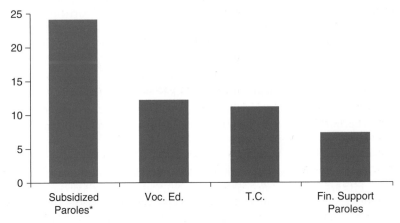

*This effect was for inmates over 27 years of age. There was no effect for younger adults.

Figure 5.7 Washington State Study of the Average Effect Sizes of Prison Programs (average percent reduction in recidivism).

Source: Aos, S., Phipps, P., Barnoski, R., Lieb, R. (1999). *The comparative costs and benefits of programs to reduce crime: a review of national research findings with implications for Washington State*. Olympia, WA: Washington State Institute for Public Policy.

analysis to determine effect sizes on recidivism. As can be seen in Figure 5.7, they found that some programs produced reductions in recidivism, with subsidizing jobs for offenders aged 27 and over producing reductions of 24 percent.

Parole Conditions

Offenders who are granted parole are required to follow rules and conditions. Failure to do so can lead to reincarceration. With regard to the imposition of parole conditions, in a nationwide survey of 52 parolee field supervision agencies, Allen and Latessa (1980) found 49 had residency requirements as a condition of parole and 47 had an employment requirement. A Travis and Latessa (1984) survey found similar results. In a 1995 review, Hartman and colleagues found that there was a discernible movement away from treatment requirements toward conditions aimed at strengthening surveillance and control. In the most recent survey, Travis and Stacey (2010) found a substantially greater number of conditions imposed than those reported by Hartman et al. (1996), with an average of 18.6 conditions for each jurisdiction ranging from a low of 10 to a high of 24. Travis and Stacey concluded that "current parole rules reflect current and emerging technologies (drug testing, bans of possession of police radio scanners, etc.), and changing views of crime and criminals including an increased emphasis on financial responsibility for offenders (payment of fees and restitution), and risk control (reporting and home visits)."

Despite the widespread requirement of parole conditions, the literature produced only three studies that were directly related to the imposition of these conditions and parole effectiveness. Although two studies (Beasley, 1978; Morgan, 1993) showed a relationship between stability of residency and parole success, the lack of research in this area makes generalization difficult.

One of the most important conditions of parole is the requirement to report regularly to a parole officer and not to leave a prescribed area, such as the county, without permission. Offenders who fail to report or whose whereabouts are unknown are called absconders. A study by Williams et al. (2000) found that 27 percent of parolees in California were listed as absconders, and another study conducted by Schwaner (1997) in Ohio found 11 percent. Absconders have problems with alcohol abuse, have been convicted of a property crime, and have a history of prior parole violation and absence of suitable housing (Buckholtz & Foos, 1996). Despite these high numbers of absconders, there has been little research on this subject.

Parole Release

Primarily in response to the supporters of determinate sentencing, researchers have increasingly turned their attention to evaluating the success of parole supervision.

Critics of parole supervision rely on two basic arguments to support their views. The first is that parole supervision is simply not effective in reducing recidivism (Citizens' Inquiry on Parole and Criminal Justice, 1975; Wilson, 1977). The second, more philosophical argument is that supervision is not "just" (von Hirsch & Hanrahan, 1979). A more plausible conclusion is that the evidence is mixed; that parole supervision is effective in reducing recidivism rates among parolees (Flanagan, 1985).

Several studies have compared parolees to mandatory releases, but they have failed to control for possible differences in the selection of the groups (Martinson & Wilks, 1977). Other studies that controlled for differences have reported favorable results (Gottfredson, 1975; Lerner, 1977), whereas other studies have reported less positive results (Jackson, 1983; Nuttal et al., 1977; Waller, 1974). In one study, Gottfredson et al. (1982, p. 292) concluded that "much of our data does indicate an effect for parole supervision, an effect that varies by offender attributes, and an effect that appears not to be very large." In a recent study, Pew (2013) found that New Jersey parolees were less likely to be rearrested, reconvicted, and reincarcerated for new crimes than inmates who maxed out their full sentences and were released without supervision. Despite its widespread use, little is actually known about whether parole reduces recidivism. We do know that about half of parole discharges successfully complete parole. In a 2005 study of parole, the Urban Institute concluded that parole supervision has little effect on rearrest rates of released prisoners (Solomon et al., 2005). The existing evidence seems to be mixed concerning parole supervision, and there is no clear consensus as to its effectiveness.

Even the most outspoken critics of parole agree that the agencies responsible for the task of supervision are often understaffed and that their officers are undertrained, underpaid, and overworked. They are inundated with excessively large caseloads, workloads, and paperwork. Community services are either unavailable or unwilling to handle parolees; as a consequence, parole officers are expected to be all things to all people. As indicated in Chapter 7, they are also expected to perform the dual roles of surveillance–police officer and rehabilitator–treatment agent.

Some evidence suggests that by shortening the amount of time on parole, we could save a considerable amount of money and time while not seriously increasing the risk of failure. Most data seem to indicate that the majority of failures on parole occur during the first two years (Flanagan, 1982; Hoffman & Stone-Meierhoefer, 1980; Durose et al., 2014) and drop significantly thereafter. There is also some evidence that early release into the community and from parole incurs no higher risk to the community and, in fact, is justifiable on cost considerations (Holt, 1975), a conclusion echoed by MacKenzie and Piquero (1994). It is also important to note that easing the offender back into the community through community residential centers and furlough programs can facilitate the early release process. The definition and purpose of community residential centers and furloughs are found in Boxes 5.3 and 5.4, respectively.

Box 5.3
Community Residential Centers

Community residential centers (also known as halfway houses) are residential facilities where probationers, furloughees, and parolees may be placed when in need of a more structured setting. The primary purpose of a halfway house is to limit an offender's freedom while encouraging reintegration into society through employment, education, treatment, habilitation, restitution, training, compliance with financial sanctions, and other activities designed to rehabilitate the offender and deter future crime (Ohio Community Corrections Organization, 1993).

Box 5.4
Furloughs

Furlough is a phased re-entry program designed to ease the offender's transition from prison to the community. Furloughs include escorted or unescorted leaves from confinement, granted for designated purposes and time periods (funerals, dying relatives, etc.), before the formal sentence expires. Used primarily for employment, vocational training, or education, furlough in effect extends the limits of confinement to include temporary residence in the community during the last months of confinement. Furloughees are frequently required to reside in community residential centers. Furloughs allow parole boards to observe the offender's behavior in the community and may lead to faster release from parole supervision for those adjusting favorably. Because furloughees are closely screened and supervised in the community, failure rates appear to be low. For example, Ohio reports a 9 percent return to prison rate for the calendar 1992 (Ohio Community Corrections Organization, 1993).

A Washington State (1976) 10-year follow-up of parolees found that the first year of parole was critical, with more than one-half of those paroled returning to prison during this time period. In this study, there were more failures in the second six months after release than in the first. It was also found that those convicted of murder and manslaughter were less likely to recidivate and that property offenders—especially those convicted of burglary, auto theft, and forgery—had the highest failure rate. As expected, younger parolees did significantly worse than those 40 years of age or older. Blacks did slightly worse than whites after the first six months, and Native Americans did significantly worse than all other groups.

It is important to note that many of the failures on parole supervision are a result of technical violations (TVs); that is, failure to abide by the conditions imposed by the parole board. TVs can range from a positive drug test to failure to

Table 5.3 Age of Parolees and Likelihood of Failure

Age at time of prison release	Rate of return to prison by years after release from prison						
	Years						
	1	**2**	**3**	**4**	**5**	**6**	**7**
18–24 years	21%	34%	41%	45%	48%	49%	50%
25–34	12	21	28	33	37	41	43
35–44	7	14	18	22	26	30	34
45+	2	4	6	8	10	11	12
All ages	14	23	29	34	37	40	42

Source: Adapted from Beck, A. (1987). *Recidivism of young parolees*. Washington, DC: Bureau of Justice Statistics Special Report.

report as directed. Some states have implemented new policies to help reduce returns to prison for technical violations. For example, California's new realignment law requires nonviolent parolees to be supervised by local probation departments and requires violators to be placed in jail rather than sent back to prison. Studies of parole success by type of offense indicate repeatedly that those who commit murder are among the best parole risks (Neithercutt, 1972). Reasons for this conclusion vary; the explanation offered most frequently is that most murderers tend to be first offenders who have committed crimes of passion. Another reason cited is age; because most convicted murderers spend a great amount of time incarcerated, they tend to be older (and more mature) when released, usually after the high-crime-risk years of 18–29 (see Table 5.3).

In a study of murderers who had been given a death sentence and then had that sentence commuted when *Furman v. Georgia* was overturned, Vito et al. (1991) found that 43.5 percent of death row inmates in Ohio were paroled and that 25 percent were returned to prison (recidivated). These results were very similar to those found in Texas, where 19 percent of the paroled *Furman* cases recidivated (Marquart & Sorensen, 1988), and in Kentucky, which had a 29 percent failure rate (Vito & Wilson, 1988). Overall, studies examining murderers were found to generate consistent findings and conclusions over time.

A study by Austin (2001, p. 331) examined the important issue of prisoner re-entry. He concluded: "it is not clear that parolees, in the aggregate, pose as large a public safety problem as some believe."

In order to summarize, we have selected data from a national study of parole recidivism (Beck, 1987). These data confirm two important points with regard to parole effectiveness: (1) recidivism rates vary depending on the definition of recidivism, and (2) the type of offense and age are important factors in determining parole success (Table 5.4). Other findings included the following:

- Approximately 10 percent of the persons paroled accounted for 40 percent of the subsequent arrest offenses.

- About one-fifth of the subsequent arrests occurred in states other than the original paroling state.
- An estimated 37 percent of the parolees were rearrested while still on parole.
- Recidivism rates were highest in the first two years after an offender's release from prison. Within one year, 32 percent of those paroled had been arrested; within two years, 47 percent had been rearrested.
- Recidivism was higher among men, blacks, and persons who had not completed high school than among women, whites, and high school graduates.
- Almost three-quarters of those paroled for property offenses were rearrested for a serious crime compared to about two-thirds of those paroled for violent offenses.
- Approximately one-third of both property offenders and violent offenders were rearrested for a violent crime upon release from prison.

Table 5.4 Failure Rates of Parolees

Percent of Young Parolees who within Six Years of Release from Prison Were

	Rearrested	Reconvicted	Reincarcerated
All Parolees:	69%	53%	49%
Sex:			
Male	70%	54%	50%
Female	52	40	36
Race:			
White	64%	49%	45%
Black	76	60	56
Hispanic	71	50	44
Other	75	65	63
Education:			
Less than 12 years	71%	55%	51%
High school graduate	61	46	43
Some college	48	44	31
Paroling offense:			
Violent offense	64%	43%	39%
Murder	70	25	22
Robbery	64	45	40
Assault	72	51	47
Property offense:	73	60	56
Burglary	73	60	56
Forgery/fraud	74	59	56
Larceny	71	61	55
Drug offense	49%	30%	25%

Source: Adapted from Beck, A. (1987). *Recidivism of young parolees*. Washington, DC: Bureau of Justice Statistics Special Report.

- The longer the parolee's prior arrest record, the higher the rate of recidivism—more than 90 percent of parolees with six or more previous adult arrests were rearrested compared to 59 percent of first-time offenders.
- The earlier the parolee's first adult arrest, the more likely the chances for rearrest—79 percent of those arrested and charged as an adult before the age of 17 were rearrested compared to 51 percent of those first arrested at the age of 20 or older.
- Time served in prison had no consistent impact on recidivism rates—those who had served six months or less in prison were about as likely to be arrested as those who had served more than two years.

In a study of parolees in Pennsylvania, Bucklen and Zajac (2009) found that criminogenic factors were the most important determinants of success or failure while on parole. Table 5.5 shows some of the major findings from this study. These

Table 5.5 Results from Pennsylvania Study of Parole

Violators were:

- More likely to hang around with individuals with criminal backgrounds
- Less likely to live with a spouse
- Less likely to be in a stable supportive relationship
- Less likely to identify someone in their life who served in a mentoring capacity
- Less likely to have job stability
- Less likely to be satisfied with employment
- Less likely to take low-end jobs and work up
- More likely to have negative attitudes toward employment and unrealistic job expectations
- Less likely to have a bank account
- More likely to report that they were "barely making it" (yet success group reported over double median debt)
- More likely to report use of alcohol or other drugs while on parole (but no difference in prior assessment of dependency problem)
- Poor management of stress was a primary contributing factor to relapse
- Had poor problem-solving or coping skills
- Did not anticipate long-term consequences of behavior
- Failed to utilize resources to help themselves
- Acted impulsively to immediate situations
- Felt they were not in control
- More likely to maintain antisocial attitudes
- Viewed violations as an acceptable option to situation
- Maintained general lack of empathy
- Shifted blame or denied responsibility
- Had unrealistic expectations about what life would be like outside of prison

Source: Adapted from Bucklen, K.B., Zajac, G. (2009). Success and failure deprivation and thinking errors as determinants of parole but some of them don't come back (to prison!). *Prison Journal* 89, 239–264.

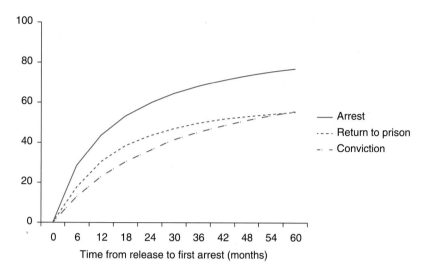

Figure 5.8 Study of Recidivism of Prisoners Released in 30 states in 2005.

Source: Durose, M.R., Cooper, A.D., Snyder, H. (2014). *Recidivism of prisoners released in 30 states in 2005: patterns from 2005 to 2010.* Washington, DC: U.S. Department of Justice, Office of Justice Programs, Bureau of Justice Statistics.

findings are consistent with the research on risk factors and the importance of targeting criminogenic areas of offenders. Not surprisingly, successes and failures did not differ in difficulty in finding a place to live after release and were equally likely to report eventually obtaining a job.

In the most recent study of recidivism of prisoners released in 30 states in 2005 (Durose et al., 2014), the Bureau of Justice Statistics found very high rates of failure when measured by arrest, return to prison, and convictions. Especially concerning is that almost 68 percent were rearrested for new crimes within three years, and almost 77 percent within five years. This study included both parolees and those released without post-release supervision. Figure 5.8 illustrates these results.

PROBATION EFFECTIVENESS

As with parole, the quality of probation research is dubious. Unlike parole, which is found on state and federal levels, probation still remains primarily a local governmental function. Facts are that (1) probation can be found at local, state, and federal levels; (2) there are municipal and county probation departments; probation (as with parole) often combines other sanctions and programs (such as electronic monitoring, referral to treatment programs, halfway houses, day reporting, etc.), and (3) probation serves both misdemeanants and felons. These, combined with the problems discussed previously, make research in probation very difficult to conduct. Indeed, much of the research has been limited to only the several probation departments to which researchers have been welcome. This event gives us a limited sense of the true picture of probation.

As with parole, the research on probation effectiveness is divided into sections. However, unlike our presentation of parole, the research on probation is divided into five groups: studies that (1) compare the performance of offenders receiving alternative dispositions; (2) simply measure probation outcome without comparison with any other form of sanction; (3) measure probation outcome and then attempt to isolate the characteristics which tend to differentiate between successful and nonsuccessful outcomes; (4) examine the cost-effectiveness of probation; and (5) examine probation combined with therapeutic drug courts.

Probation versus Alternative Dispositions

To examine the effectiveness of probation compared with other dispositions, we looked at six studies. Three of the studies compared recidivism rates of individuals placed on probation with individuals sentenced to incarceration. Babst and Mannering's (1965) study compared similar types of offenders who were imprisoned or placed on probation. The sample consisted of 7,614 Wisconsin offenders who were statistically comparable in original disposition, county of commitment, type of offense committed, number of prior felonies, and marital status. Parolees were followed for two years, and probationers were followed for two years or until discharge from probation, whichever came first. Violations were defined as the commission of a new offense or the violation of probation/parole rules. Findings of this study showed that, for offenders with no prior felony convictions, the violation rate was 25 percent for probationers and 32.9 percent for parolees. For offenders with one prior felony conviction, violation rates were 41.8 percent for probationers and 43.9 percent for parolees; for offenders with two or more felonies, rates were 51.8 percent for probationers and 48.7 percent for parolees. With respect to the difference in violation rates for first offenders, Babst and Mannering note that this finding could be a result of the fact that parolees are a more difficult group to supervise or could actually show that, at least for first offenders, incarceration does more harm than good.

Another study done in Wisconsin (Wisconsin Division of Corrections, 1965) compared the performance of burglars who had no previous felony convictions, sentenced to prison, or placed on probation. While this study also attempted to investigate the characteristics associated with successful and nonsuccessful probationers and parolees, we simply report at this point that the violation rate (based on a two-year follow-up, using the same definition of violation rate as Babst and Mannering described earlier) for burglars placed on probation was 23 percent, whereas that for burglars who were incarcerated and then placed on parole was 34 percent. Thus, it appears that, as with the Wisconsin study, probation was more successful than parole.

The Pennsylvania Program for Women and Girl Offenders, Inc. (1976) compared recidivism rates among all women placed on state probation or released on state parole during a two-year period. Recidivism was defined as any technical violation of probation or parole or any new criminal charge. Findings showed that, overall, women placed on probation had a 35.6 percent recidivism rate. When only women with no prior convictions were considered, probationers had a 24 percent recidivism rate and parolees had a 23.1 percent rate. Differences between these rates were not significant.

Vito (1978) compared regular probationers with shock probationers (who served at least 30 days in prison). He found that shock probationers had a 40 percent higher probability of failure than those released to regular supervision. Vito and Allen (1981, p. 16) concluded that:

> the fact of incarceration is having some unknown and unmeasurable effect upon (the more unfavorable) performance of shock probationers. . . . It could be that the negative effects of incarceration are affecting the performance of shock probationers.

Whereas these four studies compared probation with some form of incarceration, a California study (California Department of Justice, 1969) compared violation rates among offenders placed on probation, offenders sentenced to probation following a jail term, and offenders given straight jail sentences. The study examined the performance of a cohort of offenders, all of whom had an equal exposure of one full year in the community. For the probation group, cohort status was gained on the date of the beginning of the probation period; for the group receiving jail sentences, cohort status began on the date of release from jail. To evaluate the relative effectiveness of these dispositions, three violation levels were used: "none" or no known arrest for a technical violation or a new offense, "minor" or at least an arrest and perhaps a conviction resulting in a jail sentence of less than 90 days or probation of one year or less, and "major," signifying at least a conviction resulting in a jail sentence of not less than 90 days or a term of probation exceeding one year. Because each case was followed for only one year, the final outcome of a violation occasionally did not occur until after the year was over. If it could be inferred that the disposition or sentence was the result of an arrest that did occur within the follow-up year, the action was included in the violation rate.

The findings of this study are illustrated in Table 5.6. Those offenders receiving jail sentences without the benefit of probation services have the worst record of recidivism.

Table 5.6 Violation Levels of Sentenced Offenders in California

Violations

Sentence	None	Minor	Major
Probation only	64.7%	23.7%	11.6%
Jail, then probation	50.3%	31.7%	18.0%
Jail only	46.6%	29.5%	23.9%

Source: California Department of Justice (1969). *Superior court probation and/or jail sample: one-year follow-up for selected counties.* Sacramento, CA: Division of Law Enforcement, Bureau of Criminal Statistics.

These studies illustrate that, as a disposition, probation appears to be more effective than incarceration, even for a short period of time. This may be due, in part, to the fact that probationers immediately return to the community, their jobs, and their families.

Finally, an Alaska study (Alaska Department of Health and Social Services, 1976) utilized an experimental design to compare the performance of misdemeanant offenders receiving probation supervision with offenders officially on probation but not required to report to the probation unit. The groups were created by random assignment to the experimental group (under supervision) or the control group (no supervision) and were followed for periods ranging from two months to slightly more than two years. Performance was assessed by means of recidivism, defined as the conviction for a new offense. Findings of the study showed that 22 percent of experimental group members and 24 of control group members had been convicted of new offenses during the follow-up period.

Given the paucity of research and the caution with which recidivism data must be approached, it is nearly impossible, not to mention inappropriate, to attempt to draw any definitive conclusions from these studies about the effectiveness of probation compared to other alternative dispositions. Nonetheless, it appears from the limited research that has been conducted that the following tentative conclusions can be reached. Of studies that compared probation to incarceration, it tentatively appears that probation may have a significant impact on first offenders. It may also be suggested that the severity of violations appears to increase in proportion to the severity of the disposition. It does not appear that the provision of probation supervision for misdemeanants is more effective than an unsupervised probation period.

Probation Outcome

In a large-scale study of probation and other community correctional programs used in conjunction with supervision, Lowenkamp et al. (2006) examined community correctional programs, including intensive supervision probation, day reporting centers, and electronic monitoring programs, and found that programs that targeted higher-risk offenders and provided treatment and services were more effective than those that did not. When higher-risk offenders were targeted and given increased supervision and more services, there were reductions in recidivism. Table 5.7 and Figure 5.9 illustrate these findings. They also examined the quality of the programming, and found that high-quality supervision programs had the most effect on recidivism. Figure 5.10 shows that poorly designed and implemented probation programs actually increased recidivism while high-quality, well-implemented programs were the most effective.

Lowenkamp and his colleagues (2010) also examined the effects of the philosophy of the probation department (control-oriented or service-oriented) and found that the most effective probation departments were those that had a rehabilitation orientation. Figure 5.11 shows these results.

Table 5.7 Type of Community Supervision Program did not matter: Four Factors were Significantly Related to Outcome

---

■ Proportion of higher-risk offenders in program (at least 75% of offenders in programs were moderate- or high-risk)
■ Level of supervision for higher-risk offenders (high-risk offenders averaged longer periods of supervision than low-risk offenders)
■ More treatment for higher-risk offenders (at least 50% more time spent in treatment)
■ More referrals for services for higher-risk offenders (at least three referrals for every one received by low risk)

Source: Lowenkamp, C.T., Pealer J., Smith, P., Latessa., E.J. (2006). Adhering to the risk and need principles: does it matter for supervision-based programs? *Federal Probation* 70(3), 3–8.

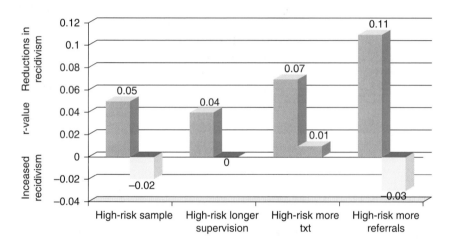

Figure 5.9 Changes in Recidivism for Probation Programs.

Source: Lowenkamp, C., Pealer J., Smith, P, Latessa, E. (2006). Adhering to the risk and need principles: does it matter for supervision-based programs? *Federal Probation* 70(3).

A number of studies reported recidivism rates only for probationers. Thirteen of these were reviewed, but one should remember that definitions of failure, follow-up periods, and types of offenders differ significantly from one study to another. Table 5.8 includes the author, types of instant offenses committed by the probationers in the study, and the definition of failure used in the study, the length of follow-up, and failure rates.

These summary descriptions illustrate many of the problems associated with attempting to assess probation effectiveness. The types of offenders constituting the samples (as represented by instant offenses) vary, as do the definitions used in each study to characterize failure. Four studies computed failure rates while

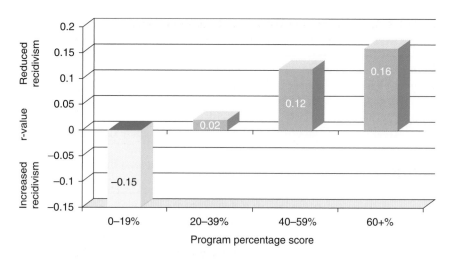

Figure 5.10 Program Integrity—Relationship Between Program Integrity Score and Treatment Effect for Community Supervision Programs.

Source: Lowenkamp, C.T., Latessa, E.J. (2005). *Evaluation of Ohio's CCA Programs.* Cincinnati, OH: Center for Criminal Justice Research, University of Cincinnati.

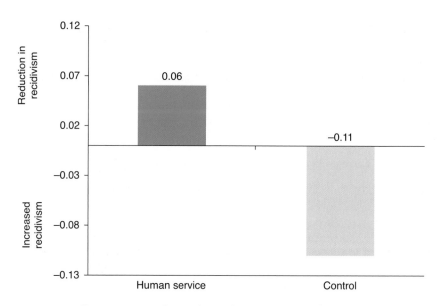

Figure 5.11 Changes in Recidivism by Probation Department Philosophy.

Source: Lowenkamp, C., Flores, A., Holsinger, H., Makarios, M., Latessa, E. (2010). Intensive supervision programs: Does program philosophy and the principles of effective intervention matter? *Journal of Criminal Justice* 38, 368–375.

Table 5.8 Studies Reporting Recidivism Rates for Probationers

Study	Instant offense	Failure	Follow-up	Failure rate (%)
Caldwell (1951)	Internal revenue laws (72%)	Convictions	Postprobation 5.5–11.5 years	16.4
England (1955)	Bootlegging (48%) and forgery	Convictions	Postprobation 6–12 years	17.7
Davis (1955)	Burglary, forgery, and checks	Two or more violations (technical and new offense)	To termination 4–7 years	30.2
Frease (1964)	Unknown	Inactive letter, bench warrant, and revocation	On probation 18–30 months	20.2
Landis et al. (1969)	Auto theft, forgery, and checks	Revocation (technical and new offense)	To termination	52.5
Irish (1972)	Larceny and burglary	Arrests or convictions	Postprobation Minimum 4 years	41.5
Missouri Div. Probation & Parole (1976)	Burglary, larceny, and vehicle theft	Arrests and convictions	Postprobation 6 months– 7 years	30.0
Kusuda (1976)	Property	Revocation	To termination 1–2 years	18.3
Comptroller General (1976)	Unknown	Revocation and postrelease conviction	Postprobation 20 months average	55.0
Irish (1972)	Property	Arrests	Postprobation 3–4 years	29.6
Petersilla (1985)	Felony probationers	Arrests	Tracked over 40 months	65.0
McGaha et al. (1987)	Felony probationers	Arrests	Tracked over 40 months	22.3
Vito (1986)	Felony probationers (excluding drug offenses)	Arrests	Tracked over 40 months	22.0
Maxwell et al. (2000)	Felony probationers	Revoked	Tracked over 30 months	47.0

Source: Adapted and updated from Allen, H., Carlson, E., Parks, E. (1979). *Critical issues in adult probation*. Washington, DC: National Institute of Law Enforcement and Criminal Justice.

offenders were on probation, and the length of follow-up periods ranged from several months to many years.

Most of the studies reviewed here stated that their purpose was to assess "probation effectiveness"; however, unlike the five studies examined earlier, none of these studies defined a base (such as a failure rate for comparable parolees or offenders on summary probation) against which to compare findings in order to support a claim that probation is an effective alternative for rehabilitating offenders.

In a study of 1,700 probationers in Michigan, Maxwell and colleagues (2000) found that only 24 percent of probationers had no technical violations during a 30-month follow-up period. Results are summarized in Figure 5.12. Treatment-related violations, such as dirty urine or failing to attend treatment programs, accounted for the largest proportion of violations, followed by failure to appear. Only 13 percent of the violations were for a new crime.

MacKenzie et al. (1999) studied the impact of probation on the criminal activities of offenders. They concluded that probation alone had an effect on property and dealing crimes. Probation was not significantly associated with reductions in personal crimes of forgery and fraud offenses. The conclusion reached by the authors was that "probation may be more effective than previously thought."

In one of the more critical studies of probation effectiveness, Petersilia (1985) examined 1,672 felony probationers from two counties in California over a 40-month period. She found that more than 67 percent were rearrested and 51 percent were convicted for a new offense. Petersilia concluded that felony probationers posed a significant risk to the community. Critics of the Petersilia study quickly pointed out that two urban counties in California are not representative of

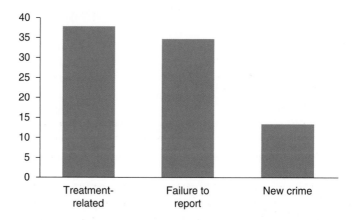

Figure 5.12 Michigan Study of Probationer Recidivism (percentage).

Source: Maxwell, S., Bynum, T., Gray, M., Combs, T. (2000). Examining probationer recidivism in Michigan. *Corrections Compendium* 25(12), 1–4, 18–19.

Box 5.5
Probationers Rearrested for a Felony within Three Years

State courts in 32 counties across 17 states sentenced 79,000 felons to probation in 1986. Within three years of sentencing, while still on probation, 43 percent were rearrested for a felony. An estimated 18 percent of the arrests were for a violent crime (murder, rape, robbery, or aggravated assault); 33 percent were for a drug offense (drug trafficking or drug possession).

Of each 100 felony probationers tracked for three years:

- 26 went to prison
- 10 went to jail
- 10 absconded.

These findings are based on a follow-up survey of felons on probation using a sample that represented a quarter of the total 306,000 felons sentenced to probation in 1986. The survey used state criminal history files and probation files to obtain information. It was not based on a nationally representative sample; 39 percent of the follow-up cases were from a single state (California). Nevertheless, based on 12,370 sample cases representing 79,043 felons placed on probation in the counties and states studied, the follow-up represents the largest survey of its kind ever done.

Source: Bureau of Justice Statistics (1996).

---

the rest of the states or the country. Two replication studies, one in Kentucky (Vito, 1986) and one in Missouri (McGaha et al., 1987), found quite different results. In both Kentucky and Missouri, felony probationers were rearrested at about one-third of the rate of those in California.

Morgan (1993) studied 266 adult felony probationers in Tennessee to determine factors associated with favorable probation outcome and those that would predict success. She found that only 27 percent of the probationers failed and that females, married probationers, and those with higher levels of education were most likely to succeed. Factors significantly related to probation failure were prior felonies, prior probation, prior institutional commitment, and probation sentence length (the longer the sentence, the more likely the failure).

The review of these studies demonstrates that little progress has apparently been made in recent years toward an adequate assessment of probation. Conclusions drawn by the authors of these studies, however, appear to suggest that an unwritten agreement or rule of thumb exists that probation can be considered to be effective and that a failure rate above 30 percent indicates it is not effective. This tendency is suggested by the comments in Table 5.9.

Table 5.9 Evaluations of Effectiveness of Probation

Year	Author	Failure rate	Comments
1951	Caldwell	16%	[P]robation is an effective method of dealing with federal offenders . . .
1955	England	18%	A reconviction rate of less than one-fifth or one-quarter . . . is an acceptable performance for a probation service.
1976	Missouri	30%	Probation is an effective and efficient way of handling the majority of offenders in the State of Missouri.
1976	Comptroller	55%	[P]robation systems we reviewed were achieving limited success in protecting society and rehabilitating offenders.
1972	Irish	30%	[S]upervision program is effectively accomplishing its objective.
1985	Petersilia	65%	Felony probation does present a serious threat to public safety.
1986	Vito	22%	Felony probation supervision appears to be relatively effective in controlling recidivism . . .
1987	McGaha et al.	22%	In Missouri, it does not appear that the current use of felony probation poses a high risk to the security of the community.
1991	Whitehead	40%	[C]alls for drastically reduced use of probation for felony offenders are only partially in order.
1993	Morgan	27%	[I]nadequate employment and unemployment are major impediments to achieving successful probation adjustment and . . . outcome.
1997	Mortimer & May	18%	Electronic monitoring and probation orders yield comparable success rates.

Source: Adapted and updated from Allen et al. (1979), Petersilla (1985), Vito (1986), McGaha et al. (1987), Whitehead (1991), Morgan (1993), and Mortimer and May (1997).

Probation Outcome and Statistics

In addition to measuring the effectiveness of probation, a number of studies have also attempted to isolate characteristics that could be related to offender rehabilitation. Table 5.10 presents a summary of the major factors that were found in each study to be statistically correlated with failure. Keeping in mind the methodological differences among the studies in terms of definition of failure and specification of follow-up period, it appears that the one characteristic found to be associated most commonly with failure is the probationer's previous criminal histories. Other factors frequently cited are the youthfulness of the probationer, marital status other than married, unemployment, and educational level below 11th grade.

Factors such as employment and education are dynamic factors that are correlated with outcome. Because these areas can be addressed during supervision, one can reasonably view these factors positively; we have a clear indication of offender needs, and they can be improved. However, a question remains as to whether probation and parole officers are addressing these needs adequately. When probation and parole agencies fail to meet offender needs that are correlated with outcome, the result is often higher failure rates.

Box 5.6
Shock Probation

Shock probation (also known as "reconsideration of sentence" or "shock therapy") is a program allowing sentencing judges to reconsider the offender's original sentence to imprisonment and then recall the inmate for a sentence to probation within the community under conditions deemed appropriate. It is presumed that a short term of incarceration would "shock" the offender into abandoning criminal activity and into pursuit of law-abiding behavior. It can be seen as an alternative disposition for sentencing judges who wish to control probationer behavior through deterrence and tourniquet sentencing. It is a last-ditch program used by some judges in the difficult decision of how best to protect the public while maximizing offender reintegration. In some instances it became a "front-end" solution to prison overcrowding.

Vito (1985b) found reincarceration rates to range from 10 to 26 percent across many studies; Boudouris and Turnbull (1985) found a rearrest/revocation rate of 39 percent in Iowa over a longer follow-up period. The latter also found that sex and substance abuse offenders were most responsive to shock incarceration and that the cost savings of sentencing offenders to shock probation would be substantial.

COST-EFFECTIVENESS

While the public has demanded tougher sentences, it has become increasingly apparent that the cost associated with more incarceration and prison construction is astronomical. Estimates place the cost of constructing a maximum-security prison at approximately $100,000 per bed, and while the annual cost of maintenance and housing inmates varies from state to state, average costs are more than $31,000 per year per inmate and range from $14,603 in Kentucky to $60,076 in New York (Henrichson & Delaney, 2012). While the construction boom of the 1990s has

Table 5.10 Studies Reporting Factors Related to Probationer Recidivism

Study	Previous criminal history	Youth	Status other than married	Not employed	Low income (below $400)	Education below 11th grade	Abuse of alcohol or drugs	Property offender	On-probation maladjustment	Imposition of conditions
Caldwell (1951)	Significant correlation	Significant correlation	Significant correlation	Significant correlation	Significant correlation	Significant correlation		—[a]		
England (1955)	Significant correlation	Significant correlation	Significant correlation	Significant correlation	Significant correlation	Significant correlation		—[a]		Significant correlation
Davis (1955)	Significant correlation	Significant correlation						Significant correlation	Significant correlation	
Frease (1964)	Significant correlation		Significant correlation		—[b]	Significant correlation	Significant correlation			Significant correlation
Landis et al. (1969)	Significant correlation	Significant correlation	Significant correlation	Significant correlation	Significant correlation	Significant correlation	Significant correlation		Significant correlation	
Irish (1972)	Significant correlation	Significant correlation	Significant correlation	Significant correlation	Significant correlation	Significant correlation	Significant correlation	Significant correlation	—[a]	
Missouri (1976)	Significant correlation	Significant correlation	Significant correlation	Significant correlation	—[c]	Significant correlation	Significant correlation	Significant correlation		
Kusuda (1976)	Significant correlation	Significant correlation	Significant correlation	Significant correlation	—[b]	—[a]	Significant correlation	—[a]		

Study				
Comptroller General (1976)		—[a]		—[a]
Irish (1972)	Significant correlation		Significant correlation	Significant correlation
Petersilia (1985)	Significant correlation	Significant correlation	Significant correlation	Significant correlation
Benedict et al. (1998)	Significant correlation	Significant correlation	Significant correlation	Significant correlation

[a]In these studies, instant and postprobation offenses committed by probationers were predominantly "property"; however, a correlation between property offenses and recidivism was not investigated.

[b]Correlation only with income between $100 and $400; those who made less than $100 and those who made above $400 both had an equal probability of success.

[c]Correlation only with income between $100 and $700; those who made less than $100 or above $700 both had an equal probability of success.

Source: Adapted from Allen, H., Carlson, E., Parks, E. (1979). *Critical issues in adult probation*. Washington, DC: National Institute of Law Enforcement and Criminal Justice.

slowed considerably, 371 new prisons have opened since 1991 (Camp & Camp, 2000), and prison space remains a scarce resource. Many states have re-examined their love affair with incarceration, and many legislators have grown reluctant to vote for new prison construction. Recently, the Bureau of Justice Assistance teamed up with Pew and the Council of State Governments (CSG) to fund a Justice Reinvestment initiative. CSG describes Justice reinvestment as a data-driven approach to improve public safety, reduce corrections and related criminal justice spending, and reinvest savings in strategies that can decrease crime and reduce recidivism. States participating in the process include Alabama, Arizona, Connecticut, Hawaii, Idaho, Indiana, Kansas, Nebraska, New Hampshire, North Carolina, Ohio, Oklahoma, Pennsylvania, Rhode Island, Texas, Vermont, Washington, West Virginia, and Wisconsin. Because of the increasingly high cost associated with incarceration, researchers have begun to focus on the cost-effectiveness of alternatives.

In light of these factors, and in addition to research aimed at measuring effectiveness in terms of recidivism, there have been attempts to demonstrate **cost-effectiveness** of probation. Typically, with criminal justice agencies, costs are usually divided into three types: processing, program, and client-centered. Processing costs include monies spent in identifying and selecting individuals for a given program. Program costs are expenditures associated with incarceration and include direct costs, such as loss of earnings, and indirect costs, such as psychological effects of alienation/prisonization, social stigma, and other detrimental effects upon the prisoner's marriage and family (Nelson, 1975).

Similarly, benefits generated by probation could include savings to society through the use of diversion, wages, and taxes generated by the participants, and reduced crime or recidivism rates (Vito & Latessa, 1979). In addition, there are the costs associated with failure, such as the monetary loss, cost of new case processing, and grief experienced by the victims.

Box 5.7
Probation as a Correctional Alternative

Morgan reviewed the probation outcome literature through 1991 and concluded that probation is effective as a correctional alternative. Failure rates ranged from 14 to 60 percent for a group that had already committed crime; success rates vary from 40 to 86 percent.

Factors associated more frequently with failure on probation included age, sex, marital status, low income, prior criminal record, and employment status. Those most likely to fail were unemployed or underemployed young males with a low income and prior criminal record. The reconviction offenses of those who failed were more likely to be minor misdemeanors rather than felonies. Probationers who were adequately employed, married with children, and had lived in their area for at least two years were most often successful when placed on probation.

Source: Morgan (1993).

Table 5.11 Cost Benefit of Selected Correctional Interventions

Program	Benefit to cost ratio*
Correctional education in prison	$19.65
Vocational programs in prison	$13.23
Mental health courts	$6.76
Risk, need, responsivity supervision (high/moderate risk offenders)	$3.73
Sex offender treatment in the community	$8.18
CBT for high- and moderate-risk offenders	$24.76
TC in the community	$4.76
Work release	$11.20
Outpatient intensive drug treatment in community	$10.87
Intensive supervision with treatment	$1.57
Intensive supervision (surveillance only)	$0.59
Drug courts	$1.26
Domestic violence treatment	$4.61

*Denotes return for every dollar spent. For example, for every dollar spent on mental health courts taxpayers received $6.76. Conversely, for every dollar spent on intensive supervision without treatment taxpayers received only 59 cents.

Source: Adopted from Washington State Institute for Public Policy: www.wsipp.wa.gov/BenefitCost.

Studies that provided the most thorough financial comparisons were those that treated the cost–benefit analysis as their primary focus and considered direct and indirect costs and benefits.

In a review of seven cost–benefit analysis studies conducted on correctional alternatives, Welsh and Farrington (2000) found that for each dollar spent on programs, the public received a return of $1.13 to $7.14 in various savings. Likewise, Cohen (1998) determined the monetary value of saving a high-risk youth at between $1.7 and $2.3 million. In a recent study comparing community placement of juveniles versus residential or institutional placement, Latessa et al. (2014) found that Ohio saved between $13.60 to $40.40 for every $1.00 spent on community programming instead of placing a youth in a residential or state facility. Perhaps the best examples of cost–benefit analyses are conducted by the Washington State Institute of Public Policy. Over the years they have examined a wide range of programs and calculated the cost savings from selected correctional programs based on expected reductions in recidivism rates (see Table 5.11).

SUMMARY

There are now several meta-analytic reviews of the correctional treatment literature conducted by different authors, and the results have been replicated with remarkable consistency. These findings are collectively referred to as the "what works" literature, and have been summarized into the "principles of effective intervention" with offender populations. In general, these meta-analyses have been very critical of the "nothing works" doctrine proposed by Martinson and others. Furthermore, the results have not supported the use of intermediate sanctions (e.g., electronic monitoring, house arrest, restitution, etc.) and other, more punitive approaches. At the same time, there are certain strategies and programs that are well supported by the literature. Specifically, programs (including probation and parole agencies) that incorporate elements of the risk, need, and responsivity framework into their interventions have produced larger average reductions in recidivism.

Review Questions

1. What are some of the indicators of effectiveness used in correctional research?
2. List the three major ways that research studies are summarized.
3. List some of the factors that are related to successful outcomes for parolees.
4. Describe the principles of effective intervention.
5. Describe what does not work to reduce recidivism in offender populations.
6. What factors are important for parole and probation agencies to consider in order to achieve meaningful reductions in recidivism?

Recommended Readings

Andrews, D.A., Bonta, J. (2010). *The psychology of criminal conduct,* 4th edn. New Providence, NJ: LexisNexis Matthew Bender (Anderson Publishing).

Latessa, E.J., Listwan, S., Koetzle, D. (2014). *What works (and doesn't) in reducing recidivism*. Boston, MA: Elsevier (Anderson Publishing).

References

Alaska Department of Health and Social Services (1976). *Misdemeanants probation project*. Juneau, AK: Division of Corrections.

Allen, H., Latessa, E. (1980). *Parole effectiveness in the United States: An assessment.* San Jose, CA: San Jose State University Research Foundation.

Allen, H., Carlson, E., Parks, E. (1979). *Critical issues in adult probation*. Washington, DC: National Institute of Law Enforcement and Criminal Justice.

Andrews, D., Zinger, I., Hoge, R., Bonta, J., Gendreau, P., Cullen, F. (1990). Does correctional treatment work? A clinically relevant and psychologically informed meta-analysis. *Criminology* 28, 369–404.

Antonowicz, D., Ross, R. (1994). Essential components of successful rehabilitation programs for offenders. *International Journal of Offender Therapy and Comparative Criminology* 38, 97–104.

Aos, S. (2005). *Correctional industries programs for adult offenders in prison: Estimates of benefits and costs*. Olympia, WA: Washington State Institute for Public Policy.

Aos, S., Miller, M., Drake, E. (2006). *Evidence-based adult corrections programs: What works and what does not*. Olympia, WA: Washington State Institute for Public Policy.

Aos, S., Phipps, P., Barnoski, R., Lieb, R. (1999). *The comparative costs and benefits of programs to reduce crime: a review of national research findings with implications for Washington State*. Olympia, WA: Washington State Institute for Public Policy.

Applegate, B., Cullen, F., Fisher, B. (1997). Public support for correctional treatment: The continuing appeal of the rehabilitative ideal. *Prison Journal* 77, 237–258.

Austin, J. (2001). Prisoner reentry: Current trends, practices, and issues. *Crime & Delinquency* 47, 314–334.

Ayers, D., Duguid, S., Montague, C., Wolowidnyk, S. (1980). *Effects of the University of Victoria Program: A post-release study*. Ottawa, CN: Ministry of the Solicitor General of Canada.

Babst, D., Mannering, J. (1965). Probation versus imprisonment for similar types of offenders. *Journal of Research in Crime and Delinquency* 2, 60–71.

Beasley, W. (1978). *Unraveling the process of parole: An analysis of the effects of parole residency on parole outcome*. Paper presented at the meeting of the American Society of Criminology, Atlanta, GA.

Beck, A. (1987). *Recidivism of young parolees*. Washington, DC: Bureau of Justice Statistics Special Report.

Benedict, W., Huff-Corzine, L., Corzine, J. (1998). 'Clean up and go straight': Effects of drug treatment on recidivism among felony probationers. *American Journal of Criminal Justice* 22(2), 169–187.

Bennett, W., Dilulio, J. Jr., Walters, J. (1996). *Body count: Moral poverty and how to win America's war against crime and drugs*. New York: Simon and Schuster.

Boudouris, J., Turnbull, B. (1985). Shock probation in Iowa. *Journal of Offender Counseling, Services and Rehabilitation* 9(4), 53–67.

Bouffard, J., MacKenzie, D., Hickman, L.J. (2000). Effectiveness of vocational education and employment programs for adult offenders: A methodology-based analysis of the literature. *Journal of Offender Rehabilitation* 31, 1–42.

Bucholtz, G., Foos, R. (1996). *Profiling parole violators at large*. Columbus, OH: Department of Rehabilitation and Correction.

Bucklen, K.B., Zajac, G. (2009). Success and failure deprivation and thinking errors as determinants of parole but some of them don't come back (to prison!). *Prison Journal* 89, 239–264.

Bureau of Justice Statistics (1996). *National update*. Washington, DC: U.S. Department of Justice, p. 10.

Caldwell, M. (1951). Review of a new type of probation study made in Alabama. *Federal Probation* 15(2), 3–11.

California Department of Justice (1969). *Superior court probation and/or jail sample: One year follow-up for selected counties*. Sacramento, CA: Division of Law Enforcement, Bureau of Criminal Statistics.

Camp, C., Camp, G. (2000). *The 2000 corrections yearbook: Adult corrections*. Middletown, CT: Criminal Justice Institute.

Citizens' Inquiry on Parole and Criminal Justice (1975). *Prison without walls: Report on New York parole.* New York: Praeger.

Clear, T.R., Stout, B., Kelly, L., Hardyman, P., Shapiro, C. (1992). *Prisoners, prisons and religion: Final report.* New Jersey: School of Criminal Justice, Rutgers University.

Cohen, M. (1998). The monetary value of saving a high-risk youth. *Quantitative Criminology* 14, 5–32.

Comptroller General of the United States (1976). *State and county probation: Systems in crisis, report to the congress of the United States.* Washington, DC: U.S. Government Printing Office.

Council of State Governments. http://csgjusticecenter.org/jr.

Cullen, F., Applegate, B. (1998). *Offender rehabilitation.* Brookfield, MA: Ashgate Dartmouth.

Cullen, F., Gendreau, P. (1989). The effectiveness of correctional rehabilitation: Reconsidering the "nothing works" debate. In: L. Goodstein, D. MacKenzie (eds) *American prisons: Issues in research and policy.*: New York: Plenum, pp. 23–44.

Currie, E. (1985). *Confronting crime: An American dilemma.* New York: Pantheon.

Davis, G.F. (1955). A study of adult probation violation rates by mean of the cohort approach. *Journal of Criminal Law, Criminology and Police Science* 55 (March 1964), 70–85.

Davis, L.M., Bozick, R, Steele, J.L., Saunders, J., Miles, J.N.V. (2013). *Evaluating the effectiveness of correctional education: A meta-analysis of programs that provide education to incarcerated adults.* Santa Monica, CA: Rand Corporation.

Durose, M.R., Cooper, A.D., Snyder, H. (2014). *Recidivism of prisoners released in 30 states in 2005: Patterns from 2005 to 2010.* Washington, DC: U.S. Department of Justice, Office of Justice Programs, Bureau of Justice Statistics.

Egg, R., Pearson, F.S., Cleland, C.M., Lipton, D.S. (2000). Evaluations of correctional treatment programs in Germany: A review and meta-analysis. *Substance Use and Misuse* 35, 1967–2009.

Eichman, C. (1965). The impact of the Gideon decision upon crime and sentencing in florida: A study of recidivism and socio-cultural change. Unpublished Master's thesis, Tallahassee, FL: Florida State University.

England, R. (1955). A study of postprobation recidivism among five hundred federal offenders. *Federal Probation* 19(3), 10–16.

Eskridge, C., Newbold, G. (1994). Corrections in New Zealand. *Federal Probation* 57(3), 59–66.

Farabee, D. (2005). *Rethinking rehabilitation: Why can't we reform our criminals?* Washington, DC: AEI Press.

Flanagan, T. (1982). Risk and the timing of recidivism in three cohorts of prison releasees. *Criminal Justice Review* 7, 34–45.

Flanagan, T. (1985). Questioning the "other" parole: The effectiveness of community supervision of offenders. In: L. Travis (ed.) *Probation, parole and community corrections.* Prospect Heights, IL: Waveland, pp. 167–184.

Frease, D. (1964). *Factors related to probation outcome.* Olympia, WA: Washington Department of Institutions, Board of Prison Terms and Paroles.

French, S.A., Gendreau, P. (2006). Reducing prison misconducts. *Criminal Justice and Behavior* 33, 185–218.

Fulton, B., Latessa, E., Stichman, A., Travis, L. (1997). The state of ISP: Research and policy implications. *Federal Probation* 61(4), 65–75.

Gendreau, P. (1996). The principles of effective intervention with offenders. In: A. Harland (ed.) *Choosing correctional options that work: Defining the demand the evaluating the supply.* Thousand Oaks, CA: Sage.

Gendreau, P., Andrews, D. (1990). Tertiary prevention: What the meta-analysis of the offender treatment literature tells us about "what works". *Canadian Journal of Criminology* 32, 173–184.

Gendreau, P., Paparozzi, M. (1995). Examining what works in community corrections. *Corrections Today* (February), 28–30.

Gendreau, P., Ross, R. (1987). Revivification of rehabilitation: Evidence from the 1980s. *Justice Quarterly* 4, 349–407.

Gendreau, P., Goggin, C., Cullen, F., Andrews, D. (2000). The effects of community sanctions and incarceration on recidivism. *Forum on Corrections Research* 12, 10–13.

Gottfredson, D. (1975). *Some positive changes in the parole process.* Paper presented at the meeting of the American Society of Criminology.

Gottfredson, D., Gottfredson, M., Adams, M. (1982). Prison behavior and release performance. *Law and Policy Quarterly* 4, 373–391.

Gottfredson, D., Gottfredson, M., Garofalo, J. (1977). Time served in prison and parolee outcomes among parolee risk categories. *Journal of Criminal Justice* 5, 1–12.

Gottfredson, M., Mitchell-Herzfeld, S., Flanagan, T. (1982). Another look at the effectiveness of parole supervision. *Journal of Research in Crime and Delinquency* 18, 277–298.

Hartman, J., Travis, L, Latessa, E. (1996). *Thirty-nine years of parole rules.* Paper presented at the annual meeting of the Academy of Criminal Justice Sciences, Las Vegas, NV, March.

Henrichson, C., Delaney, R. (2012). *The price of prisons: What incarceration costs taxpayers.* New York: Vera Institute.

Hoffman, P., Stone-Meierhoefer, B. (1980). Reporting recidivism rates: The criterion and follow-up issues. *Journal of Criminal Justice* 8, 53–60.

Holt, N. (1975). *Rational risk taking: Some alternatives to traditional correctional programs.* Proceedings: Second national workshop on corrections and parole administration, Louisville, Kentucky.

Irish, J. (1972). *Probation and its effects on recidivism: An evaluative research study of probation in Nassau County, New York.* New York: Nassau County Probation Department.

Jackson, P. (1983). *The paradox of control: Parole supervision of youthful offenders.* New York: Praeger.

Johnson, B.R. (1984). Hellfire and corrections: A quantitative study of Florida prison inmates. Doctoral dissertation, Florida State University.

Johnson, B.R., Larson, D.B., Pitts, T.C. (1987). Religious programs, institutional adjustment, and recidivism among former inmates in prison fellowship programs. *Justice Quarterly* 14, 501–521.

Knight, K., Simpson, D., Hiller, M. (1999). Three-year reincarceration outcomes for in-prison therapeutic community treatment in Texas. *Prison Journal* 79, 337–351.

Kusuda, P. (1976). *Probation and parole terminations.* Madison, WI: Wisconsin Division of Corrections.

Lab, S., Whitehead, J. (1988). An analysis of juvenile correctional treatment. *Crime & Delinquency* 28, 60–85.

Landis, J., Mercer, J., Wolff, C. (1969). Success and failure of adult probationers in California. *Journal of Research in Crime and Delinquency* 6, 34–40.

Latessa, E., Lowenkamp, C. (2006). What works in reducing recidivism. *St. Thomas Law Journal* 3(3).

Latessa, E.J., Moon, M.M. (1992). The effectiveness of acupuncture in an outpatient drug treatment program. *Journal of Contemporary Criminal Justice* 8, 317–331.

Latessa, E.J., Lovins, B.K., Lux, J.L. (2014). *Evaluation of Ohio's RECLAIM Programs: Cost benefit analysis supplemental report.* Cincinnati, OH: University of Cincinnati Corrections Institute.

Latessa, E.J., Travis., L.F., Holsinger, A. (1997). *Evaluation of Ohio's Community Corrections Act, programs and community based correctional facilities final report.* University of Cincinnati, OH: Center for Criminal Justice Research.

Lerner, M. (1977). The effectiveness of a definite sentence parole program. *Criminology* 15, 32–40.

Lightfoot, L. (1999). *Treating substance abuse and dependence in offenders: A review of methods and outcome.* In: Latessa, E.J. (ed.) *What works strategic solutions: International Community Corrections Association examines substance abuse.* Lanham, MD: American Correctional Association.

Linden, R., Perry, L. (1982). The effectiveness of prison education programs. *Journal of Offender Counseling, Services and Rehabilitation* 6, 43–57.

Lipsey, M. (1999). Can intervention rehabilitate serious delinquents? *Annals of the American Academy of Political and Social Science* 564, 142–166.

Lipsey, M., Wilson, D. (1997). Effective interventions for serious juvenile offenders. In: R. Loeber, D. Farrington (eds) *Serious and violent juvenile offenders: Risk factors and successful interventions.* Thousand Oaks, CA: Sage, pp. 313–345.

Logan, C., Gaes, G. (1993). Meta-analysis and the rehabilitation of punishment. *Justice Quarterly* 10, 245–263.

Lowenkamp, C.T. (2003). *A program level analysis of the relationship between correctional program integrity and treatment effectiveness.* Doctoral Dissertation. University of Cincinnati.

Lowenkamp, C.T., Latessa, E.J. (2003). *Evaluation of Ohio's halfway houses and community based correctional facilities.* University of Cincinnati, Cincinnati, OH: Center for Criminal Justice Research.

Lowenkamp, C.T., Latessa, E.J. (2005a). *Evaluation of Ohio's CCA Programs.* Cincinnati, OH: Center for Criminal Justice Research, University of Cincinnati.

Lowenkamp, C.T., Latessa, E.J. (2005b). *Evaluation of Ohio's reclaim funded programs, community correctional facilities, and DYS facilities.* Cincinnati, OH: Center for Criminal Justice Research, University of Cincinnati.

Lowenkamp, C.T., Pealer, J., Smith, P, Latessa, E.J. (2006). Adhering to the risk and need principles: Does it matter for supervision-based programs? *Federal Probation* 70(3).

Lowenkamp, C., Flores, A., Holsinger, H., Makarios, M., Latessa, E. (2010). Intensive supervision programs: Does program philosophy and the principles of effective intervention matter? *Journal of Criminal Justice* 38, 368–375.

MacKenzie, D.L. (2012). The effectiveness of corrections-based work and academic and vocational education programs. In: J. Petersilia, K.R. Reitz (eds) *The Oxford Handbook of Sentencing and Corrections*. Oxford: Oxford University Press.

MacKenzie, D., Browning, L., Skroban, S., Smith, D. (1999). The impact of probation on the criminal activities of offenders. *Journal of Research in Crime and Delinquency* 36(4), 423–453.

MacKenzie, D., Hickman, L. (1998). *What works in corrections? An examination of the effectiveness of the type of rehabilitation programs offered by Washington State Department of corrections*. Department of Criminology and Criminal Justice, University of Maryland: College Park, MD Report to the State of Washington Legislature Joint Audit and Review Committee.

MacKenzie, D., Piquero, A. (1994). The impact of shock incarceration programs on prison crowding. *Crime & Delinquency* 40, 222–249.

Marquart, J., Sorensen, J. (1988). Institutional and post-release behavior of furman-commuted inmates in Texas. *Criminology* 26, 667–693.

Martin, S., Butzin, C., Saum, C., Inciardi, J. (1999). Three-year outcomes of therapeutic community treatment for drug-involved offenders in Delaware. *Prison Journal* 79, 294–320.

Martinson, R. (1974). What works? Questions and answers about prison reform. *The Public Interest*, pp. 22–54.

Martinson, R., Wilks, J. (1977). Save parole supervision. *Federal Probation* 42(3), 23–27.

Maxwell, S., Bynum, T., Gray, M., Combs, T. (2000). Examining probationer recidivism in Michigan. *Corrections Compendium* 25(12), 1–4, 18–19.

McGaha, J., Fichter, M., Hirschburg, P. (1987). Felony probation: A re-examination of public risk. *American Journal of Criminal Justice* 12, 1–9.

Missouri Division of Probation and Parole (1976). *Probation in Missouri, July 1, 1968 to June 30, 1970: Characteristics, performance, and criminal reinvolvement*. Missouri: Jefferson City.

Morgan, K. (1993). Factors influencing probation outcome: A review of the literature. *Federal Probation* 57(2), 23–29.

Morris, N. (1978). *Conceptual overview and commentary on the movement toward determinacy. Determinate sentencing: Proceedings of the special conference on determinate sentencing.* : Washington, DC: National Institute of Law Enforcement and Criminal Justice.

Mortimer, E., May, C. (1997). *Electronic monitoring in practice*. London: Home Office.

Neithercutt, M. (1972). Parole violation patterns and commitment offense. *Journal of Research in Crime and Delinquency* 9, 87–98.

Nelson, C.W. (1975). Cost–benefit analysis and alternatives to incarceration. *Federal Probation* 39(4), 45–50.

Nuttal, C.P. Associates (1977). *Parole in England and Wales. Home Office Research Studies No. 38*. London: Her Majesty's Stationery Office.

Ohio Community Corrections Organization (1993). *Ohio's community corrections bench book*. Columbus, OH: OCCO.

Pennsylvania Program for Women and Girl Offenders, Inc. (1976). *Report on recidivism of women sentenced to state probation and released from SCI Muncy 1971–73*. Philadelphia, PA: PPWGW.

Petersilia, J. (1985). Probation and felony offenders. *Federal Probation* 49(2), 4–9.

Petersilia, J. (1992). California's prison policy: Causes, costs, and consequences. *Prison Journal* 72, 8–36.

Petersilia, J. (1997). Probation in the United States. In: M. Tonry (ed.) *Crime and justice: A review of research,* Vol. 22. Chicago, IL: University of Chicago Press, pp. 149–200.

Petersilia, J., Cullen, F.T. (2014). Liberal but not stupid: Meeting the promise of downsizing prisons. *Stanford Journal of Criminal Law and Policy,* summer.

Pew Charitable Trusts. Pew Center on the States (2012). *Public opinion on sentencing and corrections policy in America. Public safety performance project (Washington, DC). Public opinion strategies (Alexandria, VA); Mellman Group (Washington, DC).* Washington, DC: Pew.

Pew Charitable Trusts (2013). *The impact of parole in New Jersey.* Washington, DC: Pew.

Porporino, F., Zamble, E. (1984). Coping with imprisonment. *Canadian Journal of Criminology* 264(4), 403–421.

Redondo, S., Sanchez-Meca, J., Garrido, V. (1999). The influence of treatment programmes on the recidivism of juvenile and adult offenders: A European meta-analytic review. *Psychology, Crime and Law* 5, 251–278.

Roberts, R., Cheek, E. (1994). Group intervention and reading performance in a medium security prison facility. *Journal of Offender Rehabilitation* 20, 97–116.

Schwaner, S. (1997). They can run, but can they hide? A profile of parole violators at large. *Journal of Crime and Justice* 20(2), 19–32.

Sherman, L., Gottfredson, D., MacKenzie, D., Eck, J., Reuter, P., Bushway, S. (1998). *Preventing crime: What works, what doesn't, what's promising.* Maryland: National Institute of Justice Research in Brief.

Smith, M.O., Aponte, J., Bonilla-Rodriquez, R., Rabinowitz, N., Cintron, F., Hernandez, L. (1984). Acupuncture detoxification in a drug and alcohol treatment setting. *American Journal of Acupuncture* 12 (July–September), 251–255.

Smith, M.O., Squires, R., Aponte, J., Rabinowitz, N., Bonilla-Rodriquez, R. (1982). Acupuncture treatment of drug addiction and alcohol abuse. *American Journal of Acupuncture* 10 (April–June), 161–163.

Smith, P., Gendreau, P. (2007). The relationship between program participation, institutional misconduct and recidivism among federally sentenced adult male offenders. *Forum on Corrections Research* 19, 6–10.

Smith, P., Goggin, C., Gendreau, P. (2002). *The effects of prison sentences and interme- diate sanctions on recidivism: General effects and individual differences.* Ottawa,

Ontario: Solicitor General of Canada. A Report to the Corrections Research Branch.

Solomon, A.L., Kachnowski, V., Bhati, A. (2005). *Does parole work?* Washington, DC: Urban Institute.

Sperber, K., Latessa, E.J., Makarios, M.D. (2013). Examining the interaction between level of risk and dosage of treatment. *Criminal Justice and Behavior* 40(3), 338–348.

Spiegler, M.D., Guevremont, D.C. (2009). *Contemporary behavior therapy*, 5th edn. Belmont, CA: Wadsworth.

Sumter, M.T. (1999). Religiousness and post-release community adjustment. Florida State University: Doctoral Dissertation.

Taxman, F. (2000). Unraveling "what works" for offenders in substance abuse treatment services. *National Drug Court Institute Review* II, 2.

Travis, L., Latessa, E. (1984). A summary of parole rules—thirteen years later: Revisited thirteen years later. *Journal of Criminal Justice* 12, 591–600.

Travis, L., Stacey, J. (2010). A half century of parole rules: Conditions of parole in the United States. *Journal of Criminal Justice* 38, 604–608.

Van Voorhis, P. (1987). Correctional effectiveness: The high cost of ignoring success. *Federal Probation* 51(1), 56–62.

Vito, G. (1978). Shock probation in Ohio: A comparison of attributes and outcomes. Ohio State University: Columbus unpublished doctoral dissertation.

Vito, G. (1985a). Developments in shock probation: A review of research findings and policy implications. *Federal Probation* 48(2), 22–27.

Vito, G. (1985b). Putting prisoners to work: Policies and problems. *Journal of Offender Counseling Services and Rehabilitation* 9, 21–34.

Vito, G. (1986). Felony probation and recidivism: Replication and response. *Federal Probation* 50(4), 17–25.

Vito, G., Allen, H. (1981). Shock probation in Ohio: A comparison of outcomes. *International Journal of Offender Therapy and Comparative Criminology* 25, 70–75.

Vito, G., Latessa, E. (1979). Cost analysis in probation research: An evaluation synthesis. *Journal of Contemporary Criminal Justice* 1, 3–4.

Vito, G., Wilson, D. (1988). Back from the dead: Tracking the progress of Kentucky's Furman-commuted death row population. *Justice Quarterly* 5, 101–111.

Vito, G., Wilson, D., Latessa, E. (1991). Comparison of the dead: Attributes and outcomes of Furman-commuted death row inmates in Kentucky and Ohio. In: R.M. Bohm (ed.) *The death penalty in America: Current research*. Cincinnati, OH: Anderson Publishing Co., pp. 101–111.

von Hirsch, A., Hanrahan, K. (1979). *The question of parole: Retention, reform, or abolition*. Cambridge, MA: Ballinger.

Waller, I. (1974). *Men released from prison*. Toronto, CN: University of Toronto Press.

Washington Department of Social and Health Sciences (1976). *Who returns? A study of recidivism for adult offenders in the State of Washington*. Olympia, WA: WDSHS.

Washington State Institute for Public Policy: www.wsipp.wa.gov/BenefitCost.

Welsh, B., Farrington, D. (2000). Correctional intervention programs and cost–benefit analysis. *Criminal Justice and Behavior* 27, 115–133.

Wensel, L. (1990). *Acupuncture in medical practice*. Reston, VA: Reston.

Wexler, H., Melnick, G., Lowe, L., Peters, J. (1999). Three-year reincarceration outcomes for amity in-prison therapeutic community and aftercare in California. *Prison Journal 79*, 321–337.

Whitehead, J. (1991). The effectiveness of felony probation: Results from an Eastern State. *Justice Quarterly 8*, 525–543.

Whitehead, J., Lab, S. (1989). A meta-analysis of juvenile correctional treatment. *Journal of Research in Crime and Delinquency 26*, 276–295.

Widahl, E.J., Garland, B, Culhane, S.E., McCarty, W.P. (2011). Utilizing behavioral interventions to improve supervision outcomes in community-based corrections. *Criminal Justice and Behavior 38*(4).

Williams, F., McShane, M., Dolny, H.M. (2000). Predicting parole absconders. *Prison Journal 80*, 24–39.

Wilson, D., Gallagher, C.A., MacKenzie, D.L. (2000). A meta-analysis of corrections based education, vocation, and work programs for adult offenders. *Journal of Research in Crime and Delinquency 37*, 347–368.

Wilson, D., Gallagher, C., Coggeshall, M., MacKenzie, D. (1999). Corrections-based education, vocation, and work programs. *Corrections Management Quarterly 3*(4), 8–18.

Wilson, R. (1977). Supervision (the other parole) also attacked. *Corrections Magazine 3*(3), 56–59.

Wisconsin Division of Corrections (1965). *A comparison of the effects of using probation versus incarceration for burglars with no previous felony convictions*. Madison, NY: WDC.

Young, M., Gartner, J., O'Connor, T. (1995). Long-term recidivism among federal inmates trained as volunteer prison ministers. *Journal of Offender Rehabilitation 22*(1/2), 97–118.

Zeisel, H. (1982). Disagreement over the evaluation of the controlled experiment. *American Journal of Sociology 88*, 378–389.

Chapter 6

JUVENILES AND COMMUNITY CORRECTIONS

Key Terms

decarceration
deinstitutionalization
diversion
drug courts
juvenile court
juvenile probation

juvenile probation officers
parens patriae
selective incapacitation
status offender
waiver

> When we are out of sympathy with the young, then I think our work in
> the world is over.—George MacDonald

THE JUVENILE CRIME PROBLEM

The challenge of crime in the United States remains a major social problem that
has serious and sometimes deadly consequences; however, over the past decade
and a half, the size of the problem has abated as the nature of crime has changed.
For example, the Federal Bureau of Investigation (2013) reports that the crime rate
continued to decreased between 1998 and 2012.

The juvenile crime rate is considered a problematic aspect of the crime problem.
Youths under age 18 commit about 10 percent of the most serious crimes in the
nation but account for nearly 40 percent of the arrests for arson and about 20
percent of the arrests for robbery and property crimes (see Figure 6.1). Once
arrested, many youths are then processed through the juvenile justice system.
While serious crime by youth is always a concern, the good news is that arrests for
juveniles have been declining significantly over the past few years. Not only has
the percentage of crimes committed by juveniles been declining, but every serious
crime has also shown a decline. Table 6.1 illustrates the percentage change in
arrests for juveniles between 2008 and 2012 (Federal Bureau of Investigation,
2013).

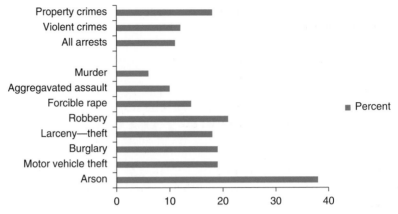

Figure 6.1 Total Arrests Involving Juveniles in 2012.

Source: Federal Bureau of Investigation (2013). *Crime in the United States 2012.* Washington, DC: U.S. Department of Justice.

Table 6.1 Percentage Change in Arrests for Juveniles between 2008 and 2012

Arson	−33%
Motor vehicle theft	−46%
Burglary	−36%
Larceny—theft	−30%
Robbery	−39%
Forcible rape	−22%
Aggregated assault	−35%
Murder	−44%
Total	−34%
Violent crimes	−36%
Property crimes	−32%

Source: Federal Bureau of Investigation (2013). *Crime in the United States, 2012.* Washington, DC: U.S. Department of Justice.

While these recent trends are all positive, it was not so long ago that juvenile crime was seen as out of control by many experts. Much of the juvenile crime in the 1980s and early 1990s was due to the emergence of crack cocaine, juvenile gangs, and violence as major aspects of gang culture (Allen & Simonsen, 2001). These crime issues and changes caused the society as a whole to rethink rehabilitation, to advocate "get-tough" approaches, to waiver in their acceptance of juvenile courts, and to bind juveniles over for trial in adult courts. Fortunately, most juvenile offenders who come to the attention of the juvenile court will receive treatment and noncustodial dispositions. As was the case with adult offenders, the development of community corrections has led to probation, currently the most frequently used disposition for juvenile offenders.

Probation for juvenile offenders is defined as a legal status created by a court of juvenile jurisdiction. It usually involves the following:

1. A judicial finding that the behavior of the child has been such to bring him within the purview of the court.
2. The imposition of conditions upon his continued freedom.
3. The provision of means for helping him meet those conditions and for determining the degree to which he meets them.

(President's Commission, 1967, p. 130)

Probation thus implies more than indiscriminately giving the child "another chance." Its central thrust is to give him or her positive assistance in adjustment in the free community.

Box 6.1
Juvenile Probation

Juvenile probation is the oldest and most widely used vehicle through which a range of court-ordered services is rendered. Probation may be used at the "front end" of the juvenile justice system for first-time, low-risk offenders or at the "back end" as an alternative to institutional confinement for more serious offenders. In some cases, probation may be voluntary, in which the youth agrees to comply with a period of informal probation in lieu of formal adjudication. More often, once adjudicated and formally ordered to a term of probation, the juvenile must submit to the probation conditions established by the court.

Source: Office of Juvenile Justice and Delinquency Prevention (1996).

HISTORICAL BACKGROUND

The historical precursors of juvenile probation are as generally outlined earlier. The legal underpinnings of modern juvenile probation were established in England during the early Middle Ages, under the principle of *parens patriae*: "The King, being father of His country, must protect the welfare of the children."

As with adult probation, John Augustus is viewed as the "father of juvenile probation," as many of his charges were female juveniles in trouble with the law. His work contributed to the development of the first visiting probation agent systems in Massachusetts (1869) and the passage of the first enabling legislation establishing probation for juveniles (1878). In the same era, the Society for the Prevention of Cruelty to Children (1875) was established. Their proposed policies and activism contributed directly to the first juvenile court in America specifically set up to address the care, treatment, and welfare of juvenile offenders: the Cook County (Chicago, Illinois) juvenile court in 1899.

The Cook County juvenile court emerged from the concerns of a group of compassionate, humanitarian, and wealthy women in Chicago who wished each child to receive the care, custody, and treatment as their natural parents should have provided (Lindner & Savarese, 1984). The juvenile court was one project devised to attain these objectives[1] and utilized individualized treatment based on extensive diagnosis of the child's personality and needs, with the judge serving as a counselor to the patient (juvenile). It was widely argued that the juvenile court would safeguard presumed superconstitutional rights[2] (the child would receive more than his or her just deserts) and avoid the stigma of criminal conviction through informal court proceedings based on benevolent attention, understanding the juvenile, humanitarian intervention, solicitous care, and regenerative and restorative[3] treatment. To attain these objectives, procedural safeguards guaranteed under the U.S. Constitution were abandoned; the focus was on the child, not the deed. Box 6.2 contains three selected Amendments to the U.S. Constitution that pertain to rights guaranteed to adults.

Box 6.2
Selected Amendments to the U.S. Constitution

Fourth Amendment: The right of the people to be secure in their persons, houses, papers, and effects, against unreasonable searches and seizures, shall not be violated, and no warrants shall issue, but upon probable cause, supported by oath or affirmation, and particularly describing the place to be searched, and the person or things to be seized.

Fifth Amendment: No person shall be held to answer for a capital, or otherwise infamous crime, unless a presentment or indictment of a Grand Jury, except in cases arising in land or naval forces, or the Militia, when in actual service in time of War or public danger; nor shall any person be subject for the same offense twice put in jeopardy of life or limb; nor shall be compelled in any criminal case to be a witness against himself, nor to be deprived of life, liberty or property, without due process of law; nor shall private property be taken for public use, without just compensation.

Sixth Amendment: In all criminal prosecutions, the accused shall enjoy the right to a speedy and public trial, by an impartial jury of the state or district wherein the crime shall have been committed, which district shall have been previously ascertained by law, and to be informed of the nature and the cause of the accusation; to be confronted with the witnesses against him, to have compulsory process for obtaining witnesses in his favor, and to have the Assistance of Counsel for his defense.

Juvenile court proceedings were informal, conducted in the absence of legal counsel, closed to the public, and individualized to maximize guidance and outcome. To protect and serve the "best interests of the child," records were confidential. Legal challenges were rare.

Juvenile courts were established quickly throughout the various states, federal government, and Puerto Rico. By 1927, all but two states had enacted enabling legislation establishing both juvenile court and probation. The theoretical assumption of juvenile probation was that providing guidance, counseling, resources, and supervision would assist low-risk juveniles to adapt to constructive living, thus avoiding the necessity of institutionalization.

The primary goals of probation became to assist juveniles in dealing with their individual problems and social environments. Resolving underlying causes of the youthful offenders would permit their reintegration into the community. It was argued that probation, rather than incarceration, should be the disposition of choice, because:

1. Probation provides for community safety while permitting the youthful offender to remain in the community for reintegration purposes.
2. Institutionalization leads to prisonization, the process of learning the norm, and culture of institutional living (Clemmer, 1940). This decreases the ability of the juvenile to function as a law-abiding citizen when released, thus leading to further involvement as an adult offender.[4]
3. The stigma of incarceration is avoided (Schur, 1971).
4. The negative labeling effects of being treated as a criminal are avoided.
5. Reintegration is more likely if existing community resources are used and the youth continues to engage in social and familial support systems (family, school, peers, extracurricular activities, employment, friends, etc.).
6. Probation is less expensive than incarceration, arguably more humanitarian, and is at least as effective in reducing further delinquent behavior as is institutionalization.[5]

The "child-saving movement" underlying the development of the juvenile court is clearly seen here.[6]

THE LEGAL RIGHTS OF JUVENILES

It is obvious that the juvenile court, as it developed over the twentieth century, addressed juvenile offenders under civil rather than criminal procedures (civil suits deal with individual wrongs, whereas criminal prosecutions involve public wrongs). The most important objective of the original creators of the juvenile court was to create a separate court system for delinquent, dependent, and neglected children. Following the doctrine of *parens patriae*, the juvenile court system suspended or ignored the legal rights constitutionally guaranteed to all citizens: the right to trial and against self-incrimination and other rights. Constitutional rights were thought unnecessary for juveniles, as the court would focus on and uphold the best interests of a child in a civil setting. Many juvenile judges and child advocates perceived inequity and attempted to provide constitutional safeguards. Beginning in the 1960s, questions about juvenile court proceeding fairness and the constitutionally guaranteed rights of juveniles were brought to the U.S. Supreme Court. Significant changes were made. It is necessary to review those decisions to comprehend their impact on the juvenile justice system, especially contemporary juvenile probation.

Kent v. United States

In 1966, the U.S. Supreme Court was asked to consider the issue of the transfer ("waiver") of a juvenile to the criminal court system.[7] The issue was the legislative waiver of the juvenile court procedures (Grisso & Schwartz, 2000). The court stated:

> There is much evidence that some juvenile courts . . . lack the personnel, facilities, and the techniques to perform adequately as representatives of the State in a *parens patriae* capacity, at least with respect to children charged with law violation. There is evidence, in fact, that here may be grounds for concern that the child receives the worst of both worlds: that he gets neither the protections accorded to adults nor the solicitous care and regenerative treatment postulated for children (*Kent v. United States*, 1966).

This case portended more important issues on which the court was asked to rule (Merlo et al., 1997).

In re Gault

In 1967, the court decided its first major issue in the area of juvenile court procedures. In Arizona, Gerald Gault, then aged 16, allegedly telephoned a female neighbor and used obscene phrases and words. The use of such language over the telephone violated an Arizona statute. Gerald Gault was subsequently adjudicated a juvenile delinquent after a proceeding in which he was denied basic procedural safeguards otherwise guaranteed to any adult. This landmark decision[8] categorically granted the following to all juveniles charged with delinquent acts that might result in such grievous harm as commitment to a correctional institution:

1. The right to know the nature of the charges against them, to prepare for trial;
2. the right to counsel;
3. the right against self-incrimination;
4. the right to confront and cross-examine accusers and witnesses.

The *Gault* decision not only returned procedural rights to juveniles, it also ended the presumption that juvenile courts were beyond the purview and scope of due process protections (Sanborn, 1994a).[9]

In re Winship

This 1970 decision further defined the rights of juveniles. Proof used in a court finding of delinquency must show "beyond a reasonable doubt" that the juvenile committed the alleged delinquent act (Sanborn, 1994b), the same proof standard used for adults in criminal trials. The court specifically found unpersuasive the argument that juvenile proceedings were noncriminal and intended to benefit the child (*In re Winship*, 1970).[10] Currently, juveniles in juvenile court do not have the constitutional right to trial by jury (*McKeiver v. Pennsylvania*, 1971), although some states have extended this right to juveniles.

These three major decisions by the U.S. Supreme Court created the due process model for the juvenile court. The *McKeiver* decision seemed to indicate that the court was moving away from increased rights for juveniles, but in 1975 the court ruled in *Breed v. Jones* that once tried as a juvenile, a person cannot be tried as an adult on the same charges.[11] Currently, juveniles in juvenile court do not have the constitutional right to trial by jury (*McKeiver v. Pennsylvania*, 1971), although some states have extended this right to juveniles. In 1979 (*Fare v. Michael C.*), the court ruled on interrogation and indicated that a child cannot voluntarily waive his or her privilege against self-incrimination without first speaking to his or her parents and without first consulting an attorney.[12] In 1984, the court distinctly departed from the trend toward increased juvenile rights by reaffirming *parens patriae* (*Schall v. Martin*, 1984). As Allen and Simonsen (1998, p. 643) note:

> As a result of Supreme Court cases, the juvenile court is now basically a court of law. . . .

Thus far, the procedural rights guaranteed to a juvenile in court proceedings are as follows:

1. The right to adequate notice of charges against him or her;
2. the right to counsel and to have counsel provided if the child is indigent;
3. the right of confrontation and cross-examination of witnesses;
4. the right to refuse to do anything that would be self-incriminatory;
5. the right to a judicial hearing, with counsel, prior to transfer of a juvenile to an adult court;
6. the right to be considered innocent until proven guilty beyond a reasonable doubt.

Juvenile probation, as seen in court proceedings and used in juvenile courts, is currently vacillating between these two models (Rogers & Mays, 1987). On the one hand, we see liberal reformers who call for increased procedural and legal safeguards for juveniles; on the other hand, we have a conservative movement that focuses on the victim (Torbert et al., 1996) and seriousness of the crime (Clear & Cole, 1990).[13] As one conservative put it, "You are just as dead if a 15-year-old shoots you as you are if a 25-year-old does."[14]

While this is undoubtedly true, in 2005, the court held that the Eighth and Fourteenth Amendments forbid the execution of offenders who were under the age of 18 when their crime was committed (*Roper v. Simmons*, 2005).

CRITICISMS OF THE JUVENILE COURT AND *PARENS PATRIAE*

Criticisms of and disenchantment with the *parens patriae* juvenile court and its procedures (Moore & Wakeling, 1997) have been voiced by such groups as the American Bar Association, the judiciary, the federal government, practitioners, private nonprofit organizations, researchers, and voluntary organizations, among others. Such efforts, when coupled with decisions by the U.S. Supreme Court, have created major changes in the juvenile justice system and particularly diversion of offenders, status offenders, decriminalization, and deinstitutionalization. We will see these changes as we review the contemporary juvenile justice system and juveniles in community corrections.

THE CONTEMPORARY JUVENILE JUSTICE SCENE

Juvenile Court Processing

Although there are some similarities between adult and juvenile systems, there are also some fundamental differences. Figure 6.2 shows a simplified version of case flow through the juvenile justice system. Figure 6.3 shows the ages of juveniles upon referral to juvenile court. As has been the pattern for many decades, the highest rate was for 16 year olds, followed closely by 15 year olds and then 17 year olds. Very few were under age 13.[15] Figure 6.4 shows the referral offense for male and female juvenile offenders. Males continue to be referred more than females for all types of crime, with property crimes the most frequent type for females.

Figure 6.5 compares the number of youths arrested for running away in 1996 and 2009. Almost 55 percent of those arrested for running away from home were female, but the good news is that the number of runaway youths has declined significantly over the years and is less than half of what it once was. Curfew violations and running away from home are viewed as status offenses that can only be committed by juveniles.

Juvenile court processing of delinquency cases can be handled in several ways. At intake, referred cases are often screened by an intake officer who might decide to dismiss the case for lack of legal sufficiency or to resolve the matter formally or informally. Informal dispositions could include a voluntary referral to a social agency for services, informal probation, or payment of fines or restitution. Formally handled cases are petitioned to juvenile court and scheduled to an adjudication (or waiver) hearing. Of those youths referred to juvenile court, about 19 percent were dismissed at intake, while another 26 percent were handled

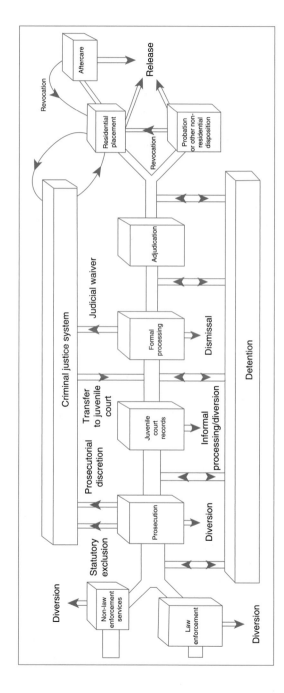

Figure 6.2 The Juvenile Justice System Flowchart.

Source: Office of Juvenile Justice and Delinquency Prevention (2001). *Caseflow diagram*. Washington, DC: OJJDP.

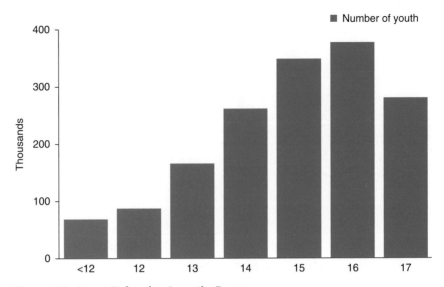

Figure 6.3 Age at Referral to Juvenile Court.

Source: Sickmund, M., Sladky, A., Kang, W. (2010). *Easy access to juvenile court statistics: 1985–2007*. Washington, DC: Office of Juvenile Justice and Delinquency Prevention.

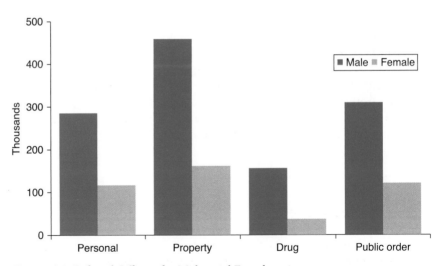

Figure 6.4 Referral Offense for Males and Females.

Source: Sickmund, M., Sladky, A., and Kang, W. (2010). *Easy access to juvenile court statistics: 1985–2007*. Washington, DC: Office of Juvenile Justice and Delinquency Prevention.

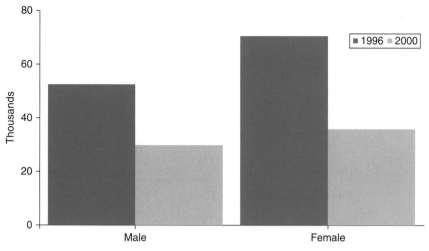

Figure 6.5 Arrests for Runaway: 1999 and 2009.

Source: Federal Bureau of Investigation (2009). *Crime in the United States, 2008*. Washington, DC: U.S. Department of Justice.

[Note: Beginning in 2010 the FBI stopped tracking arrests for runaways.]

informally. The remaining 56 percent were referred to juvenile court jurisdiction, and of those about 5 in 1,000 were waived to criminal or adult court.

Box 6.3
Status Offenders

A **status offender** is generally a juvenile who has come into contact with juvenile authorities based on conduct that is an offense only when committed by a juvenile. A status offense is conduct that would not be defined as a criminal act when committed by an adult (Maxson & Klein, 1997).

Box 6.4
Juvenile Probation Officers

There are an estimated 18,000 to 20,000 **juvenile probation officers** impacting the lives of juveniles in the United States. Eighty-five percent of these professionals are involved in the delivery of basic intake, investigation, and supervision services at the line officer level; the remaining 15 percent are involved in the administration of probation offices or in the management of probation staff.

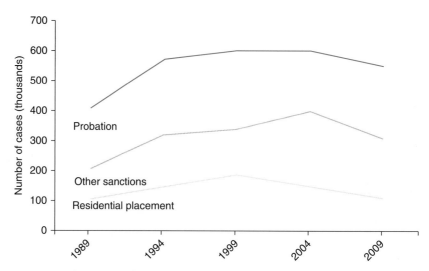

Figure 6.6 Placement of Juveniles, 1987–2009.

Source: Livsey, S. (2012). *Juvenile delinquency probation caseloads, 2009.* Washington, DC: Office of Juvenile Justice and Delinquency Prevention.

At the disposition hearing, the juvenile court judge determines the more appropriate sanction or set of sanctions, generally after reviewing a predisposition ("presentence") report prepared by a probation department. Here the range of options available to the judge is wide and typically includes commitment to an institution, placement in a foster or group home or other residential facility, probation, referral to an outside agency, day treatment or attendance center, mental health program, community correctional center (halfway house), or imposition of a fine, restitution, or community service. As shown in Figure 6.6, probation is the sentence most often imposed. For some youths, out-of-home placement can occur. Residential placement could be in a public or private facility, and Figure 6.7 provides details on juveniles in facilities intended to hold juvenile offenders. In 1996, there were more than 105,000 youths in residential facilities. By 2003 this number had decreased and in 2010 it was 70,793. Most of these juveniles resided in public facilities owned and operated exclusively by state or local governmental agencies. Private facilities are those owned and operated by various nongovernmental organizations that provide services to juvenile offenders. It should be noted that an out-of-home placement can be a very traumatic experience for a juvenile, and suicide is a constant worry.

Juveniles Waived to Criminal Court

All states set an upper age jurisdiction for juvenile courts, and it should be noted that all states have legal mechanisms that, under certain circumstances, permit youths to be tried in criminal court as if they were adults. These

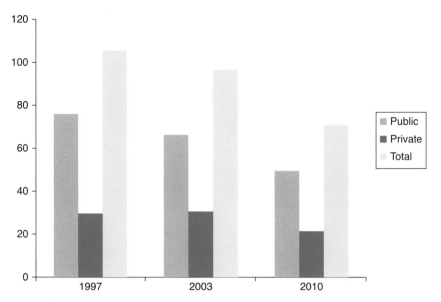

Figure 6.7 Residential Placement for Juvenile Offenders.

Source: Hockenberry, S. (2013). *Juveniles in residential placement, 2010.* Washington, DC: Office of Juvenile Justice and Delinquency Prevention.

mechanisms were developed primarily in the last part of the twentieth century (Feld, 2001) and are major changes from previous philosophical bases of juvenile court proceedings.

Such changes were brought about in part by *Kent v. United States*, a case in which the U.S. Supreme Court began to require due process in juvenile waivers and lawmakers tried to construct simple and expedient alternatives to juvenile waiver hearings. Mechanisms included automatic exclusion based on specific age or offense criteria, authorization of prosecutors to direct-file juvenile cases in criminal court, or empowering judges to sentence directly to adult correctional institutions or blend dispositions by imposing a juvenile institutional commitment followed by commitment to adult criminal facilities (Ullman, 2000). These changes were fueled in part by alarm over an increase in juvenile violence, an expanding caseload of juvenile drug offenders, and judicial assessments that many adjudicated delinquents were no longer amenable to treatment (Snyder et al., 2000). In addition, offense exclusion provided a politically attractive strategy for "get-tough" public officials who proposed to "crack down" on increased youth crime. Figure 6.8 shows juveniles waived to criminal court from 1994 through 2009, the most recent available picture. Offenses for which waivers were sought included offenses against the person and property, drug law violations, and public order. Waivers have generally decreased since 1994, when they peaked.

Advocates of juvenile waiver mechanisms asserted that juvenile court sanctions and service constitute neither just nor effective responses to predatory and

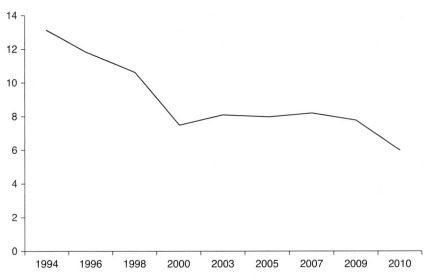

Figure 6.8 Number of Juveniles Waived to Adult Court, 1993–2010.

Source: Puzzanchera, C., Addie, S. (2014). *Delinquency cases waived to criminal court, 2010.* Washington, DC: U.S. Department of Justice, Office of Juvenile Justice and Delinquency Prevention.

savvy youthful offenders and that criminal prosecution would ensure more proportionate punishment, more effective deterrence, and greater incapacitation. It was believed that by focusing on the offense rather than the offender, public safety would be strengthened and recidivism would be reduced. It was also believed that habitually violent juveniles belonging to gangs, abusing substances, and wielding guns should be arrested, charged as adults, and sentenced to prison. In sum, authority was shifted from the judiciary to the prosecutor, although some states increased the authority of both. The correctional objective was selective incapacitation. It is important to note that the number of both juvenile arrests and cases waived to criminal court have declined since 1994 (Puzzanchera et al., 2010), reflecting the similar trend of decreasing involvement of juveniles in lives of crime and violence.

Studies of the effectiveness of waiver programs are ongoing, but so far the evidence has consistently shown that waiver to adult court results in higher recidivism rates than those retained in the juvenile system. Risler and colleagues (1998) examined the impact of Georgia's waiver legislation and found no significant reduction in the mean arrest rates (no deterrence) and suggested that such laws do not reduce serious violent crime. Redding (1999) argues that while juveniles are more likely to receive a longer and more serious sentence in criminal court, they may actually serve less time than they would in a juvenile facility. He found that criminal court adjudication generally produces higher recidivism rates for most offenders and that juveniles incarcerated in adult facilities receive fewer age-appropriate rehabilitative medical, mental health, and educational services.

Bishop (2000) reviewed the effects of juvenile waiver and concluded that expansive transfer policies send many minor and nonthreatening offenders to the adult system, exacerbate racial disparities (McNulty, 1996), and move youths with special and severe needs into correctional systems that are ill-prepared to provide treatment. Bishop also argued that creditable evidence shows that prosecution and punishment in the adult system increase recidivism and expose young people to heightened vulnerability and to potentially damaging experiences and penal outcomes.

Experts have identified several possible explanations for the higher recidivism rates for juveniles tried in adult courts versus those adjudicated in juvenile courts (Bazemore & Umbreit, 1995; Myers, 2003; Thomas & Bishop, 1984; Winner et al., 1997):

- The stigmatization and other negative effects of labeling juveniles as convicted felons.
- The sense of resentment and injustice juveniles feel about being tried and punished as adults.

Box 6.5
Selective Incapacitation

This doctrine of isolating the juvenile offender, or "social disablement," proposes a policy of incarcerating those whose criminal behavior is so damaging or probable that nothing short of isolation will prevent recidivism. This "nothing-else-works" approach would require correctly identifying those offenders who would be eligible for long-term incarceration and diverting others into correctional alternatives. Thus, we would be able to make maximum effective use of detention cells, a scarce resource, to protect society from the depredations of such dangerous and repetitive offenders.

Current correctional technology does not permit correctly identifying those who require incapacitation. Rather, the evidence is that we would probably incarcerate numerous nondangerous juveniles (a "false-positive" problem). However, there is evidence of the effectiveness of some prediction scales to identify low-rate juvenile offenders for selective early release (Hayes & Geerken, 1997; Lovins & Latessa, 2013). This would be selective "decapacitation!" Whatever benefits might accrue to this sentencing doctrine have thus far eluded corrections. However, chronic repeat offenders (those with five or more arrests by age 18), who make up a very small proportion of all offenders, commit a very high proportion of all crimes. More research into persistent criminal behavior over the life course is needed.

- The learning of criminal mores and behavior while incarcerated with adult offenders.
- The decreased focus on rehabilitation and family support in the adult system.
- The loss of a number of civil rights and privileges further reduces opportunities for employment and community reintegration (Redding, 2003, 2010).

Community Corrections

It should be obvious that the juvenile court makes decisions about youthful offenders based on assessments of needs, risks, and rehabilitation. Whether working on an informal basis in the smallest juvenile court or using structured prediction and actuarial instruments that are combined with clinical experience, as in the most sophisticated and largest juvenile settings, the juvenile justice system is winnowing cases, attempting to match sanctions with needs and control. Allen and Simonsen (2001, p. 95) refer to the process as "filtering" offenders into sanction options that address individual needs, community safety, and reintegration.

In the juvenile court, disposition decisions are based on individual and social factors, offense severity, and youths' offense history. The dispositional philosophy includes a significant rehabilitation emphasis as well as many dispositional options that cover a wider range of community-based and residential services. Dispositional orders can be and often are directed to people other than the offender (family members, in particular), and dispositions may be indeterminate, based on progress toward correctional goals and treatment objectives. In some cases, authority of the juvenile court can extend to majority age (as defined by individual states).

As fascinating as "detention" and "incarceration" might be, and they are certainly necessary for some offender control, our focus here is on prevention, alternatives to incarceration, probation, and a variety of programs designed to divert juveniles from residential settings and provide treatment and control in the community.

Box 6.6
Detention

Juvenile courts sometimes hold youths in secure detention facilities during court processing. The court may decide detention is necessary to protect the community from the juvenile's behavior, ensure a juvenile's appearance at subsequent court hearings, or secure the juvenile's own safety. Detention may also be ordered for the purpose of evaluating the juvenile. About one in five of all delinquency cases are detained. Property offenders are least likely to involve detention.

Juvenile Probation

Probation is the oldest and most widely used community-based corrections program. During probation, the juvenile usually remains in the community and can continue such normal activities as attending school or work. In exchange for this freedom, the juvenile must comply with a number of conditions. This compliance could be voluntary as in informal probation in lieu of formal adjudication, but it may also be mandatory. If the disposition results from a formal adjudication and probation, the juvenile must comply with conditions of probation as imposed by the court. Slightly more than one-half of the juvenile probation dispositions are informal (enacted without formal court adjudication or court order).

A juvenile might be required to meet regularly with a probation officer or supervisor, attend counseling, observe a strict curfew schedule, and/or complete a specified period of community service or even restitution. Such orders also imply the authority of the court to revoke probation should the juvenile violate conditions. If there is a revocation hearing, the court may reconsider its original disposition, impose additional conditions, or impose such severe alternatives as placement in a state youth authority.

At juvenile probation intake, juveniles are frequently assigned to caseloads based on their identified "risks" and "needs." High-risk youths who may be in danger of becoming chronic offenders may be assigned to special programs with strict supervision and individually designed treatment programs, including involvement of the youths' families in court-ordered activity (e.g., parenting classes). Treatment might also include counseling on alcohol and other drug abuse, mental health interventions, employment preparation and job placement, community service projects, and after-school programs. Such programs seek to reduce the number of chronic recidivists through a coordinated program of aggressive early intervention and treatment.

Investigation and diagnosis of other juveniles, usually at the intake or predisposition report level, may suggest treatment needs for mental health care, drug-abusing behavior (of juveniles and their families), or other precipitating factors contributing to the acting-out behavior of juveniles before the court. Some are diverted from further court processing, and others are placed in residential facilities, sometimes run by private-sector service providers. Probation officers are sometimes required to supervise these juveniles. We first examine diversion programs and then aftercare ("parole") of juveniles exiting residential settings.

Diversion of Juveniles

The *Gault*, *Kent*, and *Winship* cases defined those constitutionally guaranteed rights that must be accorded to every juvenile and formed the basis of the due process model noted earlier. This model requires adherence to minimally guaranteed legal procedures,[16] a voluntary and helping relationship, and the least restrictive environment necessary to treat the juvenile. It also requires a demonstrated need for detention[17] and, in the absence of this, a mandatory noncommitment to an institution (del Carmen, 1984; del Carmen et al., 1998).[18]

The question of whether incarcerated juveniles have a mandatory right to treatment has been addressed in several federal cases. The most significant of these was *Nelson v. Heyne* (1974), which upheld a categorical right to treatment for confined juveniles under the due process clause of the Fourteenth Amendment. The appellate court stated that the *parens patriae* principle of the juvenile court could be justified only if committed delinquent youths receive treatment:

> the right to treatment includes the right to minimum acceptable standards of care and treatment for juveniles and the right to individualized care and treatment. Because children differ in their needs for rehabilitation, individual need for treatment will differ. When a state assumes the place of a juvenile's parents, it assumes as well the parental duties, and its treatments of its juveniles should, so far as can be reasonably required, be what proper parental care would provide. Without a program of individual treatment, the result may be that the juveniles will not be treated, but warehoused.

There appears to be no consensus on which youths are best served by residential (vs. community) care, although one study found that youths at all risk levels (as measured by a validated risk assessment tool: the Ohio Youth Assessment System) responded best to community placement (Latessa et al., 2014). Figure 6.9 shows the results from this study.

The due process model and the *Nelson* requirements have significantly contributed toward the diversion process of juveniles. Cost is another factor; a recent study in Ohio found that the cost of incarcerating a youth in a state facility was over $166,000 versus $6,800 for probation (Lovins & Lux, 2014).

Allen and colleagues (2007, pp. 336–337) define diversion as:

> The official halting or suspension, at any legally prescribed processing point after a recorded justice system entry, of formal juvenile justice proceedings against an alleged offender, and referral of that person to a treatment or care program administered by a nonjustice agency or to a private agency. Sometimes no referral is given.

Diversion programs function to divert juveniles out of the juvenile justice system, encourage the use of existing correctional facilities and agencies for such offenders, and avoid formal contact with the juvenile court. These programs include remedial education programs,[19] foster homes, group homes, community drug treatment,[20] attendance centers,[21] and local counseling facilities and centers. The effectiveness

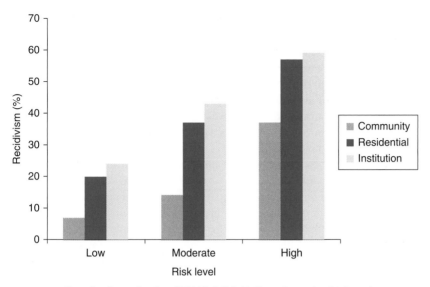

Figure 6.9 Results from Study of RECLAIM: Failure Rates by Risk and Placement Type.

Source: Latessa, E., Lovins, B., Lux, J. (2014). *Evaluation of Ohio's RECLAIM programs.* Cincinnati, OH: Center for Criminal Justice Research, University of Cincinnati.

of such programs is not yet definitively documented but preliminary evaluation reports indicate high efficacy.

Drug Courts and Diversion

The predisposition report may have also discovered that youths, either status offenders or those who have committed offenses, are experimenting, abusing, or chemically dependent on controlled substances, pharmaceuticals prescribed for others but coming under the control of juveniles, or other illicit drugs. In an increasing number of jurisdictions, such youths are afforded access to individually tailored treatment programs under juvenile **drug courts**. There, a formidable array of specific services may be available and may address not only the juvenile but family, friends, and employers. Unfortunately, the research on the effectiveness of juvenile drug courts is mixed, and a recent study of nine sites nationwide found higher recidivism rates for juveniles in drug courts than those receiving probation (Sullivan et al., 2014). These researchers speculated that there may be several reasons for these negative findings including: (1) a lack of motivation by juveniles to engage in substance abuse treatment, (2) drug courts providing too much intervention given the actual need of many juveniles, most of whom are using alcohol and marijuana, (3) the mixture of low- and higher-risk youth, and (4) the lack of evidence-based treatment. Clearly additional research is needed in this area.

Box 6.7
Juvenile Drug Courts

Juvenile drug courts are intensive treatment programs established within and supervised by juvenile courts to provide specialized services for eligible drug-involved youths and their families. Cases are assigned to a juvenile drug court docket based on criteria set by local officials to carry out the goals of the drug court program.

Juvenile drug courts provide (1) intensive and continuous supervision over delinquency and status offense cases that involve substance-abusing juveniles and (2) coordinated and supervised delivery of an array of support services necessary to address the problems that contribute to juvenile involvement in the justice system. Service areas include substance abuse treatment, mental health, primary care, family, and education. Since 1995, more than 439 juvenile drug courts have been established in the United States.

Source: National Drug Court Institute.

Deinstitutionalization

The concept of **deinstitutionalization**, also known as **decarceration**, is recent; 1969 is considered its inception. In that year, Jerome Miller began deinstitutionalization of incarcerated juvenile offenders in Massachusetts. Asserting that the era of confinement of children in larger correctional facilities was over and that an era of more humane, decent, and community-based care for delinquents had begun, Miller closed the major juvenile institutions. Confined youth were placed in small homes, using other, already existing community-based correctional programs and services (Sherrill, 1975a, 1975b).

Although no other state has fully followed the lead of Massachusetts, several have developed smaller, more community-based facilities. Utah, for instance, closed a 350-bed training school and placed the 290 youths in community-based programs modeled on Massachusetts' program. There was strong evidence that Utah saved considerable money when compared to past correctional practices (Krisberg et al., 1987). Missouri has also closed many of its larger facilities in favor of smaller "group" homes dispersed throughout the state so that youth can remain closer to home. Called the "Missouri Model," other states have looked at this model as an example of how youths can be given high-quality care outside of a large institution. Most researchers have concluded there is no evidence that public safety is compromised.

In 1995, Ohio began a program entitled RECLAIM Ohio (Reasoned and Equitable Community and Local Alternatives to Incarceration of Minors). This statewide initiative is designed to assist counties in providing community services to adjudicated juvenile offenders. Essentially, local juvenile courts are

---

Box 6.8
Costs and Benefits of Early Childhood Intervention

A series of small-scale programs attempted to assess the costs and benefits of early childhood (prenatal through age 4) intervention, asking if early interventions targeted at disadvantaged children benefit participating children and their families, and might government funds invested early in the lives of children yield compensating decreases in later government expenditures?

Peter Greenwood examined five of the most rigorously designed programs for younger children; programs had a matched control group that was assigned randomly at program onset. In particular, he found:

- IQ differences between program participants and control group members approached or exceeded 10 points at the end of the program.
- The difference in rates of special education and grade retention at age 15 exceeded 20 percent (Abecedarian project).
- Participating children experienced 33 percent fewer emergency room visits through age 4 than children in the control group (Elmira, NY Prenatal/Early Infancy Project).
- Mothers were on welfare 33 percent less time in the same Elmira Project.
- Earnings at age 27 were 60 percent higher among program participants (Perry Preschool Program).
- Benefits outweighed costs, and savings were $25,000 versus $12,000 for each family participating in the Perry program, and $24,000 versus $6,000 for each higher-risk family participating in the Elmira program.

In addition, other advantages to program participants (relative to those in the control group) were decreased criminal activity, improved educational outcomes, and improved health-related indicators such as decreased child abuse, improved maternal reproductive health, and reduced substance abuse.

Carefully targeted early childhood interventions can yield measurable benefits, and some of those benefits endure for some time after the program has ended.

Source: Greenwood (1999). See https://www.ncjrs.gov/pdffiles1/fs9994.pdf.

---

given an allocation of funds to use for community-based alternatives. In turn, they must pay for most youths who are incarcerated in a state institution from their allocation.

In 2009, Targeted RECLAIM began, which focused on the counties with the largest commitment rates. In addition to reductions in commitments, each Targeted RECLAIM county was required to develop evidence-based programs.

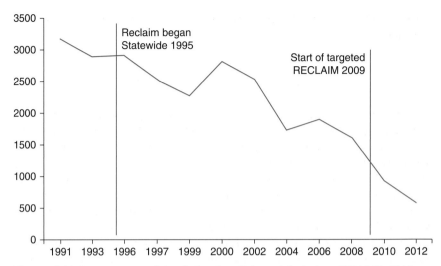

Figure 6.10 Department of Youth Services Felony Admissions FY 1991–2012.

Source: Ohio Department of Youth Services (2014) *DYS admissions*. Ohio: Ohio Department of Youth Services, 1991–2007.

Research results indicated that they are successfully reducing the commitment rate of juveniles to state facilities. Figure 6.10 shows the number of admissions to state facilities before and after the implementation of RECLAIM and later Targeted RECLAIM. As shown, there has been a significant reduction in commitments to state institutions within the Department of Youth Services. The costs savings have also been impressive, with more than $40 saved for every $1 spent on RECLAIM programs. RECLAIM has also strengthened local juvenile courts; private-sector service providers increased their participation; and cooperation across prosecutor, court, and court services increased. Failure rates were not unusually high, and the percentage of youths participating in RECLAIM who were eventually committed to state institutions has remained low. RECLAIM is a constructive example of a strategic policy decision that included coordination and use of community corrections to avoid sending youths to secure institutions (Lowenkamp & Latessa, 2005; Latessa et al., 2014).

Those favoring placement of juveniles in secure institutions cite the public's fear of violent youth crime as a rationale for incarcerating young offenders. They also argue that "getting those thugs off the streets" prevents further offending (selective incapacitation), provides the structure and control necessary for treatment and educational programs (rehabilitation), and prevents other juveniles from committing serious offenses (general deterrence). Deinstitutionalization advocates counter that many incarcerated juveniles were not committed for serious violent offenses, institutionalization is costly, the deterrence evidence is almost nonexistent, the evidence of effective rehabilitation in correctional facilities is weak, and community alternatives are just as effective. Finally, opponents of institutionalization argue that local community alternatives, when coupled with child advocates, can substantially reduce commitments to state juvenile correctional institutions.[22]

Aftercare and Community Corrections

The majority of juveniles committed to state-managed residential facilities and training schools are serious, chronic offenders. They will eventually be released to the community through parole and onto aftercare. Previous research has shown that recidivism rates among juvenile parolees are unacceptably high, ranging from 53 to 75 percent (Krisberg et al., 1991; Ohio Department of Youth Services, 2014). A large percentage of previously incarcerated juvenile offenders continue their criminal involvement into adulthood. A major portion of the problem is that a juvenile corrections and aftercare system that fails to utilize evidence-based programs is likely to continue to face the kinds of youths whom the system had either ignored or failed: serious, chronic offenders. What is needed with this population are effective interventions, intensive supervision and services, a focus on reintegration while incarcerated, and a gradual transition process that utilizes community resources and social networks. This includes aftercare planning, parole officer contact during the institutional phase, and community-based providers working within the residential setting. The latter would include working more closely with families, developing cognitive-behavioral treatment programs, supervised trips to the community, overnight or weekend home passes, substance abuse services, and mental health treatment. Virginia, Colorado, and Nevada are implementing such efforts (Office of Juvenile Justice and Delinquency Prevention, 2000).

THE FUTURE OF JUVENILE PROBATION AND COMMUNITY CORRECTIONS

Several conclusions are suggested by this review of current trends and developments. It is obvious that juvenile justice and juvenile probation are in a period of rapid change and that juvenile policy is vacillating between the old *parens patriae* and the newer due process model. Further, the roles and functions of the juvenile probation officer are undergoing change and enlargement. The various state juvenile systems and jurisdictions are moving toward diversion, waiver of juvenile offenders into the criminal justice arena, removal of the status offender from juvenile court jurisdiction, and deinstitutionalization of juveniles. In addition, faced with legal constraints, requirements for treatment of incarcerated youths, and high costs of juvenile institutions, probation officers are facing emerging and divergent demands. Finally, to divert and refer juveniles to social services, there must be increased community and private service programs and agencies to provide local community services to juveniles. States can encourage these developments with subsidies and legislation that enable local and county community corrections (Harris, 1996). Of course, many of the programs and practices used

Box 6.9
Working with Families

Effective Practices in Community Supervision (EPICS)
The purpose of the EPICS model is to teach juvenile probation and parole officers how to apply some of the core principles of effective intervention with youth on community supervision. Juvenile parole officers are taught to increase dosage to higher-risk youth; to stay focused on criminogenic needs, including antisocial thoughts, attitudes, and beliefs; and to use a social learning, cognitive-behavioral approach during interactions with offenders.

With the EPICS model, community supervision officers follow a structured approach when meeting with offenders (see Chapter 9 for more information on the model).

Family EPICS
Since 2006, the EPICS model has been used to train and coach juvenile probation and parole officers throughout Ohio and in several other states, and they are now practicing it. The family intervention extension of EPICS incorporates the components of EPICS for use with parents and guardians of youth on community supervision.

The family intervention is designed to be delivered in the same format as EPICS, with community supervision officers conducting a structured Check-In, Review, Intervention, Rehearsal, and Homework assignment with parents/guardians. Each session is intended to be delivered in approximately 30 to 50 minutes at a convenient location where parents/guardians feel comfortable and can focus on the skills to be learned. The intervention may be delivered in the home, community supervision office, or other mutually agreed upon location.

with adult offenders are also applied to juveniles. Other chapters explore privatization of services; technologies applied to supervision (electronic monitoring, classification devices, specialized service providers, and so on); and supervision strategies, such as house arrest, day attendance centers, intensive supervised probation, and specialized caseloads. Reintegrative and restorative approaches are being implemented across the nation, including restitution, victim–offender mediation, compensation, and community work orders, and many of these approaches are used successfully with juveniles.

Because juvenile probation services, as agents of court supervision for young offenders, depend on the philosophy of the juvenile court, court administrators, and referral agencies, a patchwork of temporizing procedures, responses, and programs is emerging. Some federal funding of coordinated efforts suggests that it is possible to implement intensive community-based aftercare programs. Yet with a shortfall in resources facing almost every court agency, innovation and strategic planning are required. There is no quick fix for the quandary of juvenile probation and corrections, and we conclude this section by pointing out that new demands will continue to emerge.

SUMMARY

Our examination of the development of juvenile probation identified those historical events of the nineteenth and twentieth centuries that contributed first to the development of the juvenile court and then to a re-examination of the legal rights of juveniles. Beginning with the first juvenile court in Chicago (1899), the constitutionally guaranteed rights of juveniles were ignored in favor of a benevolent venue intended to provide each child such care, treatment, and welfare as should have been provided by natural parents.

By the 1960s, child advocates and concerned organizations began to ask if the juvenile court was running roughshod over the rights of its charges while, at the same time, perhaps not delivering on promised benefits. A series of U.S. Supreme Court decisions eventually reasserted such constitutionally guaranteed protections as the right to trial, to remain silent, to present evidence on one's own behalf, to question and challenge the evidence presented against the charge, and most other rights available to adults.

Three major changes emerged. First, many jurisdictions undertook deinstitutionalization, moving their charges from state-controlled institutions into community corrections. Second, the emergence of juvenile drug gangs and increased violence led to demands for more punishment, such as waiver to adult court to stand trial as adults and presumably be punished more severely. Third, increasingly productive efforts were made to marshal a coordinated network of social and treatment programs that would provide rehabilitative and reintegrative services to youths and their families. Evidence of effectiveness as indicated by research on program outcomes suggests that such a coordinated program can yield significant reductions in juvenile delinquency, violence, and recidivism. The three major changes continue, and perhaps the best prediction of future directions in juvenile probation would be that change will increase in speed and intensity. There is much work yet to be done to prevent delinquency and increase public safety, but fortunately we have appeared to turn the corner, at least in terms of less focus on incarceration and punitive sanctions.

Review Questions

1. Why was probation established across the nation much earlier for juveniles than for adult offenders?
2. Why should probation be the disposition of choice with juvenile offenders?
3. Identify and describe three major court cases that have affected juveniles.
4. What is deinstitutionalization, and what state led the way in this movement?

5. Argue the case for binding over serious juvenile offenders as adults. Argue against this practice.
6. How can public safety be enhanced with juvenile aftercare?
7. Identify five major innovations in juvenile community corrections.
8. Can early childhood intervention reduce juvenile offending?
9. Do drug courts reduce recidivism?
10. How has juvenile probation changed in the past decade?
11. What has been the effect of RECLAIM on Ohio's incarceration rate of juveniles? Why do you think this has occurred?

Notes

1   Chicago courts continue to innovate to handle juvenile offenders. See U.S. Bureau of Justice Statistics (1994). For a critical view of the Illinois juvenile justice system, see Berger (1994). See also Getis (2000).
2   Critics argue that this has not happened. See Feld (1993) and Getis (2000).
3   Umbreit (1994). See also Umbreit (1995); and Umbreit and Vos (2000).
4   The perceived relationship between juvenile delinquency and adult criminality has been seriously challenged by recent research. Arguing that evidence is not sufficient to establish accurate predictions about whether juvenile delinquents would eventually become adult offenders, Lyle Shannon also found that the relationship that does exist can, in large part, be explained by the effects of processes within the juvenile and criminal justice systems, as well as the continued delinquent behavior of the juvenile. See Shannon (1982).
5   See Solomon and Klein (1983).
6   Not all scholars agree that the moving force behind early juvenile court development was benevolent. For example, A.M. Platt believes that the rationale for saving youths was part of a larger social movement that attempted to strengthen the position of corporate capitalism in the United States. He argues that the juvenile court was a means of preserving the existing class system. See Platt (1977).
7   Lee (1994). See also Jenson and Metzger (1994); and Merlo et al. (1997).
8   *In re Gault*, 387 U.S. 1 (1967). See also Sanborn (1994b); and Manfredi (1998).
9   See also Sanborn (1994a); and Feld (1999).
10   Historical data identifying main sources of the growth of juvenile prosecutions in London Court (1790–1820) can be found in King and Noel (1994).
11   This would be a grievous case of double jeopardy. See also Sanborn (1994a).
12   In *Fare v. Michael C.* (1979), a juvenile murder suspect consented to interrogation after he was denied the opportunity to consult with his probation officer. The U.S. Supreme Court ruled that there is no constitutional mandate to allow a suspect to speak with his or her probation officer. The court indicated that the trial court judge should take into consideration the totality of the circumstances of the youth's waiver of his or her rights. Factors such as age, maturity, intelligence, and experience should be taken into consideration.

13 Berger (1994). Cohn (1994) is more pessimistic.
14 See Sheley et al. (1995); Bastian and Taylor (1994); and Rapp-Paglicci and Wodarski (2000).
15 Office of Juvenile Justice and Delinquency Prevention (1998a).
16 Sanborn (1994a).
17 Bazemore (1994).
18 Bazemore (1994).
19 An example of this is Project READ, San Jose State University.
20 Mauser et al. (1994); and Sarre (1999).
21 McDevitt et al. (1997).
22 Macallair (1994). See also Macallair (1993).

Recommended Readings

Howell, J.C. (2008). *Preventing and reducing juvenile delinquency: A comprehensive framework*, 2nd edn. Thousand Oaks, CA: Sage.
Howell, J.C., Lipsey, M.W., Wilson, J.J. (2014). *A handbook for evidence-based juvenile justice systems*. Lanham, MD: Lexington Books.

References

Abt Associates (1994). *Conditions of confinement: Juvenile detention and corrections facilities*. Washington, DC: Office of Juvenile Justice and Delinquency Prevention.
Allen, H., Simonsen, C. (1998). *Corrections in America*. Upper Saddle River, NJ: Prentice Hall.
Allen, H., Simonsen, C. (2001). *Corrections in America*. Upper Saddle River, NJ: Prentice Hall.
Allen, H., Latessa, E., Ponder, B., Simonsen, C. (2007). *Corrections in America*. Upper Saddle River, NJ: Prentice Hall.
American Correctional Association (1986). *Directory of juvenile and adult correctional departments, institutions, agencies and paroling authorities*. College Park, MD: ACA.
American Correctional Association (1997). *Directory of juvenile and adult correctional departments, institutions, agencies and paroling authorities*. Lanham, MD: ACA.
American Correctional Association (2001). *Directory of juvenile and adult correctional departments, institutions, agencies and paroling authorities*. Lanham, MD: ACA.
Bastian, L., Taylor, B. (1994). *Young black male victims*. Washington, DC: Bureau of Justice Statistics.
Bazemore, G. (1994). Understanding the response to reform limiting discretion: Judges' views on restrictions on detention intake. *Justice Quarterly* 11(2), 429–452.

Bazemore, G., Umbreit, M. (1995). Rethinking the sentencing function in juvenile court: Retributive or restorative response to youth crime. *Crime & Delinquency* 41(3), 296–316.

Berger, R. (1994). Illinois juvenile justice: An emerging dual system. *Crime & Delinquency* 40(1), 54–68.

Bishop, D. (2000). Juvenile offenders in the adult criminal justice system. In: M. Tonry (ed.) *Criminal and justice: A review of research*, vol. 27. Chicago, IL: University of Chicago Press, pp. 81–167.

Breed v. Jones, 421 U.S. 519 (1975).

Clear, T.R., Cole, G.F. (1990). *American corrections*. Pacific Grove, CA: Brooks/Cole.

Clemmer, D. (1940). *The prison community*. New York: Rinehart and Company.

Cohn, A. (1994). The future of juvenile justice administration: Evolution v. revolution. *Juvenile and Family Court Journal* 45(3), 51–63.

del Carmen, R. (1984). *Legal issues and liabilities in community corrections*. Paper presented at the annual meeting of the Academy of Criminal Justice Sciences, Chicago, IL.

del Carmen, R., Parker, M., Reddington, F. (1998). *Briefs of leading cases in juvenile justice*. Cincinnati, OH: Anderson.

Dembo, R., Seeberger, W., Shemwell, M., Klein, L., Rollie, M., Pacheco, K., Schmeidler, J., Hartsfield, A., Wothke, W. (2000). Psychological functioning among juvenile offenders 12 months after family empowerment intervention. *Journal of Offender Rehabilitation* 32(1/2), 1–56.

Fare v. Michael C., 442 U.S. 707 (1979).

Federal Bureau of Investigation (2009). *Crime in the United States, 2008*. Washington, DC: U.S. Department of Justice.

Federal Bureau of Investigation (2013). *Crime in the United States, 2012*. Washington, DC: U.S. Department of Justice.

Feld, B. (1993). Criminalizing the American juvenile court. In: M. Tonry (ed.) *Crime and justice: A review of research*. Chicago, IL: University of Chicago Press, pp. 197–280.

Feld, B. (1999). *Bad kids: Race and the transformation of the juvenile court*. New York: Oxford University Press.

Feld, B. (2001). Race, youth violence, and the changing jurisprudence of waiver. *Behavioral Sciences & The Law* 19, 3–22.

Getis, V. (2000). *The juvenile court and the progressives*. Chicago, IL: University of Chicago Press.

Gottfredson, D., Barton, W. (1993). Deinstitutionalization of juvenile offenders. *Criminology* 31(4), 591–610.

Government Accounting Office (1994). *Residential care: Some high risk youth benefit but more study is needed*. Washington, DC: U.S. Government Accounting Office.

Greenwood, P. (1999). *Costs and benefits of early childhood intervention*. Factsheet 94. Washington, DC: Office of Juvenile Justice and Delinquency Prevention.

Grisso, T., Schwartz, R. (2000). *Youth on trial: A developmental perspective on juvenile justice.*: Chicago, IL: University of Chicago Press.

Harris, K. (1996). Key differences among community corrections acts in the United States: An overview. *Prison Journal* 76(2), 192–238.

Haumschilt, G. (2001). The responsibility to the public in parole. *CYA Today* 2(1), 4.

Hayes, H., Geerken, M. (1997). The idea of selective release. *Justice Quarterly* 14(2), 353–370.

Hockenberry, S. (2013). *Juveniles in residential placement, 2010*. Washington, DC: Office of Juvenile Justice and Delinquency Prevention.

In re Gault, 1967 387 U.S. 1 (1967).

In re Winship, 397 U.S. 358 (1970).

Jenson, E., Metzger, L. (1994). A test of the deterrent effect of legislative waiver on violent juvenile crime. *Crime & Delinquency* 40(1), 96–104.

Kent v. United States, 383 U.S. 54 (1966).

King, P., Noel, J. (1994). The origins of the problem of juvenile delinquency: The growth of juvenile prosecution in London. In: L. Knafla (ed.) *Criminal justice history: An international volume*. Westport, CT: Greenwood Press, pp. 17–41.

Koetzel-Shaffer, D. (2006). Reconsidering drug court effectiveness: A meta-analytic review. University of Cincinnati: Doctoral dissertation.

Krisberg, B., Austin, J., Steele, P. (1991). *Unlocking juvenile corrections*. San Francisco, CA: National Council on Crime and Delinquency.

Krisberg, B., Austin, J., Joe, K., Steele, P. (1987). *The impact of court sanctions*. San Francisco, CA: National Council on Crime and Delinquency.

Latessa, E., Lovins, B., Lux, J. (2014). *Evaluation of Ohio's RECLAIM programs*. Cincinnati, OH: Center for Criminal Justice Research, University of Cincinnati.

Latessa, E., Moon, M., Applegate, B. (1995). *Preliminary evaluation of the Ohio department of youth services RECLAIM Ohio Pilot Project*. Cincinnati, OH: University of Cincinnati.

Latessa, E., Shaffer, D., Lowenkamp, C. (2002). *Outcome evaluation of Ohio's drug court efforts: Final report*. Cincinnati, OH: Center for Criminal Justice Research, University of Cincinnati.

Lee, L. (1994). Factors determining waiver to a juvenile court. *Journal of Criminal Justice* 22(4), 329–340.

Lindner, C., Savarese, M. (1984). The evolution of probation: Early salaries, qualifications and hiring practices. *Federal Probation* 48(1), 3–9.

Livsey, S. (2012). *Juvenile delinquency probation caseloads, 2009*. Washington, DC: Office of Juvenile Justice and Delinquency Prevention.

Lovins, B., Latessa, E.J. (2013). Creation and validation of the Ohio Youth Assessment System (OYAS) and strategies for successful implementation. *Justice Research and Policy* 15, 67–93.

Lovins, B., Lux, J. (2014). *Cost benefit analysis of Ohio's RECLAIM, CCF and DYS programs and facilities*. Cincinnati, OH: Center for Criminal Justice Research, University of Cincinnati.

Lowenkamp, C., Latessa, E. (2005). *Evaluation of Ohio's RECLAIM funded programs, community corrections facilities, and DYS facilities*. Cincinnati, OH: University of Cincinnati, Center for Criminal Justice Research.

Macallair, D. (1993). Reaffirming rehabilitation in juvenile justice. *Youth and Society* 25(1), 104–125.

Macallair, D. (1994). Disposition case advocacy in San Francisco juvenile justice system: A new approach to deinstitutionalization. *Crime & Delinquency* 40(1), 84–95.

Manfredi, C. (1998). *The Supreme Court and Juvenile Justice.* Lawrence, KS: University Press of Kansas.

Mauser, E., Van Stelle, K., Moberg, P. (1994). The economic impacts of diverting substance-abusing offenders into treatment. *Crime & Delinquency* 40(4), 568–588.

Maxson, C., Klein, M. (1997). *Responding to troubled youth.* New York: Oxford University Press.

McCord, J., Sanchez, J. (1983). The treatment of deviant children: A twenty-five year follow-up study. *Crime & Delinquency* 29(2), 238–253.

McDevitt, J., Domino, M., Brown, K. (1997). *Metropolitan day reporting center: An evaluation.* Boston, MA: Center for Criminal Justice Policy Research, Northeastern University.

McKeiver v. Pennsylvania, 403 U.S. 528 (1971).

McNulty, E. (1996). *Arizona juvenile transfer study.* Phoenix, AZ: Administrative Office of the Courts, Arizona Supreme Court.

Merlo, A., Benekos, P., Cook, W. (1997). "Getting tough" with youth: Legislative waiver as crime control. *Juvenile and Family Court Journal* 48(3), 1–15.

Moore, M., Wakeling, S. (1997). Juvenile justice: Shoring up the foundations. In: M. Tonry (ed.) *Crime and justice: A review of research.* Chicago, IL: University of Chicago Press, pp. 253–301.

Myers, D.L. (2003). The recidivism of violent youths in juvenile and adult court: A consideration of selection bias. *Youth Violence and Juvenile Justice* 1(79), 101.

Nelson v. Heyne, 491 F.2d 352 (7th Cir.) (1974).

Office of Juvenile Justice and Delinquency Prevention (1996). *Juvenile probation: The workhorse of the juvenile justice system.* Washington, DC: OJJDP. www.ncjrs. org/pdffiles/workhors.pdf.

Office of Juvenile Justice and Delinquency Prevention (1998a). *The youngest offenders.* 1996. Washington, DC: OJJDP.

Office of Juvenile Justice and Delinquency Prevention (1998b). *What about girls?* Washington, DC: OJJDP.

Office of Juvenile Justice and Delinquency Prevention (1999). *Costs and benefits of early childhood intervention.* Washington, DC: OJJDP.

Office of Juvenile Justice and Delinquency Prevention (2000). *Implementation of the intensive community-based aftercare program.* Washington, DC: OJJDP.

Office of Juvenile Justice and Delinquency Prevention (2001a). *Caseflow diagram.* Washington, DC: OJJP.

Office of Juvenile Justice and Delinquency Prevention (2001b). *Juvenile court statistics, 2005.* Washington, DC: OJJDP.

Office of Juvenile Justice and Delinquency Prevention (2001c). *The 8% solution.* Washington, DC: OJJDP.

Ohio Department of Youth Services (2014). *DYS admissions.* Ohio: Ohio Department of Youth Services, 1991–2007.

Orange County Probation Office (2001). *8% problem study findings.* Orange County: OCPO.

Platt, A. (1977). *The child savers: The invention of delinquency.* Chicago, IL: University of Chicago Press.

Podkopacz, M.R., Feld, B.C. (2001). The back-door to prison: Waiver reform, "blended sentencing" and the law of unintended consequences. *Journal of Criminal Law and Criminology* 91, 997–1071.

President's Commission on Law Enforcement and Administration of Justice (1967). *Juvenile delinquency and youth crime.* Washington, DC: U.S. Government Printing Office.

Puzzanchera, C. (2013) *Juvenile arrests 2011.* Washington, DC: U.S. Dept. of Justice, Office of Juvenile Justice and Delinquency Prevention.

Puzzanchera, C., Adams, B., Sickmund, M. (2010). *Juvenile court statistics, 2006–2007.* Pittsburgh: National Center for Juvenile Justice.

Puzzanchera, C., Addie, S. (2014). *Delinquency cases waived to criminal court, 2010.* Washington, DC: U.S. Dept. of Justice, Office of Juvenile Justice and Delinquency Prevention.

Rapp-Paglicci, L., Wodarski, J. (2000), Antecedent behaviors of male youth victimization. *Deviant Behavior* 21(6), 519–536.

Rausch, S., Logan, C. (1982). *Diversion from juvenile court: Panacea or Pandora's box?* Paper presented at the annual meeting of the American Society of Criminology, Toronto, Canada.

Redding, R.E. (1999). Juvenile offenders in criminal court and adult prison. *Juvenile and Family Court Journal* 50(1), 1–20.

Redding, R.E. (2003). The effects of adjudication and sentencing juveniles as adults: Research and policy implications. *Youth Violence and Juvenile Justice* 1, 128–155.

Redding, R.E. (2010). *Juvenile transfer laws: An effective deterrent to delinquency? Juvenile Justice Bulletin.* Washington, DC: Office of Juvenile Justice and Delinquency Prevention.

Risler, E., Sweatman, T., Nackerud, L. (1998). Evaluating the Georgia legislative waiver's effectiveness in deterring juvenile crime. *Research on Social Work Practice* 8(6), 657–667.

Rogers, J., Mays, G. (1987). *Juvenile delinquency and juvenile justice.* New York: John Wiley.

Roper v. Simmons, 543 U.S. 551 (2005).

Sanborn, J. (1994a). Constitutional problems of juvenile delinquency trials. *Judicature* 78(2), 81–88.

Sanborn, J. (1994b). Remnants of parens patriae in the adjudicatory hearing. *Crime & Delinquency* 40(4), 599–615.

Sarre, R. (1999). Destructuring and criminal justice reform. *Current Issues in Criminal Justice* 10(3), 259–272.

Schall v. Martin, 467 U.S. 253 (1984).

Schumaker, M., Kurtz, G. (2000). *The 8% solution.* Thousand Oaks, CA: Sage.

Schur, E. (1971). *Labeling deviant behavior: Its sociological implications.* New York: Harper and Row.

Shannon, L. (1982). *Assessing the relationship of adult career criminals to juvenile careers.* Washington, DC: U.S. Government Printing Office.

Sheley, J., McGee, Z., Wright, J. (1995). *Weapons-related victimization in selected inner-city high school samples.* Washington, DC: Bureau of Justice Statistics.

Sherrill, M. (1975a). Jerome Miller: Does he have the answers …? *Corrections Magazine* 1(2), 24–28.

Sherrill, M. (1975b). Harvard recidivism study. *Corrections Magazine* 1(2), 21–23.

Sickmund, M., Sladky, A., Kang, W. (2008). *Census of juveniles in residential placement databook.* Washington, DC: Office of Juvenile Justice and Delinquency Prevention.

Sickmund, M., Sladky, A., Kang, W. (2010). *Easy access to juvenile court statistics: 1985–2007.* Washington, DC: Office of Juvenile Justice and Delinquency Prevention.

Snyder, H. (2005). *Juvenile arrests 2003.* Washington, DC: U.S. Office of Juvenile Justice and Delinquency Prevention.

Snyder, H., Sickmund, M., Poe-Yamagata, E. (2000). *Juvenile transfers to criminal court in the 1990s.* Washington, DC: Office of Juvenile Justice and Delinquency Prevention.

Snyder, H., Sickmund, M., Yamagata, E. (1996). *Juvenile offenders and victims.* Washington, DC: U.S. Office of Juvenile Justice and Delinquency Prevention.

Solomon, K., Klein, M. (1983). *National evaluation of the deinstitutionalization of status offender programs.* Washington, DC: Office of Juvenile Justice and Delinquency Prevention, U.S. Department of Justice.

Sourcebook of Criminal Justice Statistics. *Criminal Justice Statistics 2003* (31st edn). Online. www.albany.edu/sourcebook.

Sullivan, C., Blair, L., Latessa, E.J., Sullivan, C.C. (2014). Juvenile drug courts and recidivism: Results from a multisite outcome study. *Justice Quarterly.* Published online May 2014.

Thomas, C.W., Bishop, D.M. (1984). The impact of legal sanctions on delinquency: A longitudinal comparison of labeling and deterrence theories. *Journal of Criminal Law and Criminology* 75, 1225–1245.

Torbert, P., Gable, R., Hurst, H. (1996). *State responses to serious and violent juvenile crime.* Washington, DC: U.S. Office of Juvenile Justice and Delinquency Prevention.

Ullman, R.P. (2000). Federal juvenile waiver practices: A contextual approach to the consideration of prior delinquency records. *Fordham Law Review* 68, 1329–1369.

Umbreit, M. (1994). *Victim meets offender: The impact of restorative justice and mediation.* Monsey, NY: Criminal Justice Press.

Umbreit, M. (1995). The development and impact of victim–offender mediation in the United States. *Mediation Quarterly* 12, 263–276.

Umbreit, M., Vos, B. (2000). Homicide survivors meet the offenders prior to execution. *Homicide Studies* 4(1), 63–87.

U.S. Bureau of Justice Assistance (1994). *Drug night courts.* Washington, DC: USBJS.

U.S. Bureau of Justice Statistics (1994). *Night drug courts: The Cook County Experience.* Washington, DC: USBJS.

Winner, L., Lanza-Kaduce, L., Bishop, D.M., Frazier, C.E. (1997). The transfer of juveniles to criminal court: Reexamining recidivism over the long term. *Crime and Delinquency* 43, 548–563.

Wu, B. (2000). Determinants of public opinion toward juvenile waiver decisions. *Juvenile and Family Court Journal* 50(1), 9–20.

Chapter 7

ROLES OF PROBATION AND PAROLE OFFICERS

Key Terms

concrete needs counseling
emotional needs counseling
investigation
protective officer

punitive officer
supervision
surveillance
welfare officer

> A parole officer can be seen going off to his/her appointed rounds with Freud in one hand and a .38 Smith and Wesson in the other hand. It is by no means clear that Freud is as helpful as the .38 in most areas where parole officers venture. . . . Is Freud backup to the .38? Or is the .38 carried to support Freud?—David Fogel

As Fogel (McCleary, 1978) succinctly indicates, the role of the probation or parole officer (PO)[1] has traditionally been viewed as a dichotomy (American Correctional Association, 1995). The supervision role involves maintaining surveillance over (societal protection) as well as helping or treating the offender (counseling, rehabilitation, reintegration). Community supervision officers are often left to their own devices with regard to which role would be most appropriate in supervising their caseloads. This dilemma is likely to remain even though calls from several quarters of the criminal justice system point toward impending changes in the role of the supervising officer (Smith et al., 2012; Bonta et al., 2008; Reinventing Probation Council, 2001; Taxman & Byrne, 2001; Trotter, 1999). This chapter describes and outlines the boundaries of this role conflict as it has developed over time, the problems associated with it, and the responsibilities of probation and parole agencies.

RESPONSIBILITIES OF PROBATION AND PAROLE AGENCIES

To begin, it is necessary to examine what duties and responsibilities are held in common by probation and parole agencies. O'Leary (1974) has argued that parole resembles probation in several ways. With both, information is gathered and presented to a decision-making authority (either a judge or a parole board). This authority has the power to release (parole) or suspend the sentence (probation) of the offender. In turn, the liberty that the offender enjoys is subject to certain conditions that are imposed by the decision-making authority. If these conditions are not obeyed, the offender may be sentenced, or returned, to prison.

However, parole differs from probation in distinct ways. The offender on parole has served a portion of his or her sentence in a correctional facility. The decision to release the offender from prison is usually an administrative one, made by the parole board. The decision to grant probation lies entirely with the court. As Wallace (1974, p. 950) has written, "Probation is more than a process; it connotes an organization, basically a service agency, designed to assist the court and to perform particular functions in the administration of criminal justice."

Despite these differences, probation and parole agencies share one particular and significant function: they provide supervision of offenders in the community. The basic question remains: What is the purpose of supervision? To Wallace, the function of supervision, drawn from the social work field, is based on the casework model. **Supervision** is the basis of a treatment program. The officer uses all information available about the offender to make a diagnosis of that person's needs and to design a treatment plan. One example of a treatment plan for probationers, emphasizing the need for reintegration, was first suggested by the President's Commission on Law Enforcement and Administration of Justice (1967, p. 30):

> developing the offender's effective participation in the major social institutions of the school, business and church . . . which offer access to a successful career.

However, providing treatment is only one aspect of supervision. In addition, the PO is expected to maintain surveillance of those offenders who make up the caseload.

A classic definition of surveillance was provided by the National Conference of Parole (Studt, 1978, p. 65):

> Surveillance is that activity of the parole officer which utilizes watchfulness, checking, and verification of certain behavior of a parolee without contributing to a helping relationship with him.

Although these statements indicate that the treatment and surveillance roles of the probation/parole officer are almost diametrically opposed, several authors have indicated that they coexist as a part of the agency's mission. In fact, Carlson and

Parks (1979, pp. 155–157) have listed four major responsibilities of a probation or parole agency:

- **Surveillance**: While the term "surveillance" usually means simply "watching" in a police sense, it should be pointed out that a helping purpose is also intended. When surveillance is carried out properly, the client is continually sensitized to the possible results of a course of action that has made him or her vulnerable in the past. Just as an alcoholic or narcotics addict who is trying to change his or her life derives support from frequent contact with others who have conquered their problems successfully, so also can many clients derive beneficial results from frequent meetings with the probation officer.
- **Investigation**: The investigation function includes reporting violative behavior, or actual violation on the part of probationers, and gathering facts about arrests and reporting suspicions to supervisors.
- **Concrete needs counseling**: This type of counseling includes the following areas: employment, education, training, housing, clothing, financial, medical, dental, legal, and transportation.
- **Emotional needs counseling**: The services that a probation officer provides depend on the needs of clientele they serve. These needs can include marital/family relationships, companions, emotional stability, alcohol and other drug use, mental ability, and sexual behavior.

ROLE TYPOLOGIES

In one of the first studies of types of officers, Ohlin et al. (1956, pp. 211–225) developed the following typology of PO styles:

- The **punitive officer**, who perceives himself [*sic*] as the guardian of middle-class morality; he attempts to coerce the offender into conforming by means of threats and punishment and emphasizes control, the protection of the community against the offender, and the systematic suspicion of those under supervision.
- The **protective officer**, who vacillates literally between protecting the offender and protecting the community. His tools are direct assistance, lecturing, and, alternately, praise and blame. He is perceived as ambivalent in his emotional involvement with the offender and others in the community as he shifts back and forth in taking sides with one against the other.
- The **welfare officer**, who has as his ultimate goal the improved welfare of the client, achieved by aiding him in his individual adjustment within limits imposed by the client's capacity. Such an officer believes that the only genuine guarantee of community protection lies in the client's personal adjustment, as external conformity will only be temporary and, in the long run, may make a successful adjustment more difficult. Emotional neutrality permeates his relationship. The diagnostic categories and treatment skills that he employs stem from an objective and theoretically based assessment of the client's needs and capacities.

Glaser (1969) later extended this typology to include, as a fourth category, the passive officer, who sees his job as a sinecure, requiring only minimum effort. For example, Erickson (1977, p. 37) has satirically offered the following gambit to officers who wish to "fake it" and have an "ideal, trouble-free caseload":

> "I'm just so busy—never seem to have enough time." A truly professional execution of this ploy does require some preparation. Make sure that your desktop is always inundated with a potpourri of case files, messages, memos, unopened mail, and professional literature. . . . Have your secretary hold all your calls for a few days and schedule several appointments for the same time. When, after a lengthy wait, the probationer is finally ushered into your presence, impress him (or her) with the volume of your business. . . . Always write while conversing with the subject, and continue to make and receive telephone calls. Interrupt your dialogue with him to attend to other important matters, such as obtaining the daily grocery list from your wife or arranging to have your car waxed. Apologize repeatedly and profusely for these necessary interruptions and appear to be distracted, weary, and slightly insane. Having experienced the full treatment, it is unlikely that the probationer will subsequently try to discuss with you any matters of over-whelming concern. He could even feel sorrier for you than he does for himself. You should henceforth be able to deal with him on an impersonal basis, if indeed he tries to report anymore at all.

The complete typology is presented in tabular form in Figure 7.1. The key distinction in this figure is the manner in which the supervising officer personally views the purpose of the job of supervision. Personal preference and motivations of the PO will often determine the style of supervision that is followed.

A similar typology was developed by Klockars (1972), based on the working philosophy of the officer. The first style that he presented is that of the "law enforcer." Such officers are motivated primarily by (1) the court order and obtaining offender compliance with it, (2) the authority and decision-making power of the PO, (3) officer responsibility for public safety, and (4) police work—the PO as police officer of the agency.

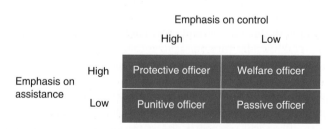

Figure 7.1 Typology of Probation Officer Supervision Styles.

Source: Jordan, F., Sasfy, J. (1974). *National impact program evaluation: A review of selected issues and research findings related to probation and parole.* Washington, DC: Mitre Corp.

The second category is that of the "time server." This person feels that the job has certain requirements to be fulfilled until retirement—"I don't make the rules; I just work here." The third type is the "therapeutic agent," a supervising officer who accepts the role of administrator of a form of treatment (usually casework-oriented) to help the offender.

Finally, the "synthetic officer" attempts to blend treatment and law enforcement components by "combining the paternal, authoritarian, and judgmental with the therapeutic." The synthetic officer attempts to solve what Miles (1965a) terms criminal justice (offender is wrong but responsible for own behavior) with treatment (casework, offender is sick) goals. In sum, Klockars's typology rounds out the original scheme developed by Ohlin et al. (1956) by providing an example through which the PO can integrate the best of each possible role.[2]

Czajkoski (1973) expanded on the law enforcement role of the officer's job by outlining the quasi-judicial role of the probation officer. He develops his thesis on five lines of functional analysis. The first line examines the plea bargaining; Czajkoski cites Blumberg's (1974) argument that the probation officer serves to "cool the mark" in the confidence game of plea bargaining by assuring the defendant of how wise it was to plead guilty. In this fusion, the PO certifies the plea-bargaining process—a task that can significantly undermine the helping/counseling role of the PO.

The second line of quasi-judicial functioning by the probation officer occurs at the intake level. For example, at the juvenile level, the officer is often asked which cases are appropriate for judicial processing. Like the prosecutor, this function permits the probation officer to have some control over the intake of the court.

The third quasi-judicial function of the probation officer concerns setting the conditions of probation, a power the judge often gives the probation officer. This often leads to discretionary abuses, as indefinite conditions (often moralistic or vague in terms of the offender's behavior) can become a vehicle for maintaining the moral status quo as interpreted by the probation officer. In addition, probation conditions can become substitutions for, or even usurp, certain formal judicial processes. For example, the monetary obligations[3] of the probationer (such as supporting dependants) can be enforced by the probation officer rather than by a court that is designed specifically to handle such matters (Schneider et al., 1982).

The fourth quasi-judicial role is concerned with probation violation procedures. Czajkoski contends that such procedures are highly discretionary, especially in view of the vague and all-encompassing nature of the probation conditions, which are usually not enforced until the officer has reason to believe that the probationer is engaged in criminal activity. Petersilia and Turner (1993) noted that increased surveillance increases the incidence of technical violations (Marciniak, 2000), jail terms, and incarceration rates, as well as program and court costs.

The final quasi-judicial role of the probation officer concerns the ability to administer punishment. Because the officer may restrict the liberty of his or her charge in several ways, this is tantamount to punishment. In this fashion, Czajkoski highlights some of the actions officers take that relate to his or her function as a quasi-judicial official and illustrates more ways in which the PO uses discretionary power in judicial-like ways.

Tomaino (1975) also attempts to reveal some of the hidden functions of probation officers. Figure 7.2 summarizes the Tomaino typology. Once again, concern for control is contrasted with concern for rehabilitation. To Tomaino, the key probation officer role is the "Have It Make Sense" face. This role attempts to integrate the often-conflicting concerns of societal protection and offender rehabilitation. Accordingly, Tomaino recommends that the officer stress goals, not offender personality traits, to "organize legitimate choices through a collaborative relationship which induces the client to act in accord with prosocial expectations." Perhaps, as Lindner (1975) suggests, the probation officer can create a learning situation for the offender and induce a desire for change.

In sum, these authors indicate that the supervising officer has a range of choices concerning the style of supervision to be followed and the ultimate goal of the entire

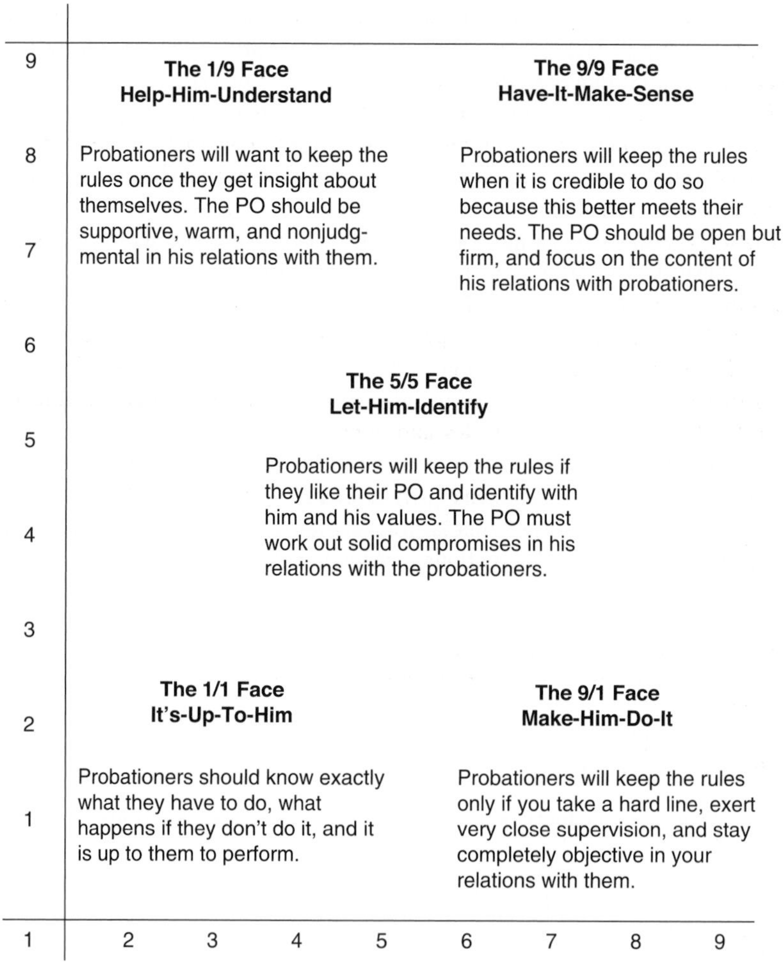

9	**The 1/9 Face** **Help-Him-Understand**	**The 9/9 Face** **Have-It-Make-Sense**
8	Probationers will want to keep the rules once they get insight about themselves. The PO should be supportive, warm, and nonjudg- mental in his relations with them.	Probationers will keep the rules when it is credible to do so because this better meets their needs. The PO should be open but firm, and focus on the content of his relations with probationers.
7		
6		
	The 5/5 Face **Let-Him-Identify**	
5		
	Probationers will keep the rules if they like their PO and identify with him and his values. The PO must work out solid compromises in his relations with the probationers.	
4		
3		
	The 1/1 Face **It's-Up-To-Him**	**The 9/1 Face** **Make-Him-Do-It**
2		
	Probationers should know exactly what they have to do, what happens if they don't do it, and it is up to them to perform.	Probationers will keep the rules only if you take a hard line, exert very close supervision, and stay completely objective in your relations with them.
1		
	2 3 4 5 6 7 8 9	

Figure 7.2 The Five Faces of Probation Supervision.

Source: Tomaino, L. (1975). The five faces of probation. *Federal Probation* 39(4), 41–46.

probation/parole process. There is a strong emphasis here upon blending the need for control with the need for counseling. The officer must choose which style to adopt based on the individual client (severity of the offense, amenability to treatment) and the nature of the situation. Supervising officers clearly have the discretionary power to either enforce the law (i.e., conditions of supervision) or offer help and treatment. No doubt, the world view of the PO also plays a crucial role in this decision.

CHARACTERISTICS OF EFFECTIVE CHANGE AGENTS

What are the characteristics of effective probation and parole officers? Research by Gendreau and Andrews (2001), as well as others, suggests that the most effective change agents possess several characteristics. First, they are able to develop a strong collaborative relationship with offenders. Warmth, genuineness, and flexibility characterize such relationships. Second, effective change agents are firm but fair, have a sense of humor, and believe that offenders can change. Third, they are able to model behavior in concrete and vivid ways. Fourth, they are a source of not simply punishment, but of reinforcement for positive behavior. Finally, an effective change agent discourages negative attitudes and behaviors with strong, emphatic statements of disagreement. Table 7.1 shows the core correctional practices that are fundamental to POs as agents of change.

Unfortunately, as Shichor (1978, p. 37) points out, such characteristics often stand in sharp contrast to current probation and parole practices that are more oriented toward "people processing" than "people changing." Research has also confirmed that the vast majority of officers do not target major criminogenic needs (such as antisocial attitudes and social supports for crime) and do not commonly use skills (such as prosocial modeling and effective reinforcement) to influence long-term behavioral change in offenders (Bonta et al., 2008).

Most recently, training curricula designed to teach community supervision officers how to apply core correctional practices in their face-to-face interactions

Table 7.1 Core Correctional Practices

1. Effective reinforcement
2. Effective disapproval
3. Effective use of authority
4. Quality interpersonal relationships
5. Cognitive restructuring
6. Anti-criminal modeling
7. Structured learning/Skill building
8. Problem-solving techniques

Source: Andrews, D.A., Kiessling, J.J. (1980). Program structure and effective correctional practices: A summary of the CaVIC research. In R.R. Ross and P. Gendreau (eds), *Effective correctional treatment*. Toronto: Butterworth, pp. 441–463.

with offenders have been piloted in many jurisdictions (see Bonta et al., 2008; Robinson et al., 2011; Latessa et al., 2013; Smith et al., 2012; Trotter, 1999). Research by Bonta and his colleagues (2008) has indicated that traditional officer–offender interactions are often not effective using traditional approaches. Table 7.2 summarizes their findings. Fortunately, results from several studies have demonstrated that trained officers achieve greater reductions in recidivism when compared to untrained officers (Bonta et al., 2010; Robinson, et al., 2011, Latessa et al., 2013). Figures 7.3 and 7.4 show results from studies in Canada and Ohio.

Table 7.2 Traditional Officer–Offender Interactions

Traditional officer–offender interactions are often not effective because:
- They are too brief to have an impact
- Conversations focus almost exclusively on monitoring compliance conditions (and therefore emphasize external controls on behavior rather than developing an internal rationale for pro-social behavior)
- Relationship is often more confrontational and authoritarian in nature than helpful
- What is targeted is not always based on assessment
- More areas discussed = less effective

Source: Bonta, J., Rugge, T., Scott, T., Bourgon, G., Yessine, A.K. (2008). Exploring the black box of community supervision. *Journal of Offender Rehabilitation* 47, 248–270.

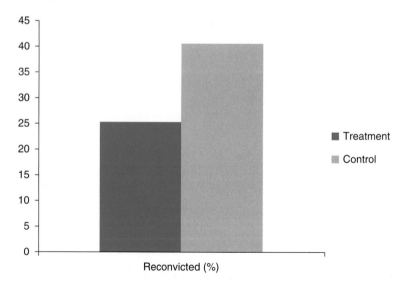

Figure 7.3 Two-Year Recidivism Results from Canadian Study: POs Utilize Core Correctional Practices.

Source: Bonta, J., Bourgon, G., Rugge, T., Scott, T., Yessine, A.K., Gutierrez, L., Li, J. (2010). *The strategic training initiative in community supervision: Risk-need-responsivity in the real world.* Ottawa: Public Safety Canada.

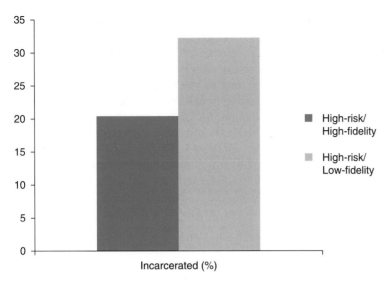

Figure 7.4 Recidivism Results from Ohio Study Looking at Fidelity and High-Risk-Offenders (both adult and juvenile) Using Core Correctional Practices.

Source: Latessa, E., Smith, P., Schweitzer, M., Labrecque, R. (2013). *Evaluation of the Effective Practices in Community Supervision Model (EPICS) in Ohio.* Cincinnati, OH: School of Criminal Justice, University of Cincinnati.

Additional research on this topic is forthcoming and will undoubtedly contribute to our understanding of how parole and probation officers can be better used as agents of change.

THE SELF-IMAGE OF PROBATION AND PAROLE OFFICERS

How do probation and parole officers see themselves and their work? Over the years several studies have focused on agents to secure their views about what the appropriate goals of supervision should be and, within the criminal justice system, where such agents primarily identify with their allegiance.

Box 7.1
All Things to All People

For larger probation departments, specialization has become more common. There are presentence investigation units, assessment units, fugitive and warrant units, surveillance officers, and specialized caseload units. In rural departments it is still common to have every probation officer perform all of these tasks.

In an early study, Miles (1965b) surveyed all 116 probation and parole officers on duty in Wisconsin on a single day. In addition, 48 officers were interviewed and accompanied into the field by the researchers. On the basis of these data, Miles discovered that a majority of these officers basically identified with the field of corrections (61.5 percent). The clear majority of individuals identified themselves as probation officers when dealing with judges (81 percent), social agencies (69 percent), and potential client employers (79 percent). These officers emphasized their identification with correctional work and did not wish to have this primary link absorbed by another area (e.g., social work). The survey also uncovered what is considered to be the basic dilemma of probation in terms of its primary goal: offender rehabilitation versus societal protection.

In a study of job tasks, Colley and colleagues (1987) surveyed 70 juvenile probation officers in Illinois. Table 7.3 illustrates the tasks performed by at least 40 percent of the sample. While most studies of probation officers have been conducted in urban areas, it is important to note what appear to be differences in

Table 7.3 Tasks Performed by at Least 40 Percent of Respondents on a Weekly or Daily Basis

Skills	Percent
COURT	
Attends court hearings with client	58.6
Takes court notes on court proceedings of clients	47.2
Confers with State's Attorney about cases	64.2
SUPERVISION—CASELOAD MANAGEMENT	
Meets with minor in office, home, and at school	57.1
Listens to complaints and problems	72.9
Asks minors about any general problems and disturbances	56.5
Inquires about police contacts	44.3
Consults teachers, therapists, significant others, community services agencies	44.3
Intervenes in crisis situations	42.9
Counsels parents	47.8
Confers with dean of students or school counselors	47.8
CASE NOTING	
Accounts for the entire history of the case	65.7
MONTHLY STATISTICS	
Documents all intakes, transfers, terminations, etc.	44.9
STAFFINGS	
Confers with other staff on informal basis about cases	60.8

Source: Colley, L., Culbertson, R., Latessa, E. (1987). Juvenile probation officers: A job analysis. *Juvenile and Family Court Journal* 38(3), 1–12.

the roles and tasks performed between urban and rural probation officers. Rural officers perform a wider range of tasks than urban officers and are less specialized (Colley et al., 1986).

Overall, the studies examined reveal that POs are aware of the surveillance/treatment dichotomy that exists with regard to style of supervision. A number of factors (age, education, years of job experience) are related to or influence the PO's style and method of supervision. Yet, in general, there is a distinct lack of consensus over which style of supervision should dominate.

Social Work or Law Enforcement?

The split between treatment and surveillance has attracted a great deal of attention, but very little in terms of empirical studies. Most authors seem to interpret role conflict as somehow tragic, intractable, and overwhelming. The most common solution has been to advocate that one orientation must be emphasized over all others (Gettinger, 1981). Simply put, is it the role of the probation or parole officer or that of the helper or the cop?[4]

The roots of role conflict are often attributed to inconsistencies that exist in the three main functions of supervision: to enforce the legal requirements of supervision (the "law enforcement" role), to assist the offender in establishing a successful community adjustment (the "social worker" role), and to carry out the policies of the supervision agency (the "bureaucrat" role). The existence of this role conflict has been seen as a major source of staff burnout (Lindquist & Whitehead, 1986; Whitehead, 1989). Others have recommended abandoning one of the roles, either social work (Barkdull, 1976) or law enforcement (Stanley, 1976). Interestingly, no one seems to believe seriously that the bureaucratic role can ever be eliminated (Lipsky, 1980; Rosecrance, 1987; Takagi, 1967).

One critic of surveillance is Conrad (1979, p. 21), who writes:

> We can hardly justify parole services on the basis of the surveillance model. What the parole officer can do, if it should be done at all, can better be done by the police. The pushing of doorbells, the recording of "contacts," and the requirement of monthly reports all add up to expensive pseudoservices. At best they constitute a costly but useless frenzy of activity. But more often than not, I suspect, they harass and humiliate the parolee without gaining even the illusion of control.

Clear and Latessa (1993, p. 442) believe that role conflict is common to most professions.

> College professors face the age-old conflict of research and teaching; lawyers confront the conflicting demands of client advocacy and case management; even ministers must consider whether they represent the interest of deities to the world or the needs of lost souls (and requisite bodies) in the world.

Certainly, probation or parole officers have no monopoly on role conflict. Many feel that the true "professional" finds a way of integrating various role expectations, balancing them and weighing the appropriateness of various expressions of the roles. There is even some evidence that the roles of "social worker" and "law enforcer" are not incompatible and that organizational policy can have a direct impact on the attitudes and behavior of probation and parole officers (Clear & Latessa, 1993).

A recent development in PO work is the increased level of assault by clients, leading to demand for arming of, or increased firepower (or both) for, POs (North Carolina Department of Corrections News, 1999). The exact number of critical incidents is unknown, as there is no state of federal bank that tracks the dangers faced by probation, parole, and even pretrial persons. However, a survey of probation and parole officers in Minnesota (Arola & Lawrence, 1999) found that 19 percent reported one or more physical assaults during their career, and 74 percent reported being threatened verbally or physically at least once. A similar study in Florida in 1999 found one in 20 probation and parole officers were battered each year (Florida Corrections Commission, 2000). With the emerging emphasis on supervision and surveillance within community corrections, the potential for crisis will increase. Another study of the extent of serious assault on community correctional personnel (Bigger, 1993) found 1,818 incidents since 1980, probably only the tip of the iceberg. Camp and Camp (2003) reported more than 16,400 assaults by inmates on prison correctional staff in 2002; about one in four required medical attention. A national study concluded that 14 percent of juvenile justice institutional staff were assaulted in 1998 (Office of Juvenile Justice and Delinquency Prevention, 1998).

Not only is there a need for a central information bank that would track critical incidents, there is a need for in-service training and orientation that would lessen the incipient danger. Brown (1993) suggested that PO safety could be enhanced by physical training, as well as learning skills to respond to such crises, including de-escalation techniques, understanding the continuum of force, and how to make effective use of authority. Perhaps there is "no farewell to arms" in the offing, and administrators might implement training sessions to reduce liability and protect workers (Janes, 1993; Chavaria, 1994; National Institute of Corrections, 2001).

Box 7.2
Motivating Offenders

Recently, many probation departments have begun training officers on motivational interviewing. First developed by Miller and Rollnick (1991) and based on Prochaska and DiClemente's (1983) stages of change, motivational interviewing is a technique designed to help prepare offenders to change their lifestyles. Officers are taught skills that can be used to overcome resistance to treatment and encourage offenders to think about the benefits of changing negative attitudes and behaviors.

EDUCATION AND TRAINING OF PROBATION AND PAROLE OFFICERS

During the past 40 years, several national commissions and studies have recommended formal education as a means of significantly improving the delivery of justice in this country (American Bar Association, 1970; National Advisory Commission, 1973; National Manpower Survey of the Criminal Justice System, 1978; President's Commission on Law Enforcement and Administration of Justice, 1967; Sherman, 1978). Graduate-level education and frequent in-service training for probation and parole officers have also been advocated for many years. The emerging philosophy now requires undergraduate degree education as a prerequisite for quality probation and parole service, and continuous in-service training as a means of maintaining and improving both service and skills (Loughery, 1975; National Advisory Commission, 1973; President's Commission on Law Enforcement and Administration of Justice, 1967; Senna, 1976).

Since 1959, the National Probation and Parole Association has recommended that all probation and parole officers should hold at least a bachelor's degree, supplemented by at least one year of graduate study or full-time field experience. This recommendation reflects the assumption that an educated officer is more competent and mature and thus is in a better position to perform the varied functions of probation and parole efficiently. However, it was not until the 1967 President's Commission on Law Enforcement and Administration of Justice Task Force Report, which led to the Law Enforcement Education Program, that federal funds were made available for higher education of justice system personnel, including a college education for probation and parole officers. In 1970, the American Bar Association (1970) reaffirmed the National Probation and Parole Association's minimum standards and suggested that probation and parole officers should hold a Master's degree. It is also important to note that the American Correctional Association Accreditation Guidelines for Probation and Parole (1981) require entry-level probation and parole officers to possess a minimum of a Bachelor's degree. They consider this an important guideline for accreditation.

The vast majority of jurisdictions in this country now require at least a Bachelor's degree for initial employment of probation and parole officers. In addition, many jurisdictions require specific areas of college study, as well as various levels of training and experience. While there is some consensus as to the level of education needed (Bachelor's degree), however, the exact content of undergraduate study is still a matter of some debate. Generally speaking, however, aspiring probation and parole personnel would better prepare themselves for agency entry by enrolling in various criminal justice, sociology, counseling, social work, and psychology courses. There is also some evidence that a comprehensive approach to training and development can effectively instill in officers the supervision attitudes that are most conducive to promoting offender change (Stichman et al., 1997).

SUMMARY

In summary, the conflict between counseling and surveillance is simply part of the job of the PO and a duality that makes his or her position in the criminal justice system vital, unique, and necessary. While some see role conflict as a reason for eviscerating some of the less salient tasks, others believe that the profession can find a way of integrating and balancing various role expectations.

The roles of probation and parole agencies are varied and range from investigating violations to assisting offenders in obtaining employment. Accordingly, the skills and education required of probation officers are often considerable. The need for college-educated staff has been advocated for many years and is becoming a reality. There has come to be a general acceptance of formal education as a prerequisite of quality probation and parole service and of in-service development as a means of maintaining and improving that service. This need has been identified and encouraged by several national commissions and organizations, as well as by numerous individual writers and researchers. A decade from now, the entry-level educational requirement could be a Master's degree.

Finally, although in many ways probation and parole officers perform the same basic duties that they did when the profession first began, there are many who argue that a change is in order. Current research has clearly demonstrated that when officers employ some core correctional practices they can become more effective agents of change and can have a significant effect on reducing recidivism.

Review Questions

1. What are the four primary responsibilities of a probation or parole agency?
2. What are the quasi-judicial roles of probation officers?
3. How does a probation/parole officer serve a law enforcement role? A social work role?
4. List those tasks that a probation or parole officer can undertake to assist an offender and those to control an offender.
5. List the seven categories of tasks ranked by probation officers in the von Langingham study.
6. According to Andrews, what are the characteristics of effective agents of change?
7. What does the research show when POs utilize core correctional practices?

Notes

1 Throughout this chapter, when the abbreviation PO is used, it is meant to designate both probation and parole officers. Their views with regard to their role, as well as the dilemmas that they face, are related so intimately that this abbreviation will not misrepresent the opinions, findings, and conclusions of the various authors.

2 Nowhere is the dichotomy of rehabilitation–casework versus surveillance–control more evident than between juvenile and adult probation officers. Juvenile officers support the former by a wide margin, but felony probation officers, particularly males, are more likely to endorse law enforcement strategies. See Sluder and Reddington (1993); and Brown and Pratt (2000).
3 Most probationers satisfy financial obligations as ordered by the court (Allen & Treger, 1994).
4 For a discussion of law enforcement officers as agents of reintegrative surveillance see Guarino-Ghezzi (1994).

Recommended Readings

Conrad, J. (1979). Who needs a doorbell pusher? *Prison Journal* 59(1), 17–26. [Building upon his experience as a probation officer, a noted scholar gives his opinions on the role of supervision.]
Ditton, J., Ford, R. (1994). *The reality of probation: A formal ethnography of process and practice.* Aldershot, UK: Avebury.
McCleary, R. (1978). *Dangerous men: The sociology of parole.* Beverly Hills, CA: Sage. [Based on participant observation, this is an in-depth examination of a parole agency and the supervision styles of its officers.]
Parent, D., Wentworth, D., Burke, P. (1994). *Responding to probation and parole violators.* Washington, DC: U.S. National Institute of Justice.
Ward, R., Webb, V. (1981). *Quest for quality.* New York: University Publications. [This is the report of the Joint Commission on Criminology and Criminal Justice Education and Standards. It examines the issues surrounding the education of criminal justice professionals.]

References

Allen, G., Treger, H. (1994). Fines and restitution orders: Probations' perceptions. *Federal Probation* 58(2), 34–40.
American Bar Association (1970). *Standards relating to probation.* New York: American Bar Association.
American Correctional Association Accreditation Guidelines for Probation and Parole (1981). *Standards for adult probation and parole field services.* Rockville, MD: Commission on Accreditation for Corrections, ACA.
American Correctional Association (1995). *Field officer resources guide.* Laurel, MD: ACA.
American Correctional Association (2008). *Directory of adult and juvenile correctional departments, institutions, agencies, and probation authorities.* Alexandria, VA: ACA. [Before 1996, agencies combining probation and parole caseloads were not separated.]
Arola, T., Lawrence, R. (1999). Assessing probation officer assaults and responding to officer safety concerns. *Perspectives* 23(3), 32–35.

Barkdull, W. (1976). Probation: Call it control and mean it. *Federal Probation* 40(4), 3–8.

Bigger, P. (1993). Officers in danger. *APPA Perspectives* 17(4), 14–20.

Blumberg, A. (1974). *Criminal justice*. New York: New Viewpoints.

Bonta, J., Rugge, T., Scott, T., Bourgon, G., Yessine, A.K. (2008). Exploring the black box of community supervision. *Journal of Offender Rehabilitation* 47, 248–270.

Bonta, J., Bourgon, G., Rugge, T., Scott, T., Yessine, A.K., Gutierrez, L., Li, J. (2010) *The strategic training initiative in community suopervision: Risk-need-responsivity in the real world*. Toronto, ONT: Public Safety Canada.

Brown, M., Pratt, J. (eds) (2000). *Dangerous offenders: Punishment and social order 2000*. London: Routledge.

Brown, P. (1993). Probation officer safety and mental conditioning. *Federal Probation* 57(4), 17–21.

Camp, C., Camp, G. (2003). *The corrections yearbook: Adult corrections 2002*. Middletown, CT: The Criminal Justice Institute.

Carlson, E., Parks, E. (1979). *Critical issues in adult probation*. Washington, DC: National Institute of Law Enforcement and Criminal Justice.

Chavaria, F. (1994). Building synergy in probation. *Federal Probation* 58(3), 18–22.

Clarkson, C. (2000). Corporate risk-taking and killing. *Risk Management* 2(1), 7–16.

Clear, T., Latessa, E. (1993). Probation officer roles in intensive supervision: Surveillance versus treatment. *Justice Quarterly* 10, 441–462.

Colley, L., Culbertson, R., Latessa, E. (1986). Probation officer job analysis: Rural–urban differences. *Federal Probation* 50(4), 67–71.

Colley, L., Culbertson, R., Latessa, E. (1987). Juvenile probation officers: A job analysis. *Juvenile and Family Court Journal* 38(3), 1–12.

Conrad, J. (1979). Who needs a door bell pusher? *Prison Journal* 59, 17–26.

Czajkoski, E. (1973). Exposing the quasi-judicial role of the probation officer. *Federal Probation* 37(2), 9–13.

Erickson, C. (1977). Faking it: Principles of expediency as applied to probation. *Federal Probation* 41(3), 36–39.

Florida Corrections Commission (2000). *Special risk for correctional probation officers*. Florida: FCC.

Gendreau, P., Andrews, D.A. (2001). *The Correctional Program Assessment Inventory-2000 (CPAI 2000)*. Saint John: University of New Brunswick.

Gettinger, S. (1981). Separating the cop from the counselor. *Corrections Magazine* 7, 34–41.

Glaser, D. (1969). *The effectiveness of a prison and parole system*. Indianapolis, IN: Bobbs-Merrill.

Guarino-Ghezzi, S. (1994). Reintegrative police surveillance of juvenile offenders: Forging an urban model. *Crime & Delinquency* 40, 131–153.

Janes, R. (1993). Total quality management: Can it work in federal probation? *Federal Probation* 57(4), 28–33.

Jordan, F., Sasfy, J. (1974). *National impact program evaluation: A review of selected issues and research findings related to probation and parole*. Washington, DC: Mitre Corp.

Klockars, C. (1972). A theory of probation supervision. *Journal of Criminal Law, Criminology and Police Science* 63, 550–557.

Latessa, E., Smith, P., Schweitzer, M., Labrecque, R. (2013). *Evaluation of the Effective Practices in Community Supervision Model (EPICS) in Ohio*. Cincinnati, OH: School of Criminal Justice, University of Cincinnati.

Lindner, C. (1975). The juvenile offender's right to bail. *Probation and Parole* 7(3), 64–68.

Lindquist, C., Whitehead, J. (1986). Correctional officers as parole officers: An examination of a community supervision sanction. *Criminal Justice and Behavior* 13, 197–222.

Lipsky, M. (1980). *Street level bureaucracy*. New York: Russell-Sage.

Loughery, D. (1975). College education: A must for probation officers? *Crime and Corrections* 3, 1–7.

McCleary, R. (1978). *Dangerous men: The sociology of parole*. Beverly Hills, CA: Sage.

Marciniak, L. (2000). The addition of day reporting to intensive supervision probation. *Federal Probation* 64(2), 34–39.

Miles, A. (1965a). The reality of the probation officer's dilemma. *Federal Probation* 29(1), 18–22.

Miles, A. (1965b). Wisconsin studies the function of probation and parole. *American Journal of Corrections* 25, 21–32.

Miller, W., Rollnick, S. (1991). *Motivational interviewing: Preparing for change*. New York: Guilford Press.

National Advisory Commission on Criminal Justice Standard and Goals (1973). *Criminal justice system*. Washington, DC: U.S. Government Printing Office

National Institute of Corrections (2001). *Topics in community corrections: Collaboration an essential strategy*. Washington, DC: National Institute of Corrections.

National Manpower Survey of the Criminal Justice System (1978). Washington, DC: U.S. Government Printing Office.

North Carolina Department of Corrections News (1999). *Officer and staff safety a top priority for Department of Corrections*. www.doc.state.nc.us/NEWS/1999/9909news/dcc.htm1999.

Office of Juvenile Justice and Delinquency Prevention (1998). *Youth gangs: An overview*. Washington, DC: OJJDP.

Ohlin, L., Piven, H., Pappenfort, M. (1956). Major dilemmas of the social worker in probation and parole. *National Probation and Parole Association Journal* 2, 21–25.

O'Leary, V. (1974). Parole administration. In: D. Glaser (ed.) *Handbook of criminology*. New York: Rand McNally, pp. 909–948.

Petersilia, J., Turner, S. (1993). Intensive probation and parole. *Crime and Justice: A Review of Research* 17, 281–336.

President's Commission on Law Enforcement and Administration of Justice (1967). *Task force report: Corrections*. Washington, DC: U.S. Government Printing Office.

Prochaska, J., DiClemente, C. (1983). Stages and processes of self-change in smoking: Toward an integrative model of change. *Journal of Consulting and Clinical Psychology* 51(3), 390–395.

Reinventing Probation Council (2001). *Transforming probation through leadership: The "Broken Windows" model.* www.manhattan-institute.org/html/broken_windows.htm.

Robinson, C.R., Van Benschoten, S.W., Alexander, M., Lowenkamp, C.T. (2011). A random (almost) study of staff training aimed at reducing re-arrest (STARR): Reducing recidivism through intentional design. *Federal Probation* 7 (2): 57–63.

Rosecrance, J. (1987). Getting rid of the prima donnas: The bureaucratization of a probation department. *Criminal Justice and Behavior* 14, 138–155.

Schneider, P., Griffith, W., Schneider, A. (1982). Juvenile restitution as a sole sanction or condition of probation: An empirical analysis. *Journal of Research in Crime & Delinquency* 19, 47–65.

Senna, J. (1976). The need for professional education in probation and parole. *Crime & Delinquency* 22, 67–74.

Sherman, L. (1978). *The quality of police education.* San Francisco, CA: Jossey-Bass.

Shichor, D. (1978). The people changing versus people processing organizational perspective: The case of correctional institutions. *LAE–Journal of the American Criminal Justice Association* 4(3), 37–44.

Sluder, R., Reddington, F. (1993). An empirical examination of work ideologies of juvenile and adult probation officers. *Journal of Offender Rehabilitation* 22, 115–137.

Smith, P., Schweitzer, M., Labreque, R., Latessa, E.J. (2012). Improving probation officers' skills: An evaluation of the EPICS model. *Journal of Crime and Justice* 35(2).

Stanley, D. (1976). *Prisoners among us: The problem of parole.* Washington, DC: Brookings Institute.

Stichman, A., Fulton, B., Latessa, E., Travis, F. (1997). *From preference to performance: Exploring the relationship between role definition and role performance among probation officers.* Paper presented at the Academy of Criminal Justice Sciences, Louisville, KY.

Studt, E. (1978). *Surveillance and service in parole.* Washington, DC: U.S. Department of Justice: National Institute of Corrections.

Takagi, P. (1967). *Evaluation and adaptations in a formal organization.* Berkeley, CA: University of California.

Taxman, F., Bryne, J. (2001). Fixing broken windows: Probation. *Perspectives* 25(2), 23–29.

Tomaino, L. (1975). The five faces of probation. *Federal Probation* 39(4), 41–46.

Trotter, C. (1999). *Working with involuntary clients: A guide to practice.* Thousand Oaks, CA: Sage.

Wallace, J. (1974). Probation administration. In: D. Glaser (ed.) *Handbook of criminology.* New York: Rand McNally, pp. 949–969.

Whitehead, J. (1989). *Burnout in probation and corrections.* New York: Praeger.

Chapter 8

OFFENDER ASSESSMENT

Key Terms

actuarial prediction
clinical prediction
dynamic risk predictors
false negatives
false positives
major risk factors
need
reassessment

reliability
responsivity
risk
risk management
static risk predictors
risk reduction
validity

Assessment is the engine that drives effective interventions.—Edward
Latessa

INTRODUCTION

Over the years, the assessment of offenders has evolved from using a "gut feeling"
to instruments that focused on past behavior (static indicators) to what are now
called fourth-generation instruments. The latest instruments combine static and
dynamic factors together to provide a more accurate prediction of risk, and they
identify the crime-producing needs that should be targeted for change in correctional treatment programs.

IMPORTANCE OF ASSESSMENT AND CLASSIFICATION

There are a number of reasons that classification and assessment of offenders are
important in community corrections. First, assessment and classification help
guide and structure decision making and provide important information that
correctional practitioners and officials can use for basing decisions such as parole
release. Second, it helps to reduce bias by eliminating extralegal factors, such as
race and gender, from consideration. Third, it enhances public safety by allowing

---

Box 8.1
Static versus Dynamic Risk Predictors

Static risk predictors refer to those factors or characteristics of an offender that cannot change. An example would be criminal history. For example, the number of prior arrests, age at first arrest, number of times incarcerated, and so on are good predictors of risk. However, once in place they cannot change. **Dynamic risk predictors** are those factors or characteristics of an offender that contribute to their risk, but are changeable; for example, peer associations, substance abuse, criminal thinking, and lack of employment. These factors also help predict reoffending and provide the probation or parole officer with areas to target. It should be noted that there are two types of dynamic factors: acute and stable. *Acute factors* can change quickly (such as employment), whereas *stable factors* are areas that take more time to change (such as attitudes and values).

---

court and correctional agencies to identify higher-risk offenders. Fourth, it helps manage offenders in a more efficient manner. This allows agencies to develop caseloads and workloads around risk and needs and to conserve scarce resources for those who need them most. Finally, the use of these instruments can aid in legal challenges. It is much easier to justify a decision based on a structured process that has been validated than on "gut feelings" (or so-called "expert opinion"). Perhaps the most important reason to conduct good assessments of offenders is that it improves the effectiveness of correctional programs. This is best illustrated by looking at the principles of effective intervention.

PRINCIPLES OF OFFENDER CLASSIFICATION

Through the work of a number of researchers, our understanding of classification and assessment and the important role it plays in community corrections is becoming more apparent (Andrews, 1982, 1989; Bonta, 2002; Bonta & Motiuk, 1985; Gendreau et al., 1996; Jones, 1996; Kennedy & Serin, 1997; Latessa & Lovins, 2010).

The key findings of meta-analyses (or quantitative reviews) of the corrections literature have been summarized into a framework that is referred to as the "principles of effective intervention." Let us now review these principles in more detail.

- **Risk**: WHO we should target for intervention. Higher-risk offenders are characterized by greater criminogenic needs; use a valid and reliable measure to assess offender risk; target higher-risk offenders for treatment.
- **Need**: WHAT we should target for intervention. Match offenders to programs that address their criminogenic needs; target more criminogenic needs than noncriminogenic needs.

- **Responsivity**: HOW we should target problem behaviors (including antisocial and criminal behaviors). Use potent behavior change strategies (i.e., social learning, cognitive-behavioral approaches); deliver intervention in a style and mode consistent with the ability and learning style of the offender and recognize that individuals may be more responsive to certain staff.
- **Professional discretion**: Having considered risk, need, and responsivity, decisions are made as appropriate under present conditions.

Risk

For our purposes, **risk** refers to the probability that an offender will reoffend. Thus, high-risk offenders have a greater probability of reoffending than low-risk offenders. It is important to remember that seriousness of the offense usually trumps "risk." That is, someone who commits a violent offense may be incarcerated, even if they are at low risk to reoffend.

The risk principle involves predicting future criminal behavior and matching interventions and supervision to the risk level of the offender. This principle states that interventions should be focused primarily on higher-risk offenders. The reason is simple: they have the highest chances of reoffending. Besides, why should we devote resources to those offenders who have a low probability of coming back again? Here is another way to think about it. Suppose that half of all offenders who leave prison never return. Are we worried about this group? Well, not as much as the half that will return. This is the group we are most concerned about and the one where we should place most of our efforts. Of course, in order to meet this principle, it is necessary to know who is the higher-risk offender, a process that involves a valid and reliable assessment process. Not only is it a question of resources, but it is also an effectiveness question. A number of studies have shown that placing lower-risk offenders into intense programs and higher levels of supervision can actually increase their failure rates.

[handwritten margin note: Too intensive too bad & Over intervention is bad Intervention on low-risk is bad]

Figure 8.1 shows the results from a study of intensive rehabilitation supervision in Canada. Data showed that higher-risk offenders placed in the intensive rehabilitation supervision program had a 32 percent recidivism rate after the two-year follow-up. Higher-risk offenders not placed in the program had a 51 percent recidivism rate. This is a 19 percent reduction in recidivism for higher-risk offenders. However, low-risk offenders placed in the treatment program reported the same recidivism rate as their high-risk counterparts. Conversely, lower-risk offenders not placed in the program

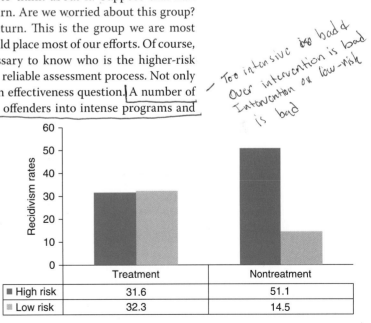

	Treatment	Nontreatment
■ High risk	31.6	51.1
■ Low risk	32.3	14.5

Figure 8.1 Study of Intensive Rehabilitation Supervision in Canada.

Source: Bonta, J., Wallace-Capretta, S., Rooney, J. (2000). A quasi-experimental evaluation of an intensive rehabilitation supervision program. *Criminal Justice and Behavior* 27(3), 312–329.

Low risk	↑ recidivism by 3%
Moderate risk	↓ recidivism by 6%
High risk	↓ recidivism by 14%

Figure 8.2 Average Difference in Recidivism by Risk for Halfway House Offenders.

Latessa, E.J., Lovins, L.B., Smith, P. (2010). *Follow-up evaluation of Ohio's community based correctional facility and halfway house programs—outcome study.* Cincinnati, OH: School of Criminal Justice, University of Cincinnati.

reported a recidivism rate almost 20 percent lower. In a nutshell, the intensive rehabilitation supervision program worked for higher-risk offenders, but actually increased recidivism rates for lower-risk offenders.

The risk principle can also be seen in a study that Latessa et al. (2010b) conducted in Ohio. This study examined the effectiveness of 44 halfway houses and 20 community-based correctional facilities and involved more than 20,000 offenders. Figure 8.2 shows average changes in recidivism based on the risk level of the offender. Low-risk offenders actually showed an increase in recidivism, while there was a reduction in recidivism for high-risk offenders.

The question is: Why do programs that have such a positive effect on high-risk offenders have such a negative effect on low-risk offenders? There are a couple of explanations. First, placing low-risk and high-risk offenders together is never a good practice. For example, if you had a son or daughter who got into some trouble, would you want them placed in a group with high-risk kids? Of course not. Second, when we take lower-risk offenders, who, by definition, are fairly prosocial (if they weren't they wouldn't be low risk) and place them in a highly structured, restrictive program, we actually disrupt the factors that make them low risk. For example, if you were sent to a correctional treatment program for six months, would you lose your job or have to drop out of school? Would you experience family disruption? Would your neighbors have a "welcome home from the correctional program" party when you got out? In other words, the criminal justice system would probably have inadvertently increased your risk by disrupting protective factors. The risk principle, then, refers to WHO should be targeted for placement in more intense services and supervision.

Need

The second principle is known as the **need principle** and is the WHAT to target. The need principle states that interventions and programs should target criminogenic risk factors, those areas highly correlated with criminal behavior.

Correlates of Criminal Conduct

What factors are correlated with criminal conduct? This is a critical question and one that criminologists have been wrestling with since criminology began. The first person to study criminals scientifically was Cesare Lombroso, who in 1876 wrote *Criminal Man*. Lombroso had personally studied more than 5,000 Italian criminals and, based on his studies, believed that about one-third of all offenders were "born" criminal, or what he called atavistic throwbacks. Lombroso believed that the born criminal could be identified through a number of factors: excessive hairiness, sloping foreheads, tattoos, solitary line in the palm of the hand, and other attributes. Despite the popularity at the time of this theory, Lombroso was incorrect and his work was flawed. The reason he is important, however, is that he was the first person to try to study criminals scientifically. Since Lombroso, there have been hundreds—if not thousands—of studies on this topic. Of course, this is part of the problem. If you start reading this literature, it will take years, and when you are done you will be just as confused as when you started. For every study that says something is a risk factor, there is another that says it isn't. So what do we believe? Fortunately, through the use of meta-analysis, researchers have been able to review large numbers of studies and determine effect sizes (how strong factors are in predicting risk).

Over the years, research by scholars such as Gendreau (1996), Simourd and Andrews (1994), and Andrews and Bonta (1996) has provided an identification of the **major risk factors** associated with criminal conduct. Table 8.1 shows the eight

Table 8.1 Major Set of Risk Factors

1. Antisocial/procriminal attitudes, values, beliefs, and cognitive emotional states
2. Procriminal associates and isolation from anticriminal others
3. Temperamental and personality factors conducive to criminal activity, including:
   - Psychopathy
   - Weak socialization
   - Impulsivity
   - Restless/aggressive energy
   - Egocentricism
   - Below-average verbal intelligence
   - A taste for risk
   - Weak problem-solving/self-regulation skills
4. A history of antisocial behavior
   - Evident from a young age
   - In a variety of settings
   - Involving a number and variety of different acts
5. Family factors that include criminality and a variety of psychological programs in the family of origin, including:
   - Low levels of affection, caring, and cohesiveness
   - Poor parental supervision and discipline practices
   - Outright neglect and abuse
6. Low levels of personal educational, vocational, or financial achievement
7. Low levels of involvement in prosocial leisure activities
   - Allows for interaction with antisocial peers
   - Allows for offenders to have idle time
   - Offenders replace prosocial behavior with antisocial behavior
8. Abuse of alcohol and/or other drugs
   - It is illegal itself (drugs)
   - Engages with antisocial others
   - Impacts social skills

major risk factors, or correlates of criminal conduct, starting with antisocial, procriminal attitudes, values, beliefs, and cognitive emotional states (such as anger and rage).

The risk factor of antisocial, procriminal attitudes, values, beliefs, and cognitive emotional states manifests itself in several important ways—negative expressions about the law, about conventional institutions, about self-management of behavior, and a lack of empathy and sensitivity toward others. In addition, offenders often minimize or neutralize their behavior. Neutralizations are a set of verbalizations which function to say in particular situations that it is okay to violate the law (see Sykes & Matza, 1957). Neutralization techniques include denial of responsibility—criminal acts are due to factors beyond the control of the individual ("I was drunk." "Some dude told me I could borrow his car."); denial of injury—the offender admits responsibility for the act, but minimizes the extent of harm or denies any harm was done ("Yeah, I beat him up, but he only went to the hospital so he could collect unemployment."); denial of the victim—reverses the role of the offender and victim and blames the victim ("She knows not to nag me." "I'm really the victim here."); system-bashing—those who disapprove of the Offenders Act are defined as immoral hypocritical, or criminal themselves ("Everyone uses drugs, I just got caught."); and appeal to higher loyalties—meaning that offenders live by a different code and the demands of larger society are sacrificed for the demands of more immediate loyalties ("You don't understand. Me and my boys have a different set of rules we live by.").

The second major risk factor is one that we are all familiar with—having procriminal friends and a lack of prosocial friends and acquaintances. As our mothers all knew, whom you hang around with is very important. Friends often act as role models, provide the context, and provide the reinforcement for criminal behavior.

The third major risk factor is one that is often ignored in assessment—temperament and personality factors. These include acting impulsively, weak socialization, being adventurous and a risk taker, and a lack of coping and problem-solving skills. Please note that egocentrism is correlated with risk. Many offenders are self-centered and have an inflated sense of self (as opposed to the commonly held perception that offenders suffer from low self-esteem). Studies are finding that criminals are more likely to be characterized as negative or hostile in interpersonal relationships, unempathetic, and lacking in self-control. However, personality is most likely working in tandem with other risk factors such as peers and attitudes. Just being egocentric will not make someone a high risk for criminal conduct. If that were the case, we would have to lock up most of the judges and professors in this country.

The fourth major risk factor is the one that is used most commonly: history. This includes criminal history and other antisocial behavior. Although history is a very strong predictor of future behavior, it has its limitations. The first limitation is that it is not very dynamic, and while it is useful for prediction, it does not provide much direction as to targets for change. The other limitation of history is that one has to have the history before it can be used in prediction. For example, it is not difficult to predict that someone who has four or five prior driving under the influence (DUI) offenses has a drinking problem and might drink and drive again. At one point, however, they had their first DUI. Undoubtedly, they probably had a number of other risk factors; however, because they had no history of DUI offenses, we would have had little on which to base prediction if we relied primarily on history. Again, this is not to say that history is not a very strong (if not the strongest) predictor of future behavior. Life course studies indicate that by age 12 up to 40 percent of later serious offenders have committed their first criminal act and that by age 14 up to 85 percent have committed their first criminal act.

The fifth major risk factor involves family factors, including criminal behavior in the immediate family, and a number of other problems, such as low levels of affection, poor parental supervision, and outright neglect and abuse.

In at six are low levels of personal educational, vocational, and financial achievement—essentially work and school are correlated with risk and round out the top six. Getting an offender a job or an education is important for several reasons (structures time, gets them around prosocial people, helps them support family and self), but if one thinks that working is for chumps, shows up late for work all the time, fights with boss or co-workers, and so forth, how long will they last on the job? Can you see why attitudes and values are so important to identifying and reducing risk? It is a critical factor in determining how we behave.

Finally, factors seven and eight would include a lack of prosocial leisure activities and interests and substance abuse. Of course, both of these allow for interaction with antisocial peers and, in the case of drugs, are usually illegal in and of themselves.

A minor set of risk factors includes lower-class origins as assessed by adverse neighborhood conditions as well as some personal distress factors, such as anxiety, depression, or being officially labeled as mentally disordered. Finally, some biological and neuropsychological indicators have also shown some correlation with criminal conduct. Again, however, these factors are relatively minor and should not be the major focus or targets for changing criminal behavior. For example, making an offender feel better about himself without reducing antisocial attitudes and values will only produce a happier offender. Many researchers believe that most of the secondary risk factors run through the first four: attitudes, values and beliefs, peer associations, personality, and history. These are referred to as the "Big Four" by Andrews and Bonta (2010).

A study conducted by researchers at the Pennsylvania Department of Corrections looked at factors related to failure for parolees. As shown in Table 8.2, most factors were related directly to attitudes, peers and associates, and personality.

Criminogenic risk factors should be the major target of programs and interventions, while noncriminogenic risk factors, such as lack of creative abilities, physical conditioning, medical needs, anxiety, and low self-esteem, are not highly correlated with criminal conduct and should not be the targets for programs.

Figure 8.3 shows results from a meta-analysis that compared effects from programs that target criminogenic versus noncriminogenic needs. As can be seen by this graph, programs that target at least four to six more criminogenic needs

Table 8.2 Results from Pennsylvania Study of Parole Failures

Social Network and Living Arrangements

Violators were:

- More likely to hang around with individuals with criminal backgrounds
- Less likely to live with a spouse
- Less likely to be in a stable, supportive relationship
- Less likely to identify someone in their life who served in a mentoring capacity

Employment and Financial Situation

Violators were:

- Slightly more likely to report having difficulty getting a job
- Less likely to have job stability
- Less likely to be satisfied with employment
- Less likely to take low-end jobs and work up
- More likely to have negative attitudes toward employment and unrealistic job expectations
- Less likely to have a bank account
- More likely to report that they were "barely making it" (yet success group reported over double median debt)

Alcohol or Other Drug Use

Violators were:

- More likely to report use of alcohol or other drugs while on parole (but no difference in prior assessment of dependency problem)
- Poor management of stress was a primary contributing factor to relapse

Life on Parole

Violators had:

- Unrealistic expectations about what life would be like outside of prison
- Poor problem-solving or coping skills
  - Did not anticipate long-term consequences of behavior
- Failed to utilize resources to help them
  - Acted impulsively to immediate situations
  - Felt they were not in control
- More likely to maintain antisocial attitudes
  - Viewed violations as an acceptable option to situation
  - Maintained general lack of empathy
  - Shifted blame or denied responsibility

Successes and failures did not differ in difficulty in finding a place to live after release

Successes and failures equally likely to report eventually obtaining a job

Source: Bucklen, K.B., Zajac, G. (2009). But some of them don't come back (to prison!) Resource deprivation and thinking errors as determinants of parole success and failure. *Prison Journal* 89(3), 239–264.

produced a 31 percent reduction in recidivism, while those programs that targeted one to three more noncriminogenic needs essentially showed no effect on recidivism. These data illustrate the importance of assessing and subsequently targeting dynamic risk factors that are highly correlated with criminal conduct. It also illustrates that the density of criminogenic needs targeted is also important. For example, most higher-risk offenders have multiple risk factors, not just one; as a result, programs that are limited to focusing on one or two targets for change may not produce much effect. Let's take, for example,

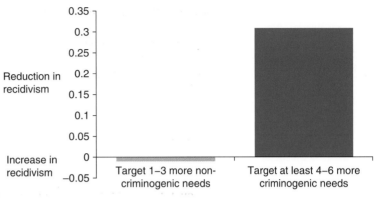

Figure 8.3 Targeting Criminogenic Need: Results from Meta-analyses.

Source: Gendreau, P., French, S.A., Taylor, A. (2002). *What works (what doesn't work) revised 2002.* Invited submission to the International Community Corrections Association Monograph Series Project.

employment. For many offenders on probation or parole, being unemployed is a risk factor, but is it a risk factor for you? If you were unemployed, would you start robbing people or selling drugs? Most of us wouldn't. What we would do if we lost our job is to go out and get another one. In other words, just being unemployed is not that big a risk factor unless, of course, you think things like "I can make more money in a day selling drugs than most can in a month," or if you hang around others who don't work, and so forth. In this case, being unemployed is a risk factor because you have a number of other critical risk factors, plus you have a lot of time on your hands to do nothing but get into trouble. Just targeting employment without including other risk factors (such as attitudes) will not produce much effect.

Responsivity

The third principle is called the responsivity principle and has two parts: general and specific. General responsivity refers to the basic approaches to intervention that are most effective (i.e., yield the largest reductions in reoffending) for most offenders. Interventions that are based on cognitive theories, behavioral theories, and social learning theories have been found to be most effective. We will discuss these approaches more in a later chapter. Specific responsivity refers to matching offenders to programs and interventions based on learning styles and ability. Responsivity factors include those characteristics of an offender related to their learning ability and program engagement. Examples would include motivation or readiness to change, social support for change, intelligence, psychological development, maturity, and other factors that can affect an offender's engagement in a program. These factors are often ignored in the assessment process. For example, say you have identified the risk and need levels of an offender, but he or she is low functioning. Because that person will not do well in a program that requires

for specific responsivity

normal functioning, this factor should be taken into consideration when matching him or her to a program, group, or caseworker.

Professional Discretion

The final principle is called professional discretion. Basically, this means that the person conducting the assessment, after having considered risk, need, and responsivity factors, should include his or her professional judgment in making a final decision about the risk to reoffend. Remember that risk and need assessments are designed to help guide decisions, not to make them. At the same time, professional override of the results of risk assessment should be used cautiously and relatively infrequently (i.e., not more than approximately 10 percent of the time).

THE EVOLUTION OF CLASSIFICATION

How is offender risk determined? This is obviously a very important question because it can affect public protection and the manner in which an offender is supervised (or whether they are even released) in the community.

The first generation of risk assessment in criminal justice refers to the use of "gut feelings" to make decisions about the risk of an offender. With this process, information is collected about the offender, usually through an interview or file review. The information is then reviewed, and a general assessment or global prediction is made: ("In my professional or expert) opinion. . . ." The problems with this approach are considerable and have been delineated by Wong (1997) and Kennedy (1998):

- predictions are subject to personal bias;
- predictions are subjective and often unsubstantiated;
- decision rules are not observed;
- it is difficult to distinguish levels of risk;
- information is overlooked or overemphasized.

The second generation of formal classification instruments was pioneered by Bruce and colleagues (1928). Development of a standardized and objective instrument was brought about by the request of the Illinois parole board, which wanted to make more informed decisions about whom to release on parole. Bruce and colleagues reviewed the records of nearly 6,000 inmates. Table 8.3 illustrates factors found by Bruce et al. (1928) in their risk prediction instrument. While many of these categories seem out of date today, the Burgess scale was one of the first attempts to develop an actuarial instrument to predict offender risk. There are several pros and cons to this approach (Kennedy, 1998; Wong, 1997):

Pros

- It is objective and accountable;
- it covers important historic risk factors;
- it is easy to use and reliable;
- it distinguishes levels of risk of reoffending.

Cons

- It consists primarily of static predictors (i.e., factors that are immutable);
- it does not identify target behaviors;
- it is not capable of measuring change in the offender.

The second generation of risk prediction recognized that risk is more than simply static predictors. The best example can be seen in the Wisconsin Case Management Classification System. First developed and used in Wisconsin in 1975, the Client Management Classification (CMC) System is designed to help identify the level of surveillance for each case, as well as determine the needs of the offender and the resources necessary to meet them. With adequate classification, limited resources can be concentrated on the most critical cases—those of high risk (Wright et al., 1984). Following Wisconsin's development of the CMC, the National Institute of Justice (1983) adopted it as a model system and began advocating and supporting its use throughout the country. It has been proven satisfactory in many jurisdictions, including Austin, Texas (Harris, 1994).

Table 8.3 Factors in the Bruce, Harno, Burgess, and Landesco Scale

---

General type of offense (e.g., fraud, robbery, sex, homicide)

Parental and marital status (parents living, offender married)

Criminal type (first timer, occasional, habitual, professional)

Social type (e.g., farm boy, gangster, hobo, ne'er-do-well, drunkard)

Community factor (where resided)

Statement of trial judge and prosecutor (recommended or protests leniency)

Previous record

Work record (e.g., no work record, casual, regular work)

Punishment record in prison

Months served prior to parole

Intelligence rating

Age when paroled

Psychiatric prognosis

Psychiatric personality type (egocentric, socially inadequate, emotionally unstable)

Source: Bruce, A., Harno, A., Burgess, E., Landesco, J. (1928). *The workings of the intermediate-sentence law and the parole system in Illinois.* Illinois: State of Illinois.

The foundation of the system is a risk/needs assessment instrument completed on each probationer at regular intervals. Cases are classified into high, medium, or low risk/needs. In turn, these ratings are used to determine the level of supervision required for each case. Figures 8.4 and 8.5 illustrate the Wisconsin risk and needs assessment components of this system.

When an offender is classified into a risk/needs level with the Wisconsin risk and needs assessment tools, a more detailed assessment of that case could be made with a profiling interview that helps determine the relationship between the officer and the offender. This element of the Wisconsin system is called the CMC system and is composed of four unique treatment modalities.

Selective Intervention. This group is designed for offenders who enjoy relatively stable and prosocial lifestyles (e.g., they are employed, established in the community, and have minimal criminal records). Such offenders have typically experienced an isolated and stressful event or neurotic problem. With effective intervention, there is a higher chance of avoiding future difficulty. Goals of treatment for these individuals include the development of appropriate responses to temporary crises and problems and the reestablishment of prolife patterns.

Environmental Structure. The dominant characteristics of offenders in this group consist of deficiencies in social, vocational, and intellectual skills. Most of their problems stem from their inability to succeed in their employment or to be comfortable in most social settings—an overall lack of social skills and intellectual cultivation/ability. Goals for these persons include (a) developing basic employment and social skills; (b) selecting alternatives to association with criminally oriented peers; and (c) improving social skills and impulse controls.

Casework/Control. These offenders manifest instabilities in their lives as evidenced by failures in employment and domestic problems. A lack of goal directedness is present, typically associated with alcohol and drug problems. Offense patterns include numerous arrests, although marketable job skills are present. Unstable childhoods, family pressure, and financial difficulties are typically present. Goals appropriate for this group include promoting stability in their professional and domestic endeavors and achieving an improved utilization of the individual's potential, along with an elimination of self-defeating behavior and emotional/psychological problems.

Limit Setting. Offenders in this group are commonly considered to be successful career criminals because of their long-term involvement in criminal activities. They generally enjoy "beating the system," they frequently act for material gain, and they show little remorse or guilt. Because of their value system, they adapt easily to prison environments and return to crime upon release. Goals for this group are problematic, but include changing the offender's basic attitudes and closely supervising his behavior within the community.

Information for the CMC is based on a structured interview with the offender. After a case has been classified, an individual treatment plan is developed. Results

File _____ of _____

CLIENT NAME _____ CASE NUMBER _____
Last   First   MI

OFFICER _____ UNIT LOCATION _____
Last   Social Security Number

DATE | | | | | | |

ARRESTED WITHIN (5) YEARS PRIOR TO ARREST FOR CURRENT OFFENSES (exclude traffic):

0 No   **4** Yes

NUMBER OF PRIOR ADULT INCARCERATIONS IN A STATE OR FEDERAL INSTITUTION:

0 No   **3** 1-2   **6** 3 and above

NUMBER OF PRIOR ADULT PROBATION/PAROLE SUPERVISIONS

0 None   **4** One or more

NUMBER OF PRIOR PROBATION/PAROLE REVOCATIONS RESULTING IN IMPRISONMENT (Adult or Juvenile):

0 None   **4** One or more

AMOUNT OF TIME EMPLOYED IN LAST 12 MONTHS:

0 More than 7 months   **1** 5 to 7 months   **2** Less than 5 months   **0** Not applicable

NUMBER OF PRIOR FELONY CONVICTIONS (or Juvenile Adjudications):

0 None   **2** One   **2** Two or more

0 None   **3** One   **6** Two or more   **7** Three or more

AGE AT ARREST LEADING TO FIRST FELONY CONVICTION (or Juvenile Adjudication):

0 24 and over   **2** 20 - 23   **4** 19 and under

AGE AT ADMISSION TO INSTITUTION OR PROBATION FOR CURRENT OFFENSE:

0 30 and over   **3** 18–29   **6** 17 and under

0 30 and over   **4** 18–29   **7** 17 and under

RATE THE FOLLOWING BASED ON PERIOD SINCE LAST REASSESSMENT

ALCOHOL USAGE PROBLEMS

0 No interference with functioning   **2** Occasional abuse; some disruption of functioning   **4** Frequent abuse; serious disruption; needs treatment

0 No interference with functioning   **2** Occasional abuse; some disruption of functioning   **3** Frequent abuse; serious disruption; needs treatment

OTHER DRUG USAGE PROBLEMS

0 No interference with functioning   **2** Occasional abuse; some disruption of functioning   **4** Frequent abuse; serious disruption; needs treatment

0 No interference with functioning   **1** Occasional abuse; some disruption of functioning   **2** Frequent abuse; serious disruption; needs treatment

ASSOCIATIONS

0 Mainly with noncriminally oriented individuals   **5** Mainly with negative individuals

TYPE OF ARRESTS (indicate most serious, excluding traffic)

0 None   **2** Technical PV only   **4** Misdemeanor arrest(s)   **8** Felony arrest

ATTITUDE

0 No adverse difficulties motivated to change   **2** Periodic difficulties/ uncooperative/dependent   **5** Frequent hostile/negative criminal orientation

Scale: Max—17 and above
      Med—9-16   TOTAL | | | | |
      Min—8 and below

Figure 8.4 Wisconsin Risk Assessment.

File _____ of _____

CLIENT NAME _____ CASE NUMBER _____
                Last   First   MI

OFFICER _____ UNIT LOCATION _____
                Last   Social Security Number

D
A | | | | | |
T
E

EMOTIONAL AND MENTAL STABILITY

0 No symptoms of emotional and/or mental instability   **2** Symptoms limit but do not prohibit adequate functioning   **3** Symptoms prohibit adequate functioning and/or has Court or Board imposed condition   **8** Severe symptoms requiring continual attention and/or explosive, threatening and potentially dangerous to others and self

| | | | | |

DOMESTIC RELATIONSHIP

0 Stable/supportive relationship   **3** Some disorganization or stress but potential for improvement   **7** Major disorganization or stress

| | | | | |

ASSOCIATIONS

0 No adverse relationships   **2** Associations with occasional negative results   **4** Associations frequently negative   **6** Associations completely negative

| | | | | |

DRUG ABUSE

0 No disruption of functioning   **2** Occasional substance abuse; some disruption of functioning and/or has Court or Board conditions   **7** Frequent abuse; serious disruptions; needs treatment

| | | | | |

ALCOHOL USAGE

0 No disruption of functioning   **2** Occasional abuse; some disruption of functioning and/or has Court or Board conditions   **7** Frequent abuse; serious disruptions; needs treatment

| | | | | |

EMPLOYMENT

0 Satisfactory employment, no difficulties reported; or homemaker, student, retired, or disabled   **2** Underemployed   **4** Unsatisfactory employment; or unemployed but has adequate job skills/motivation   **5** Unemployed and virtually unemployable; needs motivation/training

| | | | | |

ACADEMIC/VOCATIONAL SKILLS/TRAINING

0 Adequate skills, able to handle everyday requirements   **2** Low skill level causing minor adjustment problems   **6** No identifiable skills and/or minimal skill level causing serious adjustment problems

| | | | | |

FINANCIAL MANAGEMENT

0 No current difficulties   **1** Situational or minor difficulties   **5** Chronic/severe difficulties

| | | | | |

ATTITUDES

0 No adverse difficulties/motivated for change   **1** Periodic difficulties/uncooperative/dependent   **4** Frequently hostile/negative/criminal orientation

| | | | | |

RESIDENCE

0 Suitable living arrangement   **2** Adequate living, i.e., temporary shelter   **4** Nomadic and/or unacceptable

| | | | | |

MENTAL ABILITY (INTELLIGENCE)

0 Able to function independently   **1** Some need for assistance; potential for adequate adjustment   **3** Deficiencies severely limit independent functioning

| | | | | |

HEALTH

0 Sound physical health; seldom ill   **1** Handicap or illness; interferes with functioning on a recurring basis   **2** Serious handicap or chronic illness; needs frequent medical care

| | | | | |

SEXUAL BEHAVIOR

0 No apparent dysfunction   **2** Real or perceived situations or minor problems   **6** Real or perceived chronic or severe problems

| | | | | |

OFFICER'S IMPRESSION OF NEEDS

0 Low   **3** Medium   **5** Maximum

| | | | | |

Scale: Max—26 and above
      Med—13-25
      Min—12 and below

TOTAL | | | | | |

Figure 8.5 Wisconsin Risk Assessment of Client Needs.

Box 8.2
Actuarial Versus Clinical Prediction

Actuarial prediction, or statistical prediction, involves examining a group of offenders and identifying the factors associated with recidivism (or some other measure of outcome). With statistical prediction, offenders with a certain set of characteristics have a range of probabilities associated with success or failure. So, for example, if we have 100 high-risk offenders and our classification instrument indicated that the probability of failure for high-risk offenders is 75 percent, we are relatively confident that 75 out of 100 of those offenders will recidivate (assuming no intervention). Of course, we are predicting to the group and not the individual, so we do not know which 75 will fail. With **clinical prediction**, a trained professional gathers information and then uses his or her professional experience and judgment to render an opinion about the likelihood that an individual will fail or succeed. The evidence is very strong that actuarial or statistical prediction is more accurate than clinical prediction. In fact, several more recent articles have been published on the use of such measures for predicting risk with separate measures of dynamic needs in order to maximize the accuracy of risk classification (see Baird, 2009), but this idea has been rigorously debated.

---

from the CMC have found that approximately 40 percent of probation caseloads are selective intervention, 15 percent are environmental structure, 30 percent are casework control, and 15 percent are limit setting.

Despite advantages of the CMC, there are several shortcomings. One is the fact that risk and needs are assessed separately and not integrated fully. Another problem with this system is that the CMC component is time-consuming to administer and scoring is somewhat involved. In practice, many probation departments that use this instrument rely more heavily on the risk component, which is composed of mainly static predictors.

A later version of third-generation assessment instruments successfully combined risk and needs and are relatively easy to use. One example is the Level of Service Inventory-Revised (LSI-R), designed by Andrews and Bonta (1995). The LSI-R has been extensively tested and validated across North America. The LSI-R consists of 54 items in 10 areas. Information is collected primarily through a structured interview process. The LSI-R has been found to be one of the most valid instruments in predicting recidivism.

More recently, the LSI-R was updated by reorganizing the original 10 subcomponents into general and specific risk and need factors. This new instrument is considered fourth generation and is called the Level of Service/Case Management Inventory (LS/CMI) (Andrews et al., 2004). It represents an improvement over the previous version (and other third-generation classification instruments), as it

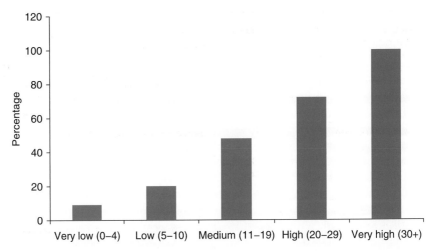

Figure 8.6 Level of Service/Case Management Inventory and Recidivism.

Source: Adapted from Andrews, D.A., Bonta, J. (2006). *The psychology of criminal conduct*, 4th edn. Newark, NJ: LexisNexis Matthew Bender (Anderson Publishing).

emphasizes the link between assessment and case management. In addition to identifying risk and need factors, the LS/CMI acknowledges the role of personal strengths and specific responsivity factors in an offender's amenability to treatment. Figure 8.6 shows recidivism results from 561 probationers whose risk was assessed using the LS/CMI (see Andrews & Bonta, 2006). Recidivism rates increase directly with LS/CMI scores. A sample of some LS/CMI categories is shown in Figure 8.7.

Another example of a fourth-generation assessment tool is the newly developed Ohio Risk Assessment System (ORAS) (Latessa et al., 2010a). Unlike previous tools, the ORAS was developed and validated by examining offenders at various decision points in the criminal justice system. The result is four assessment tools (pretrial, community supervision, prison intake, and re-entry), each designed to assess offenders based on where they are in the system. One of the primary advantages of this collection of instruments is that it establishes a common language for the purpose of case management across settings. Furthermore, several of the items are common across instruments (particularly the ones assessing static items) and can therefore reduce the time required to complete subsequent assessments in other settings.

An example of a case management plan that could be used in conjunction with a fourth-generation assessment tool is provided in Figure 8.8. Note that the need domain (i.e., dynamic risk factor) is translated into a goal (long-term behavioral change) with associated objectives and strategies.

Section 1. General Risk/Need Factors
Criminal history
  Education/employment
  Family/marital
  Leisure/recreation
  Companions
  Alcohol/drug problem
  Procriminal attitude/orientation
  Antisocial pattern

Section 2. Specific Risk/Need Factors
  Personal problems with criminogenic
  potential
    Diagnosis of "psychopathy"
    Anger management deficits
    Poor social skills
    Underachievement
  History of perpetration
    Sexual assault, extrafamilial, child/
    adolescent–female victim
    Physical assault (extrafamilial adult
    victim)
    Gang participation

Section 5. Special Responsivity
Considerations
  Motivation as a barrier
  Women, gender specific
  Low intelligence
  Antisocial personality/psychopathy

Section 9. Case Management Plan
  Program targets and intervention plan

Criminogenic		
Need	Goal	Intervention
1.		
2.		

Figure 8.7 Areas of the Level of Service/Case Management Inventory.

Source: Adapted from Andrews, D.A., Bonta, J. (2006). *The psychology of criminal conduct*, 4th edn. Newark, NJ: LexisNexis Matthew Bender (Anderson Publishing).

JUVENILE RISK/NEED ASSESSMENT TOOLS

Traditionally, there have been fewer actuarial instruments available for juvenile offenders. Recently, however, we have seen the development of a number of new instruments designed specifically for this population. The Ohio Youth Assessment System (OYAS), the Youthful LS/CMI, the Youthful Assessment and Screening Instrument (YASI), and the Youthful COMPAS are examples of risk and need assessment tools that have been developed recently for use with the juvenile population. These instruments are very similar in nature to the latest generation of adult instruments. Figure 8.9 is an example of the report generated from the Dispositional Assessment of the OYAS. This tool includes seven domains and gives the judge a view of the overall risk of the youth as well as scores in each domain.

SPECIALIZED ASSESSMENT TOOLS

There are also classification systems designed for certain types of offenders or need areas, such as the mentally disordered, sex offenders, and substance abusers.

Problem/need: Marijuana use

Need area risk level: Moderate

Strengths: Prosocial family support

Barriers: Lack of motivation

Goal: Eliminate use of marijuana

Objectives:	Strategies:	Date Initiated:	Date Completed:
Participate in substance abuse assessment by October 1.	Refer for substance abuse assessment	9/10/05	9/29/06
By next meeting, list benefits of participating in and cons for not complying with treatment	Cost–benefit analysis	10/1/06	10/15/06
Attend and participate in all substance abuse treatment activities over next 2 months	Refer for services Monitor with drug screens Updates from tx provider and offender	11/1/06	

Figure 8.8 Sample Case Management Plan.

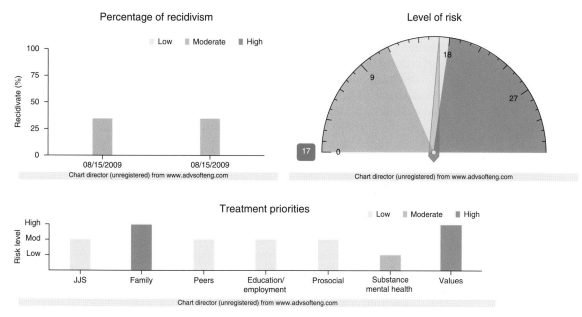

Figure 8.9 Ohio Youth Assessment System Full Report: Dispositional Tool.

Some of these tools help classify and recommend levels of intervention. Figure 8.10 shows the use of specialized assessment tools across the United States.

One of the major advantages of actuarial risk and need assessment tools is that they are standardized and objective and help distinguish levels of risk or need (e.g., high, medium, low). Because they are based on statistical studies, they also reduce bias and false positive and false negative rates (Holsinger et al., 2001).

In a national survey of probation and parole agencies concerning the use and practices surrounding class classification, Hubbard et al. (2001) found that the vast majority of agencies reported using some actuarial instrument to assess and classify offenders. A summary of their findings is presented here.

Almost 75 percent of the probation and parole agencies and about 56 percent of the community corrections service providers reported that they classify using standardized and objective instruments. Large agencies were more likely to classify clients than were smaller agencies.

More than 83 percent of the respondents reported that it was "absolutely" or "very necessary" to classify on risk and 66 percent on needs. The most widely used instrument was the Wisconsin Risk and Need instrument, followed by the LSI.

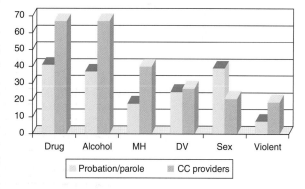

Figure 8.10 Use of Specialized Assessment Tools by Probation, Parole, and Community Corrections Service Providers (percent).

Source: Hubbard, D.J., Travis, L., Latessa, E. (2001). *Case classification in community corrections: A national survey of the state of the art.* Washington, DC: National Institute of Justice, U.S. Department of Justice.

Nearly all respondents agreed that case classification makes their job easier, benefits the offender, creates a more professional environment, helps staff make better decisions, increases effectiveness of service delivery, and enhances fairness in decision making.

The most common uses of these tools were officer workloads 75 percent, staff deployment 54 percent, development of specialized caseloads 47 percent, and sentencing decisions 20 percent.

Nearly 80 percent of the agencies reported using the various instruments to reassess offenders.

CRITICISMS OF ASSESSMENT TOOLS

Offender classification is not without its critics. Some argue that the instruments are nothing more than "educated guesses" (Smykla, 1986, p. 127), whereas others are more concerned about their proper use and accuracy (Greenwood & Zimring, 1985; Wilbanks, 1985). Some critics, such as Baird (2009), argue that risk and need factors should not be combined because risk factors are distinct from need factors. However, others contend that most of what are called "needs" are, in fact, "risk" factors (i.e., substance use, peer associations, attitudes, and values) and should be integrated into the tools. Another major concern centers on the use of a risk instrument in one jurisdiction that has been developed and validated in another. The argument is made that just because a risk instrument is accurate in one jurisdiction does not necessarily mean it will be effective in predicting outcome in another (Collins, 1990; Kratcoski, 1985; Sigler & Williams, 1994; Wright et al., 1984). As Travis (1989) stated, "ideally, a risk classification device should be constructed based on the population on which it is to be used." Most researchers, however, believe that while cut-off scores may vary across jurisdictions, risk factors are common across offender populations and jurisdictions.

Box 8.3
False Positives and False Negatives

False positives occur when offenders predicted to fail actually succeed, whereas false negatives occur when predicted successes actually fail. False negatives are potentially very costly; hence most classification strategies err on the conservative side.

The goal of most assessment and classification processes is to minimize both false positives and false negatives. Some studies of clinical assessment have found that clinicians will over-predict violence in two out of three cases!

ADVANTAGES OF ASSESSMENT TOOLS

Despite these concerns, most believe that the use of validated assessment instruments is a major advancement in offender management and treatment. For example, Clear (1988, p. 2) maintains that the implementation of these prediction instruments has two main advantages:

> First, they improve the reliability of decisions made about offenders—in a sense they make correctional officials more predictable. Second, they provide a basis on which corrections personnel can publicly justify both individual decisions and decision-making policies. In both cases, the advantage is grounded in the powerful appearance of "scientific" decision-making.

In addition to the advantages just given, the use of assessment tools based on dynamic factors provides the ability to reassess the offender to determine whether there has been a reduction in risk score. This allows an agency to move beyond risk management to risk reduction, the ultimate goal of community corrections. Figure 8.11 illustrates initial assessment and **reassessment** scores from a sample of youths supervised on probation. As shown, these data can help a probation department better focus its resources and strategies.

Another example is demonstrated in Figure 8.12, which shows results from the reassessment of offenders sentenced to an Ohio community-based correctional

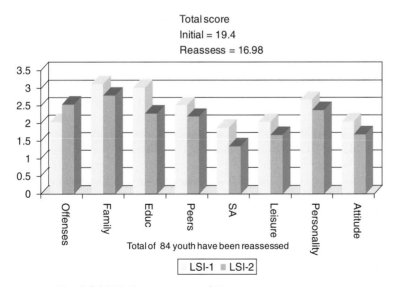

Figure 8.11 Youthful LSI: Assessment and Reassessment.

Source: Latessa, E.J., Taylor, C. (2001). *Using the youthful level of service inventory/case management in a large urban court.* Cincinnati, OH: Center for Criminal Justice Research, University of Cincinnati.

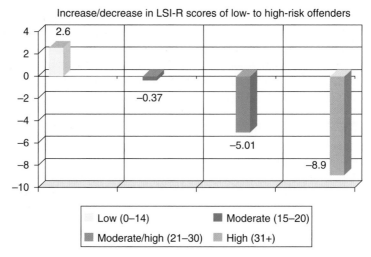

Figure 8.12 Results of Treatment as Measured by Changes in LSI-R Scores (by risk category) (*N* = 559).

Source: Latessa, E.J., Lowenkamp, C. (2001). *Testing the LSI-R in community-based correctional facilities.* Cincinnati, OH: Center for Criminal Justice Research, University of Cincinnati.

facility. The purpose of these facilities is to provide up to six months of secure, structured treatment to felony offenders who would otherwise be incarcerated in a prison. Results from this study show that the greatest reductions in risk scores were for the highest-risk offenders, while low-risk offenders actually saw their risk scores increase. In general, treatment lowers offenders' risk of recidivism. These data demonstrate the risk principle, which states that intensive treatment services should be reserved for higher-risk offenders. As can be seen from these data, when lower-risk offenders are placed in an intensive intervention program, the outcome is often detrimental to the offender. There are two reasons why this effect occurs. The first may be due to the influence of higher-risk offenders on low-risk, more prosocial individuals. The second is probably due to the disruption of prosocial networks and other social support mechanisms that low-risk offenders usually possess (or they would not be low risk!). For example, placement in a program such as the one described earlier usually results in loss of employment and disruption to the family.

Reliability and Validity

A number of important considerations with any risk need assessment process need to be considered. How easy is the instrument to use and score? How long does it take to complete? How much training is involved? Is an interview involved; if so, how do you verify the information? How much does it cost? These and other questions are important considerations when selecting a risk need assessment instrument. Of vital importance is the reliability and validity of the instrument.

Reliability refers to the consistency of the instrument. For example, if two probation officers were to use the LSI to assess the same offender, how similar would they score him or her? This is referred to as inter-rater reliability and can be a problem with more dynamic instruments. The second important consideration is **validity**, the accuracy of the instrument in predicting what it is we want it to predict. They are both important. It doesn't do any good to have an accurate tool if no one can agree on the score. Likewise, they might all agree on the score, but if it doesn't predict what we want it to, then it doesn't really matter. As a general rule, most good instruments are about 80 percent accurate. This is determined by validation studies in which we determine the correlation between the score and some outcome (usually some measure of recidivism)—the higher the correlation, the stronger the relationship. Two important factors have been found to increase the validation of assessment: training of staff on the tool and experience using the tool (Flores et al., 2006).

Points about "Good" Assessment

A number of points about classification and assessment should be considered. First, there is no one-size-fits-all approach. Each agency or jurisdiction has different needs. For example, if operating a pretrial release program, one of the considerations would be "failure to appear." This might not be important to a secure residential program. There is also no one instrument that will provide all the information needed for a comprehensive assessment. Assessment often has to be a flexible process that expands as warranted. Second, it is important to validate instruments to ensure accuracy and to determine the degree to which they can predict different outcome measures. For example, if an agency is interested in predicting sex-offending behavior, they need to make sure that the tools they are using can predict this outcome accurately. Third, classification and assessment are not one-time events. Risk can change over time. An offender who began supervision without a job, drinking, and hanging around with a bad crowd but six months later is employed, sober, and attending to family responsibilities will be lower risk than when he or she began supervision. Fourth, statistical prediction is more accurate than clinical prediction. Instruments specifically designed and validated on offender populations will more accurately predict outcome than the best clinical assessment process. Classification based on standardized factors is also more reliable, less time-consuming, and less expensive than clinical assessment. Finally, as mentioned previously, decisions based on objective criteria are less vulnerable to legal challenges.

Other Problems with Assessment

Despite the obvious problems associated with developing, norming, and validating instruments designed to predict human behavior, there are also a number of other problems associated with offender assessment.

Many agencies assess offenders, but ignore important factors. An example would be an agency that relies on a static risk assessment instrument that focuses primarily on criminal history. An offender without a long criminal history might be classified as low risk even though they may have a number of other important risk factors. Another example would be an agency that focuses primarily on substance abuse and ignores antisocial attitudes, antisocial friends, and other criminogenic risk factors. Another problem common with offender assessment are processes that assess offenders but do not produce scores or distinguish levels. These processes are usually quasi-clinical in nature. The program or probation department will gather a great deal of information about the offender, write it up in narrative form, but when finished will not be able to distinguish levels of risk or needs. A third problem is programs and agencies that assess offenders and then essentially don't use the information; everyone gets the same treatment or intervention regardless of the assessment results. A fourth problem is that some programs begin using an assessment tool without adequately training the staff on their use or interpretation. This affects the instrument's reliability and accuracy, and a host of other problems often emerges when this happens. Finally, many assessment instruments are adopted without being normed or validated on an offender population. Without this information, the accuracy of the instrument is essentially unknown.

Despite these concerns, the latest generation of classification instruments allows the probation or parole department an effective and fairly simple means of classifying and managing offenders. It is important to remember that instruments such as the CMC or LSI-R can be important and useful tools in assisting the community correctional agency and the supervising officer in case management. They neither solve all the problems faced by probation and parole agencies nor fully replace the sound judgment and experience of well-trained probation and parole officers (Klein, 1989; Schumacher, 1985).

Box 8.4
Criminogenic Needs and Promising Targets

Criminogenic needs refer to those crime-producing factors associated with criminal behavior. The new generation of risk assessment tools measures these needs. Some of the promising need factors that should be identified by researchers include the following:

- Changing antisocial attitudes
- Changing antisocial feelings
- Reducing antisocial peer associations
- Promoting familial affection and communication
- Promoting familial monitoring and supervision
- Increasing self-control and problem-solving skills
- Reducing chemical dependencies.

STANDARDS OF CLASSIFICATION

Travis and Latessa (1996) have identified 10 elements of effective classification and assessment. They include:

Purposeful. Generally, the purpose of classification and assessment is to ensure that offenders are treated differentially within a system so as to ensure safety, adequate treatment, and understanding.

Organizational fit. Organizations and agencies have different characteristics, capabilities, and needs.

Accuracy. How well does the instrument correctly assess outcome? Is the offender correctly placed within the system? Basically, reliability and validity are the key elements to accuracy. Glick and colleagues (1998, p. 73) explain reliability and validity thus: Reliability may be defined as hitting the same spot on a bull's eye all the time. If your system is reliable but not valid, you may be hitting the target consistently, but not the right spot.

Parsimony. This refers to the ease of use, the economy of composition, and achieving accuracy with the least number of factors. In other words, short and simple.

Distribution. How well does the system disperse cases across classification groups? If all offenders fall into the same group, there is little distribution.

Dynamism. Is the instrument measuring dynamic risk factors that are amenable to change? Dynamic factors also allow you to measure progress and change in the offender. It also facilitates reclassification.

Utility. To be effective, classification systems must be useful. This means that staff achieve purposes of classification and goals of the agency.

Practicality. Closely related to utility is the practical aspect of classification. The system must be practical and possible to implement. A process that is 100 percent accurate but impossible to apply in an agency does not help that agency. Similarly, a system that is easy to use but does not lead to better decisions is of no value.

Justice. An effective classification and assessment process should produce just outcomes. Offender placement and service provision should be based on offender differences that are real and measurable, and yield consistent outcomes, regardless of subjective impressions.

Sensitivity. This is really a goal of the classification process. If all elements are met, the most effective classification and assessment processes are sensitive to the differences of offenders. At the highest level, this would mean individualizing case planning.

Box 8.5
Responsivity Factors

Recognizing differences in offenders that affect their engagement in treatment and their ability to learn is part of assessing responsivity. Developing a strategy to overcome these barriers is part of developing a good case plan. Some responsivity considerations include the following:

General population	Factors more common with offenders
■ Anxiety	■ Poor social skills
■ Self-esteem	■ Inadequate problem solving
■ Depression	■ Concrete-oriented thinking
■ Mental illness	■ Poor verbal skills
■ Age	■ Social support for service
■ Intelligence	
■ Gender	
■ Race/ethnicity	
■ Motivation	

CLASSIFICATION AND FEMALE OFFENDERS

Several scholars have questioned the notion that risk factors used to predict antisocial behavior for male offenders are similar to those needed for female offenders (Chesney-Lind, 1989, 1997; Funk, 1999; Mazerolle, 1998). The neglect of female offenders has been a consistent criticism in many areas of criminological and criminal justice research, from theory development to the development of correctional interventions (Belknap & Holsinger, 1998; Chesney-Lind & Sheldon, 1992; Funk, 1999). Furthermore, the lack of instruments that discriminate between males and females has been a common criticism of current risk/need assessment efforts (Funk, 1999). The basis for this criticism is twofold: (1) different factors may be involved in risk assessment for females, and (2) the risk factors may be similar, but exposure to these factors may present different challenges for female and male offenders (Chesney-Lind, 1989; Funk, 1999; Gilligan & Wiggins, 1988).

There is no question that there has been considerably less research conducted on female offenders than males; however, several studies that have examined risk factors and gender have found that instruments such as the LSI can be useful in assessing and classifying female offenders (Andrews, 1982; Bonta & Motiuk, 1985; Coulson et al., 1996; Hoge & Andrews, 1996; Motiuk, 1993; Shields & Simourd, 1991; Smith et al., 2009). In a study examining risk prediction for male and female offenders, Lowenkamp and colleagues (2001) added to this research by looking at 317 males and 125 females. They found that the LSI-R was a valid predictive instrument for female offenders. They also found that a history of prior abuse (sexual or physical), although more prevalent in female offenders, was not correlated with outcome. Smith and colleagues (2009) conducted a meta-analysis of studies involving the use of the LSI with females. With a sample of 14,737 offenders, they concluded that the LSI-R was a valid tool for use with women. Although the debate will likely continue, it appears that the evidence is mounting that instruments such as the LSI can indeed be used to assess and classify offenders, both male and female.

Box 8.6
Risk Management vs. Risk Reduction

Risk Management: Involves determining risk level of the offender and providing appropriate sanctions and supervision.

Risk Reduction: Involves determining risk level and crime producing needs and reducing risk factors through effective interventions and appropriate supervision.

SUMMARY

This chapter discussed an important aspect of community corrections: assessment of the offender. One of the most critical aspects of supervising the offender in the community is the determination of risk and need levels. Over the years, assessment and classification have advanced beyond guesswork about whether an offender might reoffend to more scientific approaches that examine both static and dynamic factors that can assist the community correctional professional in determining "who" and "what" to target in order to meet the goal of public protection. While offender assessment is not without its critics, the vast majority of community correctional agencies utilize assessment tools, which means that it is incumbent that these tools serve the purposes they were designed for: accurately sorting offenders into levels of risk *and* identifying those characteristics of the offender that are amenable to change.

Review Questions

1. How can risk/needs assessments be used in probation?
2. What are the major correlates of criminal conduct? The "Big Four"?
3. What was the first actuarial instrument developed for predicting risk? What is the major limitation of this tool?
4. What is the difference between the Wisconsin Risk/Need assessment tools and the LSI?
5. What are the 10 standards of good classification?
6. What are the four principles of classification?
7. Give three examples of responsivity characteristics and discuss ways they can impede an offender.
8. What is the difference between a static and a dynamic predictor?
9. What are two ways to increase the validation of an assessment tool?
10. What are some of the criticisms of assessment tools?
11. Why do you think actuarial assessment tools have proven more reliable and valid than clinical assessment processes?

Recommended Reading

Van Voorhis, P. (1994). *Psychological classification of the adult male prison inmate.* Albany, NY: State University of New York Press.

References

Andrews, D. (1982). *The level of services inventory (LSI): The first follow-up.* Toronto: Ontario Ministry of Correctional Services.

Andrews, D. (1989). Recidivism is predictable and can be influenced: Using risk assessments to reduce recidivism. *Forum on Correctional Research* 1(2), 11–17.

Andrews, D., Bonta, J. (1995). *LSI-R the level of service inventory—Revised.* Toronto: Multi-Health Systems, Inc.

Andrews, D., Bonta, J., Hoge, R. (1990). Classification for effective rehabilitation rediscovering psychology. *Criminal Justice and Behavior* 17, 19–52.

Andrews, D.A. (1983). The assessment of outcome in correctional samples. In: M. Lambert, E. Christensen, S. DeJulio (eds) *The measurement of psychotherapy outcome in research and evaluation.* New York: Wiley, pp. 160–201.

Andrews, D.A., Bonta, J. (1996). *The psychology of criminal conduct.* Cincinnati, OH: Anderson Publishing.

Andrews, D.A., Bonta, J. (2006). *The psychology of criminal conduct,* 4th edn. Newark, NJ: LexisNexis Matthew Bender Anderson Publishing.

Andrews, D.A., Bonta, J. (2010). *The psychology of criminal conduct,* 5th edn. New Providence, NJ: LexisNexis Matthew Bender Anderson Publishing.

Andrews, D.A., Bonta, J., Wormith, S.J. (2004). *The level of service/case management inventory.* Toronto: Multi-Health Systems, Inc.

Baird, C. (2009). *A question of evidence: A critique of risk assessment models used in the justice system.* Madison, WI: National Council on Crime and Delinquency.

Belknap, J., Holsinger, K. (1998). An overview of delinquent girls: How theory and practice have failed and the need for innovative changes. In: R.T. Zaplin (ed.) *Female crime and delinquency: Critical perspectives and effective interventions.* Aspen: Gaithersburg, MD, pp. 31–64.

Bonta, J. (2002). Offender risk assessment: Guidelines for selection and use. *Criminal Justice and Behavior* 29(4), 355–379.

Bonta, J., Andrews, D. (1993). The level of supervision inventory: An overview. *IARCA Journal* 5(4), 6–8.

Bonta, J., Motiuk, L. (1985). Utilization of an interview-based classification instrument: A study of correctional halfway houses. *Criminal Justice and Behavior* 12, 333–352.

Bonta, J., Wallace-Capretta, S., Rooney, J. (2000). A quasi-experimental evaluation of an intensive rehabilitation supervision program. *Criminal Justice and Behavior* 27(3), 312–329.

Bruce, A., Harno, A., Burgess, E., Landesco, J. (1928). *The workings of the intermediate-sentence law and the parole system in Illinois.* Illinois: State of Illinois.

Bucklen, K.B., Zajac, G. (2009). But some of them don't come back (to prison!) Resource deprivation and thinking errors as determinants of parole success and failure. *Prison Journal* 89(3), 239–264.

Chesney-Lind, M. (1989). Girls' crime and women's place: Toward a feminist model of female delinquency. *Crime & Delinquency* 35, 5–29.

Chesney-Lind, M. (1997). *The female offender.* Thousand Oaks, CA: Sage.

Chesney-Lind, M., Sheldon, R. (1992). *Girls, delinquency, and juvenile justice.* Belmont, CA: Wadsworth.

Clear, T. (1988). Statistical prediction in corrections. *Research in Corrections* 1, 1–39.

Collins, P. (1990). Risk classification and assessment in probation: A study of misdemeanants. University of Cincinnati, Cincinnati, OH: Unpublished master's thesis.

Coulson, G., Ilacqua, G., Nutbrown, V., Giulekas, D., Cudjoe, F. (1996). Predictive utility of the LSI for incarcerated female offenders. *Criminal Justice and Behavior* 23, 427–439.

Flores, A., Lowenkamp, C.T., Holsinger, A., Latessa, E. (2006). Predicting outcome with the level of service inventory-revised: The importance of implementation integrity. *Journal of Criminal Justice* 34(4), 523–529.

Funk, S. (1999). Risk assessment for juveniles on probation. *Criminal Justice and Behavior* 26, 44–68.

Gendreau, P. (1996). The principles of effective intervention with offenders. In: A.T. Harland (ed.) *Choosing correctional options that work: Defining the demand and evaluating the supply.* Thousand Oaks, CA: Sage, pp. 117–130.

Gendreau, P., French, S.A., Taylor, A. (2002). *What works (what doesn't work) revised 2002.* Invited submission to the International Community Corrections Association Monograph Series Project.

Gendreau, P., Goggin, C., Little, T. (1996). *Predicting adult offender recidivism: What works?* Ottawa, CN: Solicitor General Canada.

Gilligan, C., Wiggins, G. (1988). The origins of morality in early childhood relationships. In: C. Gilligan, J. Ward, J. Taylor (eds) *Mapping the moral domain: A contribution of women's thinking to psychological theory and education.* Cambridge, MA: Harvard University Press, pp. 111–138.

Glick, B., Sturgeon, W., Venator-Santiago, C.V. (1998). *No time to play: Youthful offenders in the adult correctional system.* Lantham, MD: American Correctional Association.

Greenwood, P., Zimring, F. (1985). *One more chance: The pursuit of promising intervention strategies for chronic juvenile offenders.* Santa Monica, CA: The Rand Corporation.

Harris, P. (1994). Client management classification and prediction of probation outcome. *Crime & Delinquency* 40, 154–174.

Hoge, R., Andrews, D. (1996). *Assessing the youthful offender: Issues and techniques.* New York: Plenum Press.

Holsinger, A., Lurigio, A., Latessa, E. (2001). Practitioner's guide to understanding the basis of assessing offender risk. *Federal Probation* 64(2), 46–50.

Hubbard, D.J., Travis, L., Latessa, E. (2001). *Case classification in community corrections: A national survey of the state of the art.* Washington, DC: National Institute of Justice, U.S. Department of Justice.

Jones, P. (1996). Risk prediction in criminal justice. In: A.T. Harlan (ed.) *Choosing correctional options that work: Defining the demand and evaluating the supply.* Thousand Oaks, CA: Sage, pp. 33–68.

Kennedy, S. (1998). *Effective interventions with higher risk offenders.* Longmont, CO: National Institute of Corrections.

Kennedy, S., Serin, R. (1997). Treatment responsivity: Contributing to effective correctional programming. *The ICCA Journal on Community Corrections* 7(4), 46–52.

Klein, A. (1989). The curse of caseload management. *Perspectives Gerontological Nursing Association Canada* 13, 27–28.

Kratcoski, P. (1985). The functions of classification models in probation and parole: Control or treatment-rehabilitation? *Federal Probation* 49(4), 49–56.

Latessa, E.J., Lovins, B. (2010). The role of offender risk assessment: A policy maker guide. *Victims and offenders* 5(1), 203–219.

Latessa, E.J., Lowenkamp, C. (2001). *Testing the LSI-R in community-based correctional facilities.* Cincinnati, OH: Center for Criminal Justice Research, University of Cincinnati.

Latessa, E.J., Taylor, C. (2001). *Using the youthful level of service inventory/case management in a large urban court.* Cincinnati, OH: Center for Criminal Justice Research, University of Cincinnati.

Latessa, E.J., Lemke, R., Makarios, M., Smith, P., Lowenkamp, C.T. (2010a). The creation and validation of the Ohio risk assessment system (ORAS). *Federal Probation* 74(1), 16–22.

Latessa, E.J., Lovins, L.B., Smith, P. (2010b). *Follow-up evaluation of Ohio's community based correctional facility and halfway house programs—Outcome study.* Cincinnati, OH: School of Criminal Justice, University of Cincinnati.

Lowenkamp, C., Holsinger, A., Latessa, E. (2001). Risk/need assessment, offender classification, and the role of childhood abuse. *Criminal Justice and Behavior* 28(5), 543–563.

Mazerolle, P. (1998). Gender, general strain, and delinquency: An empirical examination. *Justice Quarterly* 15(1), 65–91.

Motiuk, L. (1993). Where are we in our ability to assess risk? *Forum on Correctional Research* 5(1), 14–18.

National Institute of Justice (1983). *Classification in probation and parole: A model systems approach.* Available from: www.nicic.gov/library/000936.

Proctor, J. (1994). Evaluating a modified version of the federal prison system's classification model: An assessment of objectivity and predictive validity. *Criminal Justice and Behavior* 21, 256–272.

Schumacher, M. (1985). Implementation of a client classification and case management system: A practitioner's view. *Crime & Delinquency* 31, 445–455.

Shields, I., Simourd, D. (1991). Predicting predatory behavior in a population of incarcerated young offenders. *Criminal Justice and Behavior* 18, 180–194.

Sigler, R., Williams, J. (1994). A study of the outcomes of probation officers and risk-screening instrument classifications. *Journal of Criminal Justice* 22, 495–502.

Simourd, D.J., Andrews, D.A. (1994). Correlates of delinquency: A look at gender differences. *Forum on Corrections Research* 6(1), 26–31.

Smith, P., Cullen, F.T., Latessa, E.J. (2009). Can 14,737 women be wrong? A meta-analysis of the LSI-R and recidivism for female offenders. *Criminology and Public Policy* 8(1), 183–208.

Smykla, J. (1986). Critique concerning prediction in probation and parole: Some alternative suggestions. *International Journal of Offender Therapy and Comparative Criminology* 30–31, 125–139.

Sykes, G.M., Matza, D. (1957). Techniques of neutralization: A theory of delinquency. *American Sociological Review* 22(6), 664–670.

Travis, L. (1989). *Risk classification in probation and parole.* Cincinnati, OH: Risk Classification Project, University of Cincinnati.

Travis, L., Latessa, E. (1996). Classification and needs assessment module. *Managing violent youthful offenders in adult institutions curriculum.* Longmont, CO: National Institute of Corrections.

Wilbanks, W. (1985). Predicting failure on parole. In: D. Farrington, R. Tarling (eds) *Prediction in criminology.* Albany, NY: State University of New York Press, pp. 78–94.

Wong, S. (1997). Risk: Assessing the risk of violent recidivism. *Presentation at the American Probation and Parole Association*, Boston, MA.

Wright, K., Clear, T., Dickson, P. (1984). Universal applicability of probation risk assessment instruments. *Criminology* 22, 113–134.

Chapter 9

STRATEGIES FOR MANAGING AND PROVIDING SERVICES TO OFFENDERS

Key Terms

brokerage	problem solving
case work	single-factor specialized caseload model
contracting	skills
conventional model	supervision planning
numbers game model	thought–behavior link

It is hard to change when the only model we have to copy is ourselves.—Anonymous

INTRODUCTION

In terms of community safety, the most significant responsibility of a probation or parole agency is supervising offenders. Underlying this duty are the dual objectives of protecting the community and helping offenders. As we have already learned, these objectives are not always compatible.

Depending on the jurisdiction in which the agency is located, offenders placed on probation and parole may have committed almost any type of criminal offense and may range from first-time offenders to career criminals. The number of offenders placed on probation or released on parole will also vary considerably over time, depending on political and fiscal climates in the jurisdiction, existing law in the jurisdiction, size of the prison overpopulation, and prevailing philosophy toward the use of probation and parole.

The bulk of probation and parole clients are under regular supervision, although about one in eight are under some other management program, such as intensive supervision, electronic monitoring, house arrest, or other special program (Camp & Camp, 2003). Two trends emerging over time are the increased number of

Table 9.1 Examples of Problems Faced by Offenders under Supervision

Correctional client group	Substance abuse		Mentally ill	Prior mental or physical abuse reported
	Alcohol	**Drug**		
Probationers	40%	14%	16%	16%
Jail inmates*	41	36	11	16
State prisoners	37	33	10	19

*Substance abuse for jail inmates was defined as being under the influence of drugs or of alcohol at the time of the offense.

Source: Compiled from Harlow, C. (1999). *Prior abuse reported by inmates and probationers.* Washington, DC: Bureau of Justice Statistics; Mumola, C. (1999). *Substance abuse and treatment, states and federal prisoners, 1997.* Washington, DC: U.S. Bureau of Justice Statistics; and Maruschak, L., Beck, A. (2001). *Medical problems of inmates.* Washington, DC: U.S. Bureau of Justice.

clients under correctional control and the increasing use of alternatives to regular supervision. The implications of these supervision strategies are explored here.

In addition, there is likely to be variation among probationers and parolees with respect to the type and extent of conditions imposed upon them by the court or the parole board. Finally, individuals being supervised will vary considerably in the types of problems they face (family difficulties, educational or employment needs, mental illness, alcohol or other drug abuse) (see Table 9.1). As with other major responsibilities of a probation or parole agency, supervision necessitates an organizational structure that will enable the agency to protect the community efficiently and effectively and to provide the necessary support to aid the offender.

Considering the complexity involved in complying with these duties, it is obvious that the agency will be faced with a number of critical management problems and alternatives from which to choose. Many of these, which are discussed separately, are, in reality, closely intertwined. They are not "either/or" alternatives. In fact, many strategies can easily be mixed into a variety of combinations.

This chapter addresses the broad area of service delivery and the ways in which probation and parole agencies handle offenders assigned for supervision. The philosophical models of treatment delivery are examined, as well as the planning process of supervision, different levels of caseload size, developments in the area of offender/officer interactions, and contracting for services and managing community resources.

CASELOAD ASSIGNMENT MODELS

Offenders are assigned to a probation department by the court, to a parole department by the parole board, and to other community correctional agencies, such as halfway houses, by both.[1] Because the vast majority of offenders supervised in the community are first placed on probation or parole, we will examine the ways in which offenders are assigned individually to probation or parole officers.

How cases are assigned individually to available probation and parole officers varies from jurisdiction to jurisdiction. Carter and Wilkins (1976) developed a useful typology of caseload models that includes major variations in assignment strategies. Underlying their typology is the assumption that the offender population will vary considerably across any characteristic in question (Sigler & Williams, 1994).

The first model is called the **conventional model** and ignores the differences and similarities among offenders; cases are assigned randomly to available probation and parole officers. Because of the random distribution of the offender population among caseloads, each officer handles a mixture that is generally a miniature reproduction of the entire offender population, including, of course, wide variations in personal characteristics. With the conventional caseload model, then, probation or parole officers must be able to supervise any type of offender who happens to be assigned to their caseload.

Closely related to the conventional model is what is called the **numbers game model.** This type may also ignore differences and similarities across offenders. The object of this model is to numerically balance all caseloads within the department. This balancing may take the personal characteristics of individual offenders into account because the numbers game model can be approached in two ways. First, the number of cases to be supervised can simply be divided by the number of officers available to the department. For example, if a probation department has 10 probation officers and 800 probationers, every officer will handle a caseload of 80. Alternatively, the department can select an "ideal size" for each caseload and divide the number of offenders by the ideal size, yielding the number of necessary officers. Under this method, if a department has 800 probationers and has selected 50 as its ideal size caseload, then it must provide 16 probation officers. Variations of the numbers game model may also be used with the other models discussed later.

The third assignment model is called the *conventional model with geographic considerations.* This one differs from the conventional model in one important respect: the caseload is restricted to residents in one type of geographic area (urban, suburban, or rural). Given the travel time necessary to supervise an entirely rural caseload, the size of a rural caseload is generally smaller than suburban or urban caseloads. Such caseloads, however, are not differentiated on the basis of the personal characteristics of the offenders, except to the extent that the characteristics of urban, suburban, and rural offenders may vary. In a large urban area, probation and parole departments may have satellite offices. When this is the case, geographic distinctions may be based on the side of town in which an offender resides.

The other two assignment techniques recognize the presence of important similarities and differences among offenders. The more elementary of these techniques is called the **single-factor specialized caseload model**. This groups offenders together on the basis of one single characteristic that they all share. Examples include alcohol and other drug abuse, developmental disability, sex, age, type of offense, and high potential for violent behavior ("risk"). Despite the existence of a shared characteristic, offenders on each single-factor specialized caseload may vary widely on other characteristics. For example, a caseload restricted to offenders between the ages of 18 and 21 may still include individuals who differ considerably on such variables as type of offense or potential risk to community.

Finally, the most complex assignment model, the *vertical model,* classifies offenders on the basis of two or more factors or characteristics. Often, this classification is accomplished by using one of the various prediction devices that estimate the chances of a particular offender's succeeding or failing while under supervision. Prediction devices take a wide variety of individual characteristics into account and stress the similarities among individuals. Once all offenders in the agency are screened according to their probability of success, this classificatory scheme can then be used to create caseloads composed of offenders who have roughly the same chances of success or failure. This model is called vertical because it divides the range of offender characteristics into vertical slices in order to create caseloads.

Caseload size can be varied across both single-factor and multifactor classifications. For example, the size of caseloads, when based in the vertical model, is usually varied; it can be decreased in those composed of offenders with a high risk of failure or increased for those composed of low-risk offenders.

Today, many departments employ workload formulas to determine caseload size. This technique takes into account the fact that not all offenders are the same and that some will require more attention than others. For example, higher-risk cases often have additional requirements for services and supervision (including the number of times per month that they must attend contact sessions with officers). Furthermore, higher-risk cases have higher failure rates, which means that additional time might reasonably be required in order to file paperwork for violations, etc. Here, cases are screened according to a number of factors, such as risk. Figure 9.1 shows an example of a monthly work unit ledger from the Montgomery County Adult Probation Department (Dayton, Ohio). In this particular department, a standard workload is 250 work units, based on 107.5 available hours per month. A high-risk case is equal to 4 work units, while a presentence investigation (PSI) is equal to 14. Each type of case and activity is given a weight, based on a time study that was used as the basis for their formula. This is an excellent example of how work can be distributed equally across a department by taking into account differences between offenders and certain activities.

Another creative example of how one probation department handles its caseloads can be seen in the Lucas County Adult Probation Department (Toledo, Ohio). Here, all cases are screened according to risk (high, medium, and low). In addition, screening devices are used to identify alcoholics, drug abusers, sex offenders, and offenders with high mental health needs. One probation officer, along with a team of volunteer probation officers, handles all of the low-risk offenders. High-risk offenders that do not require the assistance of a specialist are supervised in a "high-risk unit." Those special needs offenders are placed in one of the four specialty units (e.g., alcohol, mental health). Caseloads for high-risk and specialty units are considerably smaller. Offenders without these needs who fall

_____ (Team)										_____ (Month/Year)			

SUPERVISION CLASSIFICATION				INVESTIGATIONS				WORK UNITS					
OFFICER	MAX	MED	MIN	NEW	ITS	UNS	CURT	TLC	INS	INC	PATH	PSI SHCK	MISC

TOTALS

MAX—Maximum Supervision	4 work units
INS—Intercounty Transfer	1 work unit
MED—Medium Supervision	2 work units
PATH—Pay Thru	1 work unit
MIN—Minimum Supercision	1 work unit
PSI—Bond or Jail	14 work units
NEW—Not Yet Classified	5 work units
SHCK—Shock Report	2 work units
ITS—Intensive Treatment	8 work units
UNS—Unsupervised-Court	1/2 work units
MISC—Affidavit, Victim	1 work unit
CURT—Courtesy Supervision	1 work unit
TLC—Treatment in Lieu of Conviction	1 work unit

_____
(Supervisor)

Figure 9.1 Work Units Monthly Ledger Summary.

Source: Adapted from the Montgomery County Adult Probation Department.

into the medium-risk category are supervised by regular treatment officers. In addition, this department has an intensive supervision unit that handles offenders of all types, provided they have been diverted from a state penal institution. PSIs are conducted by a separate unit. Using this scheme, Lucas County is able to divert a considerable number of low-risk, minimum supervision cases and to focus their attention on offenders who require more specialized treatment or increased surveillance.

When the general strategy for managing offenders is established, officers must deliver needed services to their clients. The remainder of this chapter discusses different strategies employed by probation and parole agencies to deliver those services to offenders under supervision. Although these strategies are discussed separately, they are not mutually exclusive, and "pure" types are seldom found in actual supervision practices.

CASEWORK SUPERVISION VERSUS BROKERAGE SUPERVISION

The two major orientations or approaches to supervision are casework and brokerage. This chapter examines each approach, the assumption underlying its use, its advantages and disadvantages, and major operational concerns. We are discussing "pure" types as though the approaches were mutually exclusive, as if a department would adopt either a caseload or a brokerage approach, but could not combine any feature of the two. In reality, the two approaches are so mixed that it would be unusual if any two departments exhibited precisely the same approach as extreme positions. Most departments adopt positions somewhere along the continuum.

Casework Supervision

The traditional approach to probation and parole supervision has been the casework approach. **Casework** is not synonymous with the term "social work"; rather, it is just one of the three major specialties of social work (the others are community organization and group work). Many definitions of casework and social casework have been offered. Bowers (1950, p. 127) has provided this frequently cited definition:

> Social casework is an area in which knowledge of the science of human relations and skills in relationships are used to mobilize capacities in the individual and resources in the community appropriate for better adjustment between the client and all or any part of his total environment.

Meeker (1948, pp. 51–52) has elaborated further:

> The modern emphasis in social casework is upon discovering the positive potential within the individual and helping him exploit his own capabilities, while at the same time revealing external resources in his social and economic environment which will contribute to his ability to assume the mature responsible obligations of a well-adjusted individual.

It is apparent that the basic element in casework is the nature of the relationship between the caseworker and the individual in trouble. It is also obvious from these definitions that casework emphasizes changing the behavior of the offender through the development of a supportive one-to-one relationship. Because of the closeness, this approach views the caseworker as the sole, or at least the primary, agent of treatment for the client.

By following a casework approach, the supervising officer will also follow the basic assumptions of social work. Trecker (1955, pp. 8–9) divides these assumptions into four categories: people, behavior problems, the social worker, and the

Probation officer with an offender. *[Photo courtesy of Talbert House, Inc.]*

relationship between society and the offender. One of the assumptions about offenders is that "people can and do change in their behavior when they are given the right help at the right time and in the right amount."[2] With respect to behavior problems, it is assumed that because problems are complex and intertwined with the total living situation, treatment of those problems must be individualized. The primary treatment agent is assumed to be the social worker, and his or her most important tool is the quality of the relationship created with the client. Finally, it is assumed that the client must be motivated to participate in the treatment process; consequently, a key element of the working relationship between the social worker and the client must be the development of the client's desire to change his or her behavior.

A common thread running through these assumptions is the idea that the offender must enter the casework relationship voluntarily, or at least willingly. The relationship involved in correctional supervision, however, does not usually rest on the offender's voluntary participation, but rather on the authority of the probation or parole officer. Under the casework approach, then, it is important to resolve the conflict between the voluntary self-determination of the offender and the authority inherent in the supervising officer's position.

Many authors characterize the authority of the probation or parole officer as an important tool that can be used in the treatment process. Mangrum (1975, p. 219) refers to the use of "coercive casework" and states, "While it is true that effective casework is not something done to or for the client, but with him, it is also true that sometimes it is a matter of some action which gets his attention or holds him still long enough for him to recognize that there is motivation from within." Studt (1954, p. 24) notes that it is important for the offender to learn that "authority is power to help as well as power to limit." Hardman (1959) feels that authority, if used properly by the probation officer, can be an extremely powerful tool in the social service. He believes that all individuals, including probationers, entertain both positive and negative feelings toward authority and that a primary responsibility of the caseworker is to help the client understand and accept those conflicting feelings and to learn new ways of controlling and expressing them.

Casework is used so extensively in probation and parole supervision that it is considered the "norm" as a service provision strategy. It basically follows the medical model of corrections in which the supervising officer, through a one-to-one relationship, diagnoses the offender, formulates a treatment strategy, implements that strategy, and, finally, evaluates the offender in light of the treatment.

In reality, however, the supervising officer does not have the time or energy to devote to individual cases. Perhaps the most basic criticisms of the casework approach are that the probation and/or parole officer tries to be all things to all people, and therefore does not mobilize the community and its support systems adequately. In addition, large caseloads, staff shortages, and endless report writing leave supervising officers unable to perform all the tasks called for by casework.

Coupled with the trend away from the medical model, probation and parole administrators have initiated both the brokerage approach and community resource management teams.

Brokerage Supervision

Almost diametrically opposed to the casework approach is the brokerage approach, in which the supervising officer is not concerned primarily with understanding or changing the behavior of the offender, but rather with assessing the concrete needs of the individual and arranging for the probationer or parolee to receive services that address those needs directly. Because the officer is not seen as the primary agent of treatment or change, there is significantly less emphasis placed on the development of a close, one-on-one relationship between the officer and the offender. With the brokerage approach, the supervising officer functions primarily as a manager or broker of resources and social services already available from other agencies. It is the task of the probation or parole officer to assess the service needs of the offender, locate the social service agency that addresses those needs as its primary function, refer the offender to the appropriate agency, and follow up referrals to make sure the offender has actually received the services. Under the brokerage approach, it may be said that the officer's relationship with community service agencies is more important than the relationship with an individual client. Both the brokerage and casework approaches share the importance of the offenders' participation in developing their own supervision plans.

The National Advisory Commission on Criminal Justice Standards and Goals (1973, p. 320) recommended that the probation system should "redefine the role of probation officer from caseworker to community resource manager." The Commission report (1973, pp. 322–323) characterized this approach in the following way:

> To carry out his responsibilities as a community resource manager, the probation officer must perform several functions. In helping a probationer obtain needed services, the probation officer will have to assess the situation, know available resources, contact the appropriate resource, assist the probationer to obtain the services, and follow up on the case. When the probationer encounters difficulty in obtaining a service he needs, the probation officer will have to explore the reason for the difficulty and take appropriate steps to see that the service is delivered. The probation officer will have to monitor and evaluate the services to which the probationer is referred.

The Commission also addresses the problems of individual probation officers providing services that may be available elsewhere. They encouraged (1973, p. 32) the reliance of probation departments on other social service agencies by suggesting that

Probation systems should not attempt to duplicate services already created by law and supposedly available to all persons. The responsibility of the system and its staff should be to enable the probationer to cut through the barriers and receive assistance from social institutions that may be all too ready to exclude him.

With its emphasis on the management of community resources, the brokerage approach requires intimate knowledge of the services in the community and the conditions under which each service is available. It may not be feasible for each officer to accumulate and use this vast amount of information about all the possible community service sources. It has been suggested frequently, therefore, that the brokerage of community services might be handled more easily if individual probation or parole officers were to specialize in gaining knowledge about and familiarity with an agency or set of agencies that provide related services. For example, one officer might become extremely knowledgeable about all community agencies that offer services for individuals with drug-related problems, while another officer might specialize in all agencies that handle unemployed or underemployed individuals. Regardless of whether officers decide to specialize or would prefer to handle all types of community agencies, the essential requirements under the brokerage approach are for the supervising officer to develop a comprehensive knowledge of the resources already available in the community and to use those resources to the fullest extent for the benefit of clients.

Closely related to the brokerage approach is the role of advocate. Several authors have recently stressed the advocacy role for probation officers.[3] Recognizing the fact that some of the services the offenders need will not be available in the community, these authors suggest that instead of trying to supply those needed services themselves, probation and parole officers should concentrate on working with community agencies to develop the necessary service. This will ensure that these services will be available not only to probation or parole clients, but also to other individuals within the community who might require them.[4]

The essential tasks of the brokerage orientation to probation and parole are the management of available community resources and the use of those services to meet the needs of offenders. There is little emphasis on the quality of the relationship that develops between the officer and the offenders; rather, more emphasis is placed upon the close working relationship between the officer and the staff members of community social service agencies. Counseling and guidance are considered inappropriate activities for the probation and parole officer; no attempt is made to change the behavior of the offender. The primary function of the officer is to assess the concrete needs of each offender and make appropriate referral to existing community services. Should the needed service not be available in the community, it is the responsibility of the officer to encourage the development of that service.

In contrast to the medical model, the brokerage approach is based on the reintegration model, which emphasizes the needs of correctional clients for specialized services that can best be provided by established community agencies.

As a rehabilitation device, brokerage replaces the casework approach. The brokerage task requires the assessment of client needs and the linkage of available community services with those needs.

Obviously, a pure brokerage approach has its drawbacks. In addition to the lack of a strong relationship between the probation or parole officer and the offender, community services may not be readily available. This is often the case in more rural communities, and even if these service agencies are available, they may not be willing to accept an offender population. As a rule, there appear to be more offenders in need of specialized treatment than there is program space available. Cutbacks in government funding have also resulted in fewer programs, which raises the question: "How can a probation or parole officer be a broker if the services are not available?"

INTEGRATED MODELS

More recent attempts have been made to integrate components of the previous models into probation and parole in a manner that emphasizes both the casework supervision and brokerage elements of community supervision (see Smith et al., 2012; Taxman, 2002; Taxman et al., 2004). This discussion of casework and brokerage—the major orientations for probation and parole supervision and service provision—has highlighted the essential tasks of each approach and has emphasized their differences. Another major issue in supervision is one of form.

IMPROVING COMMUNITY SUPERVISION

Given the large caseload and varied responsibilities of probation and parole agencies, the question remains: Can probation and parole officers influence change in their offenders? Preliminary evidence from training initiatives in Canada (Bonta et al., 2008; Bourgon et al., 2010), the United States (Smith et al., 2012) as well as Australia (Trotter, 1996), has produced some promising results.

While it has been assumed that offenders benefit from community supervision much more than if they were incarcerated, recent empirical evidence on the effectiveness of community supervision challenges this assumption. For example, Bonta and colleagues have undertaken a review of the literature on the effectiveness of community supervision using meta-analytic techniques. The findings from 15 studies published between 1980 and 2006 yielded 26 effect size estimates. The average follow-up period was 17 months, and the mean effect size was *about zero*, indicating no statistically significant relationship between community supervision and recidivism.

Unfortunately, there is very little research examining how officers can influence change in offenders despite the fact that the importance of combining community supervision and "what works" literatures has been widely recognized. One pioneering study in this regard was conducted by Bonta and associates (2008, 2010). Audiotaped interviews between 62 probation officers and their offenders found relatively poor adherence to some of the basic principles of effective intervention. For the most part, probation officers spent too much time on the enforcement aspect of supervision (i.e., monitoring compliance with court conditions) and not enough time on the service delivery role of supervision. Major criminogenic needs, such as antisocial attitudes and social supports for crime, were largely ignored, and probation officers evidenced few of the **skills** (e.g., prosocial modeling, differential reinforcement) that could influence behavioral change in their offenders. This research led to the development of a strategic training initiative that has been implemented in several sites across Canada. At this point in time, it is evident that trained officers have higher caseload retention rates (i.e., fewer technical violations, new arrests, and AWOLs).

During the past decade, several attempts have been made to improve the effectiveness of community supervision by implementing RNR and other evidence-based research into community supervision practices (Bourgon et al., 2010; Robinson et al., 2012; Smith et al., 2012; Trotter, 1996, 2006). Research conducted by Trotter (1996) has also supported the use of core correctional practices in community supervision. He contends that "accurate role clarification, working with problems and goals as they are defined (in collaboration with) the offender, and modeling and reinforcing prosocial values" are necessary components of an integrated practice model. His research has also underscored the importance of the client–worker relationship, case planning, use of community resources, and training families to support behavioral change (Trotter, 1996).

Research on the principles of effective intervention coupled with the most recent research on community supervision provided the impetus for the development of a new model by the University of Cincinnati: Effective Practices in Community Supervision (EPICS). This model represents a combination of the content included in both Canadian and Australian studies. The purpose of the EPICS model is to teach probation and parole officers how to apply the principles of effective intervention (and core correctional practices specifically, including relationship skills) to community supervision practices. The EPICS model has been piloted in Indiana and Ohio, and results indicated that the trained officers are using the skills at a higher rate than untrained officers.

With the EPICS model, probation officers follow a structured approach to their interactions with their offenders. Specifically, each session includes four components: (1) *check-in*, in which the officer determines if the offender has any crises or acute needs, builds rapport, and discusses compliance issues; (2) *review*, which focuses on the skills discussed in the prior session, application of those skills, and troubleshooting continued problems in the use of those skills; (3) *intervention*, where the probation officer identifies continued areas of need, as well as trends in problems the offender experiences, teaches relevant skills, and targets problematic thinking; and (4) *homework and rehearsal*, when the offender is given an opportunity to see the model the probation officer is talking about, provided opportunities to role play, assigned homework, and given instructions to follow before the next visit.

Box 9.2 illustrates the steps of the EPICS approach. The EPICS model is designed to use a combination of monitoring, referrals, and face-to-face interactions

---

Box 9.1
Problem Solving

A problem is a specific situation or set of related situations to which a person must respond in order to function effectively. A problematic situation is one in which no effective response alternative is immediately available to the person facing the situation. One of the skills emphasized in the EPICS model is teaching the offender problem solving, which involves several steps:

1. Stop and think and identify the problem
2. Clarify goals
3. Generate alternative solutions
4. Evaluate
5. Implement the plan
6. Evaluate the plan

---

to provide the offender with a sufficient "dosage" of treatment interventions and make the best possible use of time to develop a collaborative working relationship. The EPICS model helps translate the risk, need, and responsivity principles into practice. Probation officers are taught to increase dosage to higher-risk offenders, stay focused on criminogenic needs, especially the **thought–behavior link**, and use a social learning, cognitive-behavioral approach to their interactions. The EPICs model is not intended to replace other programming and services, but rather is an attempt to more fully utilize probation officers as agents of change, thus combining the best elements of casework and brokerage. Results from the studies in Ohio and Indiana have indicated that implementation of the model was associated with reductions in recidivism, particularly for higher-risk offenders and in the case of officers who used the skills with higher fidelity (Smith et al., 2012). More recent versions of the model have further integrated EPICS with case management and motivational interviewing.

Box 9.2
Steps in EPICS

Step 1: Check in
Step 2: Review
Step 3: Intervention
Step 4: Rehearsal and homework

Box 9.3
The Thought–Behavior Link

This is the connection between what we think and how we behave. For example, we often drive over the speed limit (behavior) because of our thoughts (i.e., "I'm a safe driver," "Everyone is doing it," "I am only going 10 miles over the limit," "I'm in a hurry").

CONTRACTING FOR SERVICES

As indicated previously, recent events have called for a change in the role of the probation and parole officer. In addition to the increased demands of the surveillance aspect of supervision, other changes in this field have been geared toward enhancing the social service aspect of the probation or parole officer's role. The use of various types of contracts is one example of this development.

Contracts for a wide variety of client and administrative activities are particular to the unique responsibilities of community corrections (Jensen, 1987). These include the following:

- Residential programs (including halfway houses, house arrest, restitution centers, and facilities for juveniles, such as group or foster homes).
- Counseling and treatment programs for both general client groups and targeted offenders such as drug addicts and alcoholics.
- Administrative services for data processing, recordkeeping, evaluations, and so forth.
- Programs for victims of crime and crisis intervention. These would include traditional counseling services, as well as programs designed to aid victims as they struggle with the criminal justice system and to help them file for victim compensation.
- Programs that conduct private presentence investigation and develop sentencing alternatives for offenders.
- Dispute resolution, mediation programs, and pretrial services.
- Testing, ranging from employment/educational to urinalysis for alcohol or other drug abuse.

Stricter punishment has brought offenders that are "new" to the criminal justice system, such as drunk drivers, spouse abusers, and persons who fail to pay child support. Crowded jail facilities often cannot handle these offender categories, and it is unlikely that they will find room for such offenders in the future. As a result, many jurisdictions have turned to private providers to handle these "specialized" groups.

Contracting can be an effective way to provide services. For example, many probation and parole agencies contract with local halfway houses for beds. It is much more cost-effective to "lease" the bed space than to build and operate a halfway house. Contracting also gives the agency the flexibility of being able to terminate the contract if the service fails to meet expectations or is no longer needed.

Many of these programs represent an attempt to treat some offenders in a nontraditional fashion and provide close ties between them and community programs. Such innovations can, when used with a particular type of client (such as mentally disordered offenders or drunk drivers), help offenders and relieve the burden of heavy caseloads upon a probation department. Their use could also permit a probation department to deploy its resources in a more efficient manner.

CONTRACTING WITH THE CLIENT

Another type of contract directly focuses on the offender and the agency in an attempt to spell out fully the obligations of each party during the supervision period. As defined by Ankersmit (1976), setting the contract simply means reaching an agreement with the offender as to what goals he or she will work toward achieving. The basic idea is to use this device as a central point in the planning process, specifically including the probationer in this process. The contract, in this case, is between the supervising officer and the offender. The offender might agree to seek employment, pay child support, and study for a general education diploma. The supervising officer agrees to help the offender meet his or her goals and to provide needed assistance and support. This type of "contract" is actually an extension of the conditions of probation or parole and can be a useful tool in case planning. Although it is not known how many probation and parole agencies use "behavioral" contracts with offenders, Scott has identified two advantages of this approach:

1. The probationer is involved intimately in supervision planning from the very beginning of this process. As a result, the sentencing judge is provided with additional information on program plans and on motivations of the offender.
2. Probationers have clear specifications of what is expected of them, including the possibility of early termination. In addition, the probation officer is provided with clearly specified objectives for supervision and has a better idea of how to proceed with supervision plans. The hope is that contractual programming will result in a more efficient approach to probation management.

In short, it appears that **contracting** offers an opportunity to establish a system that strengthens and goes beyond the traditional standard special conditions of supervision. It can provide several benefits to both the offender and the department and can lead to the efficient management of community services.

SUPERVISION PLANNING

Regardless of the approach used by an agency to deliver service, an essential ingredient to successful supervision is planning (Ellsworth, 1988). This **supervision planning** includes identifying the needs and problems of the offender, identifying the resources available and arranging for them, and evaluating the effectiveness of the supervision activities. The probation and parole populations under supervision today are different than those supervised 20 years ago. Not only are we seeing higher-risk offenders on probation owing to prison and jail crowding, but the offender population is growing older (Burnett & Kitchen, 1989; McCarthy & Langworthy, 1987). With these changes comes a need to improve our planning of the actual supervision task. A solid supervision plan takes those risk, need, and responsivity factors identified in the assessment process and develops a plan or strategy to target or reduce those factors. Priorities are set, and criteria to gauge offender progress are also developed.

One example of a case plan developed from the LSI can be seen in Table 9.2. This table demonstrates how, following the assessment, the caseworker has

Table 9.2 Supervision Problem: An Example

Supervision Problems

Health: This offender has a documented history of heroin addiction
             dating back seven years and has two previous convictions for
             selling drugs to support a $100-a-day habit.

Family: Recently separated from his wife and two children but would like
             to be reunited with them. Several reports of wife abuse have been
             recorded.

Employment: Unemployed—occasional construction laborer.

For each supervision problem, a corresponding supervision objective is
developed.

Supervision Objectives

Abstain from drug use, stabilize marital relationship, and assist offender to
locate and maintain employment.

---

identified the problem area, the objectives, and the strategies used to target the
risk factor. This example also allows the identification of responsibility, time
frames, completion status, and strengths.

After problems and objectives have been identified, the supervising officer
formulates a plan for achieving those objectives. The methods selected are based
on considerations such as the nature of the problem, the abilities and expertise
of the officer, the availability of effective community resources, the attitude of
the offender, and the exercise of authority necessary to ensure the offender's
participation.

A well-thought-out initial supervision plan is the cornerstone of supervision
activities. The plan need not be lengthy, but it should specify actions to be taken by
the supervising officer, the responsibilities of the offender, and the role of any
community resources.

In addition to developing the supervision or case plan, many agencies require
periodic reviews. This review should include an evaluation of the dynamics of
the offender's supervision problems as they have emerged over time. The review
should also highlight the degree of progress achieved in meeting precisely
established objectives and goals. Finally, the officer identifies new problems and
revises the supervision plan to meet the current situation.

Undoubtedly, supervision planning varies from agency to agency, and often
from officer to officer; however, regardless of the process or the format, common
elements are involved in supervision planning: recognizing problems, selecting
objectives, developing a strategy, implementing that strategy, and, finally, evaluating
the effectiveness of the entire process.

USE OF VOLUNTEERS

Community correctional programs operate under a basic philosophy of reintegration: connecting offenders with legitimate opportunity and reward structures, and generally uniting the offender within the community. It has become quite apparent that the correctional system cannot achieve this without assistance, regardless of the extent of resources available. Reintegration requires the assistance and support of the community. One important resource for the community correctional agency is the use of volunteers. If used properly, these individuals can serve as an important asset for a community correctional agency.

This concept is certainly not a new one. The John Howard Association, the Osborne Association, and other citizen prisoners' aid societies have provided voluntary correctional-type services for many years. The volunteer movement developed in this country in the early 1820s, when a group of citizens known as the Philadelphia Society for Alleviating the Misery of Public Prisons began supervising the activities of inmates upon their release from penal institutions. This practice was later adopted by John Augustus, a Boston shoemaker, who worked with well over 2,000 misdemeanants in his lifetime (see Chapter 4).

Volunteerism is alive and well in corrections.[5] Judge Keith Leenhouts of the Royal Oak (Michigan) Municipal Court resurrected the concept some 30 years ago and continues to serve as a driving force behind this now relatively accepted, and still growing, movement. In addition to the many local programs in existence, there are several national programs supporting volunteerism, such as VISTO (Volunteers in Service to Offenders), VIP (Volunteers in Probation), and the American Bar Association-sponsored National Volunteer Aide Program. Although exact numbers are not known, it is safe to say that there are thousands of volunteers serving more than 3,000 jurisdictions nationwide.

Proponents of the volunteer concept consider it to be one of the most promising innovations in the field, claiming that it can help alleviate the problem of excessive probation and parole caseloads and contribute to rehabilitation and reintegration goals for the offender (Greenberg, 1988; Latessa et al., 1983). A good illustration of the effective use of volunteers can be seen in Lucas County (Toledo), Ohio. Here, probationers are screened according to risk. All "low-risk" probationers are assigned to one probation officer who, with the help of volunteers, supervises more than 1,000 clients.

Volunteers can range from student interns to older persons with time to devote. Some volunteers are persons who have a specific skill or talent to contribute, while others give their time and counsel.

Scope of Services

Volunteerism generally refers to situations in which individual citizens contribute their talents, wisdom, skills, time, and resources within the context of the justice system, without receiving financial remuneration. Volunteer projects operate on the premise that certain types of offenders can be helped by the services a volunteer can offer and that such services can be provided at a minimal tax dollar cost, resulting in significant cost savings.

By drawing upon the time, talents, and abilities of volunteers to assist in service delivery, community supervision officers can serve to broaden the nature of the services offered. Any community consists of persons who possess a diverse supply of skills and abilities that can be tapped effectively by volunteer programs. The National Center of Volunteers in Courts has reported that some 155 roles have actually been filled by volunteer persons in different jurisdictions. Scheier (1970) developed a list of more than 200 potential volunteer services, including the following:

addiction program volunteer	intake volunteer
case aide	newsletter editor
clerical courtroom assistance	presentence investigator
diagnostic home volunteer	recreation volunteer
educational aide	test administrator and scorer
foster parent	vocational service aide
fund-raiser	volunteer counselor.

In addition to the direct service offered, volunteers can supply a number of support services (Lucas, 1987). Volunteers often assist program operations in an administrative capacity. For example, a full-time volunteer for quite some time has supervised the well-known Royal Oak, Michigan program. The VISTO program in Los Angeles County (California) has likewise utilized volunteers to fill some of its clerical needs, such as handling supplies, photocopying, answering recruitment correspondence, and routine office contacts, as well as participating in research projects. In addition, many volunteers serve on advisory boards. Many nonprofit community agencies, such as halfway houses, rely on volunteers to serve on their boards of directors. There can be little doubt that volunteers can serve as a means of amplifying time, attention, and type of services given to clients by the system. However, it is also important that an agency not become overreliant on volunteers to the extent that they do not hire enough professional officers and staff.

SUMMARY

This chapter discussed one of the most important aspects of probation and parole: supervision of the offender. We have noted that the assignment of offenders to a probation or parole officer for supervision can follow several models. Some offenders are assigned randomly to caseloads, others are assigned based on geography or special problems, while yet others are classified through the use of prediction devices.

Once assignment is complete, the approach or philosophy of supervision usually centers on casework and brokerage. Casework follows a belief that the supervising officer should be the primary agent of change and thus "all things to all people." The brokerage approach assumes that the best place for treatment is in the community and that the primary task of the probation or parole officer is to arrange for and manage community resources. While casework is the norm, in reality most probation and parole officers and agencies use techniques for both approaches.

More recently, a new model of offender and probation officer interaction has arisen that attempts to restructure the way that POs work with offenders by focusing on criminogenic needs, skill deficits, and the thought–behavior link. By combining compliance with effective interventions, it is hoped that lower recidivism can be achieved.

Finally, the use of volunteers is not a new concept. Volunteers play an important role in community corrections and, if used properly, can be a valuable asset to a community correctional agency.

Review Questions

1. What are the assumptions of casework? Brokerage?
2. What are the limitations of casework in probation?
3. List three ways that caseloads are assigned.
4. What are the four steps in the EPICS model and how is it different from traditional approaches?
5. How can volunteers be used in probation?

Notes

1 A parole board refers to all agencies (commissions, board of charities, board of prison terms, and so on) whose duty it is to release inmates to the community, under supervision, prior to expiration of the original sentence length. Resource: www.appa-net.org.
2 This point is argued eloquently by Cullen (1994). See also Scott and Wolfe (2000).
3 For a good example of advocacy in probation and parole, see Dell'Apa et al. (1976); and Mangrum (1975).
4 For discussions of advocacy, see Macallair (1994).
5 American Correctional Association (1993). See also American Correctional Association (1987); and Celinska (2000).

Recommended Reading

Auerbach, B.J., Castellano, T.C. (1998). Successful community sanctions and services for special offenders. *Proceedings of the 1994 Conference of the International Community Corrections Association*. Lantham, MD: American Correctional Association.

References

American Correctional Association (1987). *Standards for administration of correctional agencies.* Laurel, MD: ACA.

American Correctional Association (1993). *Community partnerships in action.* Laurel, MD: ACA.

Ankersmit, E. (1976). Setting the contract in probation. *Federal Probation* 41(2), 28–33.

Bonta, J., Rugge, T., Scott, T.L., Bourgon, G., Yessine, A.K. (2008). Exploring the "Black Box" of supervision. *Journal of Offender Rehabilitation* 47(3), 248–270.

Bonta, J., Bourgon, G., Rugge, T., Scott, T.Y., Yessine, A.K., Gutierrez, L., Li, J. (2010). *Corrections research report: User report on the strategic training initiative in community supervision: Risk-need-responsivity in the real world.* Toronto: Public Safety Canada.

Bourgon, G., Bonta, J., Rugge, T., Scott, T.L., Yessine, A.K. (2010). Program design, implementation, and evaluation in "Real World" community supervision. *Federal Probation* 74(1), 1–10.

Bowers, S. (1950). The nature and definition of social casework. In: C. Kasius (ed.) *Principles and techniques in social casework.* New York: Family Services Association of America, pp. 126–139.

Burnett, C., Kitchen, A. (1989). More than a case number: Older offenders on probation. *Journal of Offender Counseling, Services and Rehabilitation* 13, 149–160.

Camp, C., Camp, G. (2003). *The corrections yearbook 2003.* South Salem, NY: The Criminal Justice Institute.

Carter, R., Wilkins, L. (1976). Caseloads: Some conceptual models. In: R.M. Carter, L.T. Wilkins (eds) *Probation, parole and community corrections.* New York: John Wiley and Sons, pp. 391–401.

Celinska, K. (2000). Volunteer involvement in ex-offenders' readjustment. *Journal of Offender Rehabilitation* 30(3/4), 99–116.

Cullen, F.T (1994). Social support as an organizing concept for criminology. *Justice Quarterly* 11, 527–560.

Dell'Apa, F., Adams, W., Jorgensen, J., Sigurdson, H. (1976). Advocacy, brokerage, community: The ABCs of probation and parole. *Federal Probation* 40(4), 37–44.

Ellsworth, T. (1988). Case supervision planning: The forgotten component of intensive probation supervision. *Federal Probation* 52(4), 28–32.

Greenberg, N. (1988). The discovery program: A way to use volunteers in the treatment process. *Federal Probation* 52(4), 39–45.

Hardman, D. (1959). Authority in casework: A bread-and-butter theory. *National Probation and Parole Association Journal* 5, 249–255.

Harlow, C. (1999). *Prior abuse reported by inmates and probationers.* Washington, DC: Bureau of Justice Statistics.

Jensen, C. (1987). *Contracting for community corrections services.* Washington, DC: U.S. Department of Justice, National Institute of Corrections.

Latessa, E., Travis, L., Allen, H. (1983). Volunteers and paraprofessionals in parole: Current practices. *Journal of Offender Counseling Services and Rehabilitation* 8, 91–105.

Lucas, W. (1987). Perceptions of the volunteer role. *Journal of Offender Counseling, Services and Rehabilitation* 12, 141–146.

Macallair, D. (1993). Reaffirming rehabilitation in juvenile justice. *Youth and Society* 25, 104–125.

Macallair, D. (1994). Disposition case advocacy in San Francisco's juvenile justice system: A new approach to deinstitutionalization. *Crime & Delinquency* 40, 84–95.

Mangrum, C. (1975). *The professional practitioner in probation.* Springfield, IL: Charles C Thomas.

Maruschak, L., Beck, A. (2001). *Medical problems of inmates.* Washington, DC: U.S. Bureau of Justice.

McCarthy, B., Langworthy, R. (1987). Older offenders on probation and parole. *Journal of Offender Counseling, Services and Rehabilitation* 12, 7–25.

Meeker, B. (1948). Probation is casework. *Federal Probation* 12(2), 51–52.

Mumola, C. (1999). *Substance abuse and treatment, states and federal prisoners, 1997.* Washington, DC: U.S. Bureau of Justice Statistics.

National Advisory Commission on Criminal Justice Standards and Goals (1973). *Corrections.* Washington, DC: U.S. Government Printing Office.

Robinson, C.R., Lowenkamp, C.T., Holsinger, A.M., Van Benschoten, S.W., Alexander, M., Oleson, J.C. (2012). A random study of Staff Training Aimed at Reducing Re-arrest (STARR): Using core correctional practices in probation interactions. *Journal of Crime and Justice* 35(2), 167–188.

Scheier, I. (1970). The professional and the volunteer: An emerging relationship. *Federal Probation* 34(2), 8–12.

Scott, K., Wolfe, D. (2000). Change among batterers: Examining men's success stories. *Journal of Interpersonal Violence* 15(8), 827–842.

Sigler, R., Williams, J. (1994). A study of the outcomes of probation officers and risk-screening instrument classifications. *Journal of Criminal Justice* 22, 495–502.

Smith, P., Schweitzer, M., Labrecque, R.M., Latessa, E.J. (2012). Improving probation officers' supervision skills: An evaluation of the EPICS model. *Journal of Crime and Justice* 35(2), 189–199.

Studt, E. (1954). Casework in the correctional field. *Federal Probation* 17(3), 17–24.

Taxman, F.S. (2002). Supervision—exploring the dimensions of effectiveness. *Federal Probation* 66(2), 14–27.

Taxman, F.S., Shepardson, E., Byrne, J. (2004). *Tools of the trade: A guide to incorporating science into practice.* Maryland: National Institute of Corrections, Maryland Division of Probation and Parole.

Trecker, H. (1955). Social work principles in probation. *Federal Probation* 19(1), 8–9.

Trotter, C. (1996). The impact of different supervision practices in community corrections: Cause for optimism. *Australian and New Zealand Journal of Criminology* 29, 1–18.

Trotter, C. (2006). *Working with involuntary clients: A guide to practice.* London: Sage.

Chapter 10

INTERMEDIATE SANCTIONS

Key Terms

boot camp
community service
day-reporting centers
diversion
electronic monitoring
enhancement

global positioning system (GPS)
home detention
intensive supervision
intermediate sanctions
net-widening
shock incarceration

If punishment makes not the will supple it hardens the offender.
—John Locke

The effects of our actions may be postponed but they are never lost.
There is an inevitable reward for good deeds and an inescapable
punishment for bad. Mediate this truth, and seek always to earn good
wages from destiny.—Wu Ming Fu

INTERMEDIATE SANCTIONS

No discussion of contemporary probation would be complete without examining the development and application of **intermediate sanctions**. Faced with overcrowded prison and jail systems, criminal justice professionals and policy makers are being forced to search for alternative ways to sanction and control criminal offenders.

A host of intermediate sanctions designed to treat the criminal offender in the community have been developed and implemented. The intermediate punishments described in this chapter include electronic monitoring, house arrest, community service, day-reporting centers, intensive supervision, drug courts, and boot camps. The purposes of these intermediate interventions are to provide correctional alternatives to confinement.

The U.S. Department of Justice (1990, p. 3) defines *intermediate sanctioning* as "a punishment option that is considered on a continuum to fall between

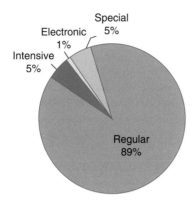

Figure 10.1 Probationers and Parolees under Different Types of Supervision.

Source: Camp, C., Camp, G. (2003) *The corrections yearbook adult corrections 2002*. Middletown, CT: The Criminal Justice Institute.

traditional probation and traditional incarceration." Intermediate sanctions were largely developed out of the need to relieve prison crowding[1] and satisfy the general public's desire for new correctional alternatives. Thus, policy makers began to experiment with programs to punish, control, and reform offenders in the community. Figure 10.1 shows the percentage of probationers under several different types of sanctions. More than 10 percent are under some form of supervision other than regular. Two major issues confronting intermediate sanctions are (1) offender diversion and (2) public safety.

Box 10.1
Intermediate Sanctions

Intermediate sanctions, ranging in severity from day fines to "boot camps," are interventions that are beginning to fill the sentencing gap between prison at one extreme and probation at the other. Lengthy prison terms may be inappropriate for some offenders; for others, probation may be too inconsequential and may not provide the degree of public supervision necessary to ensure public safety. By expanding sentencing options, intermediate sanctions enable the criminal justice system to tailor punishment more closely to the nature of the crime and the criminal. An appropriate range of punishments makes it possible for the system to hold offenders strictly accountable for their actions.

Source: Gowdy (1993).

THE NEED FOR INTERMEDIATE SANCTIONS

With prison and jail populations at an all-time high, most states have acknowledged that they will not be able to build their way out of the crisis. It should also be noted that the national annual incarceration expense for a single prisoner averaged more than $30,000 (Henrichson & Delaney, 2012). Furthermore, with more than 76 percent of correctional agencies at or exceeding capacity, it is unlikely that there will be relief in the near future. Alternatives to long-term confinement are a necessity.

Despite the ever-increasing cost of incarceration, it is necessary for alternative sanctions to gain public, legislative, and judicial support (Finn, 1991). To earn sufficient support, an alternative to confinement must "be perceived as reasonably safe; address the public's desire for punishment through community control, nonpaid labor, and victim restitution; and offer an opportunity for positive change by providing treatment and employment skills" (American Correctional Association, 1990, p. 2).

INTENSIVE SUPERVISION

The most widely used community-based intermediate sanction that attempts to meet the aforementioned criteria is **intensive supervision**. Intensive supervision is most often viewed as an alternative to incarceration. Offenders who are sentenced to intensive probation supervision are supposed to be those offenders who, in the absence of intensive supervision, would have been sentenced to imprisonment. However, intensive supervision is hardly a new idea. Previous programs of intensive supervision carried the common goal of maintaining public safety, but varied from the "new generation" of intensive supervision programs (ISPs) in very fundamental ways (Latessa, 1986).

Early versions of intensive supervision were based on the idea that increased client contact would enhance rehabilitation while allowing for greater client control. For example, California's Special Intensive Parole Unit experiments in the 1950s and the San Francisco Project in the 1960s were designed as intensive supervision, but they emphasized rehabilitation as the main goal. Later, with rehabilitation still as the main objective, experiments were "undertaken to determine the 'best' caseload size for the community supervision, despite the illogic of the proposition that a magical 'best' number could be found" (McCarthy, 1987, p. 33). Nevertheless, the failure of these experiments to produce results fueled two decades' worth of cynicism about the general utility of community-based methods.

Burkhart (1986) and Pearson (1987) contend that today's ISPs emphasize punishment of the offender and control of the offender in the community at least as much as they do rehabilitation. Further, contemporary programs are designed to meet the primary goal of easing the burden of prison overcrowding.

Box 10.2
Types of Intensive Supervision Programs

Intensive supervision programs (ISP) are usually classified as prison diversion, enhanced probation, and enhanced parole. Each has a different goal.

Diversion is commonly referred to as a "front door" program because its goal is to limit the number of offenders entering prison. Prison diversion programs generally identify incoming, lower-risk inmates to participate in an ISP in the community as a substitute for a prison term.

Enhancement programs generally select already sentenced probationers and parolees and subject them to closer supervision in the community than regular probation or parole. People placed in ISP-enhanced probation or enhanced parole programs show evidence of failure under routine supervision or have committed serious offenses deemed too serious for supervision on routine caseloads.

Treatment and service components in the ISPs included drug and alcohol counseling, employment, community service, and payment of restitution. On many of these measures, ISP offenders participated more than control members; participation in such programs was found to be correlated with a reduction in recidivism.

Source: Petersilia and Turner (1993).

Figure 10.2 illustrates differences between the objectives of the original experiments with intensive supervision and the so-called "new-generation" programs. Early models were successful at accomplishing smaller caseloads and delivering more contacts and services; however, reductions in recidivism never materialized. Similarly, the more recent programs have reduced caseloads and significantly increased control and surveillance but have not had an appreciable impact directly on prison populations.[2]

Today, no two jurisdictions define intensive supervision in exactly the same way. However, one characteristic of all ISPs is that they provide for very strict

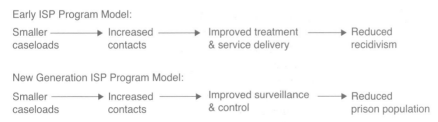

Figure 10.2 Models of Intensive Supervision Programs.

terms of probation. As Jones (1991, p. 1) points out: "Their common feature is that more control is to be exerted over the offender than that described as probation in that jurisdiction and that often these extra control mechanisms involve restrictions on liberty of movement, coercion into treatment programs, employment obligations, or all three." This increased level of control is usually achieved through reduced caseloads, increased number of contacts, and a range of required activities for participating offenders that can include victim restitution, community service, employment, random testing for substance abuse, electronic monitoring, and payment of a probation supervision fee.

Intensive supervision programs vary in terms of the number and type of contacts per month, caseload size, type of surveillance conducted, and services offered. In addition, programs vary depending on whether they are staffed by specially trained officers or regular probation officers, and whether an officer "team" approach is used.

A survey conducted by Byrne (1986) on the use of intensive supervision in the United States found that "the numbers of direct personal contacts required ranged from 2 per month to 7 per week. Some programs have specified no curfew checks, while others specified three curfew checks per week" (Pearson, 1987, p. 15). Ideally, supervising officers provide monitoring with a reduced caseload of about 15 offenders per officer. Yet, most officers carry caseloads of nearly 25 offenders. Offender entry into an intensive supervision program may be the decision of the sentencing judge, a parole board, a prison release board, or probation agency.

Table 10.1 shows some of the variations among selected ISPs. The types of clients served, the number of contacts made each month, and the recidivism rates vary greatly from program to program.

Many ISPs have revealed an increase in technical violations for ISP offenders as compared to offenders placed in other sentencing options, but no significant increase in the new offense rate (Erwin, 1987; Petersilia & Turner, 1993; Wagner & Baird, 1993). Most evaluations, however, suggest that increased contact alone does not make a difference in terms of overall recidivism rates. In a study of ISPs in Ohio, Latessa and colleagues (1997) found that offenders in ISPs were less likely to be rearrested than offenders under other forms of correctional supervision; however, they were more likely to be subsequently incarcerated. The researchers attributed this higher failure rate to revocations for probation violations. Latessa and colleagues also concluded that ISPs in Ohio were saving the state money as compared to the cost of incarceration.

As currently designed, many ISPs fail to produce significant reductions in recidivism or alleviate prison overcrowding. There does, however, appear to be a relationship between greater participation in treatment programs and lower failure rates (Jolin & Stipak, 1992; Paparozzi, n.d.; Pearson, 1987; Petersilia & Turner, 1993). This is one of the important issues facing intensive supervision. In an article summarizing the state of ISPs, Fulton et al. (1997, p. 72) made the following conclusions:

Table 10.1 Intensive Supervision Probation/Parole

Author and year	Site	Sample	Control groups	Contacts	Recidivism
Jolin & Stipak (1991)	Oregon	N = 70 drug users	100 on EM 100 on work release. Stratified random sample matched on risk	5 counseling per week and 3 self-help per week, plus curfew and EM	47% ISP 32% EM 33% WR
Erwin (1987)	Georgia	N = 200 randomly selected from ISP	N = 200 probationers N = 97 prison releasees Matched samples	5 per week ISP	40% ISP 35.5% Probation 57.8% Prison
Pearson (1987)	New Jersey	N = 554 parolees	N = 510	20 per month	24.7% ISP 34.6% CG
Byrne & Kelly (1989)	Massachusetts	N = 227 high-risk probationers	N = 834 ISP Eligible offenders plus a 35% random sample of all offenders under supervision (N = 2543)	10 month ISP 2-month probation	56.6% ISP 60.9% Probation
Latessa (1993a)	Ohio	All offenders in specialized ISP Units Alcohol = 140 Drug = 121 Sex = 64 Mental = 76	N = 424 regular probationers randomly selected	6-month alcohol and drug 4.5 month sex and mental health 1-month comparison	42% Alcohol 59% Drug 22% Sex 27% MH 46% Probation
Latessa (1992)	Ohio	N = 82 ISP randomly selected	N = 101 randomly selected from regular probation	7.5-month ISP 2.2-month probation	28% ISP 21% Probation
Latessa (1993b)	Ohio	N = 317 ISP N = 502 high-risk ISP	N = 424 randomly selected from regular probation	4-month ISP 3-month high risk 2-month probation	35% ISP 43% High 34% Probation

(Continued)

Table 10.1 (Continued)

Author and year	Site	Sample	Control groups	Contacts	Recidivism
Fallen et al. (1981)	Washington	N = 289 low-risk parolees	N = 102 matched parolees	4 per month	32.9% ISP 46.9% CG
Petersilia & Turner (1993)	Contra-Costra	N = 170	Randomly selected offenders placed in prison, probation, or parole	12 per month	29% ISP 27% CG
Petersilia & Turner (1993)	Los Angles	N = 152	Randomly selected offenders placed in prison, probation, or parole	24 per month	32% ISP 30% CG
Petersilia & Turner (1993)	Seattle	N = 173	Randomly selected offenders placed in prison, probation, or paroal	12 per month	46% ISP 36% CG
Petersilia & Turner (1993)	Ventura	N = 166	Randomly selected offenders placed in prison, probation, or parole	24 per month	32% ISP 53% CG
Petersilia & Turner (1993)	Atlanta	N = 50	Randomly selected offenders placed in prison, probation, or parole	20 per month	12% ISP 4% CG
Petersilia & Turner (1993)	Macon	N = 50	Randomly selected offenders placed in prison, probation, or parole	20 per month	42% ISP 38% CG
Petersilia & Turner (1993)	Santa Fe	N = 58	Randomly selected offenders placed in prison, probation, or parole	20 per month	48% ISP 28% CG

Petersilia & Turner (1993)	Dallas	$N = 221$ parolees	Randomly selected offenders placed in prison, probation, or parole	16 per month	39% ISP 30% CG
Petersilia & Turner (1993)	Houston	$N = 458$ parolees	Randomly selected offenders placed in prison, probation, or parole	10 per month	44% ISP 40% CG
Latessa et al. (1998)	Iowa and Northeastern state	$N = 401$	Selected from urban probation department and rural probation and parole caseload	Varied	39% ISP 40% CG
Robertson et al. (2001)	Mississippi	$N = 153$	Juvenile offenders placed on intensive probation, monitoring on regular probation, or counselling with cognitive-behavioral (CB) therapy	12 months	Benefit–cost ratio of subjects receiving CB therapy was almost twice that of intensive supervision and monitoring

Source: Compiled by authors.

- Intensive supervision programs have failed to alleviate prison crowding.
- Most ISP studies have found no significant differences between recidivism rates of ISP offenders and offenders with comparison groups.
- There appears to be a relationship between greater participation in treatment and employment programs and lower recidivism rates.
- Intensive supervision programs appear to be more effective than regular supervision or prison in meeting offenders' needs.
- Intensive supervision programs that reflect certain principles of effective intervention are associated with lower rates of recidivism.
- Intensive supervision programs provide intermediate punishment.
- Although ISPs are less expensive than prison, they are more expensive than originally thought.

Issues in Intensive Supervision

Intensive supervision, as a technique for increasing control over offenders in the community (and thereby reducing risk), has gained wide popularity.[3] As of 1990, all states, plus the federal system, had some kind of intensive supervision program in place. This widespread acceptance has provided states with the needed continuum of sentencing options so that offenders are being held accountable for their crimes while, at the same time, public safety is being maintained. This popularity of intensive supervision has generated much research, thereby raising several issues.

Current issues largely revolve around the effectiveness of intensive supervision. However, measures of success vary depending on the stated goals and objectives each program set out to address.[4] For instance, goals of a treatment-oriented program differ from goals of a program that places emphasis on offender punishment and control. However, it is possible to isolate two overriding themes of recent ISPs that raise several issues. First, "intensive probation supervision is expected to divert offenders from incarceration in order to alleviate prison overcrowding,[5] avoid the exorbitant costs of building and sustaining prisons, and prevent the stultifying and stigmatizing effects of imprisonment" (Byrne et al., 1989, p. 10). Second, ISPs are expected to promote public safety through surveillance strategies while promoting a sense of responsibility and accountability through probation fees, restitution, and community service activities (Byrne et al., 1989). These goals generate issues regarding the ability of ISP programs to reduce recidivism, divert offenders from prison, and ensure public safety.

In one study of ISPs, Lowenkamp and colleagues (2010) examined program philosophy and recidivism rates. They found that ISP programs that were "deterrence"- or control-oriented actually increased recidivism rates, whereas human service-oriented programs reduced recidivism. These results can be seen in Figure 10.3.

The debate over control versus treatment has raged for many years. In recent years, there has been a movement, initiated by the American Probation and Parole Association, to develop a more balanced approach to ISP supervision (Fulton

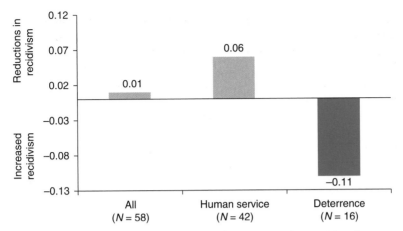

Figure 10.3 Average Change in Recidivism for Intensive Supervision Programs by Program Philosophy.

Source: Lowenkamp, C., Flores, A., Holsinger, A., Makarios, M., Latessa, E. (2010). Intensive supervision programs: Does program philosophy and the principles of effective intervention matter? *Journal of Criminal Justice* 38, 368–375.

et al., 1994, 1996). This approach continues to support strict conditions and supervision practices, but within the context of more services, and higher-quality treatment. Indeed, it appears that if ISP is going to live up to its promises, a new model must be developed.

DAY-REPORTING CENTERS

Unlike many other intermediate sanction alternatives, day reporting is of relatively recent vintage. While day reporting was used earlier in England, the first **day-reporting program** in the United States was opened in Massachusetts in 1986 (McDevitt, 1988). This inaugural program was designed as an early release from prison and jail placement for inmates approaching their parole or discharge date. Participants in the program were required to report to the center each day (hence the name, "day reporting"), prepare an itinerary for their next day's

---

Box 10.3
Day-Reporting Centers

Certain persons on pretrial release, probation, or parole are required to appear at day-reporting centers on a frequent and regular basis in order to participate in services or activities provided by the center or other community agencies. Failure to report or participate is a violation that could cause revocation of conditional release or community supervision.

> Reports indicate that offenders in these programs must not only physically report to their centers daily but also provide a schedule of planned activities and to participate in designated activities. In addition, offenders must call the centers by phone throughout the day; they can also expect random phone checks by center staff both during the day and at home following curfew. In some programs, offenders must contact their respective centers an average of 60 times weekly and, in all but one, take random drug tests.
>
> Source: Gowdy (1993).

activities, and report by telephone to the center throughout the day (Larivee, 1990). By 1992, there were six day-reporting centers in operation in Massachusetts with average daily populations ranging from 30 to more than 100 offenders

Parent (1990) reported that by the late 1980s, day-reporting programs were operational in six states, and many more states were considering the option. The characteristics of these programs and the clients they served varied considerably. As McDevitt and Miliano (1992, p. 153) noted, "Although all centers have similar program elements, such as frequent client contact, formalized scheduling, and drug testing, the operations of different DRCs (day-reporting centers) are quite varied. Therefore, it is difficult to define specifically what a day reporting center is; each center is unique."

In describing the development of day-reporting centers in Massachusetts, Larivee (1990) noted that these centers were created for the purpose of diverting offenders from confinement in local jails. Offenders live at home, but must report once each day to the center and are in telephone contact with the center four times each day. By 1990, there were seven centers serving eight counties and the state department of corrections. An evaluation of Massachusetts day-reporting centers reported that more than two-thirds of day-reporting clients completed programs successfully and only 2 percent were returned to prison or jail for new crimes or escape (Curtin, 1990). An earlier evaluation of the Hampden County center (the first opened) reported more than 80 percent successful completion of the program and only 1 percent arrested for a new crime while in the program. Larivee concluded about the Massachusetts day-reporting centers, "Every client in a day-reporting center program would otherwise be incarcerated; additionally, no client is held in the center longer than he or she would be kept in jail. . . . Only four percent of the clients were arrested for a new crime or escape, and none committed a violent offense."

Parent (1990) reported an assessment of 14 day-reporting centers known to be in operation in 1989. Only three of the centers were operated by public agencies, with the other 11 being administered by private, nonprofit organizations. Programs ranged in capacity from 10 offenders to 150, with most being able to accommodate 50 or fewer. A survey of these centers revealed that successful completion of programs varied greatly by center and by type of client. Probation and parole violators and those who had been denied discretionary parole release had successful completion rates of about one-third or less, whereas offenders received from institutional work release programs or diverted from jail had completion rates in excess of two-thirds (Parent, 1990). The survey also reported at that time a range in center costs from less than $8 per day per offender to more than $50 per day. The mean cost was nearly $15 per day.

In 1993, Parent et al. (1995) replicated this survey, this time contacting 114 day-reporting centers operating in 22 states. Fifty-four of these programs responded to the survey. Most of these responding programs indicated that they had opened after 1991. Most centers were still operated by private, nonprofit organizations and there was still a wide variety in services, programming, and contact requirements. Newer centers, however, were more likely to be operated by public agencies than older ones.

When asked to identify the goals of their day-reporting center, respondents to the survey identified four purposes of the programs. The most important purpose, according to respondents, was to provide offenders with access to treatment services. Second most important was to reduce jail and prison crowding. Additional program goals included building political support for the program and the provision of surveillance/public safety.

The survey revealed wide variations in day-reporting center organizations, populations, costs, and effectiveness. Most centers were operated at the local level by agencies affiliated with the courts. Newer day-reporting centers were likely to serve a pre-imprisonment population, whereas older centers primarily supervised offenders released from incarceration. Day-reporting center populations included pretrial releasees, offenders diverted from imprisonment, probation and parole violators, and newly released prison and jail inmates. As Parent and colleagues observed (1995, p. 22), "The average negative termination rate for all such programs is 50 percent, with a wide distribution that ranges from 14 to 86 percent." They found that characteristics of the day-reporting programs were correlated with higher rates of negative termination. The survey did not provide any information specifically concerning the rearrest rates of program participants. Rather, "negative termination" refers to offenders removed from the program for rule violations, which would include the commission of a new crime.

Centers operated by private agencies were more likely to have high negative termination rates than those operated by public agencies. Those centers offering more services and those using curfews had higher rates of negative terminations. Finally, policies toward violations of center rules were related to rates of negative termination. As would be expected, those centers with stricter policies and fewer alternatives within the program were more likely to experience high rates of negative terminations. It may also be that changes in day-reporting populations to include a variety of offender types and an increase in the number of expectations and conditions placed on these offenders (drug testing, mandatory treatment attendance, community service, curfews, etc.) combined to increase the likelihood of program failure. A final correlate of higher rates of negative terminations was line staff turnover. Programs that experienced higher rates of staff turnover also had higher rates of negative terminations. However, "it is not clear which characteristic influences the other," as Parent et al. (1995, p. 22) note.

Box 10.4
Community Service

Community service requires that the offender complete some task that helps the community. It is considered a form of restitution, with labor rather than money being supplied. Common jobs include cleaning neighborhoods, working at nursing homes, painting schools, and doing assorted chores for the elderly. Community service can be a sentence in and of itself or can be included with other sanctions, such as probation.

Day-reporting programs offered a variety of services to program participants. Most centers offered job skills, drug abuse education, group and individual counseling, job placement, education, life-skills training, and drug treatment. While most services were provided in-house, it was common for drug treatment programs to be offered by providers not located at the day-reporting center. A trend noted in the survey was the tendency for newer, public programs to co-locate social service programs with the day-reporting program. The most common in-house programs (those offered at more than three-quarters of the centers) were job-seeking skills, group counseling, and life-skills training.

The costs of these services are usually paid by the day-reporting center. For some programs, other agencies pay the costs of services such as drug treatment, transitional housing, and education and job placement assistance. Seldom are offenders required to pay for services. The costs of operation ranged from about $10 per offender per day to more than $100 per offender per day, with the average daily cost per offender being slightly more than $35. Public centers were found to generally have lower daily operating costs, and costs increased with the stringency of surveillance/supervision requirements. Costs of day reporting were found to be more than intensive probation supervision, but less than residential treatment or incarceration.

Box 10.5
The Talbert House Day-Reporting Center

Talbert House, Inc., a private, nonprofit organization, administers a day-reporting program in Cincinnati, Ohio. The program began in 1994. The objective of the program was to provide an alternative disposition for probationers facing revocation, which combines high levels of supervision and service delivery. The philosophy of the program emphasizes surveillance and compliance with probation supervision requirements. There are seven characteristics or components of the program:

1. Reporting seven days each week.
2. Development and monitoring of daily itineraries.
3. Electronic monitoring.

4. Regular, random urinalysis.
5. Breath testing.
6. Close monitoring of income to ensure payments of court financial requirements.
7. Community service work through the Hamilton County Probation Department.

The program operates with a staff of three, including two caseworkers and a manager. Day reporting is ordered as a condition of probation for all referrals. The program excludes those with a history of substance abuse, repeat violent crimes or assaultive behavior, sexual offenses against minors, a long-standing association with organized crime, or a conviction for arson. Additionally, clients are required to consent to treatment prior to acceptance to the program.

Cases referred to the center are given a risk/needs assessment. Offenders must report to the center seven days each week, provide urine and breath tests as requested, and, if unemployed, must participate in employment-seeking activities. Offenders meet with center staff each afternoon to participate in program activities until 5 PM, when they leave to return home or go to other arranged treatment activities. Offenders stay in the program between one and six months, based on judicial stipulation. The program currently serves about 10 offenders per day. The center provides in-house treatment, including individual and group counseling by appropriately licensed/registered staff. Other services include chemical dependency, case management, introduction to Alcoholics Anonymous and Narcotics Anonymous, life-skills education, HIV education, budgeting, and nutrition. Additional services available to offenders include education, parenting, financial management, community service, mental health services, and leisure. The goals of the programs are identified as follows:

1. Provide a community sanction option for probation violators.
2. Identify problems facing offenders that may lead to criminality.
3. Provide on-site or community referral to treat those problems.
4. Provide for public safety through intensive supervision, accountability, and retribution.

Unfortunately, there have not been many empirical studies of day-reporting centers. Latessa and colleagues (1998) examined five pilot day-reporting programs in Ohio. Offenders from the day-reporting programs were compared with offenders supervised under regular probation, intensive program, and those released from prison. Rearrest and incarceration rates for each group are presented in Figures 10.4 and 10.5. Rates of rearrest for the day-reporting group were slightly higher than those reported for the other groups. The incarceration rates indicate that the day-reporting group performed slightly better than those offenders

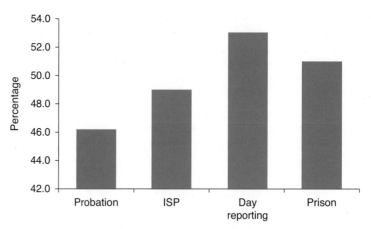

Figure 10.4 Ohio Day-reporting Study: Rearrest Rates.

Source: Latessa, E., Travis, L., Holsinger, A., Hartman, J. (1998). *Evaluation of Ohio's pilot day reporting program final report.* Cincinnati, OH: Division of Criminal Justice, University of Cincinnati.

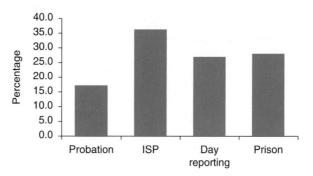

Figure 10.5 Ohio Day-reporting Study: Incarceration Rates.

Source: Latessa, E., Travis, L., Holsinger, A., Hartman, J. (1998). *Evaluation of Ohio's pilot day reporting program final report.* Cincinnati, OH: Division of Criminal Justice, University of Cincinnati.

supervised under intensive supervision, worse than those on regular probation, and similar to those released from prison. It is noteworthy that the authors also found that the quality of the treatment provided by the five day-reporting centers in this study was judged to be poor.

HOME DETENTION

House arrest, usually conjuring up images of political control and fascist repression, is court-ordered **home detention** in this nation, confining offenders to their households for the duration of their sentence (Meecham, 1986). Introduced in 1984 in Florida, home detention spread rapidly throughout a nation searching for punitive, safe, and secure alternatives to incarceration (Maxfield & Baumer, 1990). The sentence is usually in conjunction with probation but may be imposed by the court as a separate punishment (as in Florida). Florida's Community Control Program (FCCP) was designed to provide a safe diversion alternative and help address the problem of prison population escalation and associated high costs (Flynn, 1986).

Participants may be required to make victim compensation, perform community work service, pay probation fees, undergo alcohol or other drug testing, and, in some instances, wear electronic monitoring equipment to verify their presence in the residence. (In some jurisdictions, house arrest is used on a pretrial basis,[6] as an isolated sentence, in conjunction with probation or parole, or with a prerelease status such as education or work furlough.) House arrest only allows the offender to leave her or his residence for specific purposes and hours approved by the court or supervising officer, and being absent without leave is a technical violation of conditions that may result in resentencing to jail or prison (Government Accounting Office, 1990).

Home detention is a punitive sentence and was designed in most cases to relieve institutional overcrowding. For many offenders, it is their "last chance" to escape from being committed to prison. In addition to surveillance of the offender, home detention is viewed as a cost-avoidance program, a "front-end" solution to prison overcrowding, and a flexible alternative for certain offenders (such as a pregnant offender until time of delivery). The use of telemonitoring devices, discussed later as "Electronic Monitoring," can significantly increase the correctional surveillance of offenders.

The most significant critical argument[7] against home detention is that, by making a nonincarcerative control mechanism available to corrections, many petty offenders are brought under correctional control who would best be handled by diversion, fines, or mental health services. In general, such inclusive actions are viewed as "net-widening," which occurs when offenders are sentenced to community control who might otherwise have received a lesser or even no sentence.

The National Council on Crime and Delinquency conducted an evaluation of the FCCP and concluded that the impact on prison crowding, offender behavior, and state correctional costs has been positive. With an estimated prison diversion rate of 54 percent, community control is cost-effective, despite the combined effect of net widening and the punishments imposed on almost 10 percent of FCCP participants for technical violations. Furthermore, the new offense rate for community control offenders is lower than for similar offenders sentenced to prison and released without supervision. For every 100 cases diverted from prison, Florida saved more than $250,000 (Wagner & Baird, 1993).

Home detention is an option that has been widely used for many years with juvenile offenders, who are usually remanded to the care of their parents. It is also used for nonviolent adult offenders and, as mentioned previously, is often used in conjunction with electronic monitoring.

Electronic Monitoring

Home detention has a long history as a criminal penalty but its new popularity with correctional authorities is due to the advent of electronic monitoring, a

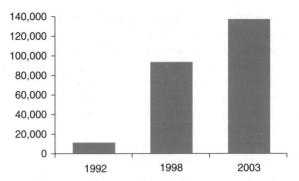

Figure 10.6 Electronic Monitoring Devices in Use.

Source: National Law Enforcement and Corrections Technology Center (1999). *Keeping track of electronic monitoring.* Washington, DC: NLECTC. Data for 2003 estimated.

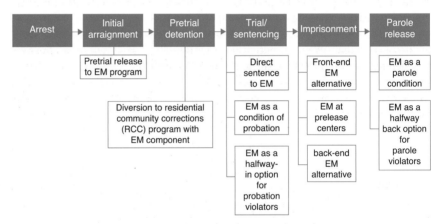

Figure 10.7 Key Decision Points Where Electronic Monitoring (EM) is Being Used.

Source: Bureau of Justice Assistance (1989). *Electronic monitoring in intensive probation and parole programs.* Washington, DC: U.S. Department of Justice.

technological link thought to make the sanction both practical and affordable (see Figure 10.6).

The concept of electronic monitoring is not new, having been proposed in 1964 by Schwitzgebel and colleagues as "electronic parole" and initially used to monitor the location of psychiatric patients.[8] The first studies of home detention enforced by electronic monitoring began in 1986 and, by early 1992, there were at least 40,000 electronic monitors in use (Gowdy, 1993). It is used almost everywhere in the justice system after arrest (see Figure 10.7).

According to the Bureau of Justice Assistance (1989, p. 3), the goals and objectives of electronic monitoring are to:

■ Provide a cost-effective community supervision tool for offenders selected according to specific program criteria.
■ Administer sanctions appropriate to the seriousness of the offense.
■ Promote public safety by providing surveillance and risk control strategies indicated by the risk and needs of the offenders.
■ Increase the confidence of legislative, judicial, and releasing authorities in ISP designs as a viable sentencing option.

Electronic monitoring can be active or passive. In active monitoring, a transmitter attached to the offender's wrist or ankle sends signals relayed by a home telephone to the supervising office during the hours the offender is required to be at home. Under passive monitoring, a computer program is used to call the offender randomly during the hours designated for home confinement. The offender inserts the wristlet or anklet into a verifier to confirm her or his presence in the residence. There does not appear to be any difference in recidivism between those on passive or active systems. Only about one in three offenders on home detention wear monitoring devices (Petersilia, 1987).

National surveys indicate that electronic monitoring was initially (1987) used for property offenders on probation but that a much broader range of offenders was being monitored (1989) than in the past. Monitoring has been expanded to include not only probationers, but also to follow-up on persons after incarceration, to control those sentenced to community corrections, and to monitor persons before trial or sentencing.

Box 10.6
Global Positioning System Monitoring in Florida

The use of active **global positioning system (GPS)** technology was implemented in Florida in 1997 and utilizes global positioning satellites to track offenders' locations in "real time." Offenders monitored with active GPS are required to wear ankle bracelets that communicate with a larger device carried by offenders at all times, called a monitoring tracking device (MTD). The MTD communicates with a satellite and transmits a signal to a monitoring center through a cell phone. The MTD has an LCD screen to display messages to the offenders from supervising officers. Officers are able to track the exact location of offenders on a computer screen to determine if they have violated the conditions of supervision by entering prohibited areas. Currently, there are more than 14,300 offenders in Florida on EM including probation, community control, and postprison. Of these, about 2,200 are on more advanced GPS.

Source: Bales et al. (2010).

A 1989 survey on telemonitoring found the following:

- Most jurisdictions using electronic monitoring tested some offenders for drug use, and many routinely tested all. Some sites charged for the testing; more than 66 percent charged offenders for at least part of the cost of leasing the monitoring equipment.
- The average monitoring term in 1989 was 79 days—the longer the period of monitoring, the higher the odds of success. The chances of termination do not vary by type of offense, except that those committing major traffic violations committed fewer technical violations and new offenses.
- There were no significant differences in successful terminations among probationers, offenders on parole, or those in community corrections. All had successful terminations rates ranging between 74 and 86 percent (West Palm Beach, Florida reported a 97 percent successful completion rate in 1992).
- Rule violations resulted in reincarceration, brief confinement at a residential facility, intensified office-reporting requirements, stricter curfews, or additional community service (Gowdy, 1993).

More recent evaluations in Oklahoma, Florida, Los Angeles, California, England and Wales,[9] Lake County, Illinois,[10] and Texas indicated some success of electronic monitoring programs, whereas others (Courtright et al., 1997) have found little evidence that there is an impact on recidivism rates. Figure 10.8 shows the program termination from an electronic monitoring program operating in Cleveland, Ohio (Latessa, 1992). This program also gave program participants an exit survey. Table 10.2 shows offender responses to selected questions.

Despite the widespread use of electronic monitoring and the support it has received by some, empirical studies have not been as favorable. A meta-analysis that included an examination of the research on electronic monitoring found that, on average, the effect size was 0.05, indicating that, on average, electronic monitoring *increased* recidivism about 5 percent over comparison groups (Gendreau et al., 2000)(see Figure 10.9). Note that the authors also examined research on Scared Straight programs and found that, on average, they *increased* recidivism rates about 7 percent.

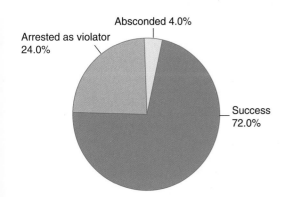

Absconded 4.0%

Arrested as violator 24.0%

Success 72.0%

Figure 10.8 Program Termination from Electronic Monitoring Program.

Source: Latessa, E. (1992). *A preliminary evaluation of the Montgomery County Adult Probation Department's Intensive Supervision Program.* Cincinnati, OH: Department of Criminal Justice, University of Cincinnati.

Perhaps the most interesting study involving electronic monitoring was conducted in Canada (Bonta et al., 2000b). In this study, offenders were first assessed with regard to risk and need factors using the Level of Supervision Inventory (LSI) and, in addition to electronic monitoring, were required to attend an intensive treatment program. Results from this study are displayed in Figure 10.10. The combination of electronic monitoring and intensive treatment services resulted in a reduction of recidivism for high-risk offenders of about 20 percent, but more than *doubled* the recidivism rates for low-risk offenders. Undoubtedly, this is another example of the harm that can come from targeting low-risk offenders with intensive treatment and supervision programs.

Table 10.2 Results from Exit Interview with Electronic Monitoring Participants

Before this program have you ever served time in prison or jail?
  No   44%
  Yes 56%

Do you think the program is better or worse than being in jail?
  Worse 5%
  Neither better nor worse   13%
  Better   82%

To what extent did you find the transmitter comfortable or uncomfortable to wear?
  Uncomfortable   25%
  Neither comfortable nor uncomfortable   44%
  Comfortable   31%

Since you have been on the monitoring program, how well do you get along with the people with whom you live?
  Better   22%
  About the same as before   72%
  Worse   6%

While you were on the monitoring program, did you find that you had more or less money than you did before?
  Less money   30%
  About the same   33%
  More money   37%

Since being on the monitoring program, do you find you have more or fewer friends?
  Fewer friends   42%
  About the same number of friends   50%
  More friends   8%

Do you have the same friends now that you had when you began the monitoring program?
  Same friends   65%
  Different friends   35%

Did you find the monitoring program better or worse than you expected it would be?
  Better   44%
  About as I expected it would be   48%
  Worse   8%

Did anyone ask what the transmitter was?
  No   30%
  Yes   70%

Were you able to violate any of the rules of the program without being caught by the monitoring equipment and/or the probation officer?
  No   87%
  Yes   13%

Source: Latessa, E. (1992). *A preliminary evaluation of the Montgomery County Adult Probation Department's Intensive Supervision Program.* Cincinnati, OH: Department of Criminal Justice, University of Cincinnati.

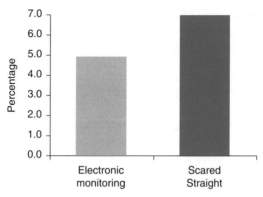

Figure 10.9 Average Effect Size from Studies of Electronic Monitoring and Scared Straight Programs: Percent Increase in Recidivism.

Source: Adapted from Gendreau, P., Goggin, C., Cullen, F., Andrews, D. (2000). The effects of community sanctions and incarceration on recidivism. *Forum* 12(2), 10–13.

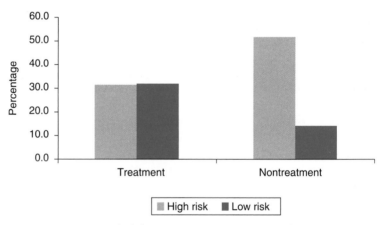

Figure 10.10 Intensive Rehabilitation Supervision in Canada.

Source: Bonta, J., Wallace-Capretta, S., Rooney, J. (2000). A quasi-experimental evaluation of an intensive rehabilitation supervision program. *Criminal Justice and Behavior* 27, 312–329.

SHOCK INCARCERATION PROGRAMS

Technically, **shock incarceration** programs, or "**boot camps**," as they are commonly known, are institutional correctional programs, not community-based ones. However, they are considered intermediate sanctions and are a distant cousin to shock probation programs.[11] The most recent shock incarceration programs appeared first in Georgia (1983) and Oklahoma (1984). The concept spread quickly and, in 2000, 54 boot camp programs had opened in 41 state correctional jurisdictions and handled more than 21,000 inmates in 2000 (Camp & Camp, 2000), in addition to many programs developed and being considered in cities and counties, and for juveniles (Gover et al., 2000).

While labeled a relatively recent innovation, the basic elements of boot camp were present in the Elmira Reformatory in 1876, designed by Zebulon Reed Brockway. In its current developments, boot camp combines elements of military basic training and traditional correctional philosophy, particularly rehabilitation. Although there is no generic boot camp because individual programs vary in form and objectives, the typical boot camp is targeted at young, nonviolent offenders.[12] Once in the camp, the participant is subjected to a regimen of (1) military drills and discipline, (2) physical exercise, (3) hard physical labor, (4) specialized education and training, and (5) counseling and treatment for substance abuse and addiction.

Most boot camp programs require the inmates to volunteer, offering as an incentive an incarceration period of a few months, compared to the much longer periods they would have spent in prison or on probation. Generally, a state boot camp graduate is released to parole, intensive supervision, home confinement, or some type of community corrections.

The philosophy behind the prison boot camps is simple. Offenders who can be turned around before they commit a major crime can improve their own opportunities for living a successful life free of incarceration. Traditional prisons generally have not been viewed as successful in rehabilitating offenders.

According to boot camp advocates, the population at greatest risk of entering prison is the young adult who is poorly educated, comes from a low-income background, has not had proper role models or discipline, has little or no work skills, and is subjected to an environment in which drug use and drug trafficking are common. Because many misdirected young persons have become productive citizens after exposure to military training, the boot camp endeavors to provide this same discipline and direction to persons who still have a chance of being diverted from a life of crime and incarceration.

Box 10.7
Shock Incarceration

[R]esearch indicates that although there is a common core of military-type drill and discipline within these programs, there are also wide variations in their operations, activities, time served, number served, release procedures, and aftercare. The rigorous physical exercise, military drill and discipline, as well as the housing barracks and other noninstitutional characteristics, distinguish correctional boot camps from traditional prisons and jails.

Michael Russell, Acting Director, National Institute of Justice, 1993.

The boot camp concept appeals to diverse elements of the justice system. For the offender, it offers a second chance. He or she generally will be returned to the community in a much shorter period without the stigma of having been in prison. For the judge, it is a sentencing option that provides sanctions more restrictive than probation but less restrictive than a conventional prison. For the correctional system, it allows the placement of individuals outside the traditional prison environment and reduces costs and crowding by moving the persons through the system in less time.

The boot camp concept also appeals to groups with diverse views on the objectives of corrections. For those who believe that corrections should focus more on rehabilitation, the shorter sentence, structured environment, supervision after release, and emphasis on training and treatment can be found in the boot camp. For those who believe that prisons should serve as punishment and a deterrent, the highly disciplined environment, military-style drills, physical exercise, and work within a correctional setting exist in the boot camp. Although boot camps are most often associated with prisons, probation and parole agencies also operate boot camps. According to Camp and Camp (2000), 19 probation and parole agencies operated 32 boot camps and served almost 3,000 offenders per year.

Results from studies of the effectiveness of boot camp programs in reducing recidivism have not been positive. Some programs have abandoned the military-style training and incorporated educational, wilderness, job corps, and industrial components (Gowdy, 1993). An outcome study conducted in Texas (1999) compared the rearrest rates of four different types of community facilities for adult offenders: boot camps, treatment centers, intermediate sanction facilities (used for probation violators), and substance abuse treatment facilities. Results are presented in Figure 10.11.

The boot camp reported rearrest rates nearly double the other programs. It should also be noted that when risk and need scores from a standardized assessment tool were compared for offenders in all four programs, the only difference was in the need scores, with boot camp residents reporting *fewer* higher-need offenders than the other options. Finally, a meta-analysis conducted by researchers

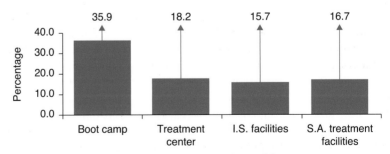

Figure 10.11 Rearrest Rates for Residents Discharged from Community Correctional Facilities in Texas: Two-year Follow-up (percent).

Source: Community Corrections Facilities Outcome Study, Texas Department of Criminal Justice, January 1999.

in Washington State (Aos et al., 1999) found that, on average, juvenile boot camps increased recidivism rates by about 11 percent. Some other findings from boot camp evaluations make the following conclusions:

- Low- or moderate-risk juvenile and adult offenders who are subjected to a high level of supervision (boot camps) actually do worse than those left on traditional probation (Altschuler & Armstrong, 1994).
- High percentages of minority youths are served by boot camps: the conclusion is that the boot camp model fails to connect with this population.
- Some evidence that the rate of recidivism declined in boot camp programs for adults where offenders spent three hours or more per day in therapeutic activity and had some type of aftercare (MacKenzie & Souryal, 1994).
- In general, studies have found similar recidivism rates for those who completed boot camps and comparable offenders who spent long periods of time in prison.

More recent evaluations of boot camps have also produced unfavorable results regarding their effectiveness in reducing recidivism (Bottcher & Ezell, 2005; Weis et al., 2005).

Despite their continued popularity, there are several reasons that boot camps are not producing the desired reductions in recidivism. Boot camps tend to:

- Bond delinquent and criminal groups together;
- target noncriminogenic needs such as physical conditioning, drill and ceremony, and self-esteem;
- mix low-, medium-, and high-risk offenders together;
- model aggressive behavior.

EFFECTIVENESS OF INTERMEDIATE SANCTIONS

There are many justifications for the use of intermediate sanctions as an alternative to incarceration. However, given the investment that many jurisdictions and states have made in these options, the question of how effective they are in reducing recidivism is an important one. In a National Institute of Justice study of what works, Sherman et al. (1998) listed a number of intermediate sanctions that have not demonstrated effectiveness. Included were correctional boot camps, shock probation, home detention with electronic monitoring, intensive supervision programs, and wildness programs for youthful offenders. In a meta-analysis of intermediate sanctions, Gendreau et al. (1996) addressed this question. They examined research results from 44 ISP programs, 16 restitution programs, 13 boot camps, 13 Scared Straight programs, nine drug-testing programs, and six electronic monitoring programs. They found virtually no effect on recidivism, and where they did find some effect it appeared that some sanctions slightly increased recidivism! They conclude that "the 'get tough' revolution has been an abject failure when it comes to reducing recidivism."

Many of the "intermediate sanctions" that have been developed over the past few years are but a few examples of correctional strategies that often fail to live up to their expectations, particularly in terms of reductions in recidivism (Latessa et al., 1997; Petersilia, 1997). These results are often attributed to policies that emphasize control and surveillance over treatment and service delivery (Fulton et al., 1997). While programs such as boot camps, Scared Straight, and other "punishing smarter" programs remain popular, there is little evidence that they will lead to reductions in recidivism. Unfortunately, evidence seems to indicate that in some cases, these so-called "punishing smarter" programs actually increase recidivism rates.

In a study funded by the National Institute of Justice, Sherman and colleagues (1998) summarized what does not work in reducing recidivism.

- Correctional boot camps using traditional military basic training;
- drug prevention classes focused on fear and other emotional appeals, including self-esteem, such as DARE;
- school-based, leisure-time enrichment programs;
- "Scared Straight" programs where juvenile offenders visit adult prisons;
- shock probation, shock parole, and split sentences adding time to probation or parole;
- home detention with electronic monitoring;
- intensive supervision;
- rehabilitation programs using vague, unstructured counseling;
- residential programs for juvenile offenders using challenging experiences in rural settings.

SUMMARY

Intermediate sanctions have become a vital component of contemporary corrections. Two developments have led to a search for innovative and cost-effective programs: prison and jail crowding and the development of new technologies, such as electronic monitoring and readily available drug testing. Not only are institutions crowded, but probation, parole, and community corrections are also impacted by the waves of offenders caught in the arms of the law.

Our review of intermediate sanctions provides insight into the reasons for the volume of clients, but also programs and strategies for managing the risks posed by different types of offenders who need differing treatments and supervision. Intermediate sanctions will likely continue, despite the mixed findings concerning their effectiveness. The critical question is whether we can take what we have learned from programs that are demonstrating reductions in recidivism and apply it to approaches that are not working. Day-reporting centers, drug courts, and other treatment-based options appear to offer the best hope that we can currently foresee for delivering effective interventions and services to offenders in the community. Change will continue. This is an exciting time for corrections as a field and for students wishing to have an impact on the futures of clients and the safety of communities.

Review Questions

1. Define intermediate sanctions.
2. Why are boot camps so popular among the general public?
3. What is "intensive supervision?"
4. What are the two basic types of electronic monitoring programs?
5. What are some of the limitations of electronic monitoring programs?
6. What do we know about the effectiveness of intensive supervision programs?
7. Why are day-reporting programs gaining popularity?
8. What are some of the reasons that boot camps have failed to reduce recidivism?

Notes

1 Blumstein argues that the nation has not to date been able to meet the demand for additional prisons to build their way out of the crowding crisis (Blumstein, 1995). See also Garland (2001).
2 Not all new generation ISP programs have abandoned the treatment approach. See Clear and Latessa (1993). The American Probation and Parole Association is working with several states to modify their ISP programs from a control/surveillance orientation to one more treatment focused (www.appa-net.org).
3 Byrne and Taxman (1994). See also Cullen et al. (1996).
4 Fulton et al. (1994). See also Cullen and Gendreau (2001).
5 For example, Whitehead et al. (1995) found that intensive probation in Tennessee resulted in both diversion and net widening. They argued that if diversion is the only objective of intensive probation then the efforts might be misguided. See Whitehead et al. (1995). See also Bonta et al. (2000a).
6 A discussion of the issues can be found in Goldkamp (1993). See also Rosen (1993); and McCann and Weber (1993).
7 See in particular Rackmill (1994). An empirical analysis can be found in Stanz and Tewksbury (2000).
8 Schwitzgebel et al. (1964). See also Gable (1986); and Lilly et al. (1986).
9 Mair (1989). See also Lilly (1990); and National Association for the Care of Offenders and the Prevention of Crime (1989).
10 Enor et al. (1992).
11 Shock probation originated in Ohio in 1965 and was designed to give first-time young adult offenders a "taste of the bars." Offenders were to be sentenced to prison and then within 30–120 days be released on probation. It was assumed that the physical and psychological hardships of prison life would "shock" the offender straight.
12 The bulk of the following section is drawn from Government Accounting Office (1993). *Prison boot camps*. Washington, DC: U.S. Department of Justice.

Recommended Readings

Latessa, E.J., Listwan, S., Koetzle, D. (2014). *What works (and doesn't) in reducing recidivism.* Boston, MA: Elsevier (Anderson Publishing).

Marciniak, L. (2000). The addition of day reporting to intensive supervised probation. *Federal Probation* 64 (2), 34–39.

Morris, N., Tonry, M. (1990). *Between prison and probation: Intermediate punishments in a rational sentencing system.* Oxford: Oxford University Press.

Sherman, L., Gottfredson, D., MacKenzie, D., Eck, J., Reuter, P., Bushway, S. (1998). *Preventing crime: What works, what doesn't, what's promising.* Washington, DC National Institute of Justice, Research in Brief: U.S. Department of Justice.

References

Altschuler, D., Armstrong, T. (1994). *Intensive aftercare for high-risk juveniles: A community care model.* Washington, DC: Program summary, Office of Juvenile Justice and Delinquency Prevention, Office of Justice Programs, U.S. Dept. of Justice.

American Correctional Association (1990). *Intermediate punishment: Community-based sanctions.* Baltimore, MD: United Book Press

Aos, S., Phipps, P., Barnoski, R., Lieb, R. (1999). *The comparative costs and benefits of programs to reduce crime: A review of the National Research findings with implications for Washington State.* Olympia, WA: Washington State Institute for Public Policy.

Bales, W., Mann, K., Bloomberg, T., McManus, B., Dhungana, K. (2010). Electronic monitoring in Florida. *The Journal of Electronic Monitoring* 22(2), 5–12.

Blumstein, A. (1995). Prisons. In: J. Wilson, J. Petersilia (eds) *Crime.* San Francisco, CA: Institute for Contemporary Studies, pp. 387–419.

Bonta, J., Wallace-Capretta, S., Rooney, J. (2000a). A quasi-experimental evaluation of an intensive rehabilitation supervision program. *Criminal Justice and Behavior* 27, 312–329.

Bonta, J., Wallace-Capretta. S., Rooney, J. (2000b). Can electronic monitoring make a difference? *Crime and Delinquency* 46(1), 61–75.

Bottcher, J., Ezell, M.E. (2005). Examining the effectiveness of boot camps: A randomized experiment with a long-term follow-up. *Journal of Research in Crime and Delinquency* 42, 309–332.

Bureau of Justice Assistance (1989). *Electronic monitoring in intensive probation and parole programs.* Washington, DC: U.S. Department of Justice.

Burkhart, W. (1986). Intensive probation supervision: An agenda for research and evaluation. *Federal Probation* 50(2), 75–77.

Byrne, J. (1986). The control controversy: A preliminary examination of intensive probation supervision programs in the United States. *Federal Probation*, June.

Byrne, J., Kelly, L. (1989). *Restructuring probation as an intermediate sanction: An evaluation of the Massachusetts intensive probation supervision program.* Washington, DC: U.S. Department of Justice, Final Report to the National Institute of Justice.

Byrne, J., Taxman, F. (1994). Crime control policy and community corrections practice. *Evaluation and Program Planning* 17, 227–233.

Byrne, J., Lurigio, A., Baird, C. (1989). The effectiveness of the new intensive supervision programs. *Research in Corrections* 2, 64–75.

Byrne, J., Lurigio, A., Petersilia, J. (1993). *Smart sentencing.* Beverly Hills, CA: Sage.

Camp, C., Camp, G. (1997). *The corrections yearbook 1997.* South Salem, NY: Criminal Justice Institute.

Camp, C., Camp, G. (2000). *The 2000 corrections yearbook: Adult Corrections.* Middletown, CT: Criminal Justice Institute.

Clear, T., Latessa, E. (1993). Probation office's roles in intensive supervision versus treatment. *Justice Quarterly* 10, 441–462.

Courtright, K., Berg, B., Mutchnick, R. (1997). Effects of house arrest with electronic monitoring on DUI offenders. *Journal of Offender Rehabilitation* 24(3/4), 35–51.

Cullen, F., Gendreau, P. (2001). From nothing works to what works: Changing professional ideology in the 21st century. *Prison Journal* 81(3), 313–338.

Cullen, F., Van Voorhis, P., Sundt, J. (1996). Prisons in crisis: The American experience. In: R. Matthews, P. Francis (eds) *Prisons 2000: An international perspective on the current state and future of imprisonment.* New York: Macmillan.

Curtin, E. (1990). Day reporting centers. In: A. Travisino (ed.) *Intermediate punishment: Community-based sanctions.* Laurel, MD: American Correctional Association, pp. 72–73.

Enor, R., Block, C., Quinn, J. (1992). *Alternative sentencing: Electronically-monitored correctional supervision.* Bristol, IN: Wyndham Hall.

Erwin, B. (1987). *Final report: Evaluation of intensive probation supervision in Georgia.* Atlanta, GA: Georgia Department of Corrections.

Fallen, D., Apperson, C., Holt-Milligan, J., Roe, J. (1981). *Intensive parole supervision.* Olympia, WA: Department of Social and Health Services, Analysis and Information Service Division, Office of Research.

Finn, P. (1991). State-by-state guide to enforcement of civil protection orders. *Response to the Victimization of Women & Children* 14(78), 3–12.

Flynn, L. (1986). House arrest. *Corrections Today* 48(5), 64–68.

Fulton, B., Gendreau, P., Paparozzi, M. (1996). APPA's prototypical intensive supervision program: ISP as it was meant to be. *Perspectives* 19(2), 25–41.

Fulton, B., Stone, S., Gendreau, P. (1994). *Restructuring intensive supervision programs: Applying what works.* Lexington, KY: American Probation and Parole Association.

Fulton, B., Latessa, E., Stichman, A., Travis, L.F. (1997). The state of ISP: Research and policy implications. *Federal Probation* 61(4), 65–75.

Gable, R. (1986). Application of personal telemonitoring to current problems in corrections. *Journal of Criminal Justice* 14, 173–182.

Garland, D. (2001). Special issue on mass imprisonment in the USA. *Punishment and Society* 3(1), 5–199.

Gendreau, P., Goggin, C., Fulton, B. (1996). Intensive supervision in probation and parole. In: C. Hollin (ed.) *Handbook of offender assessment and treatment.* Chichester, UK: John Wiley and Son.

Gendreau, P., Goggin, C., Cullen, F., Andrews, D. (2000). The effects of community sanctions and incarceration on recidivism. *Forum* 12(2), 10–13.

Goldkamp, J. (1993). Judicial responsibility for pretrial release decisionmaking and the information role of pretrial services. *Federal Probation* 57(1), 28–34.

Gordon, M., Glaser, D. (1991). The use and effects of financial penalties in municipal courts. *Criminology* 29, 651–676.

Gover, A., MacKenzie, D., Styve, G. (2000). Boot camps and traditional facilities for juveniles. *Journal of Criminal Justice* 28(1), 53–68.

Government Accounting Office (1990). *Intermediate sanctions*. Washington, DC: USGAO.

Government Accounting Office (1993). *Prison boot camps*. Washington, DC: U.S. Department of Justice.

Gowdy, V. (1993). *Intermediate sanctions*. Washington, DC: U.S. Department of Justice.

Henrichson, C., Delaney, R. (2012). *The price of prisons: What incarceration costs taxpayers*. New York: Vera Institute of Justice.

Jolin, A., Stipak, B. (1991). *Clackamas county community corrections intensive drug program: Program evaluation report*. Oregon City, OR: Clackamas County Community Corrections Division.

Jolin, A., Stipak, B. (1992). Drug treatment and electronically monitored home confinement: An evaluation of a community-based sentencing option. *Crime & Delinquency* 38, 158–170.

Jones, M. (1991). Intensive probation supervision in Georgia, Massachusetts, and New Jersey. *Criminal Justice Research Bulletin* 6(1), 1–9.

Larivee, J. (1990). Day reporting centers: Making their way from the U.K. to the U.S. *Corrections Today* (October), 86–89.

Latessa, E. (1986). Cost effectiveness of intensive supervision. *Federal Probation* 50(2), 70–74.

Latessa, E. (1992). *A preliminary evaluation of the Montgomery County Adult Probation Department's Intensive Supervision Program*. Cincinnati, OH: Department of Criminal Justice, University of Cincinnati.

Latessa, E. (1993a). *An evaluation of the Lucas County Adult Probation Department's IDU and high risk groups*. Cincinnati, OH: Department of Criminal Justice, University of Cincinnati.

Latessa, E. (1993b). *Profile of the special units of the Lucas County Adult Probation Department*. Cincinnati, OH: Department of Criminal Justice, University of Cincinnati.

Latessa, E. (2000). Incorporating electronic monitoring into the principles of effective interventions. *Journal of Offender Monitoring* 13(4), 5–6.

Latessa, E., Travis, L., Holsinger, A. (1997). *Evaluation of Ohio's community corrections act programs and community based correctional facilities final report*. Cincinnati, OH: Division of Criminal Justice, University of Cincinnati.

Latessa, E., Travis, L., Fulton, B., Stichman, A. (1998). *Evaluating the prototypical ISP: Results from Iowa and Connecticut*. Cincinnati, OH: Division of Criminal Justice, University of Cincinnati.

Latessa, E., Travis, L., Holsinger, A., Hartman, J. (1998). *Evaluation of Ohio's pilot day reporting program final report*. Cincinnati, OH: Division of Criminal Justice, University of Cincinnati.

Lilly, J. (1990). Tagging revisited. *The Howard Journal* 29, 229–245.

Lilly, J., Ball, R., Lotz, R. (1986). Electronic jail revisited. *Justice Quarterly* 3, 353–361.

Lowenkamp, C., Flores, A., Holsinger, A., Makarios, M., Latessa, E. (2010). Intensive supervision programs: Does program philosophy and the principles of effective intervention matter? *Journal of Criminal Justice* 38, 368–375.

MacKenzie, D., Souryal, C. (1994). *Multisite evaluation of shock incarceration.* Washington, DC: National Institute of Justice, Office of Justice Programs, U.S. Department of Justice.

Mair, G. (1989). *Evaluating electronic monitoring in England and Wales.* Paper presented at the annual meeting of the American Society of Criminology, San Francisco, CA.

Maxfield, M., Baumer, T. (1990). Home detention with electronic monitoring: Comparing pretrial and postconviction programs. *Crime & Delinquency* 36, 521–536.

McCann, E., Weber, D. (1993). Pretrial services: A prosecutor's view. *Federal Probation* 57(1), 18–22.

McCarthy, B. (1987). Intermediate punishment. In: McCarthy, B. (ed.) *Intermediate punishments: Intensive supervision, home confinement, and electronic surveillance.* Monsey, NY: Willow Tree Press, pp. 181–187.

McDevitt, J. (1988). *Evaluation of the Hampton County Day Reporting Center.* Boston, MA: Crime and Justice Foundation.

McDevitt, J., Miliano, R. (1992). Day reporting centers: An innovative concept in intermediate sanctions. In: J. Byrne (ed.) *Smart sentencing.* Newbury Park, CA: Sage, pp. 153–165.

Meecham, L. (1986). House arrest: The Oklahoma experience. *Corrections Today* 48, 102–110.

National Association for the Care of Offenders and the Prevention of Crime (1989). *The electronic monitoring of offenders.* London: NACRO.

National Law Enforcement and Corrections Technology Center (1999). *Keeping track of electronic monitoring.* Washington, DC: NLECTC.

Paparozzi, M. Paparozzi, M. (n.d.). *An evaluation of the New Jersey board of parole's intensive supervision program.* Unpublished report.

Parent, D. (1990). *Day reporting centers for criminal offenders—A descriptive analysis of existing programs.* Washington, DC: National Institute of Justice.

Parent, D., Byrne, J., Tsarfaty, V., Valade, L., Esselman, J. (1995). *Day reporting centers: Volume 1.* Washington, DC: National Institute of Justice.

Pearson, F. (1987). *Research on New Jersey's intensive supervision program.* New Brunswick, NJ: Administrative Office of the Courts.

Petersilia, J. (1987). *Expanding options for criminal sentencing.* Santa Monica, CA: Rand Publications.

Petersilia, J. (1997). Probation in the United States. In: M. Tonry (ed.) *Crime and justice: A review of research, Vol. 22.* Chicago, IL: University of Chicago Press, pp. 149–200.

Petersilia, J., Turner, A.S. (1993). *Evaluating intensive supervised probation/parole results of a nationwide experiment.* Washington, DC: U.S. Department of Justice.

Rackmill, S. (1994). Prisoner handbook, Camp Reams Shock incarceration program: An analysis of home confinement as a sanction. *Federal Probation* 58(1), 45–52.

Robertson, A.A., Grimes, P.W., Rogers, K.E. (2001). A short-run cost–benefit analysis of community-based interventions for juvenile offenders. *Crime & Delinquency* 47(2), 265–284.

Rosen, J. (1993). Pretrial services—A magistrate judge's perspective. *Federal Probation* 57(1), 15–17.

Schwitzgebel, R., Schwitzgebel, R., Pahnke, W., Hurd, W. (1964). A program of research in behavioral electronics. *Behavioral Scientist* 9, 233–238.

Sherman, L., Gottfredson, D., MacKenzie, D., Eck, J., Reuter, P., Bushway, S. (1998). *Preventing crime: What works, what doesn't, what's promising.* Washington, DC: U.S. Department of Justice: National Institute of Justice, Research in Brief.

Stanz, R., Tewksbury, R. (2000). Predictors of success and recidivism in home incarceration programs. *Prison Journal* 80(3), 326–344.

U.S. Department of Justice (1990). *Survey of intermediate sanctions.* Washington, DC: U.S. Government Printing Office.

Wagner, D., Baird, C. (1993). *Evaluation of the Florida Community Control Program.* Washington, DC: U.S. Department of Justice.

Weis, R., Whitemarsh, S.M., Wilson, N.L. (2005). Military-style residential treatment for disruptive adolescents: Effective for some girls, all girls, when, and why? *Psychological Services* 2, 102–122.

Whitehead, J., Miller, L., Myers, L. (1995). The diversionary effectiveness of intensive supervision and community corrections programs. In: J. Smykla, W. Selke (eds) *Intermediate sanctions: Sentencing in the 1990s.* Cincinnati, OH: Anderson Publishing, pp. 135–151.

Chapter 11

COMMUNITY RESIDENTIAL CORRECTIONAL PROGRAMS

Key Terms

community-based correctional
  facilities
community-based treatment
  centers
community residential centers
day-reporting centers
dual-diagnosed offenders

halfway house
humaneness
reintegration
residential community
  corrections programs
restitution centers
work furlough centers

> [Community residential centers] play a vital role in the criminal justice
> system. They provide additional sentencing options for the court,
> protect public safety, provide individualized and intensive service aimed
> at reducing recidivism, and are cost-effective.—Bobbie L. Huskey

Community residential programs for criminal offenders have a long history in
the United States (Hartmann et al., 1994; Latessa & Travis, 1992). Until recently,
the typical residential community correctional facility was known as a "halfway
house," a transitional residence for criminal offenders (Wilson, 1985).

Box 11.1
Halfway House

A **halfway house** is a community-based residential facility for offenders
who are either about to be released from an institution or, immediately after
release, are in the initial stages of return to society. In the past three decades,
some halfway houses have been designed as alternatives to jail or prison
incarceration, primarily for probationers. "Halfway" could now mean
halfway into, or out of, prison.

This chapter discusses such programs within the larger context of corrections in the community, explaining the historical factors that contributed to the emergence of the halfway house movements; models of halfway houses; and their current operations and practices, effectiveness, costs, and futures. We begin with an explanation of the development of the halfway house over time.

HISTORICAL DEVELOPMENT OF THE HALFWAY HOUSE IN AMERICA

The halfway house concept began first in England and Ireland during the early 1800s, advocating transitional residences for criminal offenders. It spread quickly to the United States in 1817 when the Massachusetts Prison Commission recommended establishing a temporary residence to house destitute offenders after release from prison (Cohn, 1973, p. 2):

> The convicts who are discharged are often entirely destitute. The natural prejudice against them is so strong that they find great difficulty in obtaining employment. They are forced to seek shelter in the lowest receptacles; and if they wish to lead a new course of life, are easily persuaded out of it; and perhaps driven by necessity to the commission of fresh crimes. It is intended to afford a temporary shelter in this building, if they choose to accept it, to such discharged convicts as may have conducted themselves well in prison, subject to such regulations as the directors may see fit to provide. They will here have a lodging, rations from the prison at a cheap rate, and . . . a chance to occupy themselves in their trade, until some opportunity offers of placing themselves where they can gain an honest livelihood in society. A refuge of this kind, to this destitute class, would be found, perhaps, humane and political.

The commission making this recommendation believed that ex-inmates needed an accepting transitional house immediately after release and a supportive environment to assist in the process of establishing a law-abiding and independent existence. It was also motivated by the intention to reduce the unacceptably high rate of recidivism among newly released inmates (Seiter & Carlson, 1977). Unfortunately, the Massachusetts legislature feared that ex-prisoners might "contaminate" each other if housed together, neutralizing their newly instilled crime resistance learned in prison.

The concept, however, found fertile ground in other locations and under private sponsorship. In 1845, the Isaac T. Hooper Home in New York City opened under the auspices of the Quakers and today operates as the Women's Prison Association and Hooper Home, serving female clients. Perhaps the most significant halfway house program in this earlier era was Hope House, established by Maud Booth and Ballington Booth in 1896, in New York City. Supported both financially and morally by the Volunteers of America, other Hope Halls opened across the nation (Chicago, San Francisco, New Orleans, etc.).

This earlier movement and Hope Halls in particular did not last. Parole was introduced and implemented widely in the early 1900s as a means for controlling and helping ex-inmates after release from prison. The belief in likely and malevolent contamination from association with other parolees continued. The Great Depression weakened financial support for these privately operated homes, already underfunded. Phase I of the development of the halfway house ended shortly thereafter, not to revive until the 1950s.

The rebirth of the halfway house movement resulted, in part, from a growing awareness of the ineffectiveness of institutional corrections. High-recidivism rates were interpreted as indications of ineffectiveness of prison as a venue for rehabilitation. The growing dissatisfaction with prisons was buttressed by new evidence that parolees face problems in the transition from imprisonment to a free society, evidence of the need for supportive services in the transition to community life. In 1954, numerous halfway houses opened in America (such as Crenshaw House in Los Angeles and Dismas House in St. Louis, under the direction of Father Charles Dismas), England, and Canada. Private and religious groups pioneered in both historical and revival phases of development of the halfway house.

Earlier in the revival phase, most houses used individualized treatment, counseling, employment referrals, and substance abuse counseling, reflecting the general correctional philosophy found within the prison: the medical model. Persons not yet committed to predatory criminal lifestyles, younger, and more malleable offenders were believed to be ideal clients for the medical model. Then Attorney General Robert Kennedy suggested in 1961 that federal funds be used to establish publicly operated halfway houses for juvenile and youthful offenders, leading to the establishment of the Prisoner Rehabilitation Act of 1965. This legislation authorized the Bureau of Prisons (BOP) to establish community-based residences for adult and youthful prerelease offenders, as well as to transfer federal prisoners to privately sponsored halfway houses. In 1968, the Law Enforcement Assistance Administration began to provide substantial funds for establishing nonfederal houses, a thrust that continued until 1980.

A modern halfway house. [*Photo courtesy of Connecticut Halfway Houses, Inc.*]

Substance abuse group. [*Photo courtesy of Talbert House, Inc.*]

Box 11.2
Federal Prisoner Rehabilitation Act

The attorney general may extend the limits of the place of confinement of a prisoner as to whom there is reasonable cause to believe he will honor this trust, by authorizing him, under prescribed conditions, to:

1. Visit a specifically designated place for a period not to exceed 30 days and return to the same or another institution or facility. An extension of limits may be granted only to permit a visit to a dying relative, attendance at the funeral of a relative, the obtaining of medical services not otherwise available, the contacting of prospective employees, or for any other compelling reason consistent with the public interest; or
2. work at paid employment or participate in a training program in the community on a voluntary basis while continuing as a prisoner of the institution or facility to which he is committed.

Perhaps the most significant event in Phase II was the development of the International Halfway House Association (IHHA) in 1964.[1] This group, motivated by the absence of state and local support for halfway houses, established a voluntary professional organization of halfway house administrators and personnel (Wilson, 1985). IHHA (now known as the International Community Corrections Association) conducted numerous training workshops, sponsored training programs and conferences, and affiliated with the American Correctional Association.[2] The organization grew from 40 programs in 1966 to more than 1,800 in 1982[3] and now holds annual conferences that deal with "what works" in correctional intervention. As a result of these and related efforts, few cities and counties run their own residential treatment centers, and state programs that operate halfway houses usually contract with private-sector, nonprofit halfway houses to provide services.

Box 11.3
Types of Community Centers

Day-Reporting Centers
In these community centers, adults and sometimes juvenile offenders are expected to report frequently in lieu of incarceration or as a condition of probation. A variety of community or in-house programs may also be offered, including individual and group counseling, job readiness training, Alcoholics Anonymous (AA) 12-step programs, drug abuse education, and so on. Participants usually return to their individual homes at night.

Restitution Centers

These community residential centers are for offenders ordered by the court to make financial payments to victims. Offenders may also be remanded as a condition of probation. The offender must seek and obtain employment, make restitution to victims, reimburse the center for room and board, and set aside any residual earnings for use after release. Center programs usually require curfews, strict alcohol and drug abstinence, and participation in community or in-house programs.

Work Furlough Centers

This type of residential facility is for sentenced offenders released from a correctional institution for work during the day. Residents typically spend nights and weekends in the facility and must participate in available community or in-house programs. Participants are generally charged a per diem fee for services, room, and board.

USES OF HALFWAY HOUSES

Over the past 50 years, as suggested earlier, the numbers, roles, and uses of halfway houses have increased considerably. There has been considerable role expansion in residential placements of adult (and juvenile) offenders. For the most part, the increase has been in the services provided to new groups: probationers, the accused awaiting trial, and offenders directly sentenced for treatment, ordered by a judiciary eager to secure services and supervision for offenders. Judges are usually unwilling to incarcerate clients likely to give up criminal behavior if a supportive and facilitating community environment could be provided in which the offenders remediate their needs and improve their functioning. These changes in roles, sentencing alternatives, clients, and use of halfway houses have rendered "halfway house" an obsolete term, one that has been replaced by the more accurate "community corrections residential facility." Rush (1992) defines such facilities as:

> A correctional facility from which residents are regularly permitted to depart, unaccompanied by any official, for the purposes of using community resources, such as school or treatment programs, and seeking or holding employment. This definition not only deletes the term "halfway" but also defines a correctional mission for the facility. The definition does not require centers to provide direct services to clients. Halfway houses are thus subsumed under the larger umbrella term, further reflecting the more diverse populations served, as well as broader correctional mission and such newer programs as day, restitution, and work-release centers.

Another major factor influencing the development and use of community residential centers in the United States has been a shift in the ideology of corrections, from rehabilitation to "reintegration," a term introduced by the President's Commission on Law Enforcement and Administration of Justice in 1967.

This correctional philosophy places priority on keeping offenders in the community whenever possible rather than commit them to prison. It also stresses the role of the community in corrections. Thus the new ideology, new developments stressing community placement in local correctional programs, and existing halfway houses contributed to an accelerating expansion of community correctional residential programs. This thrust was further expanded by three factors:[4] (1) widespread correctional acceptance of the reintegration mission, (2) success of the reintegration movement in the mental health field, and (3) the lower costs of halfway houses as compared to prisons.[5] Prison overcrowding in the 1980s and early 1990s, as a result of the war on drugs, further accelerated the shift (Allen et al., 2010).

From 1980 through to the present, prison inmates have increased dramatically, with well over two million prisoners held in federal or state prisons and local jails (Bureau of Justice Statistics, 2009), creating a lack of prison capacity and extensive prison overcrowding. The primary reason for the burgeoning prison population is believed to be the "war on drugs," reflecting both the conservative emphases on retributive justice and the nation's unwillingness to address the causes of crime (Allen, 1995). Three major results of this development have been (1) an increase in the number of offenders placed on probation and parole, (2) an increase in the seriousness and dangerousness of offenses of those placed into traditional community-based supervision,[6] and (3) a heightened demand for community residential treatment facilities to provide transitional placement for offenders and to respond to such special needs populations as narcotics and drug abusers, offenders driving under the influence of alcohol or other drugs, and mental health clients. Community residential facilities and programs expanded and changed to address these new demands,[7] required programs, and heightened supervision levels (Huskey, 1992).

Before addressing programs for these clients, it is necessary to understand the models on which the programs operate. The exact number of halfway houses is unknown, and no government agencies routinely gather information on them. Data indicate that in 2000, nearly 30,000 inmates were served in just over 50 percent of the states (Camp & Camp, 2000).

Mental health program. [*Photo courtesy of Talbert House, Inc.*]

MODELS OF COMMUNITY RESIDENTIAL PROGRAMS

It should be remembered that Phase II of the development of community residential programs has been under way for more than 30 years. Thus, models under which halfway houses and related community programs operate have also undergone significant change. We start by examining an earlier model in a less complex environment.

In 1976, Allen and colleagues studied halfway houses and probation. These researchers developed three alternative models of halfway houses, based on referral service. This trichotomy is useful in depicting how halfway houses interface with the criminal justice system, as well as the advantages and services these programs offer to their clients. The trichotomy can be found in Figure 11.1 (Latessa & Allen, 1982).

Model 1 is the standard and most frequent pattern of referral to halfway house programs. In this model, an inmate granted a conditional release (such as parole, shock probation, or shock parole) enters a halfway house during the initial parole

---

Box 11.6
Model

A model is a picture or representation showing the parts of a system. Models suggest the ways that segments of the criminal justice system (courts, probation, prisons, etc.) fit together and interrelate. One implication of a model is that change in one part of the system will have an impact on other parts of the system. A simplified demonstration of this is seen when law enforcement agencies increase arrests; judicial personnel, probation officers, and jail facilities face increased workloads.

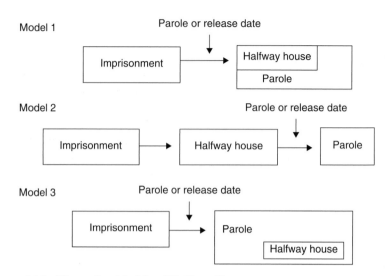

Figure 11.1 Alternative Models of Halfway Houses.

Source: Latessa, E., Allen, H. (1982). Halfway houses and parole: A national assessment. *Journal of Criminal Justice* 10, 153–163.

period. This model provides services to parolees who need support during their period of release. The length of residency in the halfway house may be specified before referral but is usually a shared decision to be made collaboratively by the supervision officer, house staff, and client. Typically, this decision is based on such factors as the resident's readiness to leave the house, employment, savings, and alternative residential plan. After leaving the house, the offender generally continues on parole supervision. This model has been found to reduce recidivism successfully (Bouffard et al., 2000).

Model 2 is similar to the first in that inmates' release plans call for placement in a halfway house as the initial phase of their release process. Unlike the first, however, halfway house residency occurs prior to formal granting of parole and subsequent supervision as a parolee. Typically, these inmates have been scheduled for a definite release date before moving from the prison to the halfway house. These clients remain inmates, serving the remainder of their sentences in residency at a halfway house. Halfway house residency provides needed and significant services in the prison–community transition. Additional benefits include continuation of jurisdiction by the referring correctional agency, ability to return the inmate to incarceration without formal violation of parole, development of a more positive attitude toward the halfway house by the resident, and less expensive aftercare service that can be more legitimately compared to imprisonment rather than the costs of parole.[8] The U.S. Bureau of Prisons was a leader in initiating this model for using halfway houses[9] and continues to use this model on a prerelease basis.[10]

The third model of halfway house use, also based on the reintegration model of corrections, differs by time of placement into the program. With Model 3, offenders on probation and inmates granted parole are assigned to the community without initially residing in a halfway house. If such clients revert to criminal

---

Box 11.7
Bureau of Prisons and Halfway Houses

The goal of BOP's halfway house program is to provide federal prison inmates with a transition back to the communities where they will live upon release from federal custody. In addition to subsistence and housing, BOP guidelines state that halfway house operators are required to offer inmates job counseling, academic and vocational training, family reconciliation services, access to substance abuse programs, postrelease housing referrals, and community adjustment services.

Source: U.S. Government Accounting Office (2001).

---

behavior or encounter unanticipated problems that might be resolved by program services of or a period of residency in a halfway house, the supervising agency may remand the offender to the residential setting for a short period. If and when conditions warrant, the client could then be returned to a lower level of supervision. It should be noted here that some residential correctional programs are large and can provide services and programs at many points in the supervision process, as explored later. Model 3 appears to best suggest the organization and practices of multiservice agencies in larger urban settings.

In addition to the models described earlier, halfway houses take on a wide range of functions and services depending on their size, mission, and resources. Figure 11.2 illustrates a continuum of types of programs based on the services they provide. Some halfway houses provide shelter, food, and minimal counseling and referral services. These programs are considered supportive halfway houses. Examples of these types of programs include shelters and drop-in centers. Halfway houses that offer a full range of services can be considered interventive programs. These are programs that offer a full range of treatment services. Most programs fall somewhere in the middle.

It should be obvious that the roles of halfway houses as residential probation and aftercare centers within the correctional process are varied in both operation and focus. Although all three models acknowledge the need for a residential setting at some point in the transition back to the community, there are various approaches and strategies for meeting these needs. To understand the range of alternatives, we examine a rural community residential treatment center, as well as a larger urban counterpart.

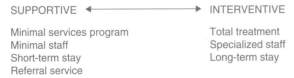

Figure 11.2 Types of Halfway Houses Based on Services.

RURAL COMMUNITY PROGRAMS

Rural correctional programs serve a wide range of offenders and are themselves diverse. Whereas the "Mom and Pop" stereotype possibly typical of the earliest developments of rural community corrections has surely died,[11] what has emerged is an increasingly diversified pattern of local programs that solidly reflect the concept of **"residential community corrections programs."**[12]

Community residential correctional programs in rural settings face differing challenges. They are generally smaller than urban programs and have fewer employment opportunities and treatment programs for offenders. Residents are drawn from a small pool of eligible offenders. These programs face and must overcome community suspicion that the center may attract recalcitrant offenders who will move their base of criminal activities to the local area, the "importation" reaction. Decreased societal tolerance for certain offender types (such as rapists, child molesters, and drug pushers), coupled with concerns over public safety and demands for increased supervision, has great potential to restrict treatment, job and educational placement, access to existing treatment programs, and funding from community sources. Many facilities must work hard to interface with referral sources (probation and parole agencies, for example) and develop liaisons with other services offered by mental health, illegal drug, alcohol, family counseling, and court agencies.

Box 11.8
Rural Community Corrections

Community corrections in its rural expression is the remnant of the grassroots folk art of the original concept. Rural programs are generally not larger than 40 beds (a *large* rural program) and are concerned about the importation of offenders regularly into their community, the meeting of the next payroll, the expense of travel to training as opposed to the cost of training itself. The rural program is generally not faced with the challenge of adequately accessing and implementing brokerages to existing treatment in their community; we are worried about how to create, fund, and perpetuate treatment. Our "community" may be a town of 12,000 serving a catchment area of several hundred miles. Our worries are not typically of gang behavior between "Crips and Bloods." They may, however, include the American Indian in any of its numerous tribal groups, the rural Hispanic or black, all in the delicately interwoven and overwoven social fabric of the lineages of a rural community. Every individual job truly means the future of our programs. The failure of one client can affect the future political support of our program; a single incident cannot only destroy a program but also the potential efforts of any program to replace it.

(Berry 1990, pp. 6–7).

These opportunities and challenges face Hilltop House,[13] a 28-bed private, nonprofit agency providing residential services to male offenders and outpatient services to delinquents and victims referred from local, state, and federal sources. In its earliest days, this small program would close in the winter and reopen in the spring, housing not more than 12 clients referred from one judicial district. It now serves a much wider catchment area, working with six district court judges.

Hilltop House began to grow in this environment, even though it encountered the conservative political swing that demanded longer sentences, less diversion, and specialized programs to assist the higher-need clients the justice system was processing. This demand was met by:

- Developing liaisons with other court referral units and probation officers.
- Working with nonincarcerated populations (such as misdemeanant offenders, persons driving under the influence, self-referred persons with alcohol and other drug abuse problems, youths referred by their parents, and so on).
- Developing new service programs in the areas of incest treatment and domestic violence, and urinalysis collection and testing for a county youth home, private schools, social services, employers, individuals, and parents.
- Developing a sexual abuse treatment team, using workers from a number of agencies and providing a service to offenders, their nonoffending spouses, victims, and other adults who had been molested as children (AMACs). This multiagency approach was expanded to include juvenile restitution, a program using many volunteers as mediators and providing subsidized employment and monitored restitution payments, as well as group therapy to reconcile victims and their offenders, and develop empathy among juvenile offenders.

Hilltop House appears to serve the specific needs of the community, to develop resources to plan and initiate specialized services, and to maximize therapeutic gains for clients, victims, and citizens. Individuals who resolve conflicts, personal problems, challenges, development problems, and the impacts of being victimized are more likely to become constructive citizens and lower the crime rate in their community.

METROPOLITAN RESIDENTIAL PROGRAMS

Residential community correctional programs for offenders located in urban areas are more numerous and diverse than those in rural areas. In addition, many of the largest programs make extensive use of existing community services, especially if these are needed adjuncts to a treatment plan for an individual client. Treatment generally falls into two categories—individual and group—and most halfway houses conduct detailed intake assessments to determine the needs of their clients. Figure 11.3 shows an example of a halfway house intake form.

Although halfway houses usually offer a range of programs and services, the most common include employment, substance abuse, and cognitive restructuring.

GENERAL INFORMATION

1. [ ][ ][ ][ ][ ][ ][ ][ ][ ][ ][ ][ ]   [ ]   [ ][ ][ ][ ][ ][ ][ ][ ][ ][ ]
   (First)   (Middle)   (Last)   Client Name

2. [ ][ ][ ][ ][ ][ ] Client T.H. ID #

3. [ ][ ]-[ ][ ]-[ ][ ][ ][ ] Client SS #

4. [ ] Admission Status:
   (1) New Admission
   (2) Re-Admission (within fiscal year)
   (3) Re-Admittance after Escape/Absconding
       (within fiscal year)
   (4) Legal Status Altered

5. [ ][ ] / [ ][ ] / [ ][ ] Date of Birth (mo/day/yr)

6. [ ] Sex (1) Male   (2) Female

7. [ ] Race
   (AI) American Indian   (OR) Oriental
   (BL) Black   (WH) White
   (HI) Hispanic   (Specify) Other _____

7a. [ ] Appalachian (1) Yes   (2) No

8. [ ] Current Marital Status
   (1) Single   (4) Married
   (2) Divorced   (5) Separated
   (3) Widowed   (6) Common Law

9. [ ][ ] Number of Dependents (financial responsibility other than self)

10. [ ][ ] Number of Children

11. [ ] Legal Responsibility for Children?   (1) Yes (2) No

12. [ ][ ][ ][ ][ ] Zip Code of Last Community Address

13. [ ] Homeless Before Arrest?   (1) Yes (2) No

14. [ ] Place to Live When Discharged?   (1) Yes (2) No

15. [ ] Primary Source of Income (at present)
   (1) Public Assistance   (5) Family
   (2) Investments   (6) No Income
   (3) Full-Time Employment   (7) Other _____
   (4) Part-Time Employment

15a. [ ][ ][ ][ ][ ] Total Income Last Year (Nearest Dollar)

16. [ ][ ][ ][ ][ ] Court Costs Owed (Nearest Dollar)

17. [ ][ ][ ][ ][ ] Restitution Owed (Nearest Dollar)

CRIMINAL HISTORY

Note: When answering questions 19-30, if the information is not available from the referral source, use client-reported answers.

18. [ ][ ][ ][ ] . [ ][ ][ ] Ohio Revised Code for which convicted.

19. [ ][ ] Number of prior felony convictions (adult/juvenile).

20. [ ][ ] Number of prior adult felony commitments in a state or federal institution (when sentenced).

21. [ ][ ] Age at admission to institution (or probation) for current offense.

22. [ ][ ] Number of offenses (including current offense) committed while under parole/probation supervision.

23. [ ][ ] Number of offenses (including current offense) involving drugs/alcohol.

24. [ ][ ] Number of prior arrests during the past five years, prior to incarceration.

25. [ ][ ] Number of offenses (including current offense) for auto theft.

26. [ ][ ] Number of offenses (including current offense) involving serious injury to the victim.

27. [ ][ ] Number of offenses (including current offense) involving the use of a weapon.

28. [ ][ ] Has this individual been previously convicted for the same offense? (1) Yes (2) No

29. [ ][ ] Was the current conviction for multiple crimes? (1) Yes (2) No

30. [ ][ ] Was the offender employed at the time of arrest? (1) Yes (2) No

Figure 11.3 Halfway House Intake Form (form A-2).

EDUCATION AND EMPLOYMENT HISTORY

31. ☐☐ Years of education attained (last grade completed).

32. ☐☐ Highest diploma/degree received and name major subject area where applicable.
    (1) None
    (2) G.E.D.
    (3) High School
    (4) College   Associate/Major   _____
                    Bachelor/Major   _____
                    Master's/Major   _____
                    Doctoral/Major   _____

33. ☐☐ Years of vocational training.

34. ☐☐ Certification of vocational training awarded
    (1) Yes _____ Trade
    (2) No

Enter 1 for YES 2 for NO for Questions 35-37

35. ☐☐ Physical/Health impairments (e.g., amputee, paraplegic, deaf, blind, serious illness, debilitating effect of age)

36. ☐☐ Mental capacity impairment (e.g., diagnosed mental retardation, diagnosed borderline MR)

37. ☐☐ Behavioral impairment (e.g., mental and/or emotional condition or disorders that require the treatment of a qualified mental health professional).

38. ☐☐ Number of jobs held in the last 2 years in the community prior to incarceration.

39. ☐☐ Longest stay on the job in the last 2 years in the community (number of months).

CLIENT/STAFF ASSISTANCE ASSESSMENT

Enter 1 for YES 2 for NO for Questions 40-55

40. ☐ Does client feel he/she needs assistance while in residency?

41. ☐ Does this individual need employment assistance?

42. ☐ Does this individual need assistance in academic or vocational training?

43. ☐ Does this individual need assistance in financial management?

44. ☐ Does individual need assistance in the area of domestic relations (e.g., marriage, family, etc.)?

45. ☐ Does this individual need assistance in the area of emotional or mental health?

46. ☐ Is this individual currently required to take medication for any psychological condition?

47. ☐ Does this individual need assistance for a substance abuse (alcohol/drug) problem?

48. ☐ Does this individual need assistance with securing suitable living arrangements?

49. ☐ Does this individual need assistance for a learning disability?

50. ☐ Has medication ever been prescribed for a psychological condition (e.g., nerves)?

51. ☐ Has client had prior psychiatric hospitalization?

52. ☐ Has client ever attempted suicide?

53. ☐ Was client ever a victim of child abuse?

54. ☐ Was client ever a victim of domestic violence?

55. ☐ Was client ever a victim of sexual abuse or incest?

DRUG/ALCOHOL HISTORY

56. ☐☐ # times client had prior drug/alcohol treatment.

57. ☐☐ # months prior outpatient treatment.

58. ☐☐ Successful? (1) Yes (2) No (3) NA

59. ☐☐ # months prior inpatient treatment.

60. ☐☐ Successful? (1) Yes (2) No (3) NA

61. ☐☐ # months prior Halfway House treatment.

62. ☐☐ Successful? (1) Yes (2) No (3) NA

63. ☐ Has client participated in a halfway house **program** before this occasion?
    (1) Yes (2) No

64. ☐☐ Longest period of drug/alcohol abstinence in community (months) **or** (99) No problem

Staff member completing form

_____

Date _____

Rev. 061992

Figure 11.3 Continued.

Box 11.9
Alcoholics and Treatment

Many community corrections center programs focus on Alcoholics Anonymous as part of the overall abstinence program. This may mean requiring residents to work the 12 steps of AA, demonstrate understanding of the program, design a postrelease plan, chair an AA meeting, and participate in the affairs of the program. The latter might include house chores (vacuuming, cleaning restrooms, shoveling snow, cleaning ashtrays, etc.), attending house meetings, remaining sober and clean, working outside the program, and seeking specialized treatment. If the resident's family unit is not broken, reconciliation counseling may be required. If appropriate, the resident might be required to participate in meetings of Adult Children of Alcoholics (ACAs) or child sexual abuse and domestic violence programs. When alcohol is the underlying cause of criminal behavior, an individually designed, monitored, and supportive program may reduce criminal activity sharply.

Employment programming usually includes job readiness training, resumé writing and interviewing skills, job placement, and transportation assistance.

Programs for drug abusers might include methadone maintenance, weekly and unscheduled urinalysis, 12-step programming, groups, Alcoholic Anonymous and Narcotics Anonymous, and detoxification. It should be noted that, on average, more than 60 percent of all male arrestees tested positive for at least one drug, including alcohol (Drug Use Forecasting, 2000), and about one in four tested positive for a major drug (PCP, heroin, crack, or cocaine). The rate for female jail inmates was even higher than for males; 28 percent tested positive for opiates compared to 17 percent for males. Alcohol and other drug abuse is a risk factor for many offenders, and such clients have high needs for treatment that community residential correctional facilities can meet.[14]

In recent years, there has been increased focus on the effectiveness of cognitive behavioral programs. These interventions involve targeting the antisocial attitudes, values, and beliefs that many offenders hold. Cognitive programming attempts to restructure the thinking of offenders and develop new skills that can be used to improve their problem-solving abilities. Many halfway houses today offer criminal thinking groups and other cognitive interventions aimed at anger and violence reduction, sexual behavior, negative peer associations, and improved problem-solving techniques.

Another group of problem offenders are those with both mental illness and substance abuse problems. County community health boards and criminal courts can both use services for these offenders. These offenders are called "dual diagnosed" and pose a special problem for community corrections. Although research indicates that major predictors of recidivism are the same for mentally disordered offenders as for nonmentally disordered offenders (Bonta et al., 1998;

Solicitor General of Canada, 1998), the availability of treatment services in the community is often lacking for this special needs group. Peters and Hills (1999, p. 95) state:

> Offenders placed under community supervision who have co-occurring mental health and substance abuse disorders are quite diverse in symptom presentation, severity and chronicity of disorders. These individuals often have severe mental health disorders, and simultaneously use different types of drugs, presenting considerable challenges to treatment programs for this population. Many offenders with co-occurring disorders would benefit from specialized treatment services in the community.

Unfortunately, relatively few programs are designed specifically to deal with the **dual-diagnosed offender**. Most of these programs are located in large urban areas. One such program is the Substance Abuse–Mental Illness (SAMI) program operated by Talbert House in Cincinnati, Ohio. This program has been in operation for more than 10 years and has served well over 500 offenders during that period of time.

Many urban communities across the nation face the problem of finding treatment opportunities that permit reintegration of high-need offenders, such as described earlier. Increasingly, these counties are turning to private-sector, for-profit, and nonprofit residential programs for assistance. Figure 11.4 suggests how such residential and community programs can interface with traditional justice agencies in provision of services.

Community residential correctional programs of these types exist across the nation and will increase in number and importance in the coming years. The private sector providing these programs, facilities, and centers will grow as cities and counties, facing fiscal and policy crises, accept and introduce these programs in their local areas.

JUVENILES IN RESIDENTIAL PLACEMENT

Although the population of juveniles in residential placement includes those in secure facilities, the use of group homes, halfway houses, and other forms of residential facilities are common in the juvenile justice system. Recent figures released by the Office of Juvenile Justice and Delinquency Prevention (Sickmund, 2010) indicate a steady decline in the number of youths placed in such facilities between 1998 and 2008. Figure 11.5 shows that the number of juveniles in residential placement peaked in 2000 and has been declining ever since. Some states, such as Missouri, have moved from large juvenile institutions to smaller, residential facilities. Box 11.10 gives an example of some new evidenced-based residential programs for youths that the state of Ohio is developing in conjunction with the University of Cincinnati.

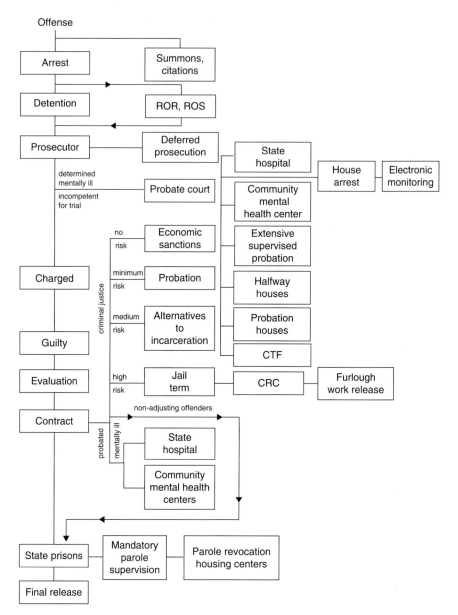

Figure 11.4 A Reintegration Model.

Source: Allen, H., Simonsen, C. (1995). *Corrections in America*. Englewood Cliffs, NJ: Prentice Hall.

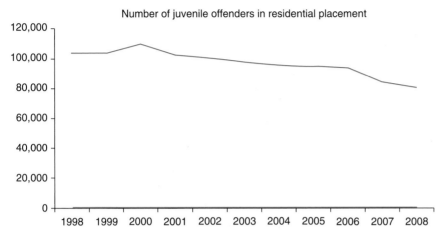

Figure 11.5 Juvenile Offenders in Residential Placement.

Source: Sickmund, M. (2010). *Juveniles in residential placement 1997–2010. OJJDP Fact Sheet.* Washington, DC: U.S. Department of Justice.

Box 11.10
Community-Based Treatment Centers (CBTC) in Ohio

The Ohio Department of Youth Services (ODYS), with the assistance of the School of Criminal Justice at the University of Cincinnati, has established several **community-based treatment centers**. The impetus for developing these programs originated from a 2005 study which indicated that moderate-risk youths placed in ODYS institutions recidivated at a substantially higher rate than similar youths placed in the community. Hence, the vision of this initiative is to create an alternative placement for moderate-risk youths committed to ODYS.

The CBTC project has the following three goals: to (1) provide a secure, intensive, high-fidelity, evidence-based treatment program for moderate-risk youths; (2) reduce the length of stay and recidivism for moderate-risk youths; and (3) provide high-quality, intensive aftercare services that support community and family reunification/stability.

The first community-based CBTC was opened in October 2009. ODYS contracted with STARR Commonwealth to operate this program. It is located in Franklin County, Ohio.

The target population for CBTCs is moderate-risk youths committed to the Department of Youth Services on a felony-level offense. Moderate risk is defined by results of an actuarial risk assessment and will include youths who fall within a moderate and high to moderate risk range.

The program is based on a cognitive-behavioral therapy model with a focus on targeting criminogenic risk factors through cognitive restructuring and skill acquisition. The total dosage of treatment approximates 300 hours. The length of the program is based on the youth's risk and needs, as well as progress in treatment, but will average 120 days of residential programming and 120 days of aftercare. STARR operates a 12-bed CBTC program. The program admits only local youth, which allows for emphasis on family intervention and aftercare.

An intensive aftercare program is an integral part of the CBTC programs. Aftercare consists of parole supervision using the Effective Practices in Community Supervision (EPICS) model. Recall from the previous chapter that this model uses a cognitive-behavioral framework to supervise offenders in the community. Likewise, youth are required to attend an eight-week aftercare group that focuses on applying those skills learned in the residential portion of the program. Finally, parole is responsible for brokerage with community resources.

In order to ensure fidelity to the program model, several layers of quality assurance are incorporated. Quality assurance consists of staff training, observation of treatment delivery with feedback, youth feedback, reassessment, program assessment, and recidivism follow-up. The University of Cincinnati is responsible for providing training and coaching of staff, as well as monitoring the fidelity of program implementation.

The Ohio Department of Youth Services has now expanded aspects of this CBTC model to many other juvenile correctional programs throughout the state.

EFFECTIVENESS OF COMMUNITY RESIDENTIAL PROGRAMS

The question of the effectiveness of halfway houses, along with other community corrections programs, was addressed previously. A brief summary statement is included here to place both phases of the halfway house movement in perspective.

Evaluation of the effectiveness of halfway houses and, more recently, residential community correctional programs requires that they be considered across three dimensions: humaneness, recidivism, and cost studies (Latessa & Allen, 1982). There is little doubt that halfway houses, during both phases, were and are more humanitarian than imprisonment. Halfway house programs were established in part to address the devastating economic and psychological effects of prisons and prisonization on most inmates. Prison crowding, gross idleness of inmates, absence of meaningful work and vocational training, unhealthy and unsafe physical plants, prison rape, and gang conflicts within prisons make prisons less than the pinnacle of humanitarianism (Donnelly & Forschner, 1987). Halfway houses are more humane, although the conservative punishment

---

Box 11.11
Humaneness of Halfway Houses

[B]ecause of the difficulty of assessing **humaneness** and behavioral changes, most researchers tend to ignore these variables to pursue more quantifiable data. However, anyone who has worked in or around halfway houses has seen positive changes of the lives of many who enter these programs.—George Wilson

---

emphasis in the last two decades raises policy questions about whether American correctional policy should be so (Latessa & Allen, 1982).

The weight of evidence to date demonstrates that halfway houses are cost-effective in terms of expenditure of public funds when compared to institutional placement. Further, their programs achieve some, if not all, stated objectives, including the maintenance of offenders' community ties and making community resources available to offender clients (Dowell et al., 1985). On average, halfway houses cost about $50 per day, and one study concluded that halfway houses tend to be more cost-effective under private rather than public management (Pratt & Winston, 1999).

The issue of recidivism is much more complex, particularly with regard to halfway houses. The diversity of halfway houses, as well as the range of types of offenders they serve (parolees, probationers, pretrial detainees, work releasees, and furloughees, not to mention state, county, and federal offenders), makes it difficult to develop adequate comparison groups for follow-up studies.[15] Recidivism studies of CRC residents that exist indicate success with about 71 percent of the clients, and in-program rearrest rates of 2 to 17 percent (Huskey, 1992). Follow-up recidivism studies of alcohol-abusing clients show success rates ranging from 70 to 80 percent; driving under the influence (DUI) rates can be reduced significantly with residential treatment, significantly raising DUI survival rates (Langworthy & Latessa, 1993, 1996; Pratt et al., 2000). For clients who graduate from CRC programs, success rates can be as high as 92 percent (Friday & Wertkin, 1995). On the whole, follow-up recidivism studies indicate that halfway house residents perform no worse than offenders who receive other correctional sanctions. There is also some evidence that offenders placed in halfway houses have more needs than other offenders (Latessa & Travis, 1991). Latessa (1998) has examined a number of halfway houses across the country. He has several criticisms that are noteworthy:

- Many halfway houses fail to assess offenders adequately, and few distinctions are made between offenders based on risk.
- In general, qualifications of staff are low, and there is a great deal of staff turnover.

- Most halfway houses offer a wide range of "eclectic" treatment, with little if any theoretically based treatment models in place.
- Despite some notable exceptions, most halfway houses can be classified as one step above "three hots and a cot."

In some studies of halfway houses, Leon and colleagues (1999) and Munden and co-workers (1999) voiced similar concerns about poor offender assessment practices, frequent staff turnover, change in leadership, inadequate resources, and insufficient emphasis on treatment. In a 2002 study of residential programs in Ohio, Lowenkamp and Latessa (2004) demonstrated the importance of assessing the risk level of offenders before assigning them to community-based correctional facilities (CBCFs). Figures 11.6 and 11.7 illustrate recidivism rates for individual CBCF programs. Consistent with the risk principle, CBCF programs generally increased the recidivism rates of low-risk offenders by 4 percent but decreased the recidivism rates of higher-risk offenders by 8 percent. In a 2010 replication study, Latessa and colleagues (2010) examined 20 CBCFs and 40 halfway houses and a sample of more than 20,000 offenders. Results from this study were very similar to the earlier one: overall recidivism *increased* by 3 percent for low-risk offenders and was *reduced* by 14 percent for high-risk offenders. As with the previous study, some programs were extremely effective, whereas others were not. The quality and implementation of the program were major factors in determining the effectiveness of the program.

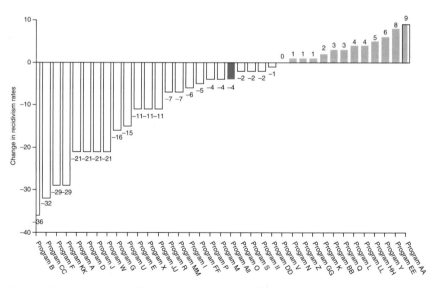

Figure 11.6 Treatment Effects for a Low-risk Offender.

Source: Lowenkamp, C.T., Latessa, E.J. (2004). Residential community corrections and the risk principle: Lessons learned in Ohio. *Ohio Corrections Research Compendium*, vol. II. Columbus, OH: Ohio Department of Research and Corrections.

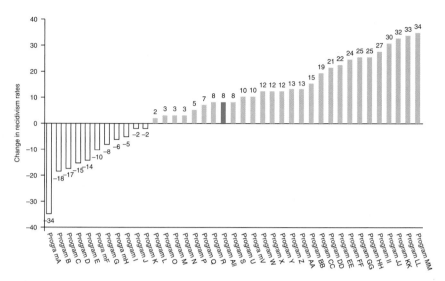

Figure 11.7　Treatment Effects for High-risk Offenders.

Source: Lowenkamp, C.T., Latessa, E.J. (2004). Residential community corrections and the risk principle: Lessons learned in Ohio. *Ohio Corrections Research Compendium,* vol. II. Columbus, OH: Ohio Department of Research and Corrections.

Box 11.12
Community-Based Correctional Facilities

In one of the more unusual attempts to provide residential treatment programs, Ohio has developed a correctional alternative called **community-based correctional facilities** (CBCFs). Currently there are 19 operating CBCFs in Ohio. The size of the facilities ranges from 54 to 200 offenders, and several serve both males and females. Funding for the CBCFs is provided by the state; however, the operation and management of the CBCFs are left to a local judicial corrections board. In some instances, local courts operate the facilities, whereas private providers are retained in others. The CBCFs are secure facilities, but treatment is the primary focus. Ohio has also developed similar juvenile programs called community correctional facilities. Some other states, such as Indiana and Texas, have similar programs. Many of these programs have demonstrated that they can effectively deliver services to offenders and reduce recidivism.

THE FUTURE OF RESIDENTIAL COMMUNITY CORRECTIONS

Predicting future correctional trends is difficult due to possible national policy changes, economic fluctuations, crime trends, and public sentiment. One thing is evident: public sentiment for increasing the punishment of offenders in the hope of lessening crime[16] remains strong. Thus, it is reasonable to expect increased numbers of offenders in jails and prisons, and on probation, parole, and other community correctional programs.

Despite the increased use of punishment, the future of residential community correctional programs appears promising. Probation populations are at an all-time high, and approximately 95 percent of prison inmates will return to the community. Halfway houses and other community-based programs will be needed to assist in their reintegration. Early release programs, such as work and educational furlough and preparole release, will also increase, furthering the demand for the services of halfway houses and related programs.

It is also likely that local units of government will increasingly turn to private-sector providers for correctional (and perhaps law enforcement) programs, contracting with larger numbers of halfway houses to provide lower-cost and diverse services that the government cannot otherwise fund. To do less would decrease reintegration services and increase the possibility of offenders returning to prisons for committing new crimes in local communities. Indeed, one of the issues facing community corrections is the increased privatization of services and programs. While nonprofit providers have always been the mainstay of traditional halfway houses, the influx of for-profit providers will likely change the face of this industry. This has not been without its critics, however, and the onus on the government to evaluate the quality of programs and services will be even greater.

Halfway houses and related programs will also need to increase the quality and effectiveness[17] of programs to serve the demands of clients, communities, and corrections. To do this, they will need to maintain relationships with justice agencies, strengthen community ties and acceptance, adopt treatment models that have demonstrated effectiveness, and assist in ensuring the safety of the community in reintegrating offenders. Future research will also be needed to address the roles and effectiveness of community residential correctional programs. Fortunately, there is a movement under way to improve the effectiveness of community correctional programs. This movement is being supported by the National Institute of Corrections[18] and the International Community Corrections Association and is based on the work of scholars such as Paul Gendreau, Don Andrews, Francis Cullen, and others. Through their research we continue to learn about "what works" with offenders (Cullen & Gendreau, 2001).

SUMMARY

Halfway houses have been part of the correctional scene since the early 1800s. Originally designed to assist offenders who had been released from prison, today many halfway houses serve as both halfway "in" and halfway "out" facilities. Often called community residential correctional programs, these facilities include both privately and publicly operated programs and range from "three hots and a cot" to programs designed to meet all of an offender's treatment needs. Although halfway houses are often overlooked, they represent an important part of community corrections.

Community corrections centers serving high-risk clients have produced evidence of both lower recidivism and cost-effectiveness. Such centers are more humane, less expensive, and more effective in ensuring public safety. Community corrections centers will remain a major segment of community corrections and will be increasingly specialized to serve a wider variety of high-risk clients. This has been the case in a number of jurisdictions throughout the United States, especially as prisons are under increasing pressure to release inmates and reduce the incarcerated population.

Review Questions

1. Why did Phase I of the halfway house movement die in the 1930s?
2. Explain the revival of the halfway house movement in the 1950s.
3. Define residential community correctional center.
4. What are some of the services offered by halfway houses?
5. What are the advantages of halfway houses?
6. What is "substance abuse?" Debate: is it a disease or a learned behavior?
7. Define "reintegration" and discuss ways that halfway houses can lower crime.
8. What are some of the criticisms of halfway houses?
9. Describe the CBTCs that Ohio is in the process of developing.

Notes

1 This organization is now known as the International Community Corrections Association; publishes the *ICCA Journal*; and sponsors local, state, regional, national, and international conferences and training programs concerned with halfway houses and community alternatives. Go to www.iccaweb.org/ for more information.
2 American Correctional Association, 206 N. Washington Street, Alexandria, VA 22314 (www.aca.org/).
3 The National Institute of Corrections lists more than 1,200 programs in its 1989 *Directory of Residential Community Corrections Facilities in the United States*. The directory does not list all small programs, particularly in rural areas. For more information, go to www.nicic.org.
4 Allen et al. (1976).
5 Halfway houses for juveniles tend to be more cost-effective than detention. Pratt and Winston (1999).
6 Petersilia et al. (1985).
7 Chapple (2000).
8 This question is explored in more detail in Hicks (1987). See also Wilson (1985); Latessa and Travis (1992); Latessa and Allen (1982).

9 Federal Bureau of Prisons (2001). See also Thevenot (2001).

10 Valentine (1991). The Bureau of Prisons underutilizes their contracted bed space, further exacerbating their prison overcrowding problem.

11 This nostalgic view of warm-hearted, older rural Americans trying to help the less successful, downtrodden, and sodden of the Depression years by feeding any who ask, putting transients to work chopping wood or hauling water, and allowing the more needy to sleep in the barn has many adherents. No doubt this pattern of early philanthropic assistance was found in many sites and continues in isolated locales. These "Mom and Pop" programs, often unofficial, were undoubtedly major sources of humanitarian assistance to the needy in some, if not most, of the nation during the early twentieth century, providing "three hots and a cot." If they exist today, they are an endangered species.

12 See the *IARCA Journal* for a description of some more successful programs in rural America and urban England (Leeds Alternative to Care and Custody Scheme, and Roundabout Group). *IARCA Journal* 3 (July, 1990).

13 See Berry (1990).

14 Barbara Owen found that alcohol frequently accompanied other drug use among parolees in California, leading to most parole violations (Owen, 1991). See also Langworthy and Latessa (1993); and Division of Criminal Justice Office of Research and Statistics (2001).

15 It is important to note that studies that do not employ a control group make it very difficult to gauge the effectiveness of programs, at least in terms of recidivism.

16 Judging from official crime statistics and victimization studies, the crime rate in the nation has been dropping for the past 10 years. However, politicians and agencies with vested interests in maintaining concern over crime have come to believe that public safety will be enhanced by "locking up criminals and throwing away the prison keys." This assumption is at least debatable and could be patently wrong.

17 There is some evidence that staff attributes within programs influence program effectiveness and recidivism. Staff selection and training, as well as program developments, could be improved by matching personality and attitudinal attributes. See Johnson and Bonta (1985).

18 For more information about this movement, write to NIC at 320 1st Street NW, Washington, DC 20534 (www.nicic.org).

Recommended Readings

Lowenkamp, C.T., Latessa, E.J. (2005). Increasing the effectiveness of correctional programming through the risk principle: Identifying offenders for residential placement. *Criminology and Public Policy* 4(2), 263–290.

Lowenkamp, C., Makarios, M.D., Latessa, E.J., Lemke, R., Smith, P. (2010). Community corrections facilities for juvenile offenders in Ohio: An examination of treatment integrity and recidivism. *Criminal Justice and Behavior* 37(6), 695–708.

References

Allen, H. (1995). The American dream and crime in the twenty-first century. *Justice Quarterly* 12, 427–445.

Allen, H., Simonsen, C. (1995). *Corrections in America.* Englewood Cliffs, NJ: Prentice Hall.

Allen, H., Latessa, E.J., Ponder, B. (2010). *Corrections in America: An introduction,* 12th edn. Upper Saddle River, NJ: Pearson/Prentice Hall.

Allen, H., Bowman, E., Carlson, E., Parks, E., Seiter, R. (1976). *Halfway houses in the United States: An analysis of the state of the art.* Paper presented at the International Halfway House Association, Guilford, England.

Berry, T. (1990). Rural community corrections and the challenge: Providing comprehensive services. *IARCA Journal* 3(July), 6–7.

Bonta, J., Law, M., Hanson, K. (1998). The prediction of criminal and violent recidivism among mentally disordered offenders: A meta-analysis. *Psychological Bulletin* 123(2), 123–142.

Bouffard, J., MacKenzie, D., Hickman, L. (2000). Effectiveness of vocational education and employment programs for adult offenders. *Journal of Offender Rehabilitation* 31(1/2), 1–42.

Bureau of Justice Statistics (2009). *Prisoners in 2008.* Washington, DC: U.S. Department of Justice.

Camp, C., Camp, G. (1997). *The corrections yearbook.* South Salem, NY: The Criminal Justice Institute.

Camp, C., Camp, G. (2000). *The 2000 corrections yearbook: Adult corrections.* Middletown, CT: Criminal Justice Institute.

Chapple, K. (2000). *Community residential programming for female offenders and their children. Responding to women offenders in the community.* Washington, DC: National Institute of Corrections, pp. 31–35.

Cohn, J. (1973). *A study of community-based correctional needs in Massachusetts.* Boston, MA: Massachusetts Department of Corrections.

Cullen, F., Gendreau, P. (2001). From nothing works to what works. *The Prison Journal* 81(3), 313–338.

Division of Criminal Justice Office of Research and Statistics (2001). *Executive summary: 2000 community corrections results.* Washington, DC: National Institute of Justice/Federal Bureau of Prisons.

Donnelly, P., Forschner, B.E. (1987). Predictors of success in a co-correctional halfway house: A discriminant analysis. *Journal of Crime and Justice* 10, 1–22.

Dowell, D., Klein, C., Krichmar, C. (1985). Evaluation of a halfway house for women. *Journal of Criminal Justice* 13, 217–226.

Drug Use Forecasting (2000). *Annual report on adult and juvenile arrestees.* Washington, DC: National Institute of Justice.

Federal Bureau of Prisons (2001) *The Bureau in brief.* www.bop.gov/resources/publications.jsp.

Friday, P., Wertkin, R. (1995). Effects of programming and race on recidivism: Residential probation. In: J. Smykla, W. Selke (eds) *Intermediate sanctions: Sentencing in the 1990s.* Cincinnati, OH: Anderson, pp. 209–217.

Hartmann, D., Friday, P., Minor, K. (1994). Residential probation: A seven-year follow-up study of halfway house discharges. *Journal of Criminal Justice* 22(6), 503–515.

Hicks, N. (1987). Halfway houses and corrections. *Corrections Compendium* 12(October), 1–7.

Huskey, B. (1992). The expanding use of CRCs. *Corrections Today* 54(8), 70–74.

Johnson, J., Bonta, J. (1985). Characteristics of staff and programs in correctional halfway houses. *Journal of Offender Counseling, Services and Rehabilitation* 9, 39–51.

Langworthy, R., Latessa, E. (1993). Treatment of chronic drunk drivers: The Turning Point project. *Journal of Criminal Justice* 21, 265–276.

Langworthy, R., Latessa, E. (1996). Treatment of chronic drunk drivers: A four-year follow-up of the turning point project. *Journal of Criminal Justice* 24, 273–281.

Latessa. E. (1998). *Public protection through offender risk reduction: Putting research into practice.* Washington, DC: National Institute of Corrections.

Latessa, E., Allen, H. (1982). Halfway houses and parole: A national assessment. *Journal of Criminal Justice* 10, 153–163.

Latessa, E., Travis, L. (1991). Halfway house or probation: A comparison of altern-ative dispositions. *Journal of Crime and Justice* 14(1), 53–76.

Latessa, E., Travis, L. (1992). Residential community correctional programs. In: J. Byrne, A. Lurigio (eds) *Smart sentencing? An examination of the emergence of intermediate sentencing.* Beverly Hills, CA: Sage, pp. 166–181.

Latessa, E., Brusman, L., Smith, P. (2010). *Follow-up evaluation of Ohio's community based correctional facility and halfway house programs—Outcome study.* Cincinnati, OH: School of Criminal Justice, University of Cincinnati. Available at www.uc.edu/criminaljustice.

Latessa, E., Langworthy, R., Thomas, A. (1995). *Community residential treatment program evaluation for Talbert House Inc.* Cincinnati, OH: Division of Criminal Justice, University of Cincinnati.

Leon, A., Dziegielewski, S., Tubiak, C. (1999). A program evaluation of a juvenile halfway house: Considerations for strengthening program components. *Evaluation and Program Planning* 22, 141–153.

Lowenkamp, C.T., Latessa, E.J. (2004). Residential community corrections and the risk principle: Lessons learned in Ohio. *Ohio Corrections Research Compendium,* vol. II. Columbus, OH: Ohio Department of Research and Corrections.

Munden, D., Tewksbury, R., Grossi, E. (1999). Intermediate sanctions and the halfway back program in Kentucky. *Criminal Justice Policy Review* 9, 431–449.

National Institute of Corrections (1989). *1989 Directory of residential community corrections facilities in the United States.* Longmont, CO: National Institute of Corrections.

Owen, B. (1991). Normative aspects of alcohol and parole performance. *Drug Problems* 18, 453–476.

Peters, R., Hills, H. (1999). Community treatment and supervision strategies for offenders with co-occurring disorders: What works? In: E. Latessa (ed.) *What works strategic solutions: The international community corrections association examines substance abuse.* Laurel, MD: ACA Press, pp. 81–136.

Petersilia, J., Turner, S., Kahan, J., Peterson, J. (1985). *Granting felons probation: Risks and alternatives.* Santa Monica, CA: Rand.

Pratt, T., Holsinger, A., Latessa, E. (2000). Treating the chronic DUI offender: "Turning Point" ten years later. *Journal of Criminal Justice* 28, 271–281.

Pratt, T., Winston, M. (1999). The search for the Frugal Grail. *Criminal Justice Policy Review* 10(3), 447–471.

President's Commission on Law Enforcement and Administration of Justice (1967). *Corrections.* Washington, DC: U.S. Government Printing Office.

Rush, G. (1992). *The dictionary of criminal justice.* Guilford, CT: Duskin.

Seiter, R., Carlson, E. (1977). Residential inmate aftercare: The state of the art. *Offender Rehabilitation* 4, 78–94.

Sickmund, M. (2010). *Juveniles in residential placement 1997–2010. OJJDP Fact Sheet.* Washington, DC: U.S. Department of Justice.

Solicitor General of Canada (1998). *Mentally disordered offenders.* www.publicsafety. gc.ca/cnt/rsrcs/pblctns/mtldrd-fndr/index-eng.aspx.

Thevenot, C. (2001). Halfway house: Training for freedom. *Las Vegas Review-Journal.* www.lvrj.com/lvrj_home/2001/Apr-15-Sun-2001/news/15812376.html.

U.S. Government Accounting Office (2001). *Prisoner releases: Reintegration of offenders into communities.* Washington, DC: U.S. Government Accounting Office.

Valentine, H. (1991). *Prison alternatives: Crowded federal prisons can transfer more inmates to halfway houses.* Washington, DC: U.S. Government Accounting Office.

Wilson, G. (1985). Halfway house programs for offenders. In: L. Travis (ed.) *Probation, parole and community corrections.* Prospect Heights, IL: Waveland, pp. 151–164.

Chapter 12

SPECIAL POPULATIONS IN COMMUNITY CORRECTIONS

Key Terms

child abuse
child molestation
criminalization of the mentally ill
dangerous sex offenders
date rape
developmentally disabled offenders
exhibitionism
forcible rape
incest

marital rape
Megan's Law
mentally disordered offenders
prostitution
psychopathy
rape
serial rapists
sex offenders
statutory rape

> Successful sex offender management requires more governmental funding. Unfortunately, public aversion to spending money on sex offenders undercuts their management.—R.J. Konopasky

INTRODUCTION

In this chapter, we review the research on special populations of offenders. We have chosen to focus on three specific types of clients in this regard: sex offenders, mentally disordered offenders, and female offenders. These categories do not exhaust the list of possible types of special category offenders.[1]

The Sex Offender

Each state has differing laws that regulate sexual conduct, and correctional systems typically deal with three special needs groups of sexual offenders: rapists, child molesters (pedophiles), and prostitutes. Each of these categories has differing motivations, modes of operation, challenges, and dangers. Almost all are handled,

---

Box 12.1
Sex Offenders

Sex offenders are persons who have committed a sexual act prohibited by law, such as rape, incest, child molestation, or prostitution for sexual, economic, psychological, or situational reasons.

On a given day, there are approximately 234,000 offenders convicted of rape or sexual assault under the care, custody, or control of corrections agencies. Nearly 60 percent of these sex offenders are under conditional supervision in the community.

The median age of the victims of imprisoned sexual assaulters was less than 13 years old; the median age of rape victims was about 22 years.

An estimated 24 percent of those serving time for rape and 19 percent of those serving time for sexual assault had been on probation or parole at the time of the offense for which they were in state prison three years earlier.

Source: Bureau of Justice Statistics (2002).

---

either initially or later, by community corrections. We begin with a brief discussion of public opinion and fear, two factors that color both legal and treatment issues with sex offenders.

Public Opinion and Fear

With the possible exception of the violent offender, no type of correctional client evokes more concern from the public than the sex offender. Sex offenders, especially child molesters, are treated with both disdain and violence. Few offenders are as stigmatized or reviled as child molesters.

Many Americans fear sexual assaulters, gang rapists, serial rapists, stranger rapists, child abductors, and child abusers. Rape is one of the most feared events as well as a frightening and misunderstood crime. Others feel that treatment of sexual assaulters is undeserved

---

Box 12.2
Prostitution

Prostitution is offering, agreeing to engage in, or engaging in a sex act with another in return for a fee, money, or other consideration.

Box 12.3
Exhibitionism

Exhibitionism is exposure of one's genitalia or other body parts to others in inappropriate circumstances or public places. An exhibitionist is the one who exposes those parts to others.

---

and ineffective. Politicians tend to follow public opinion,[2] despite evidence that there is widespread support for treatment and rehabilitation of offenders ranging from the very young to geriatric prisoners. Opinion polls overestimate the amount of support for punitive approaches to special needs clients, particularly for juveniles (Cullen & Moon, 2002). There is no doubt that public sentiment works against the establishment and funding of treatment programs and options. However, substantial evidence shows that treatment works (Lipton et al., 1999; Sherman

Table 12.1 Meta-analyses Demonstrating that Treatment Reduces Sexual Recidivism

	Number of studies	Percent reduction
Gallagher et al. (1999)	25	21
Hanson et al. (2002)	43	12
Lösel and Schmucker (2005)	69	37

et al., 1997; Yates, 2002). Specifically, three meta-analyses on the topic have been conducted (Table 12.1), and results from each review indicate that treatment has an appreciable impact on recidivism. First, Gallagher and colleagues (1999) located a total of 25 studies and found a 21 percent reduction in sexual recidivism overall. Second, Hanson et al. (2002) reviewed 43 studies involving more than 9,000 sex offenders and found a 12 percent reduction in sexual recidivism. More recently, Lösel and Schmucker (2005) quantitatively synthesized 69 studies and found a 37 percent reduction in sexual recidivism compared to controls.

Box 12.4
Dangerous Sex Offenders

Washington State's 1990 Community Protection Act was the first law authorizing public notification when **dangerous sex offenders** are released into the community. It was thought that sex offender registration laws are necessary because:

- Ex-offenders pose a high risk of reoffending after release from custody.
- Protecting the public from sex offenders is a primary governmental interest, and the rights of sex offenders take a back seat to public interest.
- Releasing certain information about sex offenders to public agencies and the general public will contribute to public safety.

It took the brutal 1994 murder–rape of Megan Kanka (1994) to prompt public demand for broad-based community notification. President Clinton signed **Megan's Law** in 1996, which allows the states discretion to establish criteria for disclosure, but compels them to make personal and private information about registered sex offenders available to the public. It was believed that such notification:

- Assists law enforcement agencies during investigations.
- Establishes legal grounds to hold offenders.
- Deters sex offenders from committing new offenses.
- Offers citizens information useful in protecting their children from victimization.

Some states mandate registration and penalize nonregistration with imprisonment. Sex offender registration has been criticized as a flawed strategy for controlling sex crime, reflecting a skewed view of sex offenders, and encouraging vigilantism. Probation and parole agents' responsibilities were impacted negatively.

Sources: Presser and Gunnison (1999); Zavitz and Farkas (2000).

The Rapist

There are many different types of rapists, including date rapists, stranger rapists, family rapists, acquaintance rapists, gang rapists, homosexual rapists, and serial rapists. All have three things in common: a victim or victims, sexual intercourse or attempted sexual intercourse with persons against their will, and force or threat of use of force. Most of the victims are female and view rape as a brutal personal assault. Many rape victims feel that the act was not so much sexually motivated as much as it was a physical assault fed by a desire for violent coercion and power. In this light, rape should be seen as an act of violence, not an act fueled primarily by sexual arousal. The female is almost never responsible for the act, although defense attorneys may use this line of argument in their efforts to blame the victim.

Forcible Rape

The definition of rape and forcible rape varies across jurisdictions, and the Federal Bureau of Investigation (FBI) (2009) defines rape as carnal knowledge of a female forcibly and against her will, including assaults and attempts to commit rape by force or threat of force. Not included are statutory rape (without force) and other sex offenses. This definition does not define rape of a male as forcible rape.

Box 12.5
Rape

Rape is sexual intercourse or attempted sexual intercourse with persons against their will, by force or threat of force. **Date rape** is forcible rape in which the victim has consented to the company of the offender but has not agreed to have sexual intercourse.

Statutory rape is sexual intercourse with a person who has consented in fact but is deemed, because of age, to be legally incapable of consent.

The extent of **forcible rape** in the nation is only estimated. In 2008, the FBI reported about 89,000 rapes of females, but the National Crime Victimization Survey (Rand, 2009) estimates that there were more than 200,000 rapes of females aged 12 and older. This suggests that not all incidents were reported to the police. Many victims fail to report because they are embarrassed; they blame themselves; they feel the police will not act; they anticipate that they, as the victim, will be blamed for the crime; or they know their rapist and fear retaliation (their assaulters were fathers, brothers, uncles, friends, or neighbors).

A darker side of rape can be seen when examining sexual assault of young children. The Bureau of Justice Statistics (2002) reported that in each sexual assault category except forcible rape, children below the age of 12 represented about half of the victims. They represent one in eight forcible rapes, and females under age 12 represent one in six of reported rapes. Almost one-half of the offenders of victims under age 6 were family members, as were four in 10 offenders who sexually assaulted juveniles aged 12 through 17. Knowing that a child under age 6 was assaulted in the residence suggests the most likely offender was a juvenile acquaintance aged 12 through 17 or a family member aged 24 through 34. Schmalleger (1996, p. 69) reports:

> 20 percent of female victims under age 12 had been raped by their fathers, 26 percent were attacked by other relatives, and 50 percent were assaulted by friends and acquaintances. Only four percent of rape victims under 12 were attacked by strangers.

Both official and victimization statistics significantly underreport rape. Other victim studies suggest that at least 20 percent of adult women and 12 percent of adolescent girls have experienced sexual abuse or assault sometime in their lives.[3]

Box 12.6
Crimes Against Children

Child molestation is any one of several forms of handling, fondling, or other contacts of a sexual nature with a child, including photographing children in lewd poses. The victim may be subject to rape, sodomy, indecent exposure, or murder. "Molester" refers to the one who commits these acts.

Child neglect is any deliberate act by the parents or legal guardian of minors that deprives minors of life's necessities, including protection, adequate sustenance, and behavioral regulation. This includes ignoring the minor. It is the willful failure to provide for one's child or ward.

Box 12.7
Child Abuse

Child abuse is any act of commission or omission that endangers or impairs a child's physical or emotional health and development: sexual abuse, exploitation, negligent treatment, and maltreatment by a person who is responsible for the child's welfare.

The major forms are (a) physical, including neglect or lack of adequate supervision; (b) emotional, including deprivation; and (c) sexual. The abuser is someone usually close to the victim, such as mother, father, stepparent, grandparent, or other caretaker who engages in a repeated pattern of behavior. Rarely is the abuser a total stranger.

Box 12.8
Incest

Incest is sexual relations between close relatives other than husband and wife.

Box 12.9
Child Victimizers

Offenders who had victimized a child are, on average, five years older than violent offenders who had committed their crimes against adults. Nearly 25 percent of child victimizers were age 40 or older, but about 10 percent of inmates with adult victims fall into that age range.

Source: Bureau of Justice Statistics (2002).

Stranger-to-Stranger Rape

When victims are attacked by strangers, the attack is likely to be more violent and the attacker is likely to be armed and to threaten the victim. The offender is likely to be a substance abuser (Hsu & Starzynski, 1990); the victim is likely to be harmed physically; and the viciously harmed female is more likely to report the attack. Most victims were not provocateurs (Warren et al., 1999).

Serial rapists (offenders raping several victims in three or more separate events) are particularly problematic among the stranger-to-stranger category for many of the victims who are killed or simply "disappear." Studies of serial rapists suggest that they are more likely to be white rather than minority status, select

---

Box 12.10
Psychopathy

Hare defines the clinical construct of **psychopathy** as a combination of interpersonal, affective, and lifestyle characteristics. Interpersonally, psychopaths are arrogant, callous, dominant, grandiose, manipulative, and superficial. Affectively, they lack guilt or anxiety and are short-tempered and unable to form strong emotional bonds with others. Interpersonal and affective characteristics are frequently found with a socially deviant lifestyle that includes impulsive and irresponsible behavior and a tendency to ignore or flagrantly violate social conventions and mores. While not all psychopaths come to the attention of the criminal justice system, they are at high risk of violence and aggression. In maximum security prisons, they may constitute 20–25 percent of the general population.

Source: Hare (2002).

---

victims based on sexual attractiveness and vulnerability (Stevens, 1999), rape their victims for longer periods of time, and use more profanity, be sadistic, and escalate levels of violence over time (Knight et al., 1998). A study of United Kingdom serial rapists indicates itinerancy and mobility. A majority of attacks were initiated within five miles of the victim's residence. Offenders tended to target locations where numbers of suitable victims were available, and rapists spent considerable time "prowling" or "hunting" over those larger areas in search of victims, occasionally stumbling upon victims during relatively sophisticated property offenses. Perpetrators are more likely to have antisocial ("psychopathic") personalities (Davies & Dale, 1996). Victims of serial rapists generally require extensive therapy over long periods of time, sometimes in therapeutic communities (Winick & Levine, 1992).

Acquaintance Rape

At least one-half of the rapes reported to police involve someone known to the victim, including family members, friends, and suitors. Victimization incidents involving female victims under age 12 suggest that this type of rape is vastly under-reported. We focus briefly on date rape and marital rape in order to comprehend the dynamics of and treatment facing offenders and the correctional system.

Date Rape

Date rape, often defined as unlawful forced sexual intercourse with a woman against her will, occurs within the context of a dating or courting relationship. Date rape is a frequent event and is not limited to this nation. A survey of Canadian college women found that one in four had sexual relations when they did not want to during the past year.[4] An estimated 15 to 25 percent of all college women in the nation are victims of rape or attempted rape. The actual incidence is probably higher, as many victims blame themselves for not being more forceful in their own defense or for using alcohol or other drugs prior to the rape. (Date rape differs from campus gang rape in that usually only one perpetrator is involved in date rape, the victim and victimizer know each other intimately, the event is not generally viewed by others, and the sexual assault is better viewed as a coercive sexual encounter than as a violent rape.)

The perpetrator may feel that he has invested so much time and money in his date that he is owed sexual relations, that sexual intimacy is a validating element in the progression of the relationship, that other couples in similarly lengthy dating processes had begun sexual activities, or that "she said 'no' but really meant 'yes'." Perhaps one in 10 date rapes is reported to the police because victims are embarrassed or frightened; some do not perceive date rape as "real rape," which they believe requires an attack by a stranger; or fear they will be stigmatized or victimized by the police. Some men (particularly adolescents) have difficulty relating to women and treat them more as sexual objects who should be responsive to their sexual appetites rather than as worthy and independent partners who should be treated as such (Kerschener, 1996). Stereotyped relations and perceptions abound in the area of rape.

Marital Rape

Marital rape, or spousal rape, is rape by a male domiciled with his wife, although the rapist/victim role can be reversed. Generally, it is spousal rape if the husband forces his wife to have nonconsensual intercourse. Until recently, a legally married man could not be prosecuted for raping his wife under the "marital exemption"; a woman entering marriage was believed to implicitly give her consent to sexual intercourse at the behest of her husband. Over the past two decades, research into spousal abuse has identified marital rape as one part of a continuing pattern of spousal abuse, sometimes accompanied by sadistic and violent beatings. Every person is worthy of protection under the law, and almost every state has now enacted legislation defining marital rape as a crime.

The extent of marital rape is unknown, but it is a persistent problem in a large number of marriages (Straus, 1988). It is underreported in part because society tends to blame and judge rape victims harshly. Women assaulted by their husbands have reported that the assault was one of a series of similar attacks (Riggs et al., 1992) occurring in three cycles: tension building, acute battering, and subsequent contrite behavior by the husband, with recurrent cycles. Considerable evidence suggests that homes in which spousal rape occurs are characterized by high levels of tension and distrust among spouses and their children (Mahoney & Williams, 1998). A study in Great Britain found 13 percent of wives had sexual intercourse with their husbands against their will and, in total, one in five had been raped either inside or outside of marriage (Painter & Farrington, 1998). Finally, multiple sexual victimization (such as incest and marital rape) is a co-occurring problem among victims and, to some extent, among perpetrators. New psychotherapy models and treatments are needed (Walker, 2000).

Treatment for Sex Offenders

The risk factors emphasized for the prediction of sexual recidivism have historically been more static in nature. Examples of static risk factors include age, previous offense history, onset of sexually deviant interests, marital status, and specific offense characteristics such as stranger victim, male victim, and contact/non-contact offense (Hanson & Bussière, 1998; Harris, 2006). More recently, however, researchers have also underscored the importance of dynamic risk factors for sexual recidivism. Furthermore, these dynamic risk factors can be further subdivided into stable (or relatively enduring) and acute (or rapidly changing) risk factors (Hanson & Harris, 2000). Stable risk factors include social influences, sexual entitlement, attitudes, sexual self-regulation, and general self-regulation (Hanson & Harris, 2000; Hanson & Morton-Bourgon, 2004). On the other hand, acute dynamic factors include access to victims, noncooperation with supervision, and anger (Hanson & Harris, 2000). Mann and colleagues (2010) have referred to these risk factors as *psychologically meaningful risk factors*.

Recall from an earlier chapter that the risk principle states that criminal behavior is predictable using actuarial assessments of both static and dynamic risk factors. The most commonly used static risk assessment tools for sexual recidivism include the Static-99 (Hanson & Thornton, 2000), Risk-Matrix-2000, and the Sex Offender Risk Appraisal Guide (Quinsey et al., 1998). In selecting risk assessment tools for sex offenders, it is important to consider both sexual and general recidivism as separate outcomes. This means that it is important for corrections professionals to assess all offenders with a composite measure of risk and need, but they should also use an additional measure to predict sexual recidivism. In fact, many sex offenders tend to score low risk for general recidivism, but at the same time they can be high risk for sexual recidivism (McGrath et al., 2011). Failure to use a sex offense specific tool could result in the misclassification of sex offenders.

Similar to general populations of offenders, offenders identified as high risk for recidivism should receive more intensive services than those identified as low risk for recidivism. In the literature, the evidence supporting the application of the risk principle to sex offenders is beginning to emerge. For example, Hanson et al. (2009) found better treatment effects with higher-risk offenders compared to lower-risk offenders. Similarly, Lovins and co-workers (2009) found that higher-risk sex offenders had lower rates of general recidivism when they received more intensive services, such as residential placement, compared with less intensive services. Finally, Wakeling and colleagues (2012) recently reviewed the literature and concluded that lower-risk sex offenders should be kept separate from higher-risk sex offenders, and treatment services should not interfere with other activities that encourage a prosocial lifestyle.

In terms of treatment, there is considerable heterogeneity of sex crimes and specific acts of violence. As a result, treatment programs are as varied as crime type; some treatment programs fail to focus on those factors contributing to the commission of the crime and thus erroneously address objectives that would not lessen reoffending. A study of sex offender treatment in Vermont outlined the goals of an institutional treatment program:

- Get the offender to accept responsibility for his actions and the harm done to the victim and others.
- Deal with distorted thinking used to justify his actions.
- Teach the offender to understand the impact of his behavior on victims and show more empathic behavior with other people around him (recognize others' emotional distress, identify another's perspective, communicate empathy toward others, etc.).
- Address such competency issues as anger management, substance abuse treatment issues, communicating with opposite gender adults, improving dating skills, and seeking therapy.
- Deal with sexual arousal to reduce inappropriate object arousal and enhance arousal with an appropriate adult partner.
- Plan relapse prevention that teaches the offender how and when to intervene in his own patterns of behavior that lead up to a sexual offense (drinking and remaining aloof, alone, and physically inactive can build up to fantasizing about a victim, and this requires such personal intervention as initiating counseling, attending Alcoholics Anonymous group meetings, and calling a designated crime prevention hotline). Relapse prevention includes teaching offenders how to recognize the chain of events leading up to their current offense and to practice strategies for breaking this chain.
- Plan for release into the community and set up a support team of people who know the offender's issues and can provide support and monitoring, including sex offender-specific outpatient treatment.

Six years after release, 5 percent of the men who completed the Vermont treatment program had committed another sexual offense and were caught, in contrast to 30 percent of the men who got only partial treatment (left the program or were expelled from the program for rules violations). Thirty percent of the incarcerated men who refused to enter the program were arrested again for some form of sexual abuse (Cumming & Finch, 2001).

A study of adolescent sexual assaulters from a Wisconsin (Nesbit et al., 2004) secure juvenile correctional institution included perpetrators of sexual assault against children, rapists of same-age or older victims, and nonsex-offense-adjudicated adolescents. The rapists and child offender groups completed a mandatory, serious sex offender treatment program that included group psychotherapy, general education, sex education, behavior management programming, and individual and family therapy. Eight years later, adolescent sex offenders were found to less frequently offend sexually than the nonsex-offending adolescent delinquents, although all three groups were significantly more likely to be involved with sexual assaults than was the general male population in the nation.

Perhaps one of the most extensive reviews of treatment effectiveness on various types of sexual offenders was published by Yates (2002), who concluded that treatment can significantly reduce sexual reoffending for a variety of offenders, both juvenile and adult, if behavioral-specific treatments are based on an assessment of needs. Effective treatments also involve the development of a treatment plan, delivery of treatment in a coherent fashion by competent therapists, and the ability to adjust treatment if it is not working. For juveniles, treatment targets include:

■ Increasing responsibility and accountability for behavior;
■ addressing cognitive, affective, and behavioral factors that support sexual offending;
■ reducing deviant sexual arousal;
■ improving relationships among family members;
■ enhancing victim empathy;
■ improving social skills;
■ developing healthy attitudes toward relationships and sex;
■ reducing the effects of personal trauma;
■ targeting cognitive distortions.

Yates reported on treatment effectiveness of adolescents six years after a comprehensive, cognitive-behavioral, relapse prevention sexual offender program. Effectiveness was measured by recidivism, comparing a treatment group with a similar nontreatment group. Results are shown in Table 12.2. Treated sex offenders recidivated significantly less frequently and less violently. Sex offender criminal behavior is amenable to intervention, and the preponderance of evidence is that treatment works for most perpetrators (although there remain considerable challenges to develop effective treatment for the relatively rare psychopathic sex offender).

Table 12.2 Comparison of Recidivism of Treated and Untreated Adolescent Sex Offenders

Group	Recidivated sexually	Recidivated violently but not sexually	Recidivated nonviolently
Treated	5.2%	18.9%	20.7%
Untreated	17.8	32.2	50.0

Source: Yates, P. (2002). What works? Effective intervention with sex offenders. In H. Allen (ed.) *What works? Risk reduction: Interventions for special needs offenders.* Lanham, MD: American Correctional Association, p. 148.

Box 12.11
Sex Offender Treatment: Does it Work?

The typical justice response to sex offenders involves punishment and inca-pacitation by eliminating offender access to victims. Because almost all sex offenders return to the community, incapacitation without treatment does not reduce reoffending. In Vermont, the cost of a relapse (justice and victim services) is estimated to be more than $138,000.

McGrath (1995) provides a synopsis of 68 outcome studies and clearly shows that treatment in the community is effective, particularly more recent programs that use relapse prevention treatment models delivered in group therapy sessions. Typical treatment goals include accepting responsibility for the offense, developing empathy with the victim, improving social compet-ence, controlling deviant sexual arousal, and developing relapse prevention skills. More recent treatment programs (since 1980) appear to be more effective.

Reoffending rates for treated offenders are 80 percent less than for untreated offenders; persons who complete treatment programs (vs. drop-ping out) are 77 percent less likely to recidivate. Sex offenders treated in relapse prevention (vs. behavioral change) groups are 73 percent less likely to reoffend. Finally, the reoffending rate for sex offenders treated since 1980 is 6 percent. Furby and colleagues (1989) argue it is no more than 10 percent but argue for longer follow-up periods after treatment.

McGrath concludes that results from the 68 sex offender outcome studies reviewed show that treatment works, is cost effective, and can be provided in communities under probation control.

Source: McGrath (1995).

MENTAL HEALTH DISORDERS

In 2005, the Bureau of Justice Statistics estimated that more than 1.2 million offenders with mental illnesses were incarcerated in the nation's jails and prisons (James & Glaze, 2006). About 56 percent of state prisoners, 45 percent of federal prisoners, and 64 percent of local jail inmates reported having a mental health problem. Most have co-occurring substance abuse problems, either alcohol or other drugs (or both).

For constitutional and policy reasons, most mental health facilities existing in the mid-twentieth century have closed; those remaining primarily service court-ordered forensic patients remanded by courts, including those not guilty by reason of insanity or guilty but mentally ill, those who are a danger to self and others, and those transferred by probate court order due to mental illnesses associated with or as a result of imprisonment. A few are dangerous sex offenders who have completed their sentences but were ordered into mental health facilities due to the perceived probability of their repeating heinous crimes.

The Sentencing Project (2002, p. 2) argues that mental disorders among prisoners occur at least five times the rate found in the general population and represent criminalization of the mentally ill: "the increased likelihood of people with mental illness being processed through the criminal justice system instead of through the mental health system." Criminalization of the mentally ill has occurred because:

- The deinstitutionalization movement that began in the 1960s was predicated on local communities providing sufficient mental health services, but funding was not forthcoming to underwrite treatment in the community.
- Of reductions in treatment spending and availability, including fragmentation of treatment services.
- Barriers arose to involuntary commitment, including a court-ordered finding that the detained are either a clear and present danger to themelves or others or are so markedly disabled by their conditions as not to be able to care for themselves. Involuntary hospitalization also requires legal representation and a full judicial hearing.

In addition, U.S. Supreme Court decisions require that persons detained involuntarily under the color of treatment must receive treatment. Many states cannot or will not fund treatment services.

Box 12.12
Probation Supervision of the Mentally Disordered Offender

Despite claims by mental health advocates that "people with mental illness pose no more of a crime threat than do other members of the general public" (National Mental Health Association, 1987), strong evidence suggests that this is not the case. However, for the correctional system, the issue of whether the mentally ill are more "dangerous" than members of the general public is not a particularly relevant question. For mentally ill individuals who have been convicted of an offense, a more appropriate question is whether they pose more of a risk than other offender groups being supervised in the community.

Latessa (1996) compared arrest, conviction, and probation outcome data for several groups under probation supervision. The probation groups included sex offenders, drug offenders, high-risk offenders, regularly supervised offenders, and mentally disordered offenders. He found that mentally disordered offenders performed as well, and in some cases better, than other probation groups and concluded that mentally ill offenders can and are being supervised in the community without increasing risk to public safety.

Source: Latessa (1996).

Box 12.13
Criminal Thinking and Mental Illness

Morgan and colleagues (2010) studied 414 adult offenders with mental illness (265 males, 149 females) and found:

- 66 percent had belief systems supportive of criminal lifestyle (based on Psychological Inventory of Criminal Thinking Scale).
- When compared to other offender samples, male offenders with mental illness scored similar or higher than nonmentally disordered offenders.
- On Criminal Sentiments Scale, 85 percent of men and 72 percent of women with mental illness had antisocial attitudes, values, and beliefs, which were higher than incarcerated sample without mental illness.

They concluded:

- Criminal thinking styles differentiate people who commit crimes from those who do not, independent of mental illness.
- Incarcerated persons with mental illness are both mentally ill *and* criminal.
- Mental illness and criminality need to be treated as co-occurring problems.

Source: Center for Behavioral Health Services Criminal Justice
Research Policy Brief, April 2010. Rutgers University.

Box 12.14
Developmentally Disabled Prisoners

Few jails or prisons have sufficient facilities and programs to handle the special needs of developmentally disabled offenders, and hospitals and other health facilities are seldom capable of administering correctional programs with sufficient security to protect society's rights. Without alternatives, judges are left with no other choice than to sentence those individuals to prison.

- Some developmentally disabled offenders require incarceration because of the seriousness of their crimes or their records as repeat offenders, but most other developmentally disabled offenders could be diverted from prison to community treatment programs while still ensuring the safety of the community.
- There is tremendous variation in estimates of the number of developmentally disabled persons incarcerated in prison: earlier research

indicates that the percentage of those offenders is higher than the percentage within the general population, while the most recent studies place the percentage at about the same level as that within the general population.

- Developmentally disabled offenders are often used by their peers, reflecting their great need for approval and acceptance. They have no long-term perspective and little ability to think in a causal way to understand the consequences of their actions.
- Developmentally disabled persons are often victimized or abused by other inmates.
- Identifying offenders who have special needs is essential for planning individualized programs. Due process, functional diagnosis, and evaluation performed by specially trained staff utilizing sophisticated assessment tools and procedures are essential.
- Because the developmentally challenged are usually undetected, violations of the legal rights of such persons are frequent.
- Criminal justice and corrections personnel are not presently trained to handle the special problems and needs of such offenders.
- Matters of competency relating to diminished mental capacity should be considered at the first point of contact with the criminal justice system and at each decision point in the continuum.
- Developmentally disabled offenders should be assigned to programs that meet their individual needs; some may be mixed in with the regular prison population; some need a segregated environment; some would benefit most from a community setting; and others might be placed in a regular developmentally disabled group home or guardianship arrangement.
- A survey of local jurisdictions revealed the need for training about the developmentally challenged for criminal justice personnel who normally do not distinguish between the developmentally challenged and mental illness; the need for early identification of such persons once they come into contact with the criminal justice system; and the need for more community resources, particularly residential programs, to serve this category of offenders.

FEMALE OFFENDERS

Male offenders constitute the majority (more than 80 percent) of adults under correctional control. The much smaller female offender population is handled primarily within the community corrections system, although the number of imprisoned females is increasing faster than that of male prisoners. This section looks at the crimes that place females under correctional control, the process by which they are assigned to and exit from community corrections, and the special problems female offenders face.

Female Corrections Populations

There are more than one million women under the care, custody, or control of adult criminal justice authorities, and almost 9,000 juvenile females were under secure and nonsecure state-managed and contract institutions. This translates into a rate of nearly 1 percent of American adult females having some correctional status on any given day. About 85 percent were supervised in the community, and 15 percent were confined in jails and prisons. Most violent female offenders are not confined; about 65,000 women convicted of violence are under supervision by probation authorities compared to some 3,300 in local jails, 21,000 in state prisons, and almost 1,000 in federal prisons. Among convicted female drug traffickers, almost 58,000 are on probation, 5,300 in local jails, 13,500 in state prisons, and almost 5,300 in federal prison (see Table 12.3).

Women Serving a Sentence

Nearly two-thirds of women under probation supervision are white, but nearly two-thirds of those confined in local jails and state and federal prisons are

Table 12.3 Types of Sentences Imposed by State Court, Female Felons

Most serious conviction offense	Percent of felons sentenced to:			
	Incarceration prison	Jail	Nonincarceration probation	Other
All offenses	25%	31%	40%	3%
Violent offenses	32%	31%	34%	3%
Murder	81	7	11	1
Sexual assault[a]	44	27	25	4
Robbery	50	24	24	1
Aggravated assault	23	35	39	3
Other violent	37	31	29	3
Property offenses	22	31	44	3
Burglary	39	43	25	3
Larceny	19	33	45	3
Fraud	22	27	48	3
Drug offenses	26	28	41	
Possession	21	30	43	6
Trafficking	29	27	40	4
Weapons	27	33	35	5
Other offenses	27	39	33	3

[a] Includes rape.

Source: Durose, M.R., Langan, P. (2005). *State court sentencing of convicted felons*. Washington, DC: Bureau of Justice Statistics, p. 23.

minority: black, Hispanic, and other races. Those on probation or in local jails are younger than those in prisons; nearly one-quarter of federal prison inmates are at least 45 years old. Adult women under correctional control are substantially less likely than the general population to never have been married.

Yet nearly seven out of 10 women under correctional sanction have minor children under the age of 18. These females report an average of 2.1 minor children; these estimates translate into more than 1.3 million minor children as the offspring of women under correctional sanction. About two-thirds of state prison inmates had lived with their children prior to entering prison.

Female prisoners generally have more difficult economic circumstances than male prisoners prior to entering prison. About four in 10 women in state prison reported that they had been employed full time prior to their arrest, but more than one-third of the employed females had earned incomes of less than $600 per month prior to arrest. Nearly 30 percent of female inmates reported receiving welfare assistance.

Health issues were more problematic for female than male offenders. About 3.5 percent of the female inmate population was HIV positive. About one-half of the confined female offenders reported they had been using alcohol, other drugs, or both at the time of the offense for which they had been incarcerated. Illicit drug use was reported more often than alcohol use. On every measure of illicit drug abuse (ever used, using regularly, using in the month before the offense, and using at the time of the offense), female offenders had higher rates of use than male offenders. Male offenders, however, had higher alcohol use on every measure of alcohol ingestion. An estimated 25 percent of women on probation, 30 percent of women in local jails and in state prisons, and 15 percent of women in federal prison had been consuming alcohol at the time of their offense. Nearly one in three women serving time in state prisons said that they had committed the offense that brought them to prison in order to obtain money to support their need for drugs.

Nearly 56 percent of women substance abusers in state prisons reported having received treatment for their alcohol and other drug abuse, and one in five said treatment had occurred since entry to prison. Another one-third said they had joined a voluntary program (such as Alcoholics Anonymous and Narcotics Anonymous) since entering prison.

Forty-four percent of women under correctional authority reported that they were assaulted physically or sexually at some time during their lives. Forty-eight percent of women reporting an assault said that it had occurred before age 18.

Women in Jail

The number of women in local jails declined from just over 100,000 in 2007 to just over 90,000 in 2012. Among convicted female inmates, nearly two-fifths reported that they had committed their first offense under the influence of drugs. Approximately four in 10 used drugs daily. About one in four convicted female jail inmates reported that they committed their current offense to get money to buy drugs. Some two-thirds of the jailed women had children under the age of 18, and most of these were with either a grandparent or father.

A study of mental illness among female jail inmates (Teplin et al., 1997) in Chicago found that 80 percent of their representative sample met criteria for at least one lifetime psychiatric disorder, most commonly substance abuse or dependence, and post-traumatic stress disorder. Rates for all psychiatric disorders (particularly depression) were significantly higher than those of the general population. Investigators concluded that few female jail inmates received in-facility treatment, primarily because inmates' needs far exceeded current resources.

Women who use drugs often have low self-esteem and little self-confidence and may feel powerless. In addition, minority women may face additional cultural and language barriers that can hinder or affect treatment and recovery. Many drug-using women do not seek treatment because they are afraid. They fear not being able to take care of or keep their children, reprisals from their spouses or boyfriends, and punishment from the authorities in the community. Many women report that their drug-using male partners initiated them into drug abuse. Finally, research indicates that drug-dependent women have great difficulty abstaining from drugs when the lifestyle of their male partner is one that supports drug use.

Approximately 40 percent of female jail inmates grew up in a single-parent household, and an additional 17 percent lived in a household without either parent. Close to one-third of all women in jail had a parent or guardian who abused alcohol or other drugs, and four in 10 reported that another family member (usually brother or sister) had been incarcerated.

This brief examination of jail inmates suggests a group of offenders with high needs who were victimized frequently as they were growing up. Broken homes, sexual and physical abuse, minority status, and parental/guardian abuse of alcohol or drugs characterize a large portion of the female population. This segment of offenders is not generally likely to receive effective treatment for the major, underlying problems. After an average stay of less than six months, most will be returned to the community to continue to break their drug dependences and, for the most part, their efforts will fail without intensive assistance. It is possible for drug-dependent women, of any age, to overcome the illness of drug addiction. Those who have been most successful have had the help and support of significant others, family members, treatment providers, friends, and the community. We discuss specific issues later in this chapter.

Women on Parole

Despite the recent emphasis on studying female offenders, relatively little is known about females on parole. In 2008, females were an estimated 12 percent of all parolees, up from

Female on street-cleaning work detail, San Francisco Jail, San Francisco Sheriff's Department/Sheriff's Work Alternative Program. [*Photo courtesy of Harry Allen.*]

8 percent in 1990. That translates into more than 100,000 female parolees. The growth in the number of female paroles reflects higher offending rates, arrests per offense, increased commitments to prison per arrest, and parole recommitments. The lifetime likelihood of a female going to state or federal prison is now more than 1 percent, although Hispanic women have a 50 percent higher likelihood than white women. Black, non-Hispanic women have a likelihood of incarceration that is seven times that of white women.

Most women sent to prison have several factors that will work against successful reintegration following parole. Alcohol and other drug use, unemployment and few occupational skills, a history of sexual abuse, and incomplete education are difficult to overcome when treatment is a low priority to resource-strapped systems. A gap exists between institutional treatment and transition to the community. Without meaningful treatment, one should not be surprised at recidivism indicators.

Women and Substance Abuse Treatment

There is widespread need for effective treatment programs for substance abuse by female offenders. Research has shown that women receive the most benefit from drug treatment programs that provide comprehensive services for meeting their basic needs, including access to the following:

- food, clothing, and shelter
- transportation
- job counseling and training
- legal assistance
- literacy training and educational opportunities
- parenting training
- family therapy
- couples counseling
- medical care
- child care
- social services
- social support
- psychological assessment and mental health care
- assertiveness training.

A comprehensive spectrum of services is needed for female offenders at every level of the criminal justice system. After all, almost all return to unconditional release into the community. Traditional drug treatment programs may not be appropriate for female offenders because those programs may not provide the services needed. In addition, research also suggests that a continuing relationship with a treatment provider is an important factor throughout treatment for female offenders. Any individual may experience lapses and relapses during the treatment process. Learning how to identify and avoid circumstances that may lead to relapse is important. This is a treatment thrust for many community programs, particularly therapeutic communities.

Jail-based projects include therapeutic communities (Sisters in Sober Treatment and Empowered Recovery or SISTERS, San Francisco, California; and Stepping Out, San Diego) that have a wide range of treatment programs (modalities). Aftercare (post-jail release) components provide intensive outpatient services and sober living, job development and placement assistance, referrals to supportive services, and a mutual-help group created for and by ex-offenders (Kassebaum, 1999). Prison-based therapeutic communities are becoming more numerous, and their clients have significantly lower relapse and recidivism rates than those who do not enroll (Nielsen et al., 1990).

The state of Georgia faced a correctional population with 10 percent of males and 27 percent of females classified as mental health cases. The Georgia Board of Pardons and Parole reported on the Georgia Treatment and Aftercare for Probationers and Parolees (TAPP) program to boost post-prison support for Georgia's mentally ill and developmentally disabled offenders. A TAPP mental health professional in each service area acts as case manager to nonviolent mental health offenders returned to the area, monitoring offenders' behavior and arranging ongoing community support and treatment. Such transitional programs are examples of the needed coordination between incarceration and gradual reintegration into the community for female offenders (Georgia Board of Pardons and Parole, 2000). Such coordination is needed throughout the community corrections system.

SUMMARY

Our discussion of special needs offenders suggests that they are not a unitary group of similarly situated offenders, but a complex combination of individuals facing the problems of living complicated by self-defeating behaviors that require change. Each group has certain distinct characteristics and problems that are related to offense situations and basic needs, almost all of which are not addressed effectively. While they are alike in that they have been convicted of criminal activities, underlying those events are unaddressed social, personal, and medical needs best handled through treatment. Future corrections will need to apply a range of classification systems to determine the most effective way to manage any group of offenders and maximize public safety.

Review Questions

1. Explain "special needs" offenders.
2. What effects have public fears had on the treatment of sex offenders?
3. Differentiate between date rape and campus gang rape.
4. Does treatment for sex offenders work?
5. Why are offenders with mental health disorders concentrated in correctional systems?

6. Explain why criminalization of the mentally ill has occurred.
7. How can corrections better respond to developmentally disabled offenders?

Notes

1 Other special needs offenders include geriatric offenders and clients with HIV. Gang members (security threat groups) are usually subsumed under institutional corrections.
2 Kerschener (1996).
3 Browne (1992).
4 DeKeseredy et al. (1993).

Recommended Readings

Hammett, R., Roberts, C., Kennedy, S. (2001). Health-related issues in prison reentry. *Crime & Delinquency* 47(3), 390–409.
Lowenkamp, C., Holsinger, A., Latessa, E. (2001). Risk/need assessment, offender classification, and the role of childhood abuse. *Criminal Justice and Behavior* 28(5), 543–563.
Sentencing Project, The (2002). *Mentally ill offenders in the criminal justice system: An analysis and prescription*. Washington, DC: TSP. www.sentencingproject.org/doc/publications/sl_mentallyilloffenders.pdf.
Travis, J. (2000). *But they all come back: Rethinking prisoner reentry*. Washington, DC: Office of Justice Programs.

References

Allen, H. (2002). In: Allen, H. (ed.) *What works? Risk reduction: Interventions for special needs offenders*. Lanham, MD: American Correctional Association.
Browne, A. (1992). Violence against women. *Journal of the American Medical Association* 267, 3184–3189.
Bureau of Justice Statistics (2000). *Probation and parole in the United States*. Washington, DC: BJS.
Bureau of Justice Statistics (2002). *Criminal offenders statistics*. Washington, DC: BJS.
Bureau of Justice Statistics (2003). *Census of state and correctional facilities, 2000*. Washington, DC: BJS.
Cullen, F., Moon, M. (2002). Reaffirming rehabilitation: Public support for correctional treatment. In: H. Allen (ed.) *What works? Risk reduction: Interventions for special needs offenders*. Lanham, MD: American Correctional Association, pp. 7–26.
Cumming, G., Finch, S. (2001). A primer on the understanding, use and calculation of confidence intervals based on central and noncentral distributions. *Educational and Psychological Measurement* 61, 530–572.

Davies, A., Dale, A. (1996). Locating the stranger rapist. *Medicine, Science and the Law* 36(2), 146–156.

DeKeseredy, W., Schwartz, M., Tait, K. (1993). Sexual assault and stranger aggression on a Canadian campus. *Sex Roles* 28(2), 263–277.

Durose, M.R., Langan, P. (2005). *State court sentencing of convicted felons, 2002.* Washington, DC: Bureau of Justice Statistics, p. 23.

Federal Bureau of Investigation (2009). *Crime in the United States 2008.* Washington, DC: Federal Bureau of Investigation.

Furby, L., Weinrott, M., Blackshaw, L. (1989). Sex offender recidivism: A review. *Psychological Bulletin* 105, 3–30.

Gallagher, C.A., Wilson, D.B., Hirschfield, P., Coggeshall, M., MacKenzie, D.L. (1999). A quantitative review of the effects of sex offender treatment on sexual reoffending. *Corrections Management Quarterly* 3, 19–29.

Georgia Board of Pardons and Parole (2000). *FY 2000 annual report.* Georgia: State Board of Pardons and Paroles. www.pap.state.ga.us.

Hanson, R.K., Bussière, M.T. (1998). Predicting relapse: A meta-analysis of sexual offender recidivism studies. *Journal of Consulting and Clinical Psychology* 66, 348–362.

Hanson, R.K., Harris, A.J. (2000). Where should we intervene? Dynamic predictors of sexual offender recidivism. *Criminal Justice and Behavior* 27(1), 6–35.

Hanson, R.K., Morton-Bourgon, K. (2004). *Predictors of sexual recidivism: An updated meta-analysis* (Corrections Research User Report No. 2004-02). Ottawa, Ontario: Public Safety Canada.

Hanson, R.K., Thornton, D. (2000). Improving risk assessment for sex offenders: A comparision of three actuarial scales. *Law and Human Behavior* 24(1), 119–136.

Hanson, R.K., Bourgon, G., Helmus, L., Hodgson, L. (2009). The principles of effective correctional treatment also apply to sexual offenders: A meta-analysis. *Criminal Justice and Behavior* 36, 865–891.

Hanson, R.K., Gordon, A., Harris, A.J.R., Marques, J.K., Murphy, W., Quinsey, V.L., Seto, M. (2002). First report of the collaborative outcome data project on the effectiveness of psychological treatment for sex offenders. *Sexual Abuse: A Journal of Research and Treatment* 14, 167–192.

Hare, R. (2002). Psychopathy as a risk factor for violence. In: H Allen (ed.) *What works: Risk reduction interventions for special needs offenders.* Lanham, MD: American Correctional Association, pp. 165–184.

Harris, A.J. (2006). Risk assessment and sex offender community supervision: A context-specific framework. *Federal Probation* 70(2), 36–43.

Hsu, L., Starzynski, J. (1990). Adolescent rapists and adolescent child sexual assaulters. *International Journal of Offender Therapy and Comparative Criminology* 34(1), 23–30.

James, D.J., Glaze, L.E. (2006). Mental health problems of prison and jail inmates. *Bureau of Justice Statistics Report* NDJ 213600.

Kassebaum, Patricia (1999). Substance abuse treatment for women offenders: Guide to promising practices. *Technical Assistance Publication Series 23* [DHHS Publication No. (SMA) 00-3454]. Rockville, MD: U.S. Department of Health and Human Services.

Kerschener, R. (1996). Adolescent attitudes about rape. *Adolescence* 31(121), 29–33.

Knight, R., Warren, J., Reboussin, R., Soley, B.J. (1998) Predicting rapist type from crime-scene variables. *Criminal Justice and Behavior* 25(1), 46–80.

Konopasky, D. (1999). *Managing sex offenders.* Kingston, Ontario: Correctional Service of Canada.

Latessa, E.J. (1996). Offenders with mental illness on probation. *Community corrections in America: New directions and sounder investments for persons with mental illness and co-disorders.* Washington, DC: National Institute of Corrections and the National Coalition for Mental and Substance Abuse Health Care in the Justice System.

Lipton, D., Pearson, F., Wexler, H. (1999). *National evaluation of the residential substance abuse treatment for state prisoners program.* New York: Development and Research Institutes.

Lösel, F., Schmucker, M. (2005). The effectiveness of treatment for sexual offenders: A comprehensive meta-analysis. *Journal of Experimental Criminology* 1, 117–146.

Lovins, B., Lowenkamp, C.T., Latessa, E.J. (2009). Applying the risk principle to sex offenders: Can treatment make some sex offenders worse?. *Prison Journal* 89, 344–357.

Mahoney, P., Williams, L. (1998). Sexual assault in marriage. In: J. Jasinski, L. Williams (eds) *Partner violence.* Thousand Oaks, CA: Sage.

Mann, R., Hanson, K., Thornton, D. (2010). Assessing risk for sexual recidivism: Some proposals on the nature of psychologically meaningful risk factors. *Sexual Abuse: A Journal of Research and Treatment* 22, 172–190.

McGrath, R. (1995). Sex offender treatment: Does it work? *Perspectives* 19, 24–26.

McGrath, R.J., Lasher, M.P., Cumming, G.F. (2011). *A model of static and dynamic sex offender risk assessment.* Washington, DC: U.S. Department of Justice, National Institute of Corrections.

Morgan, R., Fisher, W., Wolff, N. (2010). *Center for behavioral health services criminal justice research policy brief, April 2010.* New Brunswick, NJ: Rutgers University.

National Mental Health Association (1987). *Stigma: A lack of awareness and understanding.* Alexandria, VA: National Mental Health Association

Nesbit, I.A., Wilson, P.H., Smallbone, S.W. (2004). A prospective longitudinal study of sexual recidivism among adolescent sex offenders. *Sexual Abuse* 16(3), 223–234.

Nielsen, L. T., Brandenburger, A., Geanakoplos, R., McKelvey, R, Page, T. (1990). Common knowledge of an aggregate of expectations. *Econometrica, Econometric Society* 58(5), 1235–1239, September.

Painter, K., Farrington, D. (1998). Sexual and nonsexual marital aggression. *Aggression and Violent Behavior* 3(4), 369–389.

Presser, L., Gunnison, E. (1999). Strange bedfellows. *Crime & Delinquency* 45(3), 299–315.

Quinsey, V.L., Harris, G.T., Rice, M.E., Cormier, C.A. (1998). *Violent offenders: Appraising and managing risk.* Washington, DC: American Psychological Association.

Rand, M.R. (2009). *Criminal victimization 2009.* Washington, DC: Bureau of Justice Statistics.

Riggs, D., Kilpatrick, D., Resnick, H. (1992). Long-term psychological distress associated with marital rape and aggravated assault. *Journal of Family Violence* 7(4), 283–296.

Schmalleger, F. (1996). *Criminal justice today.* Upper Saddle River, NJ: Prentice Hall.

Schmalleger, F. (1999). *Criminal justice today,* 5th edn. Upper Saddle River, NJ: Prentice Hall.

Sentencing Project, The (2002). *Mentally ill offenders in the criminal justice system: An analysis and prescription.* Washington, DC: TSP. www.sentencingproject.org/doc/publications/sl_mentallyilloffenders.pdf.

Sherman, L., Gottfredson, D., MacKenzie, D., Eck, J., Reuter, P., Bushway, S.D. (1997). *Preventing crime: What works? What doesn't? What's promising?* Washington, DC: Office of Justice Programs.

Stevens, D. (1999). *Inside the mind of a serial rapist.* San Francisco, CA: Austin and Winfield.

Straus, M. (1988). In: Straus, M.(ed.) *Abuse and victimization across the life span.* Baltimore, MD: Johns Hopkins University Press, pp. 188–199.

Teplin, L., Abrams, K., McClelland, G. (1997). Prevalence of psychiatric disorders among incarcerated women. *Archives of General Psychiatry* 53(2), 505–512.

Wakeling, H., Mann, R., Carter, A.J (2012). Do low-risk sexual offenders need treatment? *The Howard Journal* 51(3), 286–299.

Walker, L. (2000). *The battered woman syndrome.* New York: Springer.

Warren, J., Reboussin, R., Hazelwood, R., Gibbs, N., Trumbetta, S., Cummings, A. (1999). Crime scene analysis and the escalation of violence in serial rape. *Forensic Science International* 100(1/2), 37–56.

Winick, C., Levine, A. (1992). Marathon therapy: Treating female rape survivors in a therapeutic community. *Journal of Psychoactive Drugs* 24(1), 49–56.

Yates, P. (2002). What works? Effective intervention with sex offenders. In: H. Allen (ed.) *What works? Risk reduction: Interventions for special needs offenders.* Lanham, MD: American Correctional Association, pp. 115–164.

Zavitz, R., Farkas, M. (2000). The impact of sex-offender notification on probation/parole in Wisconsin. *International Journal of Offender Therapy and Comparative Criminology* 44(1), 8–21.

Chapter 13[*]

DRUG AND OTHER PROBLEM-SOLVING COURTS

Key Terms

drug courts
Harrison Act of 1914
mental health courts
net widening
problem-solving courts

re-entry court
truancy courts
veterans' courts
war on drugs

> Serving a jail sentence would've been a lot easier, but I don't know if I would've come out on the other end.—*Joe M. (Drug Court Graduate)*

THE DEVELOPMENT OF DRUG COURTS

Although some people might not consider **drug courts** to be an intermediate sanction, it appears that they fall into this category when you consider that they usually combine close probation supervision with substance abuse treatment in an attempt to keep the offender from being incarcerated. Indeed, the phenomenal growth and expansion of drug courts can be largely attributed to the dissatisfaction of traditional methods of dealing with drug offenders and the belief that drug courts will reduce substance abuse and criminal behavior through close judicial monitoring and community-based treatment services. According to Belenko (1998), drug courts differ from traditional courts in several important ways. First, drug courts attempt to manage cases quickly and make provisions for the treatment to start as soon as possible after arrest. Second, drug courts have adopted a collaborative rather than an adversarial approach found in most traditional courts. Third, judges in drug courts are actively involved in the cases, holding regular status hearings, meeting regularly with treatment providers and probation officers, and providing feedback to the offender. Finally, drug courts focus on providing treatment services rather than simply increasing sanctions.

[*]The authors would like to thank Dr. Brian Lovins for his contributions to this chapter.

The United States has been waging a **war on drugs** for more than 40 years and most of that effort has been spent on law enforcement and interdiction efforts. While stopping the flow of illegal drugs is important, it is the insatiable demand that keeps the drugs coming. Indeed, we cannot even keep drug out of prisons, our most secure institutions, so what chance do we have to secure the borders?

Tired of the endless cycle of substance abusers coming through the court system and the failure of traditional approaches, many judges have begun to take the matter into their own hands by embracing drug courts as an alternative to jail or probation. Indeed, based on the drug courts model, a number of other "specialty" or therapeutic courts have emerged including mental health, veterans, driving under the influence (DUI), family, re-entry, domestic violence, gun, gambling, co-occurring disorders, and others. This chapter will examine the development and components of drug courts and some of its counterparts and look at the research concerning their effectiveness.

THE EMERGENCE OF THE DRUG COURT

There were three predominant conditions that set the stage for the emergence of the drug court. First, the war on drugs and "get-tough" sentencing provided a continuous stream of non violent drug offenders into the system. Second, the public's growing fear of drugs and violence spurred on by the media focus and political agendas. Third, the ineffectiveness of the traditional system to treat drug-addicted offenders effectively. Separately these conditions may have not had much of an effect, but together they created an opportunity for the drug court to take hold.

The War on Drugs

By 1989, the war on drugs was in full swing. Although many cite Nixon as the initial commander in chief of the war on drugs, it actually can be traced to the **Harrison Act of 1914** (Belenko, 1998). The Harrison Act was designed to limit the access drug users had to cocaine and opiates by making it illegal for medical professionals to supply addicts with drugs. In 1914 opiate and cocaine use had started to cause significant social problems including a spike in violence (Wisotsky, 1997). The Harrison Act was designed to reduce the use of cocaine and opiates by making the punishment severe enough that it would deter doctors from prescribing them to their patients. Although well intended, the Harrison Act was the first of many laws that the Federal government has enacted through the war on drugs that led to the incarceration of many non-violent drug offenders. By 1928, one-third of the federal prison population was incarcerated owing to drug use, primarily as a consequence of the Harrison Act (Jones, 1995). Of course the rise in the inmate population had a significant impact on the prison system's resources. Crowding, limited ability to supervise offenders, and lack of treatment were cited by wardens as primary problems associated with the rise in the prison population during this period (United States House of Representatives, 1928).

The next battle generally associated with the war on drugs was the Marihuana Tax Act of 1937. Initially focused on reducing the impact that hemp had on the textile and paper markets, the act leveraged a tax on all sales of hemp and any of its by-products. The maximum penalty for not paying the tax was a fine and up to four years' imprisonment for both the seller and the buyer. Although initially focused on the production of hemp, many local jurisdictions applied the law to individuals who possessed marijuana for personal use. Like the Harrison Act, the unforeseen consequence of this act was the significant spike in the number of offenders processed through the court and ultimately incarcerated (Wisotsky, 1997).

As the number of drug offenders processed through the courts increased, political responses to the war on drugs toughened. Near the middle of the century, drug users were again blamed for a significant portion of the country's violent crimes, leading to the third stage of the war on drugs (McBride & McCoy, 1997). During this time, the Boggs amendment to the Harrison Act set mandatory sentences for opiate possession, and the Narcotics Control Act increased the penalties for possession and distribution of narcotics (Sharp, 1994). By 1971, the war on drugs had reached the national spotlight. President Nixon, in a speech to the nation, identified drug abuse as a national epidemic and influenced Congress to pass the Comprehensive Drug Abuse Prevention and Control Act (Marion, 1994).

The effects of the Comprehensive Drug Abuse Prevention and Control Act of 1971 were felt immediately. The most important change was that Congress scheduled (or ranked) drugs based on their potential for harm against their medical utility. According to the new schedule, more dangerous drugs with no medical purpose, like LSD and marijuana, were reserved for Schedule I while drugs with some medicinal purposes, like cocaine and methadone, were placed in Schedule II. The Congress also provided some discretion to judges on sentencing, allowing probation to be given to drug offenders who were convicted of minor possession (Marion, 1994).

As the war on drugs progressed, the initial discretion provided to judges under the 1971 act was significantly limited. Under the original act, judges could sentence offenders to probation if the drugs were for personal use only. Under the Sentencing Reform Act of 1984 and the Anti-Drug Abuse Act of 1986, personal use was defined by the amount (or weight) of the drug, not the intent to sell, resulting in a significant spike in the number of offenders incarcerated for drug possession. By 1989, when the first drug court was implemented, almost 20 percent of the prison population was serving time for a drug crime (Snell, 1991).

Simultaneous to the war on drugs, the criminal justice system experienced a wave of "get-tough" policies, which resulted in heavier reliance on prison as a primary intervention. The "get-tough" era continued to impact drug offenders through the late 1970s and into the 1980s. The focus became less on probation and community services and more on incarceration. Mandatory minimum prison sentences were introduced across the nation. States adopted special punishments for offenders found guilty of having crack cocaine, in an effort to deter people from engaging in the violence associated with its use (Reinarman & Levine, 2004). Similar to the Harrison Act of 1914, these get-tough laws had several unintended consequences. First and foremost, the cocaine laws were routinely applied unequally across social classes. Powder cocaine use rarely resulted in prison time, while drug offenders who were caught with crack cocaine faced mandatory prison sentences. Second, for those who remained in the community, high levels of supervision were provided regardless of the risk for recidivating. While these intensive services are needed for a select few, lower-risk offenders placed on intensive supervision can actually recidivate at higher rates (Lowenkamp & Latessa, 2004). Finally, in many states, three-strikes laws resulted in lifetime sentences for violation of minor drug laws, resulting in significant overcrowding of prison populations.

Public Fear of Drugs and Violence

At the same time the first drug court was being implemented, the public concern for drug use was at a historic high (Levine & Reinarman, 1988). In August 1989, 64 percent of those polled in a *New York Times*/CBS Poll (Oreskes, 1989) identified drugs as the number one problem facing the United States. This anti-drug sentiment was a complete reversal of the favorable attitudes of the 1970s. In fact, in 1978 nearly seven out of 10 high school seniors reported that marijuana should be legalized for personal use. By 1980, 11 states had decriminalized small quantities of marijuana and several more had bills in front of their state legislatures to do the same (Johnson et al., 1989).

By 1980 however, the attitudes toward drugs started to shift. National polls suggested that the public's tolerance of drug use had begun to decrease. States like Oregon and Alaska, which had legalized marijuana in the previous decade, reversed fields and passed laws that once again criminalized personal use of marijuana (Goode & Ben-Yehuda, 1994). As the country began to adopt anti-drug sentiments, crack cocaine hit the mainstream media. With drugs regarded as instantly addictive and tied directly to violent crimes, the war on drugs gained even more momentum. Media reports suggested that crack was widely available, associated with high levels of violence, and caused significant birth defects in newborn babies (Reinarman & Levine, 2004). Television commercials depicting the effects of crack cocaine routinely aired (Oreskes, 1990). Even President George Herbert Bush, during a nationally televised primetime address, identified drugs as the most significant problem facing the nation and declared the United States at war (Kagay, 1990).

Ineffectiveness of the Criminal Justice System to Treat Drug Offenders

The third condition that set the stage for the implementation of the drug court was the lack of effective interventions for drug offenders. Since the Harrison Act was passed, the criminal justice system has struggled with managing the increased number of drug offenders. As early as 1928, wardens in the federal prisons have complained that the drug offenders presented unique challenges to a prison system (United States House of Representatives, 1928). Since then, the number of drug offenders in the state and federal system has skyrocketed. To combat increasing prison populations, the federal prison system developed alternative placements for prison coined Narcotic Camps. These minimum security camps were designed as a diversion from prison for drug offenders. They were in operation for nearly 50 years, but in 1975 after widespread reports of inmate abuses and ineffective programming they were closed (Campbell et al., 2008).

Beyond the Narcotic Camps, treatment programs were under fire. Martinson (1974) had just published an article where he and colleagues had found null effects for treatment. Although the criminal justice system had been focused on rehabilitation for the past 75 years, the goals of the system began to shift to deterrence and incapacitation. As stated earlier, the legislature began to control judges' discretion by placing mandatory minimums on specific types of drug offenses and limiting those that could be sentenced to probation. At the same time that treatment was challenged, funding for criminal justice efforts (e.g., community surveillance, incarceration) had grown 62 percent (Lock et al., 2002). Clearly, treatment had taken a back seat to strategies of incapacitation and deterrence. During this time period, the prison population grew nearly 300 percent (Lurigio, 2000).

By 2002, when drug courts were in full swing, there were nearly 200,000 drug offenders incarcerated. Processing speeds were slow, causing a log jam of offenders in the courts. Drug offenders were often arrested for new offenses before they even made it through court. Early attempts to provide pretrial services to drug offenders were fragmented and lacked continuity. There was some hope when federal funds created Treatment Alternatives for Street Crimes (TASC), but there were still significant problems with integrating treatment services into the court when TASC was introduced (Falkin, 1993).

Even with rising concerns about drug use and the lack of treatment options, the nation was still highly supportive of providing prevention and treatment in lieu of incarceration. Lock et al. (2002) found that 83 percent of those surveyed believed that the nation should maintain or increase spending on treatment, while 92 percent supported spending as much, if not more money on prevention services. The problem in the mid-1980s was finding treatment services that were effective for drug offenders.

The First Drug Court

The traditional criminal justice system clearly faced a number of barriers in addressing the needs of drug offenders. In 1989, Judge Klein of Dade County Florida formed a specialized docket for drug offenders in order to address the major gaps of the traditional system. The problem with the traditional system, as he saw it, was that it had become overburdened with the adversarial process. Drug offenders were sitting on dockets too long without treatment, and previous attempts to speed up the process resulted in just cycling the offenders through the system quicker, but with no more success. To combat these gaps, he set forth to develop a collaborative process among the courtroom work group. Its focus was no longer on guilt and innocence, but what is the best course of action to help this defendant succeed in living more prosocial life.

Freeing the prosecutor, defense attorney, judge, treatment provider, and defendant to work together to find the best option for the defendant addressed several deficiencies with the current system. First, the processing speed of the case increased significantly. Since there was limited friction between the court work group, the system could process the defendant quicker and ensure that the needs of the defendant were met in a timely fashion. Second, the defendant was available to enter treatment quicker and therefore had less time at risk before receiving help. Historically, the wait list for programming could be extremely long and research suggests that the longer a person waits for treatment the more likely he or she is to drop out (Belenko, 1998). Third, all parties are working together to help the defendant be successful; therefore, all interventions are geared toward behavioral change.

The second major area that the drug court addressed is the lack of oversight. In a traditional court, the probation officer takes the primary role of monitoring the defendant. In the drug court model, the judge or magistrate is the primary "case coordinator." The role of the judge is shifted to more of an agent of change than in a traditional court. The defendant is scheduled on a regular basis (usually weekly at the start) to attend a review hearing in which the defendant's progress is discussed with all the key personnel. Hence, the participant is being monitored on a regular and consistent basis by the court.

Third, the drug court takes an active role in the treatment of the defendant. Community providers are part of the proceedings and provide ongoing updates to the team so as to remain up-to-date on the defendant's progress. If the defendant is progressing appropriately, the court is available to provide reinforcements, and if he or she is sliding the court can provide timely interventions. Historically, treatment providers have not been active players in the court proceedings, if available at all. This model ensures that all relevant information is shared with the parties involved with the defendant. Furthermore, it promotes the integration of treatment with the court process.

Growth of Drug and Specialty Courts

Starting with the first drug court in Miami, the drug court has taken the criminal justice system by storm. Not since the separation of the adult and juvenile courts has there been such a significant change in how defendants were processed through the court system. After its initial development in 1989, the drug court concept quickly took root. Although adversaries of the drug court model predicted that the novelty would dissipate, it has grown exponentially each year (Huddleston et al., 2008). There were 10 drug courts in 1992, and by 1998 there were 275 drug courts in operation, serving an estimated 90,000 offenders (Drug Court Programs Office, 1998). As of the middle of 2013, there were 2,831 drug and other specialty

Table 13.1 Number and Types of Drug Courts

Types of Drug Courts	Number
Adult drug courts	1,485
Juvenile drug courts	422
Family drug courts	331
Tribal drug courts	119
Designated DWI courts	229
Campus drug courts	5
Re-entry drug courts	31
Federal re-entry drug courts	25
Veterans drug courts	145
Co-occurring disorder courts	39
TOTAL	**2,831**

Source: National Institute of Justice. Number as of June 30, 2013.

courts operating in the United States. Table 13.1 shows the current number of drug and specialty courts operating in the USA as of the middle of 2013.

THE DRUG COURT MODEL

Based on the lessons learned from the early drug courts, the National Association of Drug Court Professionals (1997) set forth 10 key components that should be incorporated in each adult drug court. Studies conducted since have refined these components and provided some clarification. First, the drug court should fully integrate court and treatment services. Previous attempts to target drug offenders were unsuccessful when the treatment services were not in conjunction with the court proceedings (Falkin, 1993). Second, the court work group should work collaboratively to ensure that the participant is prepared for long-term change; the adversarial approach of the traditional court should be avoided. Third, clear selection criteria should be established and participants should be referred to the drug court immediately. Fourth, the drug court should have access to an array of treatment services ranging from detox to residential care. The treatment should be responsive to the needs of the participant and involve family whenever possible. Fifth, the drug court should provide frequent and ongoing drug and alcohol urinalysis. Sixth, the court should monitor the progress of participants including results of the drug and alcohol tests. These should be shared with the court and be part of the reinforcement/punishment schedule. Although the court should recognize that relapse is typical, the expectation should always be abstinence. Seventh, the relationship between the judge and participant is essential. Cooper and Bartlett (1996) found that 88 percent of the participants of the drug court felt that the judge (or magistrate) was key in their success in the program. Drug courts that are able to retain participants are more likely to be successful at long-term change (Goldkamp et al., 1998). Eighth, ongoing quality improvement is necessary to maintain the fidelity of the drug court model. Data should be collected to ensure that participants in the program are receiving effective services. Ninth, the professionalism and training of staff is extremely important. Staff should be trained in the drug court model, core correctional practices, and behavioral change. Tenth, the drug court staff must be active in the community, garnering support for the drug court and its participants. The drug court staff cannot operate in a vacuum; staff and participants must share the successes of the program to ensure long-term support. Table 13.2 summarizes the key components.

Guided by early attempts and the drug court principles, most drug courts have evolved into a unique blend between court procedures and treatment. Although there is not a single model for how drug courts have been implemented, there are some common themes. Most are structured like traditional courts, with the presence of a judge, prosecutor, and sometimes a defense attorney. The process takes more of a treatment team approach toward addressing the defendant than the traditional adversarial procedures. The judge operates as a hybrid case manager reviewing the defendant's progress, admonishing any negative behavior

Table 13.2 Components for Drug Court Implementation

Key Component 1: Drug courts integrate alcohol and other drug treatment services with justice system case processing

Key Component 2: Using a nonadversarial approach, prosecution and defense counsel promote public safety while protecting participants' due process rights

Key Component 3: Eligible participants are identified early and promptly placed in the drug court program

Key Component 4: Drug courts provide access to a continuum of alcohol, drug, and other related treatment and rehabilitation services

Key Component 5: Abstinence is monitored by frequent alcohol and other drug testing

Key Component 6: A coordinated strategy governs drug court responses to participants' compliance

Key Component 7: Ongoing judicial interaction with each drug court participant is essential

Key Component 8: Monitoring and evaluation measure the achievement of program goals and gauge effectiveness

Key Component 9: Continuing interdisciplinary education promotes effective drug court planning, implementation, and operations

Key Component 10: Forging partnerships among drug courts, public agencies, and community-based organizations generates local support and enhances drug court program effectiveness

---

Source: *Defining drug courts: The key components January 1997.* Reprinted October 2004. Washington, DC: The National Association of Drug Court Professionals Drug Court Standards Committee.

while praising prosocial alternatives. The prosecutor and defense attorney work together with the treatment provider to determine the best course of action.

Some courts serve as a pre-adjudication court while others are operated post-disposition. For the pre-adjudication courts, the defendant agrees to participate in the program, usually with the promise of either a dismissed charge or a heavily reduced charge (e.g., felony reduced to a misdemeanor). Post-dispositional programs are offered after the rendering of guilt (usually through plea) and are part of the supervision plan for the offender, offered to mitigate the sentence, or as a post-adjudication program that offers to reduce the conviction if specific indicators are met.

Most drug courts have set exclusionary criteria including a history of violence, and motivation to participate. Once admitted, the defendant is expected to follow a set of strict rules designed to support a sober lifestyle. If these rules are violated sanctions can be provided up to and including incarceration (Peyton & Gossweiler, 2001). Kassebaum and Okamoto (2001) suggest that oversight is key to the success of drug programs. Unlike a traditional docket where there is very little oversight from the bench, the purpose of the drug court is for the judge to provide immediate feedback to the defendant, either to support the choices being made or to address them if they are leading the defendant down the wrong path (National Association of Drug Court Providers, 1997).

Box 13.1
New Jersey Drug Court Program: Testimonials

I want to thank God, the court, my probation officer. I never really respected judges and probation officers before. But here they treat you like an adult, and you're made to feel part of a larger society. The judge has been very friendly and caring. He was there for me, as well as my probation officer. Life is beautiful, but I avoided life. You can't use mood- or mind-altering chemicals and be part of life. I'm grateful. – **Tommy**

This is truly, truly a blessed day. It feels so good being clean. Now, people come to me for help! – **George**

I never liked the program, but I love what's done for me. – **Robert**

I want to thank all those who helped me believe that I can make a difference and a change in my life. – **Jo**

It was hard until I shared for the first time. They make you share. I didn't believe I had a problem at all until I shared, and then I started crying like a baby. – **Keith**

With drug court, I learned to be a man, not a kid. I'm studying music again. I don't know how to read or write, in English or Spanish, but God gave me the ability to have a band. When I go home, I kiss my instruments, because I can't believe I have this: my music, my apartment. I used to live in abandoned buildings and eat garbage. Now my eyes are open, my mind is clear. People respect me. – **Juan**

I thank God and family for giving me such a chance. Eighteen years of drug abuse. I was locked up in '99. I was scared of the real world. All I knew was selling and buying drugs. I thank drug court for helping me get this second chance at life. – **Susan**

Source: New Jersey Courts: www.judiciary.state.nj.us/index.html.

The length of the drug court varies specifically across site, but it is not uncommon to find drug courts that provide services for at least 12 months and sometimes upward to two years. The types of interventions are quite mixed. Most rely heavily on Alcoholics Anonymous (AA) or Narcotics Anonymous (NA), while others have formal agreements with substance abuse providers to deliver treatment services. Treatment targets range from criminogenic to non-criminogenic needs. Usually separated by phases, successful completion is typically based on a combination of time, a period of documented sobriety, and other behavioral indicators (e.g. obtaining employment) (Peyton & Gossweiler, 2001).

The main purpose of drug court programs is to use the authority of the court to reduce crime by changing defendants' drug-using behavior. Under this concept, in exchange for the possibility of dismissed charges or reduced sentences, defendants are diverted to drug court programs in various ways and at various stages of the judicial process, depending on the circumstances. Judges preside over drug court proceedings; monitor the progress of defendants through frequent status hearings; and prescribe sanctions and rewards as appropriate in collaboration with prosecutors, defense attorneys, treatment providers, and others. Basic elements of a drug court include the following (Huddleston, 1998; Stageberg et al., 2001):

- A single drug court judge and staff who provide both focus and leadership.
- Expedited adjudication through early identification and referral of appropriate program participants, initiating treatment as soon as possible after arrest.
- Both intensive treatment and aftercare for drug-abusing defendants.
- Comprehensive, in-depth, and coordinated supervision of drug defendants in regular (sometimes daily) status hearings that monitor both treatment progress and offender compliance.
- Enhanced and increasing defendant accountability under a graduated series of rewards and punishments appropriate to conforming or violative behavior.
- Mandatory and frequent drug (and alcohol) testing.
- Supervised and individual case monitoring.

The Expansion of Drug Courts and Problem-Solving Courts

Based on the success of the drug court model, jurisdictions were quick to broaden the scope of the drug court to meet the needs of other specialized populations that

Table 13.3 Number and Types of Other Specialty Courts

Types of Drug Courts	Number
Gun	5
Community	18
Prostitution	12
Parole violator	4
Sex offender	12
Homelessness	22
Truancy	199
Child support	50

Source: National Drug Court Resource Center. Number as of June 30, 2013.

tend to get marginalized. Specifically, drug courts expanded to juveniles and DUI drivers, while the **problem-solving courts** began to target mentally ill, families, re-entry, and veterans. Other problem-solving courts now include homeless, gun, community, prostitution, truancy, parole violator, sex offender, and child support courts (see Table 13.3). Although the problem-solving courts are fundamentally similar to the drug court, there are some distinct differences. The following section will briefly describe the models for the more widely used courts, including the juvenile drug court, the mental health court, veterans, re-entry, domestic violence and the family drug court.

Box 13.2
Truancy Courts

According to the National Drug Court Resource Center, **truancy courts** are designed to assist school-aged youth to overcome the underlying causes of truancy by reinforcing and combining efforts from the school, courts, mental health providers, families, and the community. Many courts have reorganized to form special truancy court dockets within the juvenile or family court. Guidance counselors submit reports on the youth's weekly progress throughout the school year, which the court uses to enable special testing, counseling, or other necessary services. Truancy court is often held on the school grounds and results in the ultimate dismissal of truancy petitions if the youth can be helped to attend school regularly. Consolidation of truancy cases results in speedier court dates and more consistent dispositions and makes court personnel more attuned to the needs of truant youths and their families. Community programs bring together the schools, law enforcement, social service providers, mental and physical healthcare providers and others to help stabilize families and re-engage youth in their education.

Source: National Drug Court Resource Center. www.ndcrc.org/node/360.

The Juvenile Drug Court

The first juvenile drug court was established in 1995. As of June 2013, there were 422 juvenile drug courts in operation across the United States. The juvenile drug court was initially adapted from the adult drug court model, but had to be modified rather quickly to address several challenges that were unique to juveniles (Drug Court Clearinghouse and Technical Assistance Project, 1998). Typically, juvenile drug offenders have significant barriers, including lack of family involvement, low motivation to change, and involvement with multiple systems. These barriers coupled with limited treatment options made it even more challenging to provide effective services to youth. The juvenile drug court did have one advantage over the adult drug court: juvenile courts operate more collaboratively than adult courts and are usually focused primarily on rehabilitation. The juvenile court subscribes to the *parens patriae* doctrine, so the drug court philosophy of therapeutic jurisprudence was not foreign to the juvenile proceedings.

Specialty Courts for DUI Offenders

Offenders driving while intoxicated are increasingly being placed under the jurisdiction of the drug court. Such courts are designed to reduce criminal reoffending by chemically dependent adult drivers who are at high risk to recidivate. The targeted group displays a repetitive pattern of driving under the influence of

Table 13.4 The 16 Key Strategies for Juvenile Drug Courts Recommended by the National Drug Court Institute

- Strategy 1: Collaborative planning
- Strategy 2: Teamwork
- Strategy 3: Clearly defined target population and eligibility criteria
- Strategy 4: Judicial involvement and supervision
- Strategy 5: Monitoring and evaluation
- Strategy 6: Community partnerships
- Strategy 7: Comprehensive treatment planning
- Strategy 8: Developmentally appropriate services
- Strategy 9: Gender-appropriate services
- Strategy 10: Cultural competence
- Strategy 11: Focus on strengths
- Strategy 12: Family engagement
- Strategy 13: Educational linkages
- Strategy 14: Drug testing
- Strategy 15: Goal-oriented incentives and sanctions
- Strategy 16: Confidentiality

Source: National Drug Court Institute. www.ndci.org/.

alcohol or other drugs. Such drivers otherwise cause injuries and deaths on highways, and are not deterred by usual DUI sanctions.

While DUI drug courts usually accept first-time DUI offenders, the typical court focuses on multiple violators who are sent directly to the DUI court for arraignment and adjudication. The basic intentions are to aid such offenders, protect the public by keeping offenders from reoffending, improve judicial efficiency, and reserve hard bed space for career and dangerous offenders. Georgia's DUI court is an accountability court authorized to process drug-using offenders through drug testing, intensive supervision, treatment services, and immediate incentives and sanctions. DUI courts are designed to force the offender to deal with her or his substance-abuse problems through a blend of treatment and personal accountability, as well as specialized case management. The DUI Court is a treatment court with a specialized docket managed by a specially trained judge, working with prosecutors, public defenders, probation and law enforcement officers, treatment providers, and other dedicated practitioners to compel the DUI offender to become clean and sober.

Tools used frequently in DUI courts include both early and long-term treatment intervention, frequent random drug testing, judicial supervision, intensive probation coupled later with follow-up probation, assistance with school, education, and employment, bi-weekly court appearances, frequent 12-step AA or NA meeting attendance, and home visits by compliance officers. Failure to meet requirements will cause the DUI court judge to issue immediate sanctions, such as community service, jail time, or both. Interlock devices may be installed that prevent drug court offenders from driving a vehicle. Frequent failure may lead to revocation of probation and imposition of a sentence to incarceration.

The effectiveness of DUI courts has not yet been thoroughly investigated, but preliminary results from Georgia reveal that, 12 months post-graduation, DUI court clients were almost three times less likely to have a new DUI arrest, and, 24 months post-graduation, drug court participants are 20 percent less likely to be arrested for a new felony. Hennepin County, Minnesota found that some 89 percent of program participants stayed crime-free. Keeping such offenders "off the bottle" results in one-quarter of the cost of sending a person to prison. In most drug courts, participant fees pay for treatment services (Eastern Judicial Circuit of Georgia, 2012).

Mental Health Courts

Mental health courts, like drug courts, were designed to address a growing population of offenders who face significant barriers in the traditional court system. Lamb and colleagues (1999) found that mentally ill offenders have a difficult time engaging in the traditional criminal justice system and that the system is not responsive to the needs of the mentally ill offender. The goal of the mental health court is to reduce the barriers that exist in the system while assisting the offender in stabilizing his or her mental health symptoms.

To meet this goal, the mental health court works collaboratively with the judge, court workers, community supervision officer, treatment staff, and other consumers to engage the offender and ensure that he or she complies with the identified treatment plan (Miller & Perelman, 2009). Unlike the drug courts, the mental health courts' focus is not directly on the criminal behavior. Instead, it focuses on reducing the impact of the underlying mental illness, assuming that if the symptoms are managed effectively the offender will reduce his or her involvement in the criminal justice system.

The mental health court has gone through some recent modifications. Initially focused on offenders with low-level misdemeanors, mental health courts around the nation have begun to expand their services to higher-level misdemeanants and low-level felons. With the shift to more serious offenders, the mental health court has had to reconsider some of their earlier decisions. First, many courts have shifted from a pre-adjudication to a post-adjudication model. A post-adjudication model allows for the court to secure a guilty plea up front, so if the offender fails treatment it is easier to apply the underlying sentence. Second, supervision responsibilities have transitioned from community mental health staff to probation officers. Third, the use of jail as an intermediate sanction has increased significantly (Miller and Perelman, 2009).

Common Elements in Mental Health Courts

■ Participation in a mental health court is voluntary. The defendant must consent to participation before being placed in the program.
■ Each jurisdiction accepts only persons with demonstrable mental illnesses to which their involvement in the criminal justice system can be attributed.
■ The key objective of a mental health court is to either prevent the jailing of offenders with mental illness by diverting them to appropriate community services or to significantly reduce time spent incarcerated.
■ Public safety is a high priority, and offenders with mental illness are carefully screened for appropriate inclusion in the program.
■ Early intervention is essential, with screening and referral occurring as soon as possible after arrest.
■ A multidisciplinary team approach is used, with the involvement of justice system representatives, mental health providers, and other support systems.
■ Intensive case management includes supervision of participants, with a focus on accountability and monitoring of each participant's performance.

The judge oversees the treatment and supervision process and facilitates collaboration among mental health court team members (California Courts). Recent studies have found that mental health courts are having a positive effect on the quality of life for participants, and have a small to moderate effect on recidivism (Cross, 2011; Sarteschi, 2009).

Family Drug Courts

The family drug court is one of the most unique among the problem-solving courts. Developed in 1996, there are currently 331 family drug courts in operation. Although of similar structure to the other problem-solving courts, its primary target is not criminal behavior but parental rights. The family drug court model is designed to reduce the impact that substances have on families by working with them to increase retention of their children, reunite the children if removed, or assist in permanent custody where appropriate. Referrals are typically provided by the local Department of Human Services or prenatal/ neonatal care workers. Many of the family drug courts handle both criminal and civil cases but its sole interest is to manage the child protection cases (Wheeler & Siegerist, 2003).

Re-entry Courts

With more than 600,000 inmates leaving prison each year, there has been a growing concern about re-entry into the community. The **re-entry court**, designed to assist ex-offenders with reintegration issues, was first implemented in 2001. The goal of the re-entry court was to work with ex-offenders while they were still incarcerated, so that the barriers to successful integration could be removed prior to release (Hamilton, 2010). Re-entry courts were given a significant boost when then President George W. Bush signed into law on April 9, 2008 the Second Chance Act. This legislation was designed to improve outcomes for people returning to communities after incarceration. This first-of-its-kind legislation authorizes federal grants to government agencies and nonprofit organizations to provide support strategies and services designed to reduce recidivism by improving outcomes for people returning from prisons, jails, and juvenile facilities. With this influx of federal funding, many communities developed re-entry efforts that often include a re-entry court. The re-entry court was designed to increase collaboration between community supervision officers, court personnel, and community providers. Today there are 56 re-entry courts at the local and federal levels.

Veterans' Courts

Veterans' courts are one of the newest versions of the problem-solving courts. According to the Office of National Drug Control Policy (2014), veterans' treatment courts use a hybrid integration of drug court and mental health court principles to serve military veterans, and sometimes active-duty personnel. Since veterans are often entitled to receive services through their veterans' benefits, these courts help promote sobriety, recovery, and stability through a coordinated response that involves collaboration with the traditional partners found in drug courts and mental health courts, as well as the Department of Veterans Affairs healthcare networks, Veterans Benefits Administration, State Departments of Veterans Affairs, volunteer veteran mentors, and organizations that support veterans and veterans' families.

Domestic Violence Courts

The domestic violence court's primary purpose is to increase accountability of the perpetrator. The domestic violence court started in 1998, and by 2013 there were 215 in operation. The court focuses on monitoring the offender through additional contacts, progress hearings, extended compliance monitoring of protection orders, and mandated batterer programming. Domestic violence courts are designed to address the traditional problems confronted in domestic violence cases (e.g., withdrawn charges by victims, threats to victims, lack of defendant accountability, and high recidivism). They apply intense judicial scrutiny of the defendant and close cooperation between the judiciary and social services. A designated judge works with the prosecution, assigned victim advocates, social services, and the defense to protect victims from all forms of intimidation by the defendant or his or her family or associates throughout the entirety of the judicial process; provide victims with housing and job training, where needed; and continuously monitor defendants in terms of compliance with protective orders, substance abuse treatment, and other services. Close collaboration with defense counsel ensures compliance with due process safeguards and protects defendants' rights. One variant of this model is the Integrated Domestic Operational Descriptions of Drug Courts and Other Problem-solving Courts Violence Court, in which a single judge handles multiple cases relating to one family, which might include criminal actions, protective orders, custody disputes, visitation issues, or divorce proceedings (Mazur & Aldrich, 2003). In a survey conducted by Labriola and co-workers (2009), 83 percent of the courts identified victim safety as the primary goal while 79 percent cited offender accountability as extremely important. In contrast, only 27 percent of the courts stated that rehabilitation was a very important aspect of the domestic violence court.[1]

Sex Offender Courts

Sexual offender courts are one of the newest versions of the problem-solving courts. Working to increase communication between all parties involved in addressing sexual offenders' behavior, the sex offender court focuses on community management of the sexual offender. Herman (2006) suggests that sex offender courts provide a means to track the offender effectively through the use of specialized dockets, directed supervision plans, judicial monitoring of progress, and ongoing treatment team meetings. In addition, the sex offender court typically provides an avenue for the victim to get ongoing information about the offender. Unlike the typical drug court whose primary focus is rehabilitation, the sex offender courts are predominately focused on offender management and community safety, the assumption being that if sexual offenders are monitored more effectively they will not have an opportunity to offend (Herman, 2006).

PROBLEM-SOLVING COURT EFFECTIVENESS

The body of research on adult drug courts has grown substantially over the years, and the overall conclusion that can be reached is that they are effective in reducing recidivism. Because they differ substantially among jurisdictions, it has been more difficult to identify which components or combinations of features are contributing to success or failure.

There are enough studies of drug courts available that researchers have been able to conduct meta-analysis (see Chapter 14 on Evaluating Community Corrections). Overall, these reviews have found favorable results for adult drug courts. Table 13.5 lists some of these studies over the years.

In addition to reducing recidivism, adult drug courts have been found to be cost-effective. A study done by the Washington State Institute for Public Policy estimated that the average drug court participant produces $6,779 in benefits (WSIPP, 2003). In New York, researchers estimate that $254 million in incarceration costs were saved by diverting 18,000 offenders to drug courts. Finally, California researchers concluded that drug courts in that state save $18 million per year (NPC, 2002). Compared to jail and prison, adult drug courts appear to be cost-effective and to reduce criminal conduct.

While the research has generally shown adult drug courts to be effective, studies of juvenile drug courts have not been as favorable. Most researchers have found considerably smaller effects for juvenile drug courts, and in a recent study of 9 juvenile drug courts from across the country, researchers at the University of Cincinnati (Sullivan et al., 2014) found that youths in juvenile drug courts did worse than comparison cases. The researchers speculated that in general, most youths may not be particularly well suited to the treatment and monitoring process of a juvenile drug court.[2] Other explanations include the mixing of low-risk and higher-risk youths, the predominance of marijuana and alcohol users versus more serious substances, and the lack of motivation of many juveniles to abstain from experimenting with substances. Although there is considerably less research on mental health courts, one recent meta-analysis found moderate, but

Table 13.5 Average Reductions in Recidivism for Adult Drug Courts: Results from Meta-Analysis

Aos et al. (2001)	Average 8% reduction in recidivism
Barnoski & Aos (2003)	Average 13% reduction in recidivism
Lowenkamp et al. (2005)	Average 7% reduction in recidivism
Latimer et al. (2006)	Average 14% reduction in recidivism
Wilson et al. (2006)	Average 26% reduction in recidivism
Shaffer (2011)	Average 9% reduction in recidivism
Mitchell et al. (2012)	Average 12% reduction in recidivism, similar results for DUI Courts
Drake (2012)	Average 25% reduction in recidivism

significant, average reduction in recidivism; however, there was no effect on clinical outcomes (Cross, 2011). Research on other types of problem-solving courts is just emerging, and it is too early to reach any conclusions on their effectiveness.

ISSUES FACING PROBLEM-SOLVING COURTS

Although generally supported across the nation, drug and problem-solving courts are not without their critics. Marlowe and colleagues (2003) acknowledge that research on the effectiveness of drug courts is not without its flaws. First, a majority of studies use no comparison group or do not overcome selection bias. Second, the methods used to collect data in some of the primary studies have been called into question. Third, most of the studies that show effects use successful graduates as the study population, not a sample of intent to treat. In fact, the Government Accountability Office (2005) found that only 27 of the 117 evaluations published on drug courts were acceptable methodologically.

In addition to some concerns regarding the evidence, Boldt (2002) argues that the adversarial nature of the drug courts can be problematic for vulnerable defendants. With judge, prosecutor, and defense attorney working together Boldt posited that there is little protection in place for the drug offender. Similar arguments are made for mental health courts. Critics suggest that mentally ill offenders are often underrepresented in court, are potentially forced to accept plea bargains that are not in their favor, and are coerced into maintaining compliance of psychotropic medications (O'Keefe, 2006).

Another concern centers around the challenge of funding problem-solving courts. For example, while many drug courts have been created with support from federal grants, as these funds have ended many have struggled to continue the same level of programming and services. Finally, as is often the case with correctional alternatives, there is always the possibility that **net-widening** can occur. This can happen when offenders who might otherwise be processed out of the system are brought into the problem-solving court simply because the court exists. This is a particular concern given the research that indicates that juvenile drug courts may be focusing their efforts on lower-risk youths.

Johnson and colleagues (2000) suggest that the drug courts, and presumably the problem-solving courts, have been adopted without considering the broader context of the research on effective correctional interventions. They argue that local jurisdictions should apply the broader principles of effective interventions to the drug courts in an effort to make them more effective. First, and foremost, the drug courts should adopt a method of classifying offenders into levels of risk. The drug court model is a relatively intensive intervention and should be reserved for moderate- to high-risk offenders (Andrews & Bonta, 2010; Lowenkamp & Latessa, 2004).

Second, the drug court should adopt a cognitive-behavioral model and insist that its community providers use a similar model to deliver treatment. Typically drug courts rely on community providers to deliver the treatment services to the offenders. These providers should be monitored and the court should insist on the programs using models that have been shown to be effective for treatment.

Johnson and colleagues (2000) identified some ways that drug courts can increase their effectiveness:

- Improve the assessment of offenders by using standardized and objective instruments that provide levels of risk and need and which cover all major risk and need factors, not just substance abuse.
- Use behavioral and cognitive treatment strategies.
- Provide at least 100 hours of direct treatment service and make sure the level of treatment is matched to the need and risk of the offender.[3]
- Provide structured aftercare.
- Monitor the delivery of treatment services.

In addition to the concerns regarding the context of the programs, others have challenged the use of Alcoholics Anonymous and Narcotics Anonymous that often occurs in drug courts. Drug courts were found to rely heavily on 12-step models for either primary treatment or social support (Peyton & Gossweiler, 2001). Wells-Parker and Bangert-Drowns (1995) found that AA and NA were not effective for offender populations. Specific to drug courts, Shaffer (2011) found that drug courts that mandated attendance to AA/NA had lower effect sizes than those that did not mandate these services.

SUMMARY

Drug and other problem-solving courts will continue to play an important role in community corrections. In many ways, they represent the future and the hope that we will see the collaboration of close supervision practices and high-quality and effective treatment and services for offenders. In recent years, we have seen the original concept of the drug court expanded to include other special needs populations that come into contact with the criminal justice system, such as the mentally ill, veterans, drunk drivers, sex offenders, and others. While the evidence indicates that drug courts for adults are effective in reducing recidivism, there is some indication that increased attention and involvement of the system with juveniles can be harmful, and only additional research will tell if some of the other problem-solving courts are effective. While the growth has been dramatic over the years, issues remain and it will be important for these efforts to apply what has been learned about designing effective programs from the larger body of research on correctional interventions.

Review Questions

1. Where was the first drug court, and why did the judge decide to create it?
2. What is the primary difference between drug courts and family courts?
3. Who is the target population for re-entry courts?
4. What are the issues facing drug and other problem-solving courts?

5. What are some of the steps that drug and other problem-solving courts can take to increase their effectiveness?
6. What are some of the reasons that juvenile drug courts have not been as effective as their adult counterparts?

Notes

1 This study examined 9 juvenile drug courts from across the United States and was funded by OJJDP. See Latessa et al. (2013).
2 Although 27 percent of the courts in the survey stated that rehabilitation was not very important, there was a clear distinction between New York State and the rest of the country. Only 19 percent of New York State's courts identified rehabilitation as very important, while 53 percent of the courts across the rest of the United States supported rehabilitation.
3 Recent research indicates that 100 hours is the minimum for moderate-risk offenders and that higher-risk offenders will need considerably more. See Makarios et al. (2014), and Sperber et al. (2013).

Recommended Readings

Johnson, S., Hubbard, D.J., Latessa E.J. (2000). Drug courts and treatment: Lessons to be learned from the "What Works" literature. *Corrections Management Quarterly* 4(4), 70–77.

Miller, S., Perelman A. (2009). Mental health courts: An overview and redefinition of tasks and goals. *Law & Psychology Review* 33, 113–123.

Shaffer, D.K. (2011). Looking inside the black box of drug courts: A meta-analytic review. *Justice Quarterly* 28(3), 493–521.

Sullivan, C., Blair, L., Latessa, E.J., Sullivan, C.C. (2014). Juvenile drug courts and recidivism: Results from a multisite outcome study. *Justice Quarterly*. Published online May 12, 2014.

References

Andrews, D.J., Bonta, J. (2010). *The psychology of criminal conduct*, 5th edn. New Providence, NJ: LexisNexis Matthew Bender (Anderson Publishing).

Aos, S., Phipps, P., Barnoski, R., Lieb, R. (2001). *The comparative costs and benefits of programs to reduce crime.* Olympia, WA: Washington State Institute of Public Policy.

Barnoski, R., Aos, S. (2003). *Washington State's Drug Courts for Adult Defendants: Outcome Evaluation and Cost-Benefit Analysis.* Olympia, WA: Washington State Institute for Public Policy.

Belenko, S. (1998). *Research on drug courts: A critical review.* New York: The National Center on Addiction and Substance Abuse at Columbia University.

Boldt, R. (2002). The adversary system and attorney role in the drug treatment court movement. In: J. Nolan, *Drug courts: In theory and in Practice.* New York: Aldine de Gruyter, pp. 115–143.

California Courts, Judicial Branch of California. www.courts.ca.gov/5982.htm.

Campbell, N., Olsen, J.P., Walden, L. (2008). *The narcotic farm: The rise and fall of America's first prison for drug addicts*. New York: Abrams Publishing.

Cooper, C.S., Bartlett, S.R. (1996). *Drug courts: Participant perspectives*. Washington, DC: SJI National Symposium on the Implementation and Operation of Drug Courts, Justice Programs Office.

Cross, B. (2011). Mental health courts effectiveness in reducing revidivism and improving clinical outcomes. Master's thesis, University of South Florida.

Drake, E. (2012). *Chemical dependency: A review of the evidence and benefit-cost findings*. Olympia, WA: Washington State Institute of Public Policy.

Drug Court Clearinghouse and Technical Assistance Project (1998). *Juvenile and family drug courts: An overview*. Washington, DC: American University.

Drug Court Programs Office (1998). Looking at a Decade of Drug Courts, Office of Justice Programs. Washington DC: US Department of Justice.

Eastern Judicial Circuit of Georgia, State Court DUI Court Program, at www.chathamcourts.org/StateCourt/DUICourtProgram.aspx (accessed October 26, 2012).

Falkin, G. (1993). *Coordinating drug treatment for offenders: A case study*. Report to the National Institute of Justice.

Goldkamp, J.S., White, M.D., Robinson, J. (1998). *An honest chance: Perspectives of drug court participants – findings from focus groups in Brooklyn, Miami, Seattle, Las Vegas, and San Bernadino*. Drug Court Program Office, Office of Justice Programs, U.S. Department of Justice. Philadelphia: Crime and Justice Research Institute.

Goode, E., Ben-Yehuda, N. (1994). *Moral panics: The social construction of deviance*. Oxford: Blackwell.

Government Accountability Office (2005). *Adult drug courts: Evidence indicates recidivism reductions and mixed results for other outcomes*. Washington, DC: U.S. Government Accountability Office.

Hamilton, Z. (2010). *Do reentry courts reduce recidivism?* New York: Center for Court Innovation.

Herman, K. (2006). Sex offense courts: The next step in community management? *Sexual Assault Report*. Civic Institute 9(5), 65–80.

Huddleston, C., Marlowe, D., Casebolt, R. (2008). *Painting the current picture: A national report card on drug courts and other problem-solving court programs in the United States*. New York: Bureau of Justice Assistance II(1).

Huddleston, W.C. (1998). Drug court and jail-based treatment. *Corrections Today* 60(6), 98.

Johnson, L.D., Bachman, J.G., O'Malley, P.M. (1989, February 28). National press release, *Teen drug use continues decline, according to U-M survey. Cocaine down for second straight year; crack begins to decline in 1988*. Ann Arbor, MI: University of Michigan News and Information Services.

Johnson, S., Hubbard, D.J., Latessa, E.J. (2000). Drug courts and treatment: Lessons to be learned from the "what works" literature. *Corrections Management Quarterly* 4(4), 70–77.

Jones, J. (1995). The rise of the modern addict. *American Journal of Public Health* 85(8), 1157–1162.

Kagay, Michael R. (1990). Deficit raises as much alarm as illegal drugs, a poll finds. *New York Times*, July 25, p. A9.

Kassebaum, G., Okamoto, D.K. (2001). The drug court as a sentencing model. *Journal of Contemporary Criminal Justice* 17(2), 89–104.

Labriola, M., Bradley, S., O'Sullivan, C., Rempel, M., Moore, S. (2009). *A national portrait of domestic violence courts*. New York: National Institute of Justice.

Lamb, H., Weinberger, L., Gross, B. (1999). Community treatment of severely mentally ill offenders under the jurisdiction of the criminal justice system: A review. *Psychiatric Services* 50, 907–913.

Latessa, E., Sullivan, C.C., Blair, L., Sullivan, C.J., Smith, P. (2013). *Outcome and process evaluation of juvenile drug courts*. University of Cincinnati, OH: Center for Criminal Justice Research.

Latimer, J., Morton-Bourgon, K., Chretien, J. (2006). *A meta-analytic examination of drug treatment courts: Do they reduce recidivism?* Ottawa, Ontario: Department of Justice Canada, Research and Statistics Division.

Levine, H., Reinarman, C. (1988). The politics of America's latest drug scare. In: R. Curry (ed.) *Freedom at risk: Secrecy, censorship and repression in the 1980s*. Philadelphia, PA: Temple University Press, pp. 251–258.

Lock, E.D., Timberlake, J.M., Rasinski, K.A. (2002). Battle fatigue: Is public support waning for "war"-centered drug control strategies? *Crime and Delinquency* 48(3), 380–398.

Lowenkamp, C., Latessa, E. (2004). Increasing the effectiveness of correctional programming through the risk principle: Identifying offenders for residential placement. *Criminology and Public Policy* 4(1), 501–528.

Lowenkamp, C.T., Holsinger, A., Latessa, E.J. (2005). Are drug courts effective: a meta-analytic review. *Journal of Community Corrections* XV(1), 5–10, 28.

Lurigio, A.J. (2000). Drug treatment availability and effectiveness: Studies of the general and criminal justice populations. *Criminal Justice and Behavior* 27(4), 495–528.

Makarios, M.D., Sperber, K., Latessa, E.J. (2014). Treatment dosage and the risk principle: A refinement and extension. *Journal of Offender Rehabilitation* 53, 334–350.

Marion, N. (1994). *A history of federal crime control initiatives, 1960–1993*. Westport, CN: Praeger.

Marlowe, D., Matteo, D., Festinger, D. (2003). A sober assessment of drug courts. *Federal Sentencing Reporter* 16, 153–157.

Martinson, R. (1974). What works?—Questions and answers about prison reform. *Public Interest* 35, 22–54.

Mazur, R., Aldrich, L. (2003). What makes a domestic violence court work? Lessons from New York. *Judge's Journal* 42(2), 5–10.

McBride, D.C., McCoy, C.B. (1997). The drugs–crime relationship: An analytical framework. In: L.K. Gaines, P.B. Kraska (eds) *Drugs, crime, and justice*. Prospect Heights, IL: Waveland Press, Inc.

Miller, S., Perelman, A. (2009). Mental health courts: An overview and redefinition of tasks and goals. *Law & Psychology Review* 33, 113–123.

Mitchell, O., Wilson, D., Eggers, A., MacKenzie, D. (2012). Drug courts' effects on criminal offending for juveniles and adults. *Campbell Systematic Reviews* 4.

National Association of Drug Court Professionals (1997, January). *Defining drug courts: The key components*. Washington, DC: Bureau of Justice Assistance.

NPC Research, Inc., and Administrative Office of the Courts, Judicial Council of California (2002). *California drug courts: A methodology for determining costs and avoided costs: Phase i: Building the methodology: Final report.* Portland, OR: NPC.

Office of the National Drug Control Policy (2014). www.ndcrc.org/faq/faq-categories/category/faq-categories/types-drug-courts#t32n355.

O'Keefe, K. (2006). *The Brooklyn mental health court evaluation: Planning, implementation, courtroom dynamics, and participant outcomes.* New York: New York State Office of Mental Health.

Oreskes, M. (1990). Drug war underlines fickleness of public. *New York Times,* September 6, p. A22.

Peyton, E., Gossweiler, R. (2001). *Treatment services in adult drug courts: Report on the 1999 National Drug Court Treatment Survey.* Washington, DC: National Institute of Justice.

Reinarman, C., Levine, H.G. (2004). Crack in the rearview mirror: Deconstructing drug war mythology. *Social Justice* 31(1–2), 182–199.

Sarteschi, C. (2009). Assessing the effectiveness of mental health courts: A meta analysis of clinical and recidivism outcomes. Doctoral dissertation, University of Pittsburgh.

Shaffer, D.K. (2011). Looking inside the black box of drug courts: A meta-analytic review. *Justice Quarterly* 28(3), 493–521.

Sharp, E. (1994). *The dilemma of drug policy in the United States.* New York: Harper-Collins.

Snell, T. (1991). *Corrections populations in the United States, 1989 Full Report.* Washington, DC: Bureau of Justice Statistics NCJ 130445.

Sperber, K., Latessa, E.J., Makarios, M.D. (2013). Examining the interaction between level of risk and dosage of treatment. *Criminal Justice and Behavior* 40, 338–384.

Stageberg, P., Wilson, B., Moore, R. (2001). *Final Report of the Polk County Adult Drug Court.* Des Moines, IA: Iowa Division of Criminal Justice Policy.

Sullivan, C., Blair, L., Latessa, E.J., Sullivan, C.C. (2014). Juvenile drug courts and recidivism: Results from a multisite outcome study. *Justice Quarterly.* Online First: DOI:10.1177/0093854813520603.

United States House of Representatives (1928). *Establishment of two federal narcotic farms: Hearings before the Committee on the Judiciary,* 70th Congress, 1st session, p. 28.

Washington State Institute for Public Policy (2003). *Drug courts for adult defendants: Outcome evaluation and cost benefit analysis.* Olympia, WA: WSIPP.

Wells-Parker, E., Bangert-Drowns, R. (1995). Final results from a meta-analysis of remedial interventions with drink/drive offenders. *Addiction* 90(7), 907–927.

Wheeler, M.M., Siegerist, J. (2003). *Family dependency treatment court planning initiative training curricula.* Alexandria, VA: National Drug Court Institute.

Wilson. D.B., Mitchell, O., MacKenzie, D.L. (2006). A systemic review of drug court effects on recidivism. *Journal of Experimental Criminology* 2, 459–487.

Wisotsky, S. (1997). Not thinking like a lawyer: The case of drugs in the courts. In: L.K. Gaines, P.B. Kraska *Drugs, Crime, and Justice.* Prospect Heights, IL: Waveland Press, Inc.

Chapter 14

Evaluating Community Corrections

Key Terms

ballot counting
comparison group
length of follow-up
literature review
meta-analysis

outcome measure
performance measure
program quality
recidivism

> With few and isolated exceptions, the rehabilitative efforts that have
> been reported so far have not had an appreciable effect on recidivism.
> —Robert Martinson

> The data have continued to accumulate, testifying to the potency of
> offender rehabilitation programs.—Paul Gendreau

After examining more than two decades of correctional research, Martinson's
(1974) now famous conclusion had a tremendous impact on the field of
corrections. Whatever the limitations of the Martinson study, and there
were many, the conclusion drawn by a lot of people was that treatment or
rehabilitation is not effective.[1] Thus, what became known as the "nothing works"
doctrine led to renewed efforts to demonstrate the effectiveness of correctional
programs.[2] As learned in Chapter 2, there has been a great deal of research since
Martinson that has added significantly to the body of knowledge about correctional effectiveness.

The effectiveness of community-based correctional programs has been debated
and studied for many years. As more and more offenders have been diverted or
released to the community, the question of effectiveness has become increasingly
important. Many critics of both probation and parole point to discretionary
abuses, the arbitrary nature of the indeterminate sentence, the disparity in
sentencing practices by judges, the failure of rehabilitation and supervision,
and the inadequate delivery of services. In an attempt to offset some of these

criticisms, mandatory and determinate sentencing systems have been imposed, sentencing tribunals have been formed, parole boards have adopted and implemented decision-making guidelines, probation and parole departments have tested new and innovative service delivery strategies, and intermediate sanctions have been developed. But these are also open to attack and are frequently criticized.

Much has been written about the effectiveness of probation and parole. We know that the use of discretionary parole release has declined dramatically over the past years, yet the number of offenders under supervision in the community has continued to increase. The ever-increasing number of offenders placed on probation and parole has resulted in large caseloads and workloads for probation and parole departments.

There is also an acute shortage of residential programs and halfway houses. We continually experiment with service system components, such as brokerage, casework, house arrest, electronic monitoring, day reporting, drug testing, kiosks, intensive and specialized caseloads, and volunteers. In short, there have been nearly as many innovative programs and reported results as there are probation and parole agencies. The question of how we measure and determine effectiveness remains and, because it is so essential, should be examined closely.

Perhaps the most limiting aspect of effectiveness studies has been the neglect given to other performance measures. By simply comparing recidivism rates, researchers have ignored some of the main effects that community correctional programs are designed to achieve. The quality of contacts and services provided to probationers and parolees needs to be defined and gauged adequately, as does the effect of officer style and attitude on outcome. There are also relatively few cost–benefit or cost-effectiveness studies. The importance of this type of information should not be overlooked. These types of studies can help community correctional agencies make more efficient selections in terms of the resources they will employ and the strategies used to deliver those resources. For example, Petersilia (1991) distinguishes between "passive" research designs and "active" ones. She argues that passive designs only look at the program in operation and ignore the selection of participants and levels of treatment. Without this kind of information, it is difficult to determine which attributes of a correctional program are effective.

Finally, a list of effectiveness indicators should include the degree of humaneness that community supervision affords offenders and their families and the impact of these alternatives on reducing prison populations and overcrowded conditions in jails and prisons. We have come to understand that we cannot incarcerate everyone who breaks the law. Yet, probation and parole are often an afterthought, particularly when it comes to resource allocation.

There is little doubt that recidivism, no matter how it may be defined, should remain a main criterion; however, the need to measure additional outcome indicators appears obvious. Indeed, there has been a great deal of criticism directed at research conducted in the area of correctional programming. This chapter examines some of the ways that community correctional programs are evaluated and how effectiveness is measured.

Box 14.1
Parole Violation

A parolee can be returned to prison for committing a new criminal act or failing to conform to the conditions of parole. The latter is frequently known as a technical parole violation: a rule violation that is not a criminal act but is prohibited by the conditions of the parole agreement. The latter might include persistent consumption of alcohol, failure to observe curfew, refusal to make victim restitution, failure to file required reports, and so on. In a study of parole revocations, Austin (2001) found that 54 percent of parolees in California were returned for technical violations, 36 percent in Georgia, 57 percent in Missouri, 55 percent in Ohio, and 53 percent in Texas. Drug use accounts for many of the violations, and often there are few intermediate punishments for parole officers to use. Prison treatment programs for drug abuse are generally insufficient, and community resistance to implementing treatment centers is considerable. Clearly, prisoner re-entry is a major issue facing corrections and policy makers.

LIMITATIONS OF EFFECTIVENESS STUDIES

Evaluating the effectiveness of community corrections is not easy even under the best of circumstances. First, political, ethical, and programmatic reasons may not permit random assignment of offenders to membership in the treatment or control group. Nonrandom assignment forces the evaluator to statistically make the groups comparable, an honored tradition in empirical research but one that delivers results that are sometimes hard to communicate to policy makers and program directors (and sometimes to other researchers).

Even when random assignment is achieved, for the same reasons mentioned previously, treatment or program effects "bleed over" to the control group or the intended treatment is applied inappropriately or unevenly. This makes it difficult to determine whether the treatment group members received needed treatment and whether the control group remained "treatment free." After all, no program and no client exists in a vacuum; historical accidents can impact both groups, one group more than another, or accidentally reinforce negative treatment effects in one group or another.

Another major problem in evaluating treatment effectiveness in community corrections is that it is rare to have only one treatment in operation at a time. For example, an offender ("Bob") may be sentenced initially to probation and restitution. The victim–offender interaction and mediation may have very positive effects on Bob's attitudes and behavior. His drinking problem, however, may lead the probation officer (PO) to recommend that the court tightens the conditions of probation to include mandatory participation in substance abuse treatment from which Bob derives much immediate and long-term benefit. Former antisocial friends may become reacquainted with Bob, and misdemeanor crime may occur.

Alerted by Bob's subsequent arrest, the PO may have Bob (a failure?) assigned to group counseling that includes relapse prevention techniques to assist him in identifying high-risk situations and coping with them. After three years of probation, when the victim's losses have been compensated and with Bob securely employed in a job with a future and now voluntarily participating in substance abuse treatment, it is impossible to determine which of the treatment program elements will have been most effective in turning Bob around and aiding his reintegration. Was it probation supervision? The quality of PO supervision? Mediation and remorse associated with restitution? Substance abuse treatment? Relapse prevention techniques? Employment? Or some combination of treatment elements? Because "probation" is a generic term that can refer to a combination of treatment, supervision, and intermediate sanctions ("punishing smarter"), what element should be recognized as the "best intervention"?

Finally, we need to deal with the question of whether Bob should be labeled a "success" or "failure" in corrections. Defining "failure" may mean using outcome indicators: arrest, reconviction or probation revocation, or incarceration (jail or prison). If the research design defines "success" as the absence of arrest, Bob failed: he was arrested. Yet the overall picture indicates that the arrest was just one critical incident in the long-range process of reintegration, one that Bob and his probation officer managed to overcome. However, that single arrest incident in the three-year period would, from the perspective of reintegration, misclassify the probationer into the "failure" category. The bulk of evidence, however, clearly indicates that Bob was a success.

CORRECTIONAL EFFECTIVENESS

While the debate over correctional effectiveness will surely continue for some time, those attempting to evaluate and measure the worth of various strategies and programs found in corrections face a most difficult dilemma: defining "effectiveness."

Box 14.2
Cost–Benefit Analysis

One of the basic premises of cost–benefit analysis is that many decisions are often made on the basis of how resources can be optimally used, avoiding duplication, waste, and inefficiency. Cost–benefit analysis is a tool for decision makers who need to make choices among viable competing programs (including jail and prisons) to achieve certain goals. It is important to remember that cost–benefit analysis is not necessarily designed to favor the least expensive or the costliest programs, but rather optimal programs in terms of available resources and explicit goals (Latessa, 1986). Unfortunately, cost–benefit analysis is not a wholly satisfactory tool for evaluating social programs, as it is incapable of measuring social costs and benefits accurately (Vito & Latessa, 1979). However, when combined with other measures of program effectiveness and impact, cost–benefit information can provide policy makers with a valuable perspective. Comprehensive and meaningful cost–benefit analyses of criminal justice programs have been conducted. In these analyses, the amount of money saved for each dollar spent on the program is calculated (see Aos et al., 2001).

Measuring Outcome and Recidivism

A large part of the problem lies in the desire on the part of researchers and practitioners alike to define failure or success in clear-cut, "either/or" terms. See Figure 14.1 for some of the ways that offenders are classified at termination. Unfortunately, very few programs can be categorized in definitive terms. There is a strong need to view success or failure on a continuum rather than as a success-or-failure dichotomy. For example, an offender may complete a sentence of probation yet have erratic employment and numerous technical violations. This individual is certainly not as successful as one who finishes probation, gains upward mobility in a job, makes restitution, supports a family, and incurs no new charges of any type; still, both of these cases may be classified as successes. There is also a great deal of difference between the offender who is caught on a minor

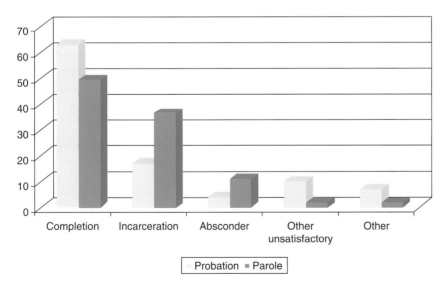

Figure 14.1 Type of Termination for Probation and Parole.

Note: Data reported for 2008.

Source: Glaze, L., Bonczar, T.P. (2009). *Probation and parole in the United States, 2008.* Washington, DC: Bureau of Justice Statistics.

charge or a technical violation and one who commits a serious new felony. For example, in California and other states, evidence shows that the number of parolees being revoked for technical violations is increasing dramatically (Austin, 2001). Some consider a new arrest a failure, whereas others count only those who are incarcerated.[3]

In addition to this problem, there is no consensus on the indicators of effectiveness. While most agree that recidivism should be a primary performance measure, there is no agreement on its definition or on the indicators used for its measurement. Indeed, one study of parole supervision found that the nature of outcome criteria had a significant effect on the interpretation of results (Gottfredson et al., 1982). Researchers tend to define recidivism in terms that fit available data, yet we know official sources are inadequate at best. Community follow-up and appropriate comparison groups are the exception rather than the rule when examining the recidivism of probationers and parolees. There is also some evidence that the amount of time given to the follow-up period may have a significant effect on the reported recidivism rates (Hoffman and Stone-Meierhoefer, 1980; Nicholaichuk et al., 2000).[4]

The correctional outcome, which is usually operationalized as recidivism, has inherent limitations. Indicators used to measure recidivism, length of follow-up, and external and internal factors affect recidivism rates. Indeed, the best way to ensure a low recidivism rate is to define it very conservatively (e.g., incarceration in a state penal institution) and to utilize a very short follow-up period.

Too often, arrest (and only arrest) is used as a primary indicator when measuring recidivism, and consequently, program success or failure. Certainly, arrest may serve as an indicator of post-program (or post-release) performance, but in and of itself arrest has many limitations. Some other factors overlooked when considering the impact of a correctional program or criminal sanction, even when arrest is being used, are time until arrest; offense for which an offender was arrested (type of offense as well as severity level); whether or not the offender was convicted; and, if convicted, the resulting disposition.

An example of this can be seen from the results of a study of community corrections in Ohio. Figure 14.2 show results from a three-year follow-up of

---

Box 14.3
Developing Comparison Groups

One of the greatest challenges in evaluating community correctional programs is identification and development of a **comparison group**. Because random assignment to correctional programs is rare, most researchers are forced to use quasi-experimental designs in which offenders in the treatment group are "matched" to those not participating in the program. Finding offenders who are similar and not receiving treatment can be one of the major issues facing researchers.

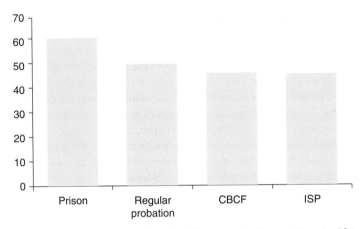

Figure 14.2 Offenders Supervised under Community Corrections in Ohio: Percent Rearrested During a Three-year Follow-up.

Source: Latessa, E., Travis, L., Holsinger, A. (1997). *Evaluation of Ohio's Community Corrections Act programs and community based correctional facilities.* Cincinnati, OH: Division of Criminal Justice, University of Cincinnati.

offenders supervised in the community. Four groups were used for this study: offenders supervised under regular probation and intensive supervised probation (ISP), those who were released from a community-based correctional facility (CBCF), and those released from prison. In this graph, the rearrest rates of the groups are presented. These data indicate that ISP and CBCF groups performed better than the regular probation and the prison groups (i.e., lower recidivism rates), at least when measured by rearrest. However, when Figure 14.3 is examined,

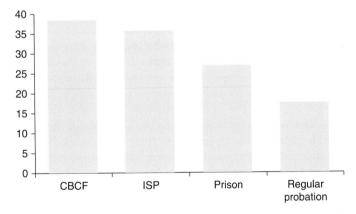

Figure 14.3 Offenders Supervised under Community Corrections in Ohio: Percent Incarcerated in a Penal Institution During a Three-year Follow-up.

Source: Latessa, E., Travis, L., Holsinger, A. (1997). *Evaluation of Ohio's Community Corrections Act programs and community based correctional facilities.* Cincinnati, OH: Division of Criminal Justice, University of Cincinnati.

we see a somewhat different picture of recidivism. In this example, incarceration rates for the same four groups are presented. Here, we see that the ISP and CBCF groups had the highest failure rates (when defined as subsequent incarceration). Of course, what this figure does not show is that the majority of those ISP and CBCF offenders who were incarcerated were a result of a technical violation. Regular probationers who received a technical violation were often placed in ISP or a CBCF and, because the majority of offenders in the prison group were released without parole supervision, they were not subject to revocation.

Despite these limitations, recidivism remains the most important measure of public protection. When legislators and other public officials ask if a program works, recidivism is what they are generally referring to. Outcome studies provide much of our knowledge about the effectiveness of correctional programs in reducing recidivism. Unfortunately, outcome studies are usually focused on the results of intervention and provide little, if any, useful information about why a program is or is not effective. Besides the measurement of outcome, another factor that can influence recidivism rates is the quality of a program.

Measuring Program Quality

Few would argue that the quality of a correctional intervention program has no effect on outcome. Nonetheless, correctional researchers have largely ignored the measurement of **program quality**. Traditionally, quality has been measured through process evaluations. This approach can provide useful information about a program's operations; however, these types of evaluations often lack the "quantifiability" of outcome studies. Previously, researchers' primary issue has been the development of criteria or indicators by which a correctional program can be measured. While traditional audits and accreditation processes are one step in this direction, thus far they have proven to be inadequate. For example, audits can be an important means to ensure if a program is meeting contractual obligations or a set of prescribed standards; however, these conditions may not have any relationship to effective intervention. It is also important to note that outcome studies and assessment of program quality are not necessarily mutually exclusive. Combining outcome indicators with assessments of program quality can provide a more complete assessment of an intervention's effectiveness. Fortunately, there has been considerable progress in identifying the hallmarks of effective programs (Andrews et al., 1990; Cullen & Applegate, 1998; Gendreau & Paparozzi, 1995; Gendreau & Ross, 1979, 1987; Lowenkamp et al., 2006; Palmer, 1995a, 1995b). This issue is examined later in this chapter.

Reviews of Research

Given all the research that is conducted, and the sometimes contradictory findings, what do we believe? Looking at one study can be a mistake. For example, there are often limitations to research, especially evaluations conducted in the real world (limited sample size, lack of generalizability, lack of adequate control groups, program changes over time, etc.). One of the ways in which we attempt to address these problems is by looking at a body of knowledge. For example, most of us believe that cigarette smoking is bad for our health. How do we know this? "Research," you say, but don't you think that given the hundreds of studies that have been conducted, there aren't studies out there that say that cigarette smoking is not that bad? If you wanted to justify smoking based on some research, you can probably find these studies out there (even though the few studies may have been funded by the tobacco industry). The reason that most of us believe that smoking is harmful is because there is a body of knowledge concerning smoking and health that says that if you smoke you increase your chances of cancer, heart disease, emphysema, and so forth. It turns out that we also have an extensive body of knowledge surrounding correctional interventions that can be summarized quantitatively. As noted in Box 14.4, there are three ways that scholars summarize research: literature reviews, ballot counting, and meta-analysis. In a narrative literature review, all the studies are qualitatively summarized by the researcher. Although this is the most common approach, it has many limitations (e.g., studies chosen to review, bias of reviewer, no quantifiable summary statistics, etc.). Ballot counting involves identifying all of the studies published on a particular subject and then sorting the results; if more studies show negative results than positive, then the researcher would conclude that the preponderance of the evidence supported negative results. This approach is also problematic for a number of reasons, not the least of which is that it more or less ignores studies that do show a positive effect. The third approach is called meta-analysis, which is now the favored approach to reviewing large numbers of studies. Some of the advantages and disadvantages of this approach are listed in Table 14.1.

Table 14.1 Meta-analyses

Advantages
- Can summarize large bodies of literature
- Easy to replicate
- Easy to extend by gathering more studies in the future
- Can estimate range of treatment effects
- Can estimate changes in magnitude of the effect depending on type of offender, dosage, and quality of research design
- From a policy perspective it provides more definitive conclusions than typical narrative reviews

Limitations
- Selection of studies—file draw problem
- Inadequacies of individual studies
- Choice of variables for coding
- Accuracy of coding is subjective

Box 14.4
Three Methods of Research Review

With all the studies conducted and published each year, it is often difficult to sort through all the research. There are three major techniques that researchers use to summarize and understand research findings:

Literature Review
The first and most common method for reviewing research is called a **literature review**. Using this approach, the researcher reads studies available on a topic and then summarizes what they think the major conclusions are from that body of research. Advantages to this approach are that most of us are familiar with the technique, it is easy to do, and it allows the reader to consider a wide range of issues. Disadvantages include the potential for bias of the reviewer, and the selection of studies to review.

Ballot Counting
The second approach is called **ballot counting**. With this technique, the researcher gathers research studies on a particular topic and then "counts" the number of studies that show or do not show some effect. This is the approach that Robert Martinson used to arrive at his now famous conclusion that "nothing works." He gathered 231 studies on correctional intervention, divided them into topics (e.g., education programs and work programs), and then determined that more studies showed no effect than those that did. Thus, his conclusion was based on a tallying of the number of studies that showed no effect (by the way, 48 percent of the studies he reviewed showed a positive effect). This approach is also relatively easy to do; however, because the majority wins, it tells us little about programs that do report positive effects.

Meta-analysis
The third approach that has become increasingly popular with researchers is called **meta-analysis**. This approach uses a quantitative synthesis of research findings in a body of literature. Meta-analysis computes the "effect size" between treatment and outcome variable—in our case, recidivism. The effect size can be negative (treatment increases recidivism), zero, or positive (treatment reduces recidivism). Meta-analysis also has some limitations. First, it is affected by "what goes into it"—what studies are included in the analysis. Second, how factors are coded can also be an important issue (e.g., into what treatment categories). There are major advantages, however, to meta-analysis. First, it is possible to control for factors that might influence the size of a treatment effect (e.g., size of sample, quality of research design, and length of treatment). Second, it provides a quantifiable result that can be replicated and tested by other researchers. Third, meta-analysis helps build knowledge about a subject such as correctional treatment in a precise and parsimonious way.

All three approaches allow us to review a large body of knowledge; however, given the advantages of meta-analysis, it is becoming more popular with researchers. As we will see, the approach is not as important as what we can learn from the research.

Meta-analysis is very helpful in summarizing the research, and because it yields an "effect size," it can show the relative strength of the intervention or subject under study. Meta-analysis is a blunt instrument, however, because though it cannot correct deficiencies or limitations in original research, it can point us in the right direction.

Recidivism as an Outcome Measure

It is important to put recidivism as an **outcome measure** in perspective. **Recidivism** is and should be the primary outcome measure by which we assess correctional program effectiveness. However, recidivism is problematic for a number of reasons. First, numerous definitions are applied, such as arrests, incarceration, technical violations, convictions, and so forth. How we define recidivism can determine the rate. For example, using a new arrest as the definition will result in higher recidivism rates than using return to prison. Second, the **length of follow-up** can be critical. For most offender groups, a two- or three-year follow-up is sufficient; however, as we have seen, for some offenders, such as sex offenders and drunk drivers, we need a much longer follow-up to adequately gauge recidivism. Third, recidivism rates can be influenced by both internal and external factors. For example, probation departments may change policies, such as increasing drug testing, which in turn can result in higher failure rates (internal), or police departments may focus on specific types of crimes, such as random stops for drunk drivers (external). Finally, recidivism is often treated as a dichotomous variable: an all-or-nothing measure, when in fact we know that variations in this outcome measure exist. That is, someone who is arrested for public intoxication is much less problematic than someone arrested for armed robbery, but we often simply count both instances as failures when examining program effectiveness. Nevertheless, recidivism is usually referenced when someone asks, "Does the program work?" This doesn't mean that we should not examine other "intermediate" measures. Let's now look at some ways this can be done.

Performance-Based Measures

In addition to long-term outcome measures, such as reductions in recidivism, we may also be interested in examining other intermediate measures. Unfortunately, in community corrections we often count activities that have little or no relationship to program or offender performance. An example would be counting the number of contacts between a probation officer and offenders. There is no empirical evidence that there is any relationship between the two factors, yet this is a common measuring stick in probation. The difference between counting an activity and a **performance measure** is illustrated in the following example:

Activity: Counting the number of job referrals made.
Performance: Number of unemployed offenders at the time of arrest and percentage employed within six months after being placed on probation.

Table 14.2 shows an example of the difference between counting activities and counting results for a juvenile court. One counts tasks, while the other counts outcomes.

Often, documenting performance in offenders will help you determine treatment effects. Examples would be:

- Reductions in dynamic risk/need assessment scores;
- changes in pre/post measures, such as improvement in test scores, changes in attitudes, behaviors, etc.;
- changes in problem areas (e.g., drug test results);
- completion of behavioral objectives (meeting treatment plan);
- substance abuse: drug tests, attitude change, day's abstinence, etc.;
- education: improvement on standardized achievement tests;
- employment: days employed, earnings, savings, contributions to support, etc.;
- mental health: days hospitalized (pre/post-treatment).

By focusing on performance rather than activities, a community correctional program can develop intermediate goals, which, if achieved, can serve as a prelude to reductions in recidivism. Osborne and Gaebler (1993) have identified seven principles for results-oriented management:

1. What gets measured gets done.
2. If you don't measure results, you can't tell success from failure.
3. If you can't see success, you can't reward it.
4. If you can't reward success, you're probably rewarding failure.
5. If you can't see success, you can't learn from it.
6. If you can't recognize failure, you can't correct it.
7. If you can demonstrate results, you can win public support.

Table 14.2 Communicating What a Juvenile Court Does: Activities vs. Results

Counting activities	Counting results
Number of contacts	Increase in number of school days attended
Number of drug tests	Percent drug-free
Number of youths on electronic monitoring	Reductions in runaways
Number of assessments completed	Average reduction in risk scores

INTRODUCTION TO PROGRAM ASSESSMENT

The characteristics and quality of a community correctional program often help determine its effectiveness. Let's now turn our attention to how we can measure the integrity of a community correctional program.

Examining the "input" of a program is usually referred to as *process evaluation*. Process evaluations usually involve a more qualitative methodology than an outcome evaluation. A process study helps determine whether the program is operating as it was designed. The problem is that a program may in fact be operating efficiently, but not effectively. For example, a drug education program may be doing a great job of teaching offenders about the harm that drugs can do to them, without being effective in reducing drug usage.

The other problem with traditional process studies is that they do not provide a "quantitative" measure. One way to think of this would be the example from offender assessment. Some assessment processes gather a great deal of information about the offender (i.e., criminal history, employment, drug use, family, education). The problem is that when they are done, they don't really have a good way to pull it all together to measure risk quantifiably. Now compare that to using the LSI or another instrument. The same information is gathered, but when you are finished, you produce a score that in turn helps tell you the probability of recidivism, as well as whether the offender scores "high," "medium," or "low" in each domain.

So how do we quantifiably measure program integrity, and what factors are examined? One tool used was developed by Gendreau and Andrews: the Correctional Program Assessment Inventory (CPAI). This instrument is based in part on results from meta-analyses of correctional effectiveness studies. It is a tool for assessing correctional programs based on empirical criteria. However, unlike traditional process evaluations or audits of adherence to standards, this process looks at the degree to which a correctional program is meeting the principles of effective intervention. This tool has been used to evaluate programs all over the United States and Canada.[5]

The CPAI examines six areas of a program (see Table 14.3).

As seen in Table 14.3, the first area looks at program leadership, as well as design and implementation of the program. The second area looks at the manner in which offenders are selected for the program and how they are assessed. As we have learned, good assessment involves the use of standardized and objective instruments that produce scores related to risk, need, and responsivity factors. The third area covered by the CPAI is treatment delivered by the program. Does the program target criminogenic risk factors? What interventions does the program use? Does it try to "talk" the offender into changing or does it use approaches that have demonstrated effectiveness in reducing recidivism, such as cognitive-behavioral curriculums? The fourth area examined is staff. Effective programs have educated, experienced, supervised, and supportive staff who are well trained. The fifth area is evaluation and quality assurance. How does the program monitor the services it delivers? We also know that effective programs routinely monitor recidivism and conduct outcome studies. Finally, miscellaneous items (such as the quality of records and the stability of the program) are examined.

Table 14.3 Correctional Program Assessment Inventory

Examines six areas:
1. Program implementation and leadership
   a. Influence and involvement of the program director
   b. Leadership and qualifications
   c. Implementation and design of the program
2. Offender assessment
   a. Selection of offenders
   b. Assessment of specific offender characteristics
   c. Manner in which offenders are assessed
3. Program characteristics
   a. Ability to target criminogenic behaviors
   b. Types of treatment used
   c. How treatments are used
   d. Preparation of offenders to return to the community
4. Staff characteristics
   a. Type and education of the staff
   b. Experience, longevity, and involvement of the staff
   c. Assessment and training of the staff
5. Evaluation
   a. Types of feedback
   b. Program assessment and evaluation
   c. Quality assurance
6. Other
   a. Ethical guidelines for intervention
   b. Completion of offender files
   c. Advisory board
   d. Community support
   e. Stability of funding and program

All told, there are 78 items scored across the six areas. Each area is scored as "very satisfactory," "satisfactory," "needs improvement," or "unsatisfactory" depending on the percentage of items scored in each area.

Although there was a great deal of variation between (and within) programs, Latessa and Holsinger (1998) summarized some of the major strengths and weaknesses in each of the CPAI areas across the programs they assessed.

■ **Program Implementation and Leadership**
Strengths: Effective programs have strong leadership and involvement of the program director. For the most part, we have found qualified and experienced program directors involved in designing the program. They tend to be involved in the hiring and training of staff; in many instances they provide some direct services to offenders. It is also important for the support of a program that the values and goals of the program be consistent with existing values in the community or institution in which it resides and that there be a documented

need for the program. Support for the program also depends on perceptions of cost-effectiveness. We usually find that most correctional programs meet these conditions.

Weaknesses: There are two flaws common in this area. Effective programs are based on strong theoretical models derived from the treatment literature. Regardless, many of the correctional intervention programs examined were basic-ally designed with little regard for the empirical research on what works with the types of offenders they were serving. In addition, effective programs are usually begun on a pilot basis to work out the logistics. Thus far, we have found few programs that piloted their treatment components before full implementation.

- **Offender Assessment and Classification**

Strengths: The vast majority of programs studied have stated criteria for admissions, receive appropriate clients, and have a rational legal/clinical basis for the exclusion of certain types of offenders. We also found that, in general, most programs attempt to assess some offender characteristics related to risk and need.

Weaknesses: While many programs did indeed attempt to assess offenders regarding risk and need, doing so did not involve incorporation of a standardized, objective, actuarial instrument. The absence of actuarial risk/needs assessment instruments was particularly evident in programs that deal with juvenile offenders. Even when a standardized assessment is being performed at some point in the offender's entry/progress, it is seldom found that the information gathered is being used to distinguish offenders by risk. In other words, even when proper (and potentially beneficial) assessments are being performed, the information is not influencing the decision-making process, let alone service delivery. In addition, it is generally found that staff assessments of offenders are based on a quasi-clinical approach that does not result in a summary score. Likewise, it has been very rare to find that programs are routinely measuring with standardized instruments responsivity characteristics, such as levels of motivation, intelligence, or psychological development.

- **Characteristics of the Program**

Strengths: Effective intervention programs focus the vast majority of their efforts on targeting criminogenic needs and behaviors. In general, we have found that many correctional intervention programs target these behaviors (although we still find programs that provide intensive services and treatment in noncrime-producing areas, such as self-esteem). Another common strength was that many programs have criteria for program completion, and upon discharge many offenders are routinely referred to programs and services that help meet their needs.

Weaknesses: Offenders typically have not been spending a significant percentage of their time in structured programs. In addition, the amount of services and treatment provided has not been varying by risk and need levels. Yet another characteristic of an effective program is the use of a treatment model that has been found to be effective. Because programs are rarely designed around a theoretical model, it was not surprising to find a lack of a consistently applied treatment model in place. In general, major shortcomings found when considering the "Characteristics of Program" portion of the CPAI include lack of programmatic structure; incomplete or nonexistent treatment manuals; few rewards to encourage program participation and compliance; ineffective use of punishment; staff being allowed to design their own interventions regardless of the treatment literature base; and a host of very obvious and definable, yet ineffective treatment models. This area of the CPAI also examines the extent to which matching occurs between offenders and staff, offenders and programs, and staff and programs. Even when matching is found to occur, it is uncommon to observe it being based on specific responsivity criteria. In addition, it is very rare to find a program that includes family and/or friends of the offender in the treatment process. Finally, many programs failed to provide aftercare services or booster sessions.

- **Characteristics and Practices of the Staff**

  Strengths: Although there is a great deal of variation from program to program regarding staff quality, for the most part we found educated and experienced staff working with offenders. Often staff were selected on personal characteristics, such as life experience, fairness, firmness, and problem-solving skills. We also found that staff usually had input in the structure of the programs and that ongoing training was provided.

  Weaknesses: Staff turnover was often a problem with some types of correctional programs (e.g., halfway houses), and we rarely found staff who had received sufficient training on the interventions and treatments utilized by the program. Clinical supervision was not provided routinely, and staff were rarely assessed on service-delivery skills.

- **Evaluation and Quality Control.** Programs that study themselves tend to be more effective than programs that do not. Data provide insight into program and offender performance, help identify who is successful and who is not, and allow adjustments to be made.

  Strengths: File review and case audits were usually conducted.

  Weaknesses: Periodic, objective, and standardized assessment of offenders to see if criminogenic factors were being reduced was uncommon. In short, most programs do not develop meaningful performance measures (to measure either program or offender performance over time). We also found that the majority of programs were not tracking offenders after they have left the program, and formal evaluations involving comparison groups were the exception.

- **Other Items**

  Strengths: Most of the programs we examined score well in this area. In general, offender records are complete and are kept in a confidential file. Changes that jeopardize programs, funding, or community support are rare.

  Weaknesses: Some programs do not have ethical guidelines for intervention, and public agencies tend not to have advisory boards, while those operated by nonprofits do.

Figure 14.4 shows average scores from nearly 400 program assessments conducted by University of Cincinnati researchers.

Two investigators have assessed the predictive validity of the CPAI. Nesovic (2003) reviewed 173 studies (including a total of 266 effect sizes) from the offender treatment literature and reported a mean correlation of $r = 0.46$ between program

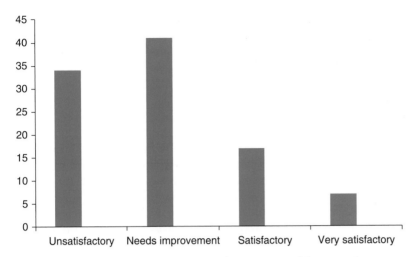

Figure 14.4 Percentage of Programs in Each Correctional Program Assessment Inventory Category.

Results are based on about 400 assessments.

scores (i.e., overall CPAI score) and recidivism. Lowenkamp and colleagues (2006) used the CPAI to conduct 38 reviews of offender treatment programs with matched controls and reported a mean correlation of $r = 0.42$ between program scores and recidivism. See Figure 14.5 for a graph demonstrating the difference in recidivism rates between treatment and comparison groups based on CPAI total scores.

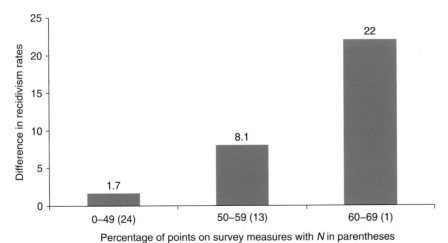

Figure 14.5 Difference in Recidivism Rates between Treatment and Comparison Groups Based on the Correctional Program Assessment Inventory Measure Total Score.

Source: Adapted from Lowenkamp, C.T., Latessa, E.J., Smith, P. (2006). Does correctional program quality really matter? The impact of adhering to the principles of effective intervention. *Criminology and Public Policy* 5(3), 201–220.

While these results indicate that the majority of correctional programs assessed are not fully meeting the principles of effective intervention, they also provide some useful information on how to improve the quality of correctional interventions.

SUMMARY

Evaluating community correctional programs is a challenge. Defining recidivism, measuring outcome, and identifying comparison groups are some of the issues confronting researchers. Summarizing research has taken several forms, but the favored approach today is meta-analysis. Meta-analysis refers to a type of research method that examines other studies on a specific subject or topic and produces an "effect size" that helps policy makers and practitioners determine best approaches.

Even though there appear to be programs and interventions that are effective, research conducted to date has been hampered by many constraints and limitations and, as a result, is less than adequate. Part of this dilemma rests with the concept of effectiveness. While, as noted earlier, most would agree that recidivism should be a primary performance measure, there is no consensus on its definition or the indicators to be used for its measurement. Researchers often ignore other performance measures of effectiveness, especially those examining the management or supervisory aspects of parole and probation, and the quality of correctional programs.

Review Questions

1. What are some of the indicators of effectiveness used in correctional research?
2. List the three major ways that research studies are summarized.
3. List some of the factors related to outcomes.
4. What are the six areas of the Correctional Program Assessment Inventory?
5. According to the research presented in the text, approximately what percentage of correctional programs can be classified as "very satisfactory" or "unsatisfactory"?

Notes

1 For a discussion of the limitations and criticism of the Martinson study, see Palmer (1975); and Cullen and Gendreau (2001).
2 Francis T. Cullen eloquently argues that rehabilitation reduces recidivism across programs by about 50 percent when interventions are based on principles of effective treatment (Cullen, 1994).
3 For a discussion of the various alternative definitions of recidivism, see Champion (1988); Palmer (1995); and National Policy Committee of American Society of Criminology (2001). *The use of incarceration in the U.S.* (http://link.springer.com/article/10.1023%2FA%3A1013111619501#page-2l).

4 Length of follow-up can affect recidivism rates. For most types of offenders, most failures will occur within three years. Exceptions to this are sex offenders and drunk drivers who, because of the lower probability of being caught, require longer follow-up periods.
5 The new version of the CPAI is called the CPAI–2010. In addition, researchers at the University of Cincinnati have developed several derivatives, including the Correctional Program Checklist (CPC), the CPC-Drug Court, CPC-Groups, and the CPC-Community Supervision Agency.

Recommended Readings

Aos, S., Phipps, P., Barnoski, R., Lieb, R. (1999). *The comparative costs and benefits of programs to reduce crime: A review of national research findings with implications for Washington State.* Olympia, WA: Washington State Institute for Public Policy.

Gendreau, P. (1996). The principles of effective intervention with offenders. In: A. Harland (ed.) *Choosing correctional options that work: Defining the demand and evaluating the supply.* Thousand Oaks, CA: Sage.

Martinson, R. (1974). What works?—Questions and answers about prison reform. *The Public Interest* 35, 22–54.

References

Andrews, D., Zinger, I., Hoge, R., Bonta, J., Gendreau, P., Cullen, F. (1990). Does correctional treatment work? A clinically relevant and psychologically informed meta-analysis. *Criminology* 28, 369–404.

Aos, S., Phipps, P., Barnoski, R., Lieb, R. (2001). *The comparative costs and benefits of programs to reduce recidivism.* Olympia, WA: Washington State Institute for Public Policy.

Austin, J. (2001). Prisoner reentry: Current trends, practices, and issues. *Crime & Delinquency* 47, 314–334.

Champion, D. (1988). *Felony probation, problems and prospects.* New York: Praeger, pp. 95–97.

Cullen, F. (1994). Social support as an organizing concept for criminology. *Justice Quarterly* 11, 52–59.

Cullen, F., Applegate, B. (1998). *Offender rehabilitation.* Brookfield, MA: Ashgate Dartmouth.

Cullen, F., Gendreau, P. (2001). From nothing works to what works. *Prison Journal* 81(3), 313–338.

Gendreau, P., Paparozzi, M. (1995). Examining what works in community corrections. *Corrections Today* (February), 28–30.

Gendreau, P., Ross, R. (1979). Effective correctional treatment: Bibliography for cynics. *Crime & Delinquency* 25, 463–489.

Gendreau, P., Ross, R. (1987). Revivification of rehabilitation: Evidence from the 1980s. *Justice Quarterly* 4, 349–407.

Glaze, L, Bonczar, T.P. (2009). *Probation and parole in the United States, 2008.* Washington, DC: Bureau of Justice Statistics.

Gottfredson, M., Mitchell-Herzfeld, S., Flanagan, T. (1982). Another look at the effectiveness of parole supervision. *Journal of Research in Crime and Delinquency* 18, 277–298.

Hoffman, P., Stone-Meierhoefer, B. (1980). Reporting recidivism rates: The criterion and follow-up issues. *Journal of Criminal Justice* 8, 53–60.

Latessa, E.J. (1986). The cost effectiveness of intensive supervision. *Federal Probation* 50(2), 70–74.

Latessa, E.J., Holsinger, A. (1998). The importance of evaluating correctional programs: Assessing outcome and quality. *Corrections Management Quarterly* 2(4), 22–29.

Latessa, E., Travis, L., Holsinger, A. (1997). *Evaluation of Ohio's Community Corrections Act programs and community based correctional facilities.* Cincinnati, OH: Division of Criminal Justice, University of Cincinnati.

Lowenkamp, C.T., Latessa, E.J., Smith, P. (2006). Does correctional program quality really matter? The impact of adhering to the principles of effective intervention. *Criminology and Public Policy* 5(3), 201–220.

Martinson, R. (1974). What works?—Questions and answers about prison reform. *Public Interest* 35, 22–54.

Nesovic, A. (2003). *Psychometric evaluation of the correctional program assessment inventory.* Dissertation Abstracts International 64(09), 4674B (UMI No. AAT NQ83525).

Nicholaichuk, T., Gordon, A. GUD. (2000). Outcome of an institutional sexual offender treatment program. *Sexual Abuse* 12, 139–153.

Osborne, D., Gaebler, T. (1993). *Reinventing government: How the entrepreneurial spirit is transforming the public sector.* New York: Penguin.

Palmer, T. (1975). Martinson revisited. *Journal of Research in Crime and Delinquency* 12, 133–152.

Palmer, T. (1995). Programmatic and nonprogrammatic aspects of successful intervention: New directions for research. *Crime & Delinquency* 41(1), 101–131.

Petersilia, J. (1991). The value of corrections research: Learning what works. *Federal Probation* 55(2), 24–26.

Vito, G.F., Latessa, E.J. (1979). Cost analysis in probation research: An evaluation synthesis. *Journal of Contemporary Criminal Justice* 1(3), 3–16.

Chapter 15

THE FUTURE OF CORRECTIONS IN THE COMMUNITY

Show people that there are programs nationwide where violent or habitual felons are assured prison beds only because many of the nuisance shoplifters, technical probation violators, or petty thieves are being punished in other meaningful ways. Make the public understand that dangerous offenders will still be put in prison; that intermediate sanctions are necessary to reintegrate offenders so they have a better chance of becoming successful citizens and not continuing lives of crime.—M. Castle, Former Governor of Delaware

INTRODUCTION

It is legitimate to ask what corrections will look like by the year 2025, and what changes will have occurred by then. Such questions offer exciting opportunities to effect closure in the area of corrections in the community. We start by looking once again at where we are, and then where we might be by the year 2025. As illustrated in Figure 15.1, in 2010 we experienced the first decline in the prison population in nearly 40 years.

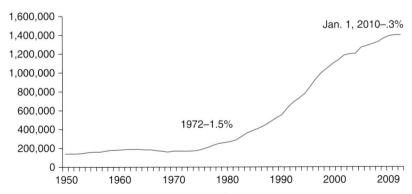

Figure 15.1 First Decline in Prison Population in 38 Years.

Source: Prisoners Series, Bureau of Justice Statistics, and Pew Center on the States, Public Safety Performance Project.

Whether this is a trend or simply the result of tough economic times is yet to be seen, but it is clear that this trend has continued over the past four years. As seen in Figure 15.2, not all states have experienced a decline. The number of Americans on probation or parole has declined slightly over the past few years,

Absolute change in state prison populations, 2008–2009.

−4,257	California
−3,260	Michigan
−1,699	New York
−1,315	Maryland
−1,257	Texas
−1,233	Mississippi
−945	Connecticut
−602	New Jersey
−479	Colorado
−371	Rhode Island
−313	Illinois
−300	Delaware
−290	Kentucky
−281	Iowa
−268	Wisconsin
−252	Massachusetts
−235	South Carolina
−204	Nevada
−195	Virginia
−173	New Hampshire
−80	Ohio
−64	Hawaii
−30	Nebraska
−11	Utah
−9	Wyoming
−2	Montana

▲
STATES WITH DECREASES
STATES WITH INCREASES
▼

Maine	31
North Dakota	34
South Dakota	92
Kansas	102
Vermont	105
Idaho	110
Tennessee	145
Minnesota	154
New Mexico	176
Alaska	190
Oregon	237
Washington	307
West Virginia	308
North Carolina	389
Arkansas	455
Oklahoma	533
Missouri	606
Georgia	843
Arizona	934
Alabama	1,053
Louisiana	1,399
Indiana	1,496
Florida	1,527
Pennsylvania	2,122

Figure 15.2 Prison Counts by State.

Note: Change is from December 31, 2008 to January 1, 2010 unless otherwise noted in the jurisdictional notes.

Source: Pew Center on the States, Public Safety Performance Project.

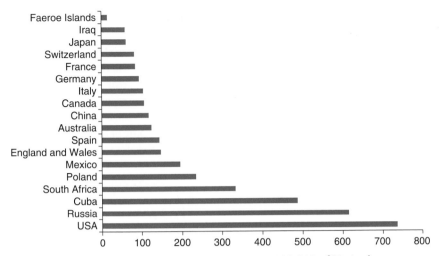

Figure 15.3 International Incarceration Rates per 100,000 of Nation's Population.

Source: International Centre for Prison Studies: University of London (www.prisonstudies.org/).

and currently totals approximately 4.8 million people, or approximately one in every 50 adult Americans. About 82 percent of those were on probation and another 12 percent on parole. Taken together, we incarcerate more adult residents in this nation (690 per 100,000 residents) than any other major Western country. These rates are illustrated in Figure 15.3 (The Sentencing Project, 2001). The incarceration rate of African-American males is more than four times that in Russia (3,250 to 690), formerly a totalitarian country now undergoing democratization. This high rate is due in large part to policies that encourage the use—and, some would say, overuse—of incarceration for property and drug offenders (Fish, 2000).

The use of imprisonment, of course, varies greatly by group. Although African Americans make up about 14 percent of the total population, they represent one-half of the jail and prison group. This turns out to be about one in 12 adult African-American men aged 14 to 54; there are more African Americans under incarceration than the total number of African-American men of any age enrolled in college throughout the nation. Disproportionate minority confinement is widespread (although the Juvenile Justice Institute in 2000 demonstrated that it can be sharply reduced).

No doubt this higher rate reflects the differential rate of involvement of African Americans in violent crimes, but it also reflects the impact of the war on drugs (Cullen et al., 1996).[1] Despite our efforts, the war on drugs has not had any major effect on the sale, distribution, or use of illicit controlled substances (General Accounting Office, 2007), but continues still.

At the present time, then, the correctional population in the United States totals more than seven million offenders. The bulk of offenders are on probation or under parole supervision. Whether these numbers will decline is yet to be seen.

INTERMEDIATE SANCTIONS

The reader will recall that intermediate sanctions are correctional interventions that fill the sentencing gap between probation and prison. Their dominant characteristic is that they allow increased surveillance and control over the offender; they have been advanced as a means of avoiding prison crowding and reintegrating offenders. These are depicted in Figure 15.4 and range across 13 distinct programs, each increasingly punitive and controlling. Some of these programs are themselves composed of different technologies and usefulness and many permit effective treatment.

PUBLIC ACCEPTANCE

The public tends to perceive corrections as being a choice between mere probation and imprisonment,[2] a false dichotomy that implies that public safety is met only when major offenders are locked away, out of sight, and for long periods of time. It should be apparent at this point that public protection does not mean only prison or that anything short of incarceration will endanger public safety.

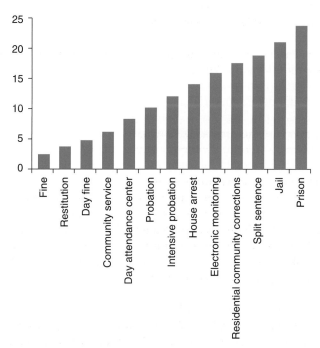

Figure 15.4 A Range of Sentencing options: Rank by Level of Punishment.

Source: Adapted from Byrne, J. (1990). The future of intensive probation service. *Crime & Delinquency* 36(1), 29.

Policy makers in the state of Delaware, convinced that it was not possible to build their way out of the prison crowding problem and that the public held strong preferences for reintegration of offenders,[3] decided to develop and expand community corrections. Their policy priorities were to (1) remove violent offenders from the community, (2) restore victims to pre-offense status by restitution and compensation, and (3) rehabilitate offenders. The result was a continuum of programs comprising five levels of increasingly restrictive and punitive sanctions that included cost-control mechanisms. The system was designed to allow offenders to earn their way out of prison by good behavior, work, and conformity to rules or to worm their way into the prison system by repeated criminal activity and nonconformity to supervision rules. The system is spread over five "levels."

- Level V is full incarceration with complete institutional control.
- Level IV is quasi-incarceration in which an offender is supervised from nine to 23 hours a day in such programs as community treatment centers, electronically monitored house arrest, attendance centers, and residential drug treatment centers.
- Level III is intensive, direct supervision over one to eight hours per day, during which offenders are subject to curfew checks, employment checks, and frequent monitoring for attendance in treatment programming.
- Level II is "normal" field supervision, generally probation, with from zero to one hour of supervision per day.
- Level I is the lowest level of supervision.

The system allows the sentencing judge wide latitude in sentencing both the offender and the offense (see Box 15.1).

Box 15.1
Community Corrections in Delaware

Administrative supervision—Level I
Offenders assigned to Level I are placed in the least restrictive form of supervision under the sentencing system. These are generally first-time offenders who pose little risk of reoffending. The majority of these offenders are required to pay a fine, make restitution, or attend a specific first-offender program. Requirements are also to monitor offenders' participation in designated programs and make progress reports on same to the court.

Probation and parole—Level II
Level II is the standard probation/parole supervision program. Offenders on Level II supervision are to meet with their probation officer on a regular schedule to comply with contact requirements based on risks/needs assessments. Level II probation/parole officers serve in the traditional roles of counseling.

Intensive supervision—Level III

The intensive supervision unit (ISU) represents Level III of the alternatives to incarceration. The officer to client ratio is 1:25. The purpose of the ISU is to closely supervise adult offenders in the community to prevent further criminal behavior while sentences are being served. Supervision is frequent and intense while also assisting the offender in making a successful return to the community. The ISU makes recommendations to move cases up or down the sanctioning levels based on the SENTAC guidelines and upon individual client progress as documented by the supervising officer. Addition of the supervised custody unit to the intensive supervision unit will augment probation/parole's capabilities to more closely supervise Level III probationers in the community.

House arrest program—Level IV

House arrest is a community custody program for offenders who are to be restricted to an approved residence in which specific sanctions are to be imposed and enforced. The house arrest program is administered by probation officers and includes continuous electronic and direct surveillance.

Pretrial Services

Pretrial services provide the courts with bail recommendations based on screening interviews with newly arrested and detained individuals. After initial screening, follow-up interviews and recommendations are made at preset intervals. Community supervision is also provided for certain released individuals as ordered by the courts. Presentence reports are completed as requested to the Wilmington Municipal Court. All pretrial services occur prior to a SENTAC level being established for an individual.

Day-reporting Center

The day-reporting center concept is designed to provide intensive supervision with treatment program participation to improve the transition of high-risk offenders from incarceration to the community.

Community Work Program

Offenders placed in this program perform various types of labor at nonprofit organizations in order to satisfy special conditions of supervision and/or to be relieved of court-ordered assessments.

Another, more recent example can be seen in Michigan. Faced with high unemployment and severe budget deficits, Michigan initiated a new program designed to reduce prison populations, save money, and maintain public safety. The Michigan Prison Reentry Initiative (MPRI) has thus far met all of these goals.

As described in Box 15.2, MPRI has been hailed as a great success. Likewise, Connecticut recognized the need to have more options and created an alternative to incarceration centers (see Box 15.3). Noteworthy is that both of these states recently experienced significant drops in their prison populations.

Box 15.2
Michigan Prisoner Reentry Initiative

The Michigan Prisoner Reentry Initiative (MPRI) has helped cut down on the number of repeat criminal offenses, inmates in prison, and the general crime rate. The success couldn't come at a better time, when the state's budget is squeezed by declining tax revenue.

A spokesman for the Michigan Department of Corrections said MPRI is at least partially responsible for a 29 percent relative rate reduction in the number of prisoners returning to the state's prisons. About 20,000 inmates have gone through the program since its inception in 2005, and the number of those returning to prison has been reduced by 1,597.

In addition, through the first six months of 2009, felony court dispositions were down 6.3 percent—a total of 1,634. The crime rate declined 16 percent in the first half of 2008, the latest period for which figures are available. Prison intake decreased 8 percent during the first seven months of 2009 compared to the same period in 2008. Michigan's Governor Granholm announced that she plans to close three prisons and five prison camps to save $118 million annually. This is in addition to two prisons and one prison camp that have already been closed.

The key to MPRI's success appears to be the network of services it offers through partnerships with other agencies. According to a study of MPRI released in 2008, the percentage of parolees returning to prison within two years dropped from 48 percent to 36 percent since the program launched. Sixty percent of parolees now go through the program.

"Michigan has shown exceptional leadership in the area of prisoner re-entry," said Amy Solomon, senior research associate for the Washington, DC-based Urban Institute. "From the start, the Michigan Prisoner Re-Entry Initiative has drawn on the best ideas from research and practice with a clear mission to protect the public and create better citizens. The MPRI also deserves high marks for reaching out to community partners and national experts alike for feedback along the way."

According to the Vera Institute, high rates of failure among people on probation and parole are a significant driver of prison populations and costs in most states. A 2004 study by the National Governors Association said that of prisoners who are released nationally, 67 percent will be rearrested and 52 percent will be reincarcerated within three years. The MPRI study said more than 90 percent of prisoners eventually return to the community, either on parole or after serving their complete sentences. Last year, nearly 12,500 prisoners were released.

Source: Adapted from Gilbert (2009).

Box 15.3
Alternative to Incarceration Centers

There are currently 18 Alternative to Incarceration Center (AIC) locations serving all areas of the state of Connecticut. The overarching goal of Connecticut's AIC program is to provide a comprehensive service delivery system that incorporates research-driven practices targeting offender behavioral change so as to lead to reductions in recidivism; assist the state to reduce both pretrial and sentenced populations at correctional facilities; and act as an alternative to incarceration for individuals with technical violations or who are in need of increased structure, supervision, and services.

The AIC program came about in response to the prison and jail over-crowding that was plaguing Connecticut's criminal justice system in the early 1980s. Federal court decrees setting population limits, legislation creating automatic release mechanisms, and extensive prison construction were major responses to the problem. However, by the mid-1980s it had become apparent that Connecticut could not address overcrowding through building alone.

In 1986, the Department of Correction and the Connecticut Prison Association, now Community Partners in Action, developed a pilot program known as the Alternative to Incarceration Center program. The program was limited to 35 slots, intended to operate only in Hartford, and designed to offer the court a meaningful alternative to incarceration. The pilot AIC was initiated without legislation; it was agreed that parole release, release on a conditional written promise to appear, and release on probation with specific conditions would be the means used to place people into the program. The AIC program relied heavily upon traditional social services (e.g., family reunification, community organizations coming to the AIC to educate offenders on domestic violence and STDs), but added three new components to its operation: (1) strict monitoring of involvement by participants in the social services program, (2) extensive community service for sentenced offenders, and (3) a mandatory reporting system.

A 1988 evaluation of the AIC concluded that the program was serving the court in such a fashion as to divert both pretrial detainees and sentenced offenders from incarceration. About the same time, Hartford-based judges and state attorneys expressed the opinion that an expansion of the AIC concept to other areas in the state would likely produce results similar to

Hartford's experience addressing the problem of prison and jail over-crowding. Connecticut Public Act 89-383 authorized the development of the Alternative to Incarceration Program across the state. For the next 17 years, the AICs operated much like reporting centers for offenders being supervised in the community, with reporting requirements based on employment status (e.g., unemployed offenders reported three hours a day, five days a week). While at the AICs, offenders were expected to participate in whatever programming was available at the time they reported.

In 2002, CSSD began its Risk Reduction program to reduce the risk of reoffense among CSSD's community corrections populations through the use of research-driven practices. The effort led to a commitment by CSSD to align its internal (adult and juvenile probation, bail services, and family services) and contracted programs with principles of effective intervention. Connecticut consulted with experts from the United States and Canada and attended trainings on evidence-based practice and, in turn, held meetings with the executive level, all regions and courts, and all probation offices to prepare the judicial branch for this new way of delivering community super-vision and services.

In 2005 and 2006, leaders made an investment to track and analyze useful, relevant, and timely information and to use those data to inform decision-making processes. This quality assurance effort continues today.

Continuing the implementation of its risk-reduction efforts, in July 2009 the state implemented a set of Risk Reduction Indicators. Indicators for AICs are intended to assess progress on both process and outcome meas-ures and include Working Alliance Inventory scores, quality assurance ratings, completion rates for the three core interventions, percentage of clients gaining employment, and 12-month recidivism rates for program completers. These indicators are reviewed quarterly with AIC providers, probation, and bail services managers.

The evidence-based interventions put in place in 2005 remain today and include cognitive-behavioral treatment, skill-based substance abuse treat-ment, employment services groups, assistance with job searches, and case management. Each location has a community service program and also conducts urinalysis and Breathalyzer services as required on a case-by-case basis.

Annually, the AICs receive around 10,000 referrals from judges, proba-tion officers, jail reinterview staff, bail commissioners, and limited depart-ment of corrections referrals.

CREATING CHANGE

Prisons will continue to play a vital role in corrections in future years, yet may be called upon to play decreasingly important functions as they cease to be the central element of corrections. This will require an agenda for change, and the most effective way would be to encourage local communities to address better ways to manage crime and criminals in their own communities. This in turn would require leadership at the state governmental level to sentence "smarter," not just tougher. Is there a politician existing in today's political environment who believes that taking a "soft" approach to crime will help in winning an election? The problem to be addressed is not "softer or harsher," but a recognition that what is needed is a philosophy for organizing corrections and the use of evidence-based practices.

When the "nothing works in corrections" argument arose, many scholars and practitioners who should have known better abandoned the rehabilitation model. Corrections lost its organizing theme or premise. Now that the abandonment of rehabilitation has been recognized as both premature and erroneous,[4] the stage is set for a considerable and acrimonious battle over the "conscience" or purpose of handling offenders. Unfortunately, that will not likely occur until we are well into the twenty-first century and will probably be triggered by fiscal crisis, as states and local jurisdictions are unable to sustain the heavy cost of correctional systems, particularly prisons and jails.

We choose to focus on boot camp programs to identify and discuss the dimensions of some of the issues. Since their inception in 1983, boot camp programs have been implemented in jurisdictions across the country, including jails, prisons, and probation/parole agencies. Advocates of this politically popular program pointed to alleged benefits of boot camps ("we will teach the offender discipline," "we will build up physical and moral fiber," "nothing works like punishment," and so on). Some programs have extensive program components, such as learning to read and write, obtaining a GED, learning "life" skills, and breaking drug dependency. Few scholars or practitioners, however, openly admit that the primary purpose of the program has a quite different objective: managing prison population growth by facilitating early release of basically low-risk offenders with drug problems who, if community corrections were more developed and coordinated, should never have been imprisoned. Boot camps became part of the correctional scene, despite negative results emerging from most program evaluations.[5]

Well over 100 evaluations of boot camp programs have been conducted, and with rare exceptions, most evaluations did not find reduced recidivism; some show that gains made during program participation evaporate quickly ("wash out") after the offender was released back into the community. Although well intentioned and mostly staffed by an enthusiastic and optimistic cadre, boot camps have several fatal flaws: for the most part they do not target criminogenic needs, they fail to treat effectively, and they model aggressive behavior.

EFFECTIVE INTERVENTIONS

Treatment can be defined as assessment of an offender's needs, design of a specific program to address criminogenic needs, application of evidence-based programs by competent staff supervised by experienced professionals, routine review of the adequacy of delivery of the service and redesign of the individual's program until it is effective, and graduated release into the community with supervision and assistance. Treatment also requires follow-up of the graduates over time and documentation of outcome, the latter to help "fine-tune" treatments for incoming offenders. Said differently, "treatment" requires assessment, classification, delivery of the intervention, and case monitoring and long-term follow-up. Contemporary community corrections are called upon to do more with less, to be more effective, and to protect through service and surveillance. Meeting this challenge will require more resources, trained professionals, competent administrators, and demonstrated effectiveness. It is no longer enough to be "well meaning." A new breed of correctional practitioner, theorist, manager, and specialist is needed; the principles of effective treatment must be implemented. And vital to achieving the new community corrections is the recognition that "more of the same" is no longer acceptable.

Lest the reader misunderstand, we are not berating boot camp programs *per se*, but are identifying the basic philosophical problem that underlies community as well as institutional corrections. The need is for vision, mission, and training. Competence, focus, assessment, classification, and use of evidence-based programs that follow well-articulated principles of effective intervention must be incorporated as part of the mission. Students entering corrections who can dedicate themselves to accepting the challenge of crime in a free society would be warmly welcomed.

SUMMARY

The nation cannot build itself out of current prison and management crises, but states and local jurisdictions can manage and control not only the prison and jail populations but also the costs and integrity of the justice system that deals with post-offense corrections. By developing a logical set of sentencing policies with clear goals and a wide range of sentencing options and sanctions, the nation would begin to address public safety on a more sound foundation. In addition, an aggressive public education and information initiative is necessary for public acceptance. In the long run, corrections must hold offenders accountable to the public and the legal system for their criminal behaviors, and politicians must be held accountable to the public for their actions.

Many issues face community corrections: risk management and handling of special needs populations, officer safety and work conditions, and the appropriate use of technology, such as drug testing and electronic monitoring. We have confidence that the field will rise to the challenge. We base this faith on our knowledge of the professionals who work in and will come to the field. Because of these dedicated individuals, the future of corrections in the community is bright, and the achievement of a logical, coherent, and safe system for handling criminal offenders is attainable. In doing this, we must remember that corrections are, above all else, a human issue, that change is not easy, and that partners in change are necessary. Community corrections have a bright future.

Review Questions

1. Why do you believe that the United States leads the world in incarceration?
2. What are considered the three least restrictive sentencing options? And what are considered the three most restrictive?
3. What does effective "treatment" require?

Notes

1 This statement is not meant to imply that nonwhites are not concerned about drugs and crime. Surveys indicate that both white and nonwhite Americans are concerned about drug abuse and the effects of drugs on communities.
2 Cullen and Moon (2002).
3 There is a clear and negative impact of welfare on crime, particularly cash and public housing programs. For bibliotherapy, see Zhang (1997); and Hirsch (2001).
4 Allen (2002).
5 Stinchcomb and Terry (2002).

References

Allen, H. (2002). Introductory remarks. In: H.Allen (ed.) *Risk reduction: Interventions for special needs offenders* 2002. Lanham, MD: American Correctional Association, pp. 1–6.

Bureau of Justice Statistics (2013). *Correctional populations in the United States, 2012.* Washington, DC: BJS.

Byrne, J. (1990). The future of intensive probation service. *Crime & Delinquency* 36(1), 29.

Castle, M. (1989). *Alternative sentencing: Selling it to the public.* Washington, DC: U.S. Department of Justice.

Cullen, F., Moon, M. (2002). Reaffirming rehabilitation: Public support for correctional treatment. In: H. Allen (ed.) *Risk reduction: Interventions for special needs offenders.* Lanham, MD: American Correctional Association, pp. 7–26.

Cullen, F., Van Voorhis, P., Sundt, J. (1996). Prisons in crisis: The American experience. In: R. Matthews, F. Francis (eds) *Prisons 2000: An international perspective on the current state and future of imprisonment.* New York: Macmillan, pp. 21–52.

Fish, J. (2000). The drug policy debate. *Fordham University Law* 28(6), 3–361.

General Accounting Office (2007). *Drug control: U.S. assistance has helped Mexican counternarcotics efforts, but tons of illicit drugs continue to flow into the United States.* Washington, DC: USGAO.

Gilbert, G. (2009). Success of Michigan prisoner re-entry initiative allows Granholm to close prisons, save money. *The Oakland Press* (September 6, 2009).

Greene, J., Schiraldi, V. (2002). *Cutting correctly: New prison policies for times of fiscal crisis.* Washington, DC: Justice Policy Institute.

Hirsch, A. (2001). The world has never been a safe place for them. *Violence against Women* 7(2), 159–175.

Juvenile Justice Institute (2002). *Reducing disproportionate minority confinement.* www.oaisd.org/juvserv/programs/juvenilejustice.

Sentencing Project, The (2001). International Centre for Prison Studies: University of London.

Pew Center on the States. (2010). *Prison count 2010.* www.cjpc.org/Prison_ Count_2010%20Pew%20%c20Center%20report.pdf.

Stinchcomb, J., Terry, W. (2002). Predicting the likelihood of rearrest among shock incarceration graduates. *Crime & Delinquency* 47(2), 221–242.

Zhang, J. (1997). The effect of welfare programs on criminal behavior: A theoretical and empirical analysis. *Economic Inquiry* 35(1), 120–137.

Glossary/Index

Page numbers in **bold** refer to figures, page numbers in *italic* refer to tables.

The authors are grateful to the Law Enforcement Assistance Administration for publication of the *Dictionary of Criminal Justice Data Terminology*, from which many of the following terms and definitions have been extracted. It is in the spirit of that effort to standardize criminal justice terminology that we have decided to include this section. It is hoped that students, especially those new to the field, will take the time to read and absorb the meanings of these tools of the trade. To obtain more detailed information about terms in this glossary, write to U.S. Department of Justice, National Criminal Reference Service, Washington, DC 20531.

document alleging the commission of one or more crimes; a single defendant; in juvenile or correctional proceedings, a person who is the object of agency action.

Case (court). A single charging document under the jurisdiction of a court; a single defendant.

case classification 238

case management plan 233–4, 235, **236**

case plans 263–4, *264*

Caseload (corrections). The total number of clients registered with a correctional agency or agent during a specified time period, often divided into active and inactive or supervised and unsupervised, thus distinguishing between clients with whom the agency or agent maintains contact and those with whom it does not. **253, 256–7, 274**

Caseload (court). The total number of cases filed in a given court or before a given judicial officer during a given period of time.

Caseload, pending. The number of cases at any given time that have been filed in a given court, or are before a given judicial officer, but have not reached disposition. **8**

casework 255

casework relationship 255–6, **256**

casework supervision 255–7, 266–7

casework/control 230

Cash bail. A cash payment for a situation in which the charge is not serious and the scheduled bail is low. The defendant obtains release by paying in cash the full amount, which is recoverable after the required court appearances are made. **94, 400**

CCH. An abbreviation for computerized criminal history.

Charge. A formal allegation that a specific person(s) has committed a specific offense(s). **66, 71, 174, 175, 193**

Charging document. A formal written accusation, filed in a court, alleging that a specified person(s) has committed a specific offense(s). **71**

Check fraud. The issuance or passing of a check, draft, or money order that is legal as a formal document, signed by the legal account holder but with the foreknowledge that the bank or depository will refuse to honor it because of insufficient funds or a closed account. *143, 151*, **152**, *229, 343*

Chicago: Cook County juvenile court 172

Child abuse. Willful action or actions by a person causing physical harm to a child. **333**

child molestation 329, 332

Child neglect. Willful failure by the person(s) responsible for a child's well-being to provide for adequate food, clothing, shelter, education, and supervision. **332**

child saving movement 173

child victimizers 333

childhood intervention 189

Chute, Charles Lionel 48

Citation (to appear). A written order issued by a law enforcement officer directing an alleged offender to appear in a specific court at a specified time in order to answer a criminal charge.

Citizen dispute settlement. The settlement of interpersonal disputes by a third party or the courts. Charges arising from interpersonal disputes are mediated by a third party in an attempt to avoid prosecution. If an agreement between the parties cannot be reached and the complainant wishes to proceed with criminal processing, the case may be referred to court for settlement.

civil suits 173

Civil War 46

class classification 237

class discrimination 20

classification system: criticisms of 238; development of 228–30, *229*, **231, 232**, 233–4, **234, 235**; false negatives 238; false positives 238; female offenders 244; importance of 219–20; principles 220–6, **221**, *223, 226*, **227**; specialized 235, **237**, 237–8; standards 243

ANNOTATION. Part I offenses are:

1. Criminal homicide a. Murder and nonnegligent (voluntary) manslaughter b. Manslaughter by negligence (involuntary manslaughter)
2. Forcible rape a. Rape by force b. Attempted forcible rape
3. Robbery a. Firearm b. Knife or cutting instrument c. Other dangerous weapon d. Strongarm
4. Aggravated assault a. Firearm b. Knife or cutting instrument c. Other dangerous weapon d. Hands, fist, feet, etc.—aggravated injury
5. Burglary a. Forcible entry b. Unlawful entry—no force c. Attempted forcible entry
6. Larceny-theft (larceny)
7. Motor vehicle theft a. Autos b. Trucks and buses c. Other vehicles

Offenses, Part II. A class of offenses selected for use in UCR, consisting of specific offenses and types of offenses that do not meet the criteria of frequency and/or seriousness necessary for Part I offenses.

ANNOTATION. Part II offenses are:
Other assaults (simple,* nonaggravated)
Arson*
Forgery* and counterfeiting*
Fraud*
Embezzlement*
Stolen property: buying, receiving, possessing
Vandalism
Weapons: carrying, possessing, etc.
Prostitution and commercialized vice
Sex offenses (except forcible rape, prostitution, and commercialized vice)
Narcotic drug law violations
Gambling offenses against the family and children
Driving under the influence*
Liquor law violations
Drunkenness disorderly conduct
Vagrancy
All other offenses (except traffic law violations)
Suspicion*

Curfew and loitering law violations (juvenile violations)
Runaway* (juveniles)
Terms marked with an asterisk (*) are defined in this glossary, although not necessarily in accord with UCR usage. UCR does not collect reports of Part II offenses. Arrest data concerning such offenses, however, are collected and published.

Pardon. An act of executive clemency that absolves the party in part or in full from the legal consequences of the crime and conviction.

ANNOTATION. Pardons can be full or conditional. The former generally applies to both the punishment and the guilt of the offender and blots out the existence of guilt in the eyes of the law. It also removes his or her disabilities and restores civil rights. The conditional pardon generally falls short of the remedies of the full pardon, is an expression of guilt, and does not obliterate the conviction.

Suspect. A person, adult or juvenile, considered by a criminal justice agency to be one who may have committed a specific criminal offense but who has not been arrested or charged.

Suspended sentence. Essentially, a threat to take more drastic action if the offender commits a crime again during some specified time period. When no special conditions are attached, it is assumed that the ends of justice have been satisfied by conviction and no further action is required, as long as the offender refrains from involvement in new offenses. Suspended sentences may be conditioned on various limitations as to mobility, associates, or activities, or on requirements to make reparations or participate in some rehabilitation program **46, 48**

Suspicion. Belief that a person has committed a criminal offense based on facts and circumstances that are not sufficient to constitute probable cause.

Theft. Larceny, or in some legal classifications, the group of offenses including larceny, and robbery, burglary, extortion, fraudulent offenses, hijacking, and other offenses sharing the element of larceny. *16*, **141**, *151*, **170**

Third-party release. A release extending to another person the responsibility for ensuring the defendant's appearance in court. This may be a person known to the defendant or a designated volunteer. Third-party release may be a condition of unsecured bail, with the third party as a cosigner.

Time served. The total time spent in confinement by a convicted adult before and after sentencing, or only the time spent in confinement after a sentence of commitment to a confinement facility. **133–4**

Training school. A correctional institution for juveniles adjudicated to be delinquent or status offenders and